TESTOSTERONE DREAMS

TESTOSTERONE DREAMS

REJUVENATION, APHRODISIA, DOPING

John Hoberman

UNIVERSITY OF CALIFORNIA PRESS

BERKELEY   LOS ANGELES   LONDON

Parts of chapter 7 are reprinted, by permission, from
J. Hoberman, 2001, "How Drug Testing Fails: The Politics
of Doping Control," in *Doping in Elite Sport: The Politics
of Drugs in the Olympic Movement,* edited by W. Wilson
and E. Derse (Champaign, Ill.: Human Kinetics), 241–74.

University of California Press
Berkeley and Los Angeles, California

University of California Press, Ltd.
London, England

Library of Congress Cataloging-in-Publication Data
Hoberman, John M. (John Milton), 1944–
    Testosterone dreams : rejuvenation, aphrodisia, doping /
John Hoberman.
        p. ; cm.
    Includes index.
    ISBN 0-520-22151-6 (cloth : alk. paper)
    1. Testosterone.   2. Hormone therapy.   3. Meno-
pause—Hormone therapy.   4. Testosterone—Therapeutic
use.   5. Testosterone—Physiological effect.   6. Longevity.
7. Aphrodisiacs.
    [DNLM: 1. Hormone Replacement Therapy—trends.
2. Testosterone—therapeutic use.   3. Aphrodisiacs.
4. Doping in Sports.   5. Rejuvenation.   WJ 875 H682t
2005]   I. Title.
QP572.T4H635   2005
615'.36—dc22   2003022824

Manufactured in the United States of America
14   13   12   11   10   09   08   07   06   05
10   9   8   7   6   5   4   3   2   1

The paper used in this publication is both acid-free and
totally chlorine-free (TCF). It meets the minimum
requirements of ANSI/NISO Z39.48–1992 (R 1997)
(Permanence of Paper).♾

This book is dedicated to my father,
Henry D. Hoberman, M.D., Ph.D.,
who taught me the dignity of medicine
and the love of science.

CONTENTS

Testosterone Dreams

Pharmacology and Our Human Future

Testosterone Dreams is an investigation of modern attitudes toward enhancing the mental, physical, and sexual powers of human beings. The
chapters that follow explore the theory and practice of human enhancement by focusing on the complex, and sometimes bizarre, history of the
synthetic hormone testosterone and the careers it has made, both inside
and outside the medical world, over the past seventy years. Testosterone
is the hormone of choice for this purpose because it has played all the
major roles in which a charismatic hormone can function: it has been regarded as a rejuvenating drug, as a sexually stimulating drug, and as a
doping drug that builds muscle and boosts athletic performance. The
first chapter of this book presents a history of testosterone therapy and
the primitive "organotherapy" that preceded it. Of particular interest
here is the medical and social status of synthetic testosterone and its derivatives, the anabolic-androgenic steroids. Why has testosterone acquired a special, even fashionable, cachet as a particularly dynamic hormone? When have testosterone drugs been viewed as harmful or benign?
Why is testosterone finally prevailing despite the law that regulates its
use? What has the pharmaceutical industry done to create a market for
testosterone products? The second chapter describes early testosterone
therapies for "frigid" women and homosexuals and explains why the
drug companies failed to create a mass market for testosterone products
after the Second World War. Chapters 3 and 4 show how the commercial

promotion of testosterone drugs has overcome these obstacles and is now mainstreaming testosterone therapy as a socially acceptable enhancement. Chapters 5 through 7 examine the role of testosterone drugs in the world of Olympic sport and the doping epidemic they have unleashed over the past forty years. We shall examine the world of high-performance athletics as a kind of parallel universe in which pharmacological performance enhancement has become a way of life for entire groups of athletes. In this subculture of drug-taking athletes we find the doctor-patient relationships that have long served as models for the hormone entrepreneurs who now offer to enhance the mental, physical, and sexual athleticism of their patients.

Testosterone dreams are the fantasies of hormonal rejuvenation, sexual excitement, and supernormal human performance that have been inspired by testosterone since it was first synthesized in 1935. This scientific achievement was driven by a competition among three teams of researchers sponsored by rival pharmaceutical companies, all dreaming of a male hormone market that would produce profits like those of the already-established market for female hormones. During the years that followed, a steady stream of medical observations pointed to exciting prospects for the "androgenic" drugs derived from testosterone. An association between testosterone treatment and muscular enlargement in male mammals was proposed in 1938. "Androgens exert a tonic and stimulating action, associated perhaps with their metabolic effects," the *Journal of the American Medical Association* stated in 1942. Scientists were already distinguishing between testosterone's effects on "sexual function" and "mental and physical vigor," between its capacities to produce "sexual stimulation" and "constitutional rehabilitation." Over the next several decades, the growing use of testosterone and its derivatives, the anabolic-androgenic steroids, would demonstrate that many people were interested in using testosterone products for a variety of purposes.

The first public advocate of testosterone therapy for aging men was the popular science journalist Paul de Kruif, whose manifesto *The Male Hormone* was published with some fanfare in 1945. Excerpted in *Reader's Digest* and promoted by a full-page review in *Newsweek* ("Hormones for He Men"), *The Male Hormone* was in some respects a prophetic book. "The male hormone," de Kruif declared, "is now ready for the trial of its possible power to extend the prime life of men." Commending his "courageous honesty," one reviewer declared that de Kruif had brought out into the open "the questions raised by the laboratory synthesis and the now unlimited production of testosterone, the male hormone."

The excitement about testosterone's medical and commercial prospects was shared by some of the major pharmaceutical companies of this era. "Of all the sex hormones," *Business Week* reported in December 1945, "testosterone is said to have the greatest market potentialities." Two companies, Schering and Glidden, had been fighting it out in court for the right to manufacture synthetic sex hormones. By 1937 testosterone propionate was being produced in sufficient quantities for use in clinical trials. By 1938 the production of testosterone had already resulted in antitrust proceedings and controversy in the pharmaceutical industry. The manufacture of testosterone, de Kruif predicted in 1945, "will make its producers wealthy."

De Kruif declared that a growing demand for testosterone would "soon bring it within reach of everybody." The availability of methyl testosterone in pill form convinced him that a practical way to administer the drug had finally been found. The potential clientele seemed to be enormous: "How many millions of American males, not the men they used to be, would flock to the physicians and the druggist, a bit shamefaced and surreptitious, maybe, but hopeful, murmuring: 'Doc, how about some of this new male hormone?' " Physicians, too, seemed to be ready for a breakthrough in treatments. Despite the warnings issued by the American Medical Association, "many physicians, and more of them all the time, were trying out testosterone on this, that, and almost every disease of the middle and later years of the lives of men." So it appeared that an inexpensive supply, a healthy demand, and favorable medical opinion would soon add up to a viable market for androgen drugs.

Testosterone became a charismatic drug because it promised sexual stimulation and renewed energy for individuals and greater productivity for modern society. Physicians described the optimal effect of testosterone as a feeling of "well-being," a term that has been used many times over the past half century to characterize its positive effect on mood. In the early 1940s testosterone was hailed as a mood-altering drug whose primary purpose was the sexual restoration and reenergizing of aging males. The sheer numbers of these potential patients suggested that they would eventually constitute a lucrative market. This idea was still in the air a decade after *The Male Hormone* was published. "The present results with steroid therapy in geriatrics are astonishing," one gerontologist wrote in 1954. "Their future possibilities stagger the imagination."

Interest in testosterone was strong enough to prompt the American Medical Association to advise that "these substances ought to be kept out of vitamin pills."

The idea that testosterone was a performance-enhancing drug that could boost the productivity of socially significant people appeared in 1939, along with the idea of the male menopause. Testosterone replacement therapy would help older men in important positions fulfill their "social and economic responsibilities." Paul de Kruif offered his readers a similar vision of drug-induced productivity that made a prophetic connection between elite athletes and their civilian counterparts. "We know how both the St. Louis Cardinals and St. Louis Browns have won championships, super-charged by vitamins," he observes. "It would be interesting to watch the productive power of an industry or a professional group that would try a systematic supercharge with testosterone[.]" Within a generation, sports audiences around the world were enjoying record-breaking performances achieved by athletes whose "productive power" was boosted by testosterone-based anabolic steroids. The "doping" of athletes with androgens and other hormones can thus be understood as one of the human enhancements that will precipitate an unprecedented crisis of human identity during the twenty-first century.

As more drugs are finding new and often unexpected uses, the distinction between illegitimate doping and socially acceptable forms of drug-assisted productivity is gradually disappearing. One consequence of this vanishing boundary is that the de facto legitimizing of a drug can also create an implicit or even explicit obligation to use it for purposes society or certain subcultures define as desirable. Compulsory doping of this kind has been observed in certain athletic subcultures for many years. Shot-putters, weightlifters, and professional cyclists are among the most obvious examples of athletes whose communities have legitimated (and effectively mandated) the consumption of illicit drugs for the purpose of staging more "productive" competitions. The former East German elite sports program practiced compulsory doping—and Olympic medal production—on a unique scale. My point is that modern societies have embarked on various kinds of pharmacological practices that exemplify what we may call compulsory or obligatory doping.

People can feel obligated to dope themselves for military, professional, or sexual purposes. The amphetamine drugs once known as "pep pills," for example, found widespread military use during the Second World War. In March 1944, the air surgeon of the United States Air Force explained to the American public that despite the "disgrace" into which Benzedrine had fallen on account of its widespread abuse by civilians, it played an essential wartime role in keeping military pilots alert while they were in action. Amphetamines were subsequently provided to pilots in the Vietnam and Gulf wars. After two U.S. Air Force pilots killed four Canadian soldiers in a "friendly-fire" incident in Afghanistan in April 2002, their lawyers argued that these men had felt compelled to take Dexedrine pills that could have affected their behavior on that fateful night. Although air force officials deny that they require pilots to take these drugs, the consent form presented to their aviators suggests otherwise.

It is not surprising that military officials are unwilling to endorse the doping of their personnel openly and unambiguously. "The aviation community and the air force community certainly don't like to talk about so-called 'performance enhancing' drugs," one defense policy expert pointed out during the Afghanistan inquiry. The blanket stigmatizing of drugs by governmental authorities forces those responsible for producing even legitimate drug-dependent performances to cover up or apologize for their pharmacological policies. In this sense, the U.S. Air Force policy that issues amphetamines to pilots and authorizes them to "self-regulate" their drug use bears a striking resemblance to the tacit drug policy followed for many years by the professional cyclists who ride in the Tour de France.

The same predicament has confronted Australian authorities, who in 1998 discovered that large numbers of soldiers in one of their elite units were using doping drugs. They responded by legitimizing these drugs and issuing guidelines for their use, on the grounds that any technique that promoted the survival of their fighting men was acceptable. In 2002 the Australian Defence Force's director of personnel operations expressed concern about an "apparent increase in illegal drug use, particularly steroid abuse" among soldiers. The *Sydney Morning Herald* reported that these military personnel were "using steroids to bulk up, boost stamina and self-esteem and to recover more quickly from injuries they have sustained." This ostensibly rational use of steroids could lead to a compulsory doping subculture if left unchecked. The director of personnel operations thus felt obliged to declare that steroid doping would subvert rather than enhance a soldier's fitness: "Drug involvement leads to reduced performance, health impairment, presents a security risk and has the potential to endanger the safety of our soldiers." As in the case of amphetamine-consuming pilots, a military establishment found itself caught between the potential utility of performance-enhancing drugs and a social stigma that threatened to become a public relations problem. The solution was to declare that any performance enhancement from these drugs came at too high a price in undesirable side effects. The problem with this argument, as we shall see, is that it offers no justification for banning performance-enhancing drugs that do not have side effects.

Compulsory doping in the workplace is a real possibility in a culture that promotes productivity and accepts pharmacological solutions to human problems. "How might a substance like Prozac enter into the competitive world of American business?" Peter D. Kramer asked in *Listening to Prozac*. As in the world of high-performance sport, it can be a short step from posing such questions to implementing performance-enhancing solutions that exert pressure on every performer. Some years later another psychiatrist answered Kramer's question by pointing out that SSRI (selective serotonin reuptake inhibitor) antidepressants like Prozac had become "all-purpose psychoanalgesics" for competitive situations. "People think they've got to keep up with the Joneses, pharmacologically—if everyone at your office is taking Zoloft to stay alert and work long hours, you've got to have it, too." This is the predicament Kramer had already anticipated in his best-selling book. The same dynamic has promoted the use of antidepressants and other psychiatric medications among American students—a trend that some find troubling. "We work against having medication used in the Olympics," says the director of psychological services at one American college, so why should drug-taking be allowed to "increase performance in school?" This flagrant discrepancy between the treatment of athletic and academic performances amounts to an unresolved cultural crisis to which we shall return later in this book.

Such scenarios show how hard it can be to determine where therapy ends and performance enhancement begins. This uncertainty about the boundary between healing and enhancement changes our sense of what is "normal" and what is not. If I become fatigued while my drug-taking coworkers stay alert, their "supernormal" stamina may well recalibrate the very idea of normal functioning. Their greater productivity might eventually legitimize their doping habit and make it compulsory for everyone. In this work environment, it is the drug-free worker who is in a state of deficiency. The ultimate drug of this kind, currently being marketed as Provigil, can apparently keep people awake and alert for days. Small wonder it "is showing signs of becoming a lifestyle drug for a sleep-deprived 24/7 society" that demands round-the-clock performance from employees. "Even as sleep disorders increase," Jerome Groopman notes, "firms are pushing their employees to disrupt their normal sleep patterns in order to provide services around the clock." In the meantime, the company that manufactures Provigil is asking the Food and Drug Administration (FDA) for permission to expand its uses to make it a billion-dollar drug.

The logic of obligatory self-medication has shaped the use of female hormone replacement therapy (HRT) for decades. The declared purposes of estrogen replacement were to enhance both the labor productivity and the sexual appeal of aging women. More than half a century ago the American Medical Association recommended estrogen replacement for all menopausal female workers during the Second World War to promote efficiency: "The employee may because of her emotional instability become irritable and thus lessen production," one concerned commentator warned. After the war, as we shall see, many physicians promoted estrogen replacement therapy (ERT) with great success as an anti-aging therapy that could provide husbands with more satisfying sexual partners and thereby save endangered marriages. The biochemistry of sexual pleasure could thus enhance social stability.

Today's version of hormone-enhanced well-being for older women is based on demands for productivity, disease prevention, and sexual fulfillment. It is important to recognize that these calls can come from institutions as well as from individuals. For example, the demand for emotionally stable female production-line workers in the 1940s eventually became a demand for emotionally stable female executives. In the 1960s the estrogen-promoting physician Robert Wilson warned: "With more and more women entrusted with decision-making posts in business, government, and in various institutions, the effects of menopause present a new type of management problem that has yet to be fully understood by the experts of corporate administration." According to Sonia McKinlay, an expert on menopause, "letting it be known that you're on HRT may become a requirement for women in upper levels of management and government to prove that they're 'in control' of possible symptoms and not declining. Margaret Thatcher made it known that she was a user" to legitimize her power in the eyes of her male colleagues.

Hormone replacement can also be presented as a cost-saving public health program:

> Hormonal replacement therapy . . . is now promoted on a large scale for preventing osteoporosis and cardiovascular diseases. If a consensus is

reached in biomedical science that menopause is a deficiency disease, this will have important implications for physicians and women alike. If the physician wants to act according to good medical practice, the prescription of hormonal replacement therapy is not only legitimated, but will be imperative. On the other hand, it is conceivable that the woman suffering from one of the aforementioned diseases, and who declines to take hormonal therapy, will be held responsible for her condition. . . .

Presenting hormonal replacement therapy in economic terms is likely to turn it into a political issue. In the worst of all scenarios, one can imagine that social security will penalize women for diseases or invalidity allegedly due to hormone deprivation.

Hormone therapy to promote sexual desire in older women can include the administration of testosterone as well as estrogen. This procedure is increasingly popular, in part because of the greater sexual demands of older men who are now taking Viagra. "Patients come in and they look you straight in the eye and say, 'I have no libido, something's wrong, fix it,' " says Dr. Mary Lake Polan, head of the department of obstetrics and gynecology at Stanford University School of Medicine. "Five years ago, nobody ever came in and said that. And I can't believe there has been a change in the way people relate to each other in that period of time." This surge in demand for aphrodisia is symptomatic of a growing medicalization of modern life that appears to create opportunities for deepening human experience. Yet a medical technique that restores sexual activity can also be experienced as a mandate to be sexually active even in the absence of desire. Constant exposure to modern society's sexual propaganda means that "many people will feel 'inadequate' when faced with evidence about extremes of sexual performance." Drug-induced sexual fitness and the concept of "performance" can turn sexual relations into an intimate competitive sport judged by quantitative norms. Thus "lifestyle" medicine appears to offer a choice as to "whether to grow old or not" as a professionally or sexually active person. In either case, whether the decision is to become more productive or to become more erotic, the availability of the hormone can create a social pressure to use it.

Why testosterone did not become a mass-market drug in the 1940s is a major theme of this book. The most important factor was the sexual conservatism of most physicians and the society they served. The belief that testosterone was a sexually stimulating drug made it a potential threat to sexual morality as well as a promising therapy. Sensational coverage had given the male hormone a quasi-pornographic image that its female counterpart had never acquired. Commenting on testosterone's unsavory reputation in 1946, *Science Digest* reported that "the uninformed continue to believe that the sole use of this innocent chemical is to turn sexual weaklings into wolves, and octogenarians into sexual athletes."

The pharmaceutical companies that sought to shape medical opinion by placing advertisements in professional journals were not yet allowed to go directly to the public and solicit customers for prescription drugs over the heads of their physicians. What is more, the aging men of the 1940s directed their requests for testosterone to male physicians who often had little interest in salvaging the sex lives of middle-aged or older people. The campaign to sexually rejuvenate senior citizens was not possible until a momentous social transformation of attitudes toward erotic experience had taken place. During the second half of the twentieth century the Kinsey Reports on human sexuality, together with the sexual freedom made possible by the birth control pill, dismantled the old cultural restraints that had prevented sexual expression from becoming an entitlement for the adult population.

■

This book tells the story of testosterone's gradual liberation from the restraints that have limited its use over the past sixty-five years. The transformation of testosterone's roles inside and outside of medicine has taken place both in the larger social sphere, where ideas about health and sexual mores shape human desires and behaviors, and within the smaller world of clinical medicine that evaluates and promotes therapeutic drugs. In the larger world the use of testosterone was once inhibited by a social conservatism that kept most doctors uninterested in the sexual problems of older people. In addition, the idea that testosterone might serve as a "tonic" for the general population has for many years made little headway against the belief that people with normal hormone levels cannot benefit from supraphysiologic doses of the drug. "The prevailing experience," the American Medical Association reported in 1941, "is that endocrine preparations almost invariably fail when they are given to otherwise normal individuals" for the purpose of stimulating sexual desire. The same principle applied when testosterone was administered to stimulate premature babies or estrogen was given to women to increase the size of their breasts. The marketing of testosterone and estrogen thus required the concept of a hormone deficiency that could be normalized by means of synthetic hormone products. Only such a deficiency legitimized hormone therapy.

Today it is the aging process that provides the deficiency that justifies hormone therapies that can include testosterone, human growth hormone, or both. The dramatic increase in the use of testosterone products is now a matter of record, even if medical authors are unable to determine how much of this trade outside doctors' control occurs on the black market. The medical publications that once decried hormone quackery now serve as a forum for a cautious but unmistakable legitimizing of hormone therapy to treat the process that has become known as the male menopause or andropause. "Improvement of clinical symptoms of andropause via androgen substitution therapy has long been recognized," one team of medical researchers noted in 2002. The list of symptoms—diminished energy, virility, fertility and a decrease in bone and muscle mass—shows how easy it is to conflate declining hormone levels and the aging process itself. Clinical guidelines for the diagnosing of low male testosterone levels (hypogonadism), published with pharmaceutical industry support in 1996, point to "symptoms that are often denied by the patient and ignored by the physician. . . . In aging men, these symptoms and signs may be difficult to appreciate because they are often attributed to 'getting older.' " This intriguing observation suggests that hormone therapy can make getting older a symptom-free experience, and it is this illusion that does much to sustain the "anti-aging" hormone market. The frequent use of terms such as *quality of life* and *psychological well-being* to describe the effects of hormone therapies employing testosterone, the adrenal hormone DHEA (dehydroepiandrosterone), or the "prohormone" androstenedione makes it clear that their purpose is life enhancement as well as therapy in the traditional sense.

Testosterone therapy is also being presented as less hazardous that it was once assumed to be. Even as "designer androgens," which would have minimal effects on the prostate and on cholesterol levels, are being developed, the long-standing medical concern that exogenous testosterone stimulates the growth of existing prostate cancers has been called into question. A 1996 study that administered supraphysiologic doses of testosterone to normal men for ten weeks detected no unhealthy side effects. The report concludes, however, with the standard warning about the possible consequences of extended use that has appeared in many such reports over the past decade.

This ongoing conflict between cautionary statements and cautious optimism about hormone therapy has created an opening for medical practices that inhabit the gray zone between scientifically based medicine and quackery. The medical literature on the promises and hazards of testosterone and human growth hormone therapy has created a disorienting situation that is easily exploited by entrepreneurial physicians who have chosen not to wait for long-term clinical trials of these hormone therapies. The stunning discovery in 2002 that the overall risks of ERT outweighed its benefits demonstrated that even decades of studies endorsing the value of a hormone treatment can be wrong. As the principal investigator of the dissenting federal study notes: "They linked up a very beneficial product for treating menopausal symptoms to the answer for treating all of a woman's aging problems," and it was the powerful appeal of a way to solve these problems that prevailed over scientific caution. According to the same study, hormone therapy for menopause did not even improve "quality of life" measures such as sexual enjoyment. Here massive anecdotal evidence of lifestyle benefits collided with the best available clinical data, leaving doctors wondering where the HRT boom had come from in the first place. Testosterone, too, has benefited from a massive anecdotal endorsement of its effects and may well prove to be vulnerable to the same kind of scrutiny that has undone the reputation of HRT for women.

Finally, access to testosterone is facilitated by the various tricks and maneuvers that patients and doctors can use to circumvent the Anabolic Steroids Control Act of 1990, which places limits on a physician's ability to prescribe anabolic steroids for patients who might need them. *Testosterone* magazine offers advice on how to find and manipulate "open-minded" doctors by inventing symptoms or producing them by means of dieting and sleep deprivation. A far more significant workaround is the legal prescription of these drugs for "off-label" uses, defined as "treatment indications with little or no proven efficacy" that also lack package insert information approved by the FDA. Even though this federal agency's approval of a drug is limited to the treatment of a specific disease, doctors are free to prescribe drugs for other uses—including anti-aging therapies. This is how every blockbuster drug, from Prozac to Provigil, becomes a marketing phenomenon. This is why "the vast majority of psychotropic medications prescribed for preschoolers are being used off-label." The use of human growth hormone (HGH) has spread in a similar fashion, since "estimates suggest that one third of prescriptions for growth hormone in the United States are for indications for which it is not approved by the Food and Drug Administration." Prescribing these drugs to patients who have off-label disorders amounts to conducting large-scale experiments on human subjects under the rubric of therapy. The male hormone, too, has inspired many such experiments. *Testosterone Dreams* can thus be read as the story of how synthetic testosterone is becoming a major off-label drug.

CHAPTER 1

Hormone Therapy and the New Medical Paradigm

ENHANCEMENTS: WHERE ARE THE LIMITS?

As the sun rises over the Palm Springs Life Extension Institute, situated amid the palm trees in the desert a hundred miles east of Los Angeles, a bare-chested patient named Bob Jones is already ascending into the foothills of the Little San Bernardino Mountains. Clasping two hiking sticks, his bodybuilder's torso dripping with sweat, the seventy-year-old prodigy wipes a lock of implanted hair out of his eyes and presses on toward the summit. His new and strenuous life under medical supervision has become a single-minded campaign against death and decay. "No one," he says, "can age with dignity without a body that works." Not surprisingly, the dignity of the body comes at a price for the institute's affluent clientele: Jones has invested $60,000 in his own rejuvenation, and it is hard to imagine how this novice bodybuilder will deal with the fact of his mortality when the end finally comes. In the meantime, he will continue his individualized regimen of "Total Hormone Replacement Therapy"—injections of testosterone and human growth hormone, topically applied testosterone gel, tablets of melatonin, and as many as six other hormones that are supposed to slow the aging process and intensify the patient's sense of well-being and sexual vigor. "Aging," the medical director of the Life Extension Institute declares, "is a disease" that can be treated with hormones. His clear implication is that only fools or masochists would refuse to take them.

Inspiring stories of hormonal rejuvenation appeared often during the 1990s. The American Academy of Anti-Aging Medicine, founded in Chicago in 1993, now has more than 11,000 members, most of them physicians, and many of them offer hormone replacement therapy. These and other proponents of hormone therapy promote the idea of a male menopause (or "andropause") to justify their medical evangelism, and the popular press has offered frequent encouragement. *Newsweek*'s "Testosterone" cover story in 1996 described the Life Extension Institute as "the vanguard of a nascent movement to reshape American manhood" and offered its own anecdotal accounts of the mental, physical, and sexual renewal of aging men. "In the next few years," Gail Sheehy told the readers of *Vanity Fair* the same year, "all kinds of people, particularly affluent boomers, will seek out anti-aging specialists for custom-designed hormone cocktails." Britain's most prominent advocate of testosterone therapy, Dr. Malcolm Carruthers, whose Harley Street clinic is said to have administered testosterone treatments to more than a thousand men, described a typical case: "The menopausal man has lost his ability, and often his will, to succeed and in consequence he is depressed." The effect of testosterone implants, according to one satisfied patient, "was like being turbo-boosted."

How can we assess the social and medical significance of such reports? First, we must keep in mind that the marketing of rejuvenation techniques has been flourishing since the latter part of the nineteenth century. So our first question is whether today's hormone therapies represent a medical advance over what came before them. Second, we cannot accept at face value journalistic reports about drug therapies in general and hormone therapies in particular. These stories tend to be too credulous and are frequently used to sell magazines rather than present the public with balanced coverage of medical advances. Finally, we want to know how many people are actually getting such hormone treatments, where these services are available, and who is providing them. "I strongly suspect that there is a significant level of testosterone and hormone replacement going on, very much the same way estrogen is used in the general population," says Dr. Charles E. Yesalis, an epidemiologist and steroid expert. "But we don't have, to my knowledge, any real hard data on the prevalence of hormone use."

I argue here that demand for hormone therapies has now achieved a momentum that is both unprecedented and unstoppable. Public interest in hormones, unregulated "dietary supplements," and the hormone substitute Viagra has created a kind of parallel medical universe, a cottage industry of hormone clinics and Internet consultants equipped with medical degrees and prescription pads. Here we find, to take another example, the so-called Swiss Rejuvenation Clinic, headquartered in the Bahamas, with offices across the United States where prospective clients can have their blood tested for hormone "deficiencies" that will qualify them for injections of testosterone and human growth hormone. Here, too, is the Palm Springs Life Extension Institute, where a diverse clientele of sick, anxious, or narcissistic people pursue rejuvenation through Total Hormone Replacement Therapy. These operations thrive in a medical twilight zone, situated somewhere between quackery and mainstream medicine, that has existed since the marketing of glandular extracts began more than a hundred years ago. A fundamental thesis of this book is that powerful social forces are now pushing many mainstream physicians into this expanding hormone therapy market and its entrepreneurial ethos in the absence of countervailing values or interest groups of comparable influence. Nor is this migration of physicians into anti-aging therapy limited to the United States. In Germany, those competing for patients include urologists, endocrinologists, internists, dermatologists, and even gynecologists whose female patients bring along their husbands as prospective clients. In November 2000 a public relations firm specializing in men's health (Medical Connection) sponsored a Men's World Day in Vienna that featured celebrities such as Mikhail Gorbachev and Simon Wiesenthal. This event, as well as recent professional congresses on "The Aging Man" (Leipzig) and "Anti-Aging Medicine" (Berlin), points to the growing influence of male hormone therapy. According to the German endocrinologist Bruno Allolio, "We are being steamrollered by the demands of the patients. A huge, uncontrolled field experiment has begun."

The search for rejuvenation through hormones and other drugs confronts us with profound questions about the role of biomedical ambition in the lives of modern people who place a premium on preserving their physical, sexual, and psychological functioning. For the "enhancing" of human capacities is now a large and expanding commercial enterprise that has created a new class of medical entrepreneurs who offer what one researcher has called "medically reinforced normality." Plastic surgeries, once an exotic enhancement procedure, are experiencing dramatic growth and acquiring a new respectability among doctors and laymen alike. The booming trade in a vast array of "supplements," an ambiguous category of manufactured substances that fall somewhere between food and drugs, is additional evidence that enormous numbers of people now accept physiological performance enhancement as a way of life. Whether these substances actually boost the human organism as the advertisements say they do is, for our purposes, less important than the widespread ambition to practice this socially acceptable form of "doping" ordinary people. "The use of dietary supplements has outstripped the science to support their use," says the director of the Office of Dietary Supplements at the National Institutes of Health. But this credibility gap has shadowed the hormone and supplements markets for most of a century without putting a dent in demand for what many people believe to be performance-enhancing substances. These new markets are also changing the economics of medicine, since they belong to the "alternative" medical practices that now compete effectively with traditional medicine. As physicians have watched their share of the medical market diminish, many of them are responding to customer demands for enhancement procedures, such as hormone therapies and cosmetic surgeries, that they once disdained. The current proliferation of hormone clinics that accelerated sharply during the 1990s is only one sign of the new age of medical enhancements that is now upon us.

Exploring the history of testosterone drugs allows us to understand modern attitudes toward a series of major medical issues bearing on the pharmacological enhancement of human beings. The sheer scope of these controversial topics can be expressed in the form of the following questions: How does a society define the "legitimate" uses of drugs? Who has the authority to manufacture and regulate drugs? How does the medical profession respond to public demand for drugs? Should people have the right to obtain all the drugs they want for "therapeutic" purposes? Will the current and dramatic expansion of "cosmetic medicine" promote the use of previously restricted drugs? How does a society confer official status on those "syndromes" and "disorders" (such as menopause) that justify a new pharmacological way of life? Can physicians use drugs to promote marital stability? Should society make available drugs that enhance sexual gratification for the hormonally impaired or for anyone at all? Will demands for productivity in the workplace eventually legitimate the use of hormonal or other drugs for this purpose? Should we object to the pharmacological enhancement of normal people? Should elite athletes be denied drugs that are generally available to others who can afford them? The unprecedented access to hormone drugs is in itself a significant event in the social history of modern pharmacology. How the expanding demand for them has circumvented the laws and regulations that were intended to restrict their use to small and carefully defined groups of patients is only one of the important stories this book recounts in the chapters that follow.

Regulating enhancements has proven to be very difficult because modern societies that run on the principles of productivity and efficiency cannot credibly oppose techniques that boost the human organism in order to enhance its mental, physical, and sexual performances. As one Nobel Prize–winning brain researcher put it in January 2002: "We are rapidly becoming a culture in which it will be normal to take drugs in order to function in an optimal way. In ten years we will have a pill that improves memory in older people, and they will take it. . . . Our view of what is normal is constantly changing as effective drugs come on the market." The question of what constitutes "normal" functioning is crucial to the promotion of hormone treatments that are marketed under the rubric of "anti-aging" therapy. This defiance of physical and mental decline among older people is based on what we may call a rhetoric of enhancement. Its doctrine consists of a set of assertions and predictions about the powers of hormone therapy that have been widely promulgated in the popular media. Each of these claims raises important questions about what a human being is as well as whether the human organism should be altered for various purposes. Its principal arguments are the following: the aging process is a disease process rather than a normal state; enhancement techniques are legitimate forms of "therapy"; entrepreneurial medicine is as legitimate as traditional medicine; the psychological and emotional origins of sexual problems are less important than hormone deficiencies; enhancement procedures are essential to well-being and self-respect; physicians are role models who can demonstrate their bona fides by taking hormones and undergoing plastic surgery along with their patients; hormone therapy is a safe procedure whose side effects can be predicted or avoided by proper dosing.

The philosophical issues raised by enhancement procedures originate in the most basic questions about what it means to be a human being. More specifically, enhancement procedures challenge our sense of human identity by moving or dissolving limits to functioning and performance that have been crucial to defining what a normal person is. And at the very core of the enhancement problem is the question of whether we should be concerned about preserving the mental and physical limitations that inhere in being normal representatives of the human species. Erik Parens introduces his penetrating study of this problem by asking why we should be concerned about limits at all: "Why worry about a new psychopharmaceutical agent that promised to enhance concentration and performance in school? What about a new psychopharmaceutical or genetic technology that promised to make us kinder and gentler?" It turns out there are two (related) reasons for such concern about enhancements. The potential for creating a caste of people who enjoy unfair competitive advantages is one. The other is the fear of creating an "inauthentic" self and thus leading an "inauthentic" life. Parens notes, "For those committed to the idea of *authenticity*, using drugs to pursue the idea of *self-fulfillment* is disturbing." Inauthenticity is the consequence of a hubris that attempts the creation or radical alteration of a self that is (and should remain) a product of nature.

This ideal of authenticity thus contains an obligation to practice self-restraint. For modern people, however, a restraint that refuses the benefits of medically sanctioned enhancements is a form of self-abnegation that stands in opposition to the declared ambitions of medical science and its evolving ideal of well-being. The problem of enhancements can thus be defined as a fateful choice between two attitudes toward biomedicine and what it can (and eventually will have to) offer to people who may want to alter themselves in nontraditional ways. The "normal function model" of health care aims at preserving or restoring people to life based on the premise that "there are natural differences and characteristics that medicine ought not to be used to erase." It assumes that there exists a normal kind of human functioning that is rooted in the "design of the organism." The enhancement model is based on the very different premise that "medicine really has no proper boundaries, and practitioners and their patients should be free to decide together what problems to count as 'diseases' and what interventions to count as 'treatments.' "

We may call this latter approach client-centered libertarian medicine: "One takes one's cues from the patient's value system, and negotiates toward interventions that can help achieve the patient's vision of human flourishing." Here is the medical ethos of the results-oriented partnerships between high-performance athletes and the physicians who treat them with banned hormones and stimulants. But a significant (and increasingly conspicuous) segment of today's medical clients is interested, as we have seen, in a broad range of enhancements that transcend mere athleticism. According to the American representative on the International Narcotics Control Board, Herbert S. Okun, the growing problem for regulators is not an appetite for illegal drugs, but rather client demand for a range of legal performance and body enhancers that require a doctor's prescription. "I'm talking about the performance-enhancing drugs or image-making drugs—anorectics for slimming, steroids for building muscles, methylphenidates sold under the trade name Ritalin for hyperactivity disorder and, of course, Viagra for sexual performance." This perspective is striking in that it turns the traditional model of drug abuse inside out. Once upon a time, respectable society feared contamination by illegal and disreputable drugs that were consumed by social deviants. Now regulators are concerned about a growing demand for legal drugs that serve socially sanctioned goals such as productivity, physical attractiveness, and sexual viability. The "threat" posed by such drugs originates in the very system of values that sanctions their use, and it is a paradox that has put regulators in an untenable position. For regulation becomes impossible once physicians allow patients—as some sports physicians have long allowed their athlete-clients—to specify their own pharmacological requirements so as to realize "the patient's vision of human flourishing."

Client-centered libertarian pharmacology of this kind means that the patient is in charge of how he or she is medicated. More coercive scenarios arise when "enhancement doctors" collude with employers, educators, and military authorities who have an interest in getting enhanced performances from employees, schoolchildren, and soldiers or aviators. *Newsweek* has noted existing practices that point ahead to a scenario in which cognitive workers would eventually be forced to drug themselves into a state of higher productivity: "Some colleagues and competitors of Ritalin-popping executives feel themselves at a disadvantage, like rules-respecting sprinters facing a steroid user. Will guidance counselors urge parents to give their kids memory pills before the SATs? Will supervisors 'suggest' workers take a little something to sharpen their concentration?" Such officially sanctioned doping of the workforce raises the prospect of "reverse drug-testing" that would enforce the consumption of performance-enhancing drugs by certain kinds of workers. As strange as such an arrangement may seem to people accustomed to the "war on drugs," it is probably closer than we think.

"Imagine," Parens wrote in 1993, "a new drug or genetic technology that enabled us to sleep less and thus be more productive." Less than a decade later we learn that such a drug already exists. Modafinil (Provigil) appears to be a safe and effective treatment for the sleep disorder known as narcolepsy. But the implications of such a drug extend far beyond the private lives of drowsy individuals. According to the Department of

Advanced Research Projects Agency (DARPA), "The capability to resist the mental and physiological effects of sleep deprivation will fundamentally change current military concepts of 'operational tempo' and contemporary orders of battle for the military services. In short, the capability to operate effectively, without sleep, is no less than a 21st Century revolution in military affairs." Another potential beneficiary of this drug is the international competitor dubbed by Jerome Groopman "the Olympian executive who can straddle time zones, bridging the Nasdaq and the Nikkei." Here, too, the world of high-performance sport offers itself as the prototype for larger-scale developments. The analogy between economic productivity and athletic efficiency points to the sports mode of functioning that now serves as the idealized paradigm for so much competitive behavior in the modern world.

Enhancement doctors serve several types of "patients" with various kinds of drugs. The East German doctors who treated unsuspecting female athletes with anabolic steroids during the 1970s and 1980s were pioneers in the field of coercive hormone therapies meant to boost the productivity of people whose performances supposedly served a greater good. Their predecessors in the field of coercive pharmacology were the American, British, German, and Japanese military authorities who administered amphetamines to their troops during the Second World War. Half a century later, the United States Air Force administered the amphetamine Dexedrine to most of the pilots who flew during the Persian Gulf War. In 1997 the Drug Enforcement Administration authorized Novartis (formerly the Ciba-Geigy Company) to produce 13,824 kilograms of the stimulant Ritalin to treat attention deficit disorder (ADD)—an overdiagnosed and almost undefinable condition—in about 3.5 million schoolchildren (mostly boys) and adults. In September 2000 lawyers filed suit in federal courts in California and New Jersey against the Novartis Pharmaceuticals Corporation, the manufacturer of Ritalin, and the American Psychiatric Association, alleging they had "conspired to create a market for Ritalin and expand its use." The alleged conspiracy presumably aimed at boosting the academic performance of distractible children along with the conspirators' income. As for promoting better adult functioning, Peter Kramer wonders whether the Prozac equivalent Sarafem, officially prescribed for premenstrual syndrome (PMS), will be used to pressure the moody woman "to respond to demands that she be a more affable colleague." For he, too, can see a future in which "medication to alter normal but undesirable traits may become unremarkable."

Modafinil is the most interesting of these drugs because it seems to have no adverse side effects. As David Dinges, a sleep researcher at the University of Pennsylvania, puts it, modafinil is "the most tempting drug for our society to come along in decades"—pure performance enhancement without physiological risk to the human organism. But it is also a drug that should compel us to ask some fundamental questions about our commitment to the ideal of productivity: "Now is the time to have an open and frank discussion on how far we will go as a culture, what are our priorities, how regularly do we want to manipulate our brain chemistry. What are the limits?"

Receptiveness to performance-enhancing or performance-enabling drugs of various kinds is a basic characteristic of modern civilization. Modern society's acceptance of these drugs has been effectively obscured by the notoriety of addictive drugs, such as heroin and cocaine, that have given the word *drugs* its ominous resonance. Yet even these and other disreputable narcotics will be tacitly accepted as performance-enhancing substances if they appear to offer some kind of social benefit. The drug habits of popular musicians such as Ray Charles or Keith Richards, to take two famous examples, are a familiar part of the pop cultural landscape. This kind of drug use is the unremarkable, and only faintly controversial, cost of providing musical entertainment for an enormous audience that could not care less about the drugs its icons consume. Nor does the public worry about how artists might benefit from composing or performing music while under the influence of psychotropic drugs. It is more likely, in fact, that many people regard an artist's drug use as a credential, as a source of creativity and inspiration. The legend of the Beat Generation novelist Jack Kerouac includes the story of how he wrote his cult novel *On the Road* (1957) during a twenty-day, amphetamine-fueled binge in 1951. The great French novelist Honoré de Balzac consumed massive amounts of cold, concentrated coffee on an empty stomach with the following result: "The ideas surge forth like army battalions on the field of battle, and the battle begins. Memories charge ahead, their flags unfurled; the light cavalry of comparisons develops at a magnificent gallop, while the artillery of logic arrives with its retinue," and so forth. It is a curious fact that neither mental doping of this kind nor the use of anxiety-reducing beta blockers by orchestral musicians provokes public disapproval. Unlike doped Olympic champions, Balzac and Kerouac are in no danger of losing their literary laurels because they resorted to enhancements to boost their mental productivity. As Parens notes, "There is something indeed odd in worrying about aiming technologies at the 'enhancement of human capacities.'"

Comparisons of socially acceptable and unacceptable doping practices point to the inconsistent, and sometimes illogical, rules that determine which drugs merit regulation and which do not. The commerce in alcohol and tobacco products, for example, is granted an exemption from effective regulation, despite the socially sanctioned harm inflicted by these drugs on millions of people. The key point here is that drug habits that do not appear to threaten the social and political equilibrium of a society will be only lightly regulated. Drugs that do not threaten the stability of a society's system of values fall under the same rule. This theory of how drugs are regulated enables us to formulate two hypotheses. The first is that the social status of a harmful or controversial drug can change over time, since commercial promotions, social fashions, or scientific discoveries can alter the images of drugs in ways that make them more or less vulnerable to regulation. The second proposition is that the new status of enhancements means that regulating performance-enhancing drugs is becoming increasingly difficult for the governmental agencies that are charged with this task. For the absence of a general consensus on the goals of medicine makes it ultimately impossible to say whether certain drugs are "treatments" or "enhancements." The regulation of testosterone products is, as we shall soon see, a cardinal example of how demand for a "charismatic" hormone enhancement can circumvent a regulatory process that was originally intended to protect the public from substances and procedures it was expected to regard as harmful rather than helpful.

Every society develops pharmacological practices that are the result of a complex process of negotiation that involves the public, the medical establishment, the pharmaceutical industry, and public and private institutions such as governments, schools, media, and religious organizations. Every pharmacological regime is, therefore, an inherently unstable arrangement that is subject to unpredictable scientific developments, corporate marketing ambitions, public curiosity about drugs, the whims of politicians, and the economic circumstances of physicians, who are already modifying their medical practices in order to enhance their incomes. A gradual shift from purely therapeutic medicine to practices that include "lifestyle" procedures such as cosmetic surgery and hormone therapies is already under way. Prescription drug laws and official anti-drug campaigns may at first make regulation seem like the order of the day, but one sign of the precarious state of this consensus is the seemingly unstoppable spread of drug sales on the Internet. While the United States government has announced its resolve to regulate this market, the legal and technological obstacles to regulation are formidable. The unstable consensus is also evident in the widespread use of legal and illegal drugs in an elite sport subculture in which unregulated self-medication, often with the aid of a sympathetic physician, has become the norm for many athletes. These alternative drug markets traffic in large volumes of hormone drugs and prohormones, such as the "dietary supplement" androstenedione, which was made famous by the baseball star Mark McGwire in 1998. Much larger markets for "alternative" medicines such as herbal remedies and dietary supplements are worth billions of dollars. Indeed, the influence of the supplements industry has already become a political force to be reckoned with.

These markets are now out of control, driven by a combination of medical needs, consumer fantasies, sexual and athletic ambitions, and hyperbolic media coverage of fashionable drugs. The enormous publicity surrounding superstar drugs such as Prozac and Viagra has further intensified the public's sense of entitlement to various kinds of therapeutic medications. Pharmaceutical companies are now allowed to advertise directly to consumers, bypassing physicians who are already besieged by drug company representatives and by the drug advertisements that subsidize major medical journals. These are the shifting sands on which our official pharmacological culture is based, and it is hard to imagine that the traditional restraints on consumption will survive the emerging populist pharmacology intact. Congressional resistance to regulation of the dietary supplements industry by the Food and Drug Administration (FDA) is a harbinger of the libertarian pharmacology that is already evident in the popularity of supplements and the proliferating pharmacopoeia of herbal remedies. A more libertarian approach to testosterone and other hormones is the logical next step.

How modern societies deal with hormones is significant for two reasons. First, decisions to legitimize or forbid the expanded use of drugs that can produce both mental and physical transformations create precedents that shape attitudes toward even more powerful medical procedures. Sex hormone therapies, including hormone replacement therapy (HRT) for women, are among the most widespread procedures that can (or are imagined to) alter the physiological foundations of moods and emotions and, consequently, human identity itself. In this sense, synthetic hormones are an antechamber to the Great Hall of genetic engineering and its more profound transformations of human identity. Second, understanding our deepest feelings about hormone therapies can help us to predict how we and our descendants will react to the biomedical innovations of the future. As this book demonstrates, modern feelings about hormone drugs have been on display throughout most of the past century. Today medical and popular attitudes toward these therapies still show signs of ambivalence, as interest in their potential benefits confronts deeply rooted inhibitions about the pharmacological transformation of "human nature." The prospect of extending hormone therapies and other psychoactive drug regimens into the lives of millions of aging but otherwise normal people is now at hand. We are, in fact, in the midst of an epochal contest between biomedical innovations and cultural restraints; the latter are gradually eroding under the constant pressure of pharmacological products that promise to repair the aging human organism and boost its various "performances."

The inhibitions of religious origin that have restrained intimate modifications of the human organism now confront the appeal of rejuvenating therapies for an affluent and middle-aged generation that feels entitled to medical advances of all kinds. This sense of entitlement has developed along with the view that desirable modifications of human beings are not violations of human identity but are actually forms of therapy that preserve or enhance the normal self. An important example of this kind of reasoning is the process of rationalization that permits modern societies to overcome traditional doubts about new reproductive technologies such as in vitro fertilization, the freezing of human embryos, and surrogate motherhood. As two fertility experts once described it, the initial response of "horrified negation" eventually gives way to "negation without horror," which is followed in turn by "slow and gradual curiosity, study, evaluation, and finally a very slow but steady acceptance." Recent societal responses to such drugs as Prozac and Viagra show that inhibitions about embarking on psychological and physiological enhancements survive now as an "instinctive" but weakening cultural reflex. Moreover, the time that passes between "horrified negation" and the acceptance of new transformational therapies is constantly growing shorter, owing to the erosion of the cultural restraints that are incarnated in the myth of Dr. Frankenstein and his "workshop of filthy creation." Indeed, the Frankenstein story continues to maintain its hold on the modern imagination precisely because it serves our biotechnological age as the last symbol of a need for restraint, as the ultimate warning against the biomedical blasphemies that are now taking shape before our eyes. But it is also a myth that will become increasingly peripheral to a modern civilization whose definition of human nature is constantly being modified by a panoply of therapies that are constantly changing our sense of what a normal person really is.

TESTOSTERONE AS THERAPY AND MYTH

Testosterone Dreams is a medical and social history of synthetic testosterone and the anabolic-androgenic steroids that are modified versions of the testosterone molecule. Testosterone has long been referred to as the "male" hormone, since more of this sex hormone circulates in men than in women, while women have higher estrogen levels than men. That both "male" and "female" hormones occur naturally in both sexes, albeit in different proportions, is not widely understood, because it does not conform to the hormonal folklore of our culture, which remains rooted in archetypes of hormonally determined masculine and feminine essences. The complex and interesting histories of the estrogenic (female) and androgenic (male) drugs that have been manufactured since the 1920s and 1930s, respectively, reach deep into the lives of modern men and women in more ways than are generally understood. The purpose of this book, therefore, is to illuminate the important and sometimes bizarre roles that testosterone drugs have assumed in clinical medicine and in the wider world of diverse personal needs and ambitions that range far beyond the therapeutic aims of the clinic. Both the medical and social histories of testosterone belong to the larger history of synthetic hormone drugs that must be numbered among the revolutionary medical advances of the twentieth century. "The quest for sex hormones exemplifies the dreams of modernity," the medical historian Nelly Oudshoorn notes, in that modernity demands a biological wisdom and a technological mastery that make possible human control over human biology. For these are the technologies that determine whether we will be healthy or diseased, comfortable or distressed, destined to live or to die.

The history of synthetic testosterone and its roles in the management of various disorders appears to be unknown to most medical professionals. Recent medical commentaries on possible uses for these drugs show little awareness of their long and controversial career in clinical medicine. "Scientists have only recently recognized how the decline in hormones affects sexual desire," according to one physician who specializes in sexually transmitted diseases. But if that is the case, then why were doctors recommending hormone replacement therapies for sexually declining "menopausal" men and women as early as the 1940s? "Is There a Role for Androgenic Anabolic Steroids in Medical Practice?" a contributor to the *Journal of the American Medical Association (JAMA)* asked in 1999. "Anabolic steroids," according to this cancer researcher, "have been used by the medical community in rare situations." In fact, they have been used often, and often unwisely, for the past sixty years. Unbeknownst to this author, papers asking the same question about the clinical value of androgenic drugs had been published over the preceding half century. This loss of contact with the past can have serious consequences: research may be duplicated, potentially valuable leads may be overlooked, scientists may be unduly influenced by lay opinion about hormones, and doctors may not understand their patients' needs and desires.

Testosterone occupies a unique status among the socially controversial drugs for several reasons. First, its public image is not comparable to those of intoxicants such as marijuana and cocaine that are widely believed to ruin the people who use them. Although testosterone is a psychoactive drug, most people associate it with building muscle rather than with dysfunctional dependencies. Its notoriety derives from its association with socially marginal people like bodybuilders and with the ethical transgressions of doped athletes rather than with a possible threat to the general population. Finally, testosterone is now undergoing a social rehabilitation because it is imagined to be a source of dynamic and useful personality traits for people of all ages. After more than half a century, testosterone's career as the rogue hormone is gradually coming to an end. A decade after the discovery of testosterone, one American physician wrote in 1946, "the uninformed continue to believe that the sole use of this innocent chemical is to turn sexual weaklings into wolves, and octogenarians into sexual athletes." Half a century later, sexual athleticism has become a socially sanctioned goal for everyone. It is, in fact, the unprecedented respectability of sexual therapies and performance norms for older people that is most influential in normalizing the status of testosterone products in the minds of many physicians and ordinary people.

Testosterone also appeals to a wide variety of younger people on both sides of the law. In Oslo, Norway, nightclub bouncers and criminal enforcers known as torpedoes take anabolic steroids to achieve the violent emotional state their jobs often require. "It is well known," says one Norwegian official, "that combining anabolic steroids and central nervous system stimulants like amphetamines produces violent, almost uncontrollable aggression. Some members of this underworld see this as a useful side effect." On the other side of the law, policemen in England take steroids to help them survive encounters with violent criminals. "Many officers around the country," the *Sunday Times* reports, "have turned to steroids as a way of minimizing their chances of being hurt or humiliated," thereby mimicking the behavior of steroid-consuming bodybuilders around the world. Steroid use by police officers in the

United States is both widespread and a virtually tabooed subject. The French customs police who initiated the 1998 Tour de France doping scandal found 160 vials of testosterone that were to be injected into professional cyclists to fortify them for their grueling ordeal. The Italian police who raided the hotel rooms of professional cyclists during the 2001 Giro d'Italia race found testosterone patches among other hormonal contraband. In the United States, increasing numbers of adolescent and even preadolescent boys and girls use steroids, but there is little public alarm. Steroid use among female adolescents increased rapidly during the 1990s, yet this epidemic of "reverse anorexia" has not attracted much interest. Of an estimated 83,000 teenage steroid users in Canada, 25,000 share needles to inject themselves, thereby creating a major threat to public health that receives much less attention than the injection of traditionally stigmatized drugs such as heroin and cocaine.

While testosterone was promoted as an anti-aging therapy just after the Second World War, its long career as a sexual stimulant prescribed by licensed physicians has remained one of the better-kept secrets of modern medicine. Nor is secrecy about this drug confined to its role as an aphrodisiac. Public discussion of users such as police officers, firefighters, and professional football players has been kept off the public policy agenda for many years, just as rampant drug use among Tour de France riders was covered up for decades by the many journalists and sports officials who might have reported it. In all of these cases, the interested parties enter into private arrangements that allow patients and athletes access to useful drugs. Today, the privacy of such arrangements is diminishing in the face of more frequent public claims from physicians and others that testosterone and other hormonal drugs can rejuvenate the muscles and the sex lives of an aging population.

The male sex hormone testosterone is well suited to be a charismatic drug. Pharmacological charisma means that public discussion of a drug takes for granted its power to significantly enhance the functioning of most people. The fact that only a small fraction of any population will ever use any charismatic drug is largely ignored. Far more conspicuous is the general belief that the drug can alter human nature in a new and exciting way. The image of the drug and its powers has mythic force that may bear little relation to its actual therapeutic value.

Hormones and the glandular extracts that preceded them were associated with biological vitality throughout the twentieth century. Both doctors and laypeople have seen hormones as the wellsprings of personality, while hormone deficiencies appeared to cause physical and psychological disorders. One persisting theme has been that hormones are the basis of personality itself. "Attempts have been made," one physician wrote in 1919, "to explain even psychic processes such as emotions and states of mind through the increase or diminution or alteration of secretions of this or that gland." While this explanation seemed radical at the time, it was also the shape of things to come. Reports that testicle transplants could reform the sexual orientation of bisexuals and homosexuals, or bring about "the transformation of a lethargic individual into an enthusiastic athlete," seemed to confirm the almost magical powers of glandular substances. "Now for the first time in human history," one hormone enthusiast declared in 1926, "we know the underlying causes of the quality called 'personality,' and we possess the practical means of shaping and directing it." Commenting in 1952 on the "lack of charm" of women who lack "good ovarian function," the author of *Glands, Sex, and Personality* confidently asserts that "personality reconstruction may well begin with appropriate hormones." More recent claims about the rejuvenating powers of various hormone replacement therapies continue this tradition, showing that popular belief in the power of hormones to shape identity remains the basis of their romantic aura.

The idea that testosterone is a potentially rejuvenating force of nature is supported by research on the correlation of testosterone levels with specific character traits and social behaviors. The American psychologist James M. Dabbs has defined "a high-testosterone approach to life" as a combination of flamboyance, directness, self-confidence, and what he calls "simple thought and action"—a set of traits that are a legacy of our primeval past. "The evolution of testosterone in human beings," he writes, "resulted in the muscles, energy, sexual interest, and combativeness needed for survival in a primitive world."

This research is the scientific basis for testosterone's popular association with male unruliness, which has become a familiar part of our hormonal folklore. *Testosterone poisoning* has found a place in colloquial speech as a sardonic diagnosis of masculine excess. Indeed, the word *testosterone* has entered the vernacular as a synonym for both male unpredictability and impressive displays of physical dynamism and virility. Of the many hormones that flow through the human body, only this one has been dressed up as a persona, an "attitude," and has acquired a kind of cachet. The potential for hormone-induced bedlam is conveyed in the phrase *'roid rage,* as illustrated by the steroid-abusing shot-putter who threw his girlfriend through a window. At the same time, vernacular references to testosterone and its derivatives, the anabolic-androgenic steroids, are commonly infused with a sense of irony or even jocular resignation, as if to acknowledge that these "male" behaviors are rooted in biological drives and instinctive preferences for bulked-up bodies—preferences about which little if anything can be done.

This semihumorous, and therefore inherently tolerant, attitude toward the male hormone and its effects has become ubiquitous in popular culture and journalistic parlance. In this vein, the animation experts at Disney engineer "the new anabolic Tarzan" for an audience of children already acculturated to hypermuscular action figures. The behemoths of the World's Strongest Man competition, a bizarre collection of "gargantuan mummies come to life," are featured in *Sports Illustrated* as the "Titans of Testosterone," most of whom will confirm off the record that they take steroids. Lifestyle magazines of "the men-behaving-badly genre" are "testosterone-driven." A book reviewer imagines "a testosterone-addled, myopic car nut." The stock market plunge that followed Mayor Rudolph W. Giuliani's crackdown on New York strip clubs is whimsically attributed to "a testosterone drought." The election of the former professional wrestler Jesse Ventura as governor of Minnesota is part of a "testosterone backlash" that has also fostered the rise of high-decibel male politicians such as Patrick Buchanan and Rudy Giuliani. "The testosterone flowed freely" when a ruggedly masculine actor shared military memories with a general at the U.S. Marine Corps Birthday Ball. The Hyundai Corporation once put its investment fund "on steroids" by harnessing the patriotic emotions of South Korean housewives. An armored military vehicle looks like "a Tonka toy on steroids." The "humorless, unnecessarily sadistic" film *Soldier* is "a blustering testosterama," "a testosterone-fueled futuristic fantasy."

Absent from all but the last of these images is anything resembling genuine alarm at the roles synthetic male sex hormones play in modern life. In fact, testosterone has become a positive and even fashionable concept in public discourse because it conveys the aura of power that is so useful to businesses and advertising agencies. When a *New York Times* columnist calls multinational companies "Corporations on Steroids," the point of the metaphor is sheer magnitude rather than unnatural growth. The same ambiance of power and charisma is invoked in a printed advertisement by the Saab automobile company that is inscribed on the muscled back of a bronzed male sculpture: "Anabolic steroids build muscle mass. More muscle increases strength. In car terms, this means a bigger engine and more horsepower." The equating of male hormones and sheer energy could not be more straightforward.

The notoriety of testosterone drugs has grown out of highly publicized and often ineffectual campaigns, dating from the 1970s, that seek to drive anabolic steroids out of the sports world. Steroids have also been stigmatized by their association with hundreds of thousands of self-injecting bodybuilders, who support a criminal black market and consume far more steroids (with far less publicity) than athletes do. In this connection, it is worth noting that the vernacular salute to testosterone as a form of pure energy has coincided with the mainstreaming of steroid-soaked entertainments such as bodybuilding and professional wrestling. Such signs of public indifference to steroid use remind us that the perceived hazards of testosterone poisoning have never been taken very seriously outside sports stadiums. Steroids trouble modern societies when they compromise fair competitions among elite athletes. Yet even sports doping can be presented today as a natural step in the development of athletic potential. "Many of baseball's most talented players," a veteran sportswriter wrote in 2001, "have discovered the wonders of nutrition, strength training, supplements and—in some cases—testosterone boosters such as steroids, combined with heavy lifting." "Devaluation?" he asks, then answers himself: "No, evolution. Survival of the fittest." Testosterone boosting, from this perspective, is a legitimate hormone therapy for athletes who are willing to train hard enough to earn its benefits. Removing the stigma of cheating now makes it possible to regard testosterone as just one more type of "supplement." Giving these drugs to senior citizens is even less problematic because it does not involve cheating of any kind. Why, after all, should society object to the use of drugs that may improve human functioning for an aging patient population that far exceeds the number of elite athletes who engage in doping? What, in the last analysis, is the difference between giving people testosterone and giving them a drug like Prozac?

"PSYCHIC STEROIDS":
PROZAC AS A PERFORMANCE-ENHANCING DRUG

The speed with which Prozac was dubbed a "psychic steroid" shows that the vernacular prestige of testosterone exceeds even that of the legendary antidepressant. Testosterone is, in this sense, the currency in which other performance-enhancing substances are measured; it is the fundamental unit of physiological power. That Prozac qualifies as a performance-enhancing drug is one more sign of the obsession with performance so characteristic of modern technological civilization.

The legend of Prozac was made possible by two collective and related fantasies about its effects: first, that it opened the door to made-to-order, off-the-shelf personalities; and second, that it is a performance-enhancing drug. Indeed, Prozac's most significant impact on the modern world may well have been the boost it gave to the idea that performance enhancement is a legitimate goal of both mainstream and alternative pharmacology. "Prozac's enormous appeal to patients and therapists," David J. Rothman observes, was forcing modern society to confront the prospect of "new medical interventions with even greater capacities for enhancing performance." In a similar vein, *Newsweek* claimed that Prozac was gaining a reputation as "an all-purpose personality enhancer."

Performance enhancement is a major theme of Peter Kramer's influential book *Listening to Prozac* (1993). Kramer believes that Prozac produces "a normal or near-normal condition called 'hyperthymia,' " or what the ancient Greeks called the sanguine temperament. In modern terms, this condition implies optimism, quick thinking, charisma, energy, and confidence. "Hyperthymia," Kramer points out, "can be an asset in business. Many top organizational and political leaders require little sleep, see crises as opportunities, let criticism roll off their backs, make decisions easily, exude confidence, and hurry through the day with energy to spare. These qualities help people succeed in complex social and work situations. They may be considered desirable or advantageous even by those who have quite normal levels of drive and optimism." Small wonder that shyness is considered pathological as the capitalist ethos reigns triumphant in an age of globalization that views competition as the prime mover of human progress. "The success of Prozac," according to Kramer, "says that today's high-tech capitalism values a very different temperament. Confidence, flexibility, quickness, and energy—the positive aspects of hyperthymia—are at a premium."

The notion that Prozac boosts performance spread quickly via news magazines and more sophisticated commentators who harbored no motive to hype the drug. Rothman, for example, calls Prozac "a quintessentially American drug[,] . . . an office drug that enhances the social skills necessary in a postindustrial, service-oriented economy." In her *Prozac Diary*, a brave and poetic memoir of depression, Lauren Slater uncomfortably weighs the possibility that Prozac is "the ultimately capitalist pill" that enables people to "produce babies and airplanes with a particularly American glee." These anxieties, based on intuitions about human nature rather than any real evidence, demonstrate how the conceptual framework of Aldous Huxley's novel *Brave New World* (1932) continues to shape our expectations about psychotropic drugs. In this scenario, Prozac is cast as a kind of "soma"—Huxley's wonder drug, which obliterates pain and unhappiness—that produces excessively active rather than excessively passive people. This is a valid diagnosis in that performance mania is, as we have seen, a quintessentially modern form of bondage.

Frequent comparisons of Prozac with anabolic steroids have also promoted the idea that it is a performance-enhancing drug. We have already seen how steroid drugs have taken on a life of their own as a popular symbol of force and energy, and it is socially significant that Prozac has acquired a similar aura. Kramer himself uses the steroid analogy in *Listening to Prozac* when he addresses the temptation to use antidepressants in ethically questionable ways. What if antidepressants become "steroids for the business Olympics" or "psychic steroids for mental gymnastics"? When Kramer suggests to a patient that she go back on medication for a job interview, she replies: "Wouldn't that be like taking steroids?" Slater is plagued by similar doubts about whether taking an effective antidepressant amounts to cheating in the game of life: "It is one thing to be dependent on a drug, but the issues get more thorny still if the substance imparts unfair advantage. Thus I wonder, am I now entering the wrestling ring of life on psychic steroids? Thinking of it this way, I feel not only the shame of dependency but the guilt of chicanery, and this, for sure, is yet another issue inherent in a long-term liaison with Prozac." She adds, "I don't think it's right to ingest psychic steroids," because "no one wants to be a cheater. No one wants to be a fake."

BACK TO THE FUTURE:
THE SEX HORMONE MARKET FROM ORGANOTHERAPY
TO "ANDRO"

The fear that some drugs may confer unfair advantages on those who take them points to the profound impact that steroid doping in sport has had on modern feelings about pharmacological enhancements. Earlier concerns about powerful drugs focused on threats to health rather than the possibility they might promote "inauthentic" performances. Even the widespread abuse of amphetamines during the 1940s and 1950s did not arouse such fears, despite an early report that Benzedrine might produce higher scores on intelligence tests. The striking fact that androgens acquired a social stigma almost entirely because of the disgrace associated with athletic cheating shows how deeply the world of sport can leave its mark on our thinking about the ethical importance of "fairness" and "a level playing field." But this social stigma's curious origin also suggests how it might be removed. Normalizing the use of drugs by athletes removes the stigma of cheating and confers on the drugs a new social (and market) status that can make their use routine. The United States Olympic Committee's $20 million sponsorship contract with the supplement manufacturer Pharmanex, covering the period 2000–2004, demonstrates that some sports officials are perfectly willing to encourage athletes to stuff themselves with chemicals if this practice can be presented as an alternative to what is officially defined as doping. Those who have the power to define doping are thus in a position to create markets for "supplements" that bear their official seal of approval. Doping is, then, a matter as much of semantics as of pharmacology. From a marketing standpoint, the ideal product would combine the power of a doping drug with the comfortable familiarity of a home remedy.

Such products are known as tonics, performance boosters that have kept their innocence, thanks to the legitimacy bestowed by society on folk medicines that are enveloped in an aura of tradition. The tonics of the nineteenth century promised to invigorate the organism without violating its natural limits. Today the term *tonic* evokes a substance that has earned its place in that popular pharmacopoeia of home remedies and herbal beverages that are simply immune to questions about "legitimate" or "illegitimate" use. It is this special status that makes the concept of the tonic interesting, since it signifies performance enhancement within limits that appear to be sanctioned by a folk tradition. When, for example, the Coca-Cola Company advertised its beverage as "the ideal brain tonic" during the 1890s, it was claiming only that this product could "invigorate the fatigued body and quicken the tired brain." The U.S. government scientist who later tried to stop this marketing of caffeine, on the grounds that it was a medically dangerous "stimulant," did not prevail. Coca-Cola prevailed in its semantic war with a government regulator by establishing that its product was a "tonic" rather than a "stimulant," and a commercial dynasty was born.

Before they were associated with athletic cheating, androgens were often regarded as tonics. For as long as they have existed, synthetic androgens and other hormones have been seen as "productive" drugs that provide energy for normal people dealing with the stresses of modern life or the aging process. Androgens, the crude testicular extracts that preceded them, and adrenaline (a famous hormone) have always been seen as energizing stimulants or as tonics. In 1921, for example, an endocrinologist called thyroxin—one of the first synthetic hormones to actually cure disease—"a general cell stimulant," "the 'tonic' *par excellence*" that could even slow down the aging process. A year later L. L. Stanley credited "testicular substance" with the "promotion of bodily well-being." "Androgens," a *JAMA* editorial reported in 1942, "exert a tonic and stimulating action, associated perhaps with their metabolic effects." For the British gerontologist Vladimir Korenchevsky, sex hormones were "natural stimulants." A 25-milligram dose of testosterone, *JAMA* told its readers in 1945, "is usually adequate when the preparation is given for its tonic effect." A year later the Chicago surgeon Victor Lespinasse called testosterone "a general body stimulant." In 1951 *Geriatrics* remarked on the "general stimulative effects of androgens," which appeared to involve "some obscure over-all enhancement of certain physiologic processes." In 1953 an Italian gynecologist recommended androgen for its "tonic and dynamogenic" effects on sexually "frigid" and depressive women. In 1971 a professor at the University of Washington School of Medicine referred to testosterone as an "anabolic tonic" and saw no reason not to inject it into aging men for its placebo effect. As we have seen, this practice continues today in private clinics. What we do not know is the extent to which testosterone is still being prescribed as a tonic in general medical practice.

These endorsements demonstrate the essentially benign image that androgens have enjoyed in the world of clinical medicine. Confidence in their safety led physicians for several decades to prescribe male hormone substances to infants and children. As early as 1920 a medical report from Paris recommended testicle organotherapy for its "tonic and stimulating influence" on children. Reports appearing in 1949 and 1961 show that doctors gave oral and injectable forms of testosterone to premature infants, both male and female, to accelerate their growth. A study published in 1950 found that methyl testosterone made babies grow faster without affecting the size of their sex organs and was therefore "perfectly safe." Testosterone was given to anorexic and underweight children as "a general growth stimulant" that was also appreciated for the "increased vigor, aggressiveness and self-confidence which accompanied the somatic improvement." Though the unwanted side effects of androgens had been known since the early 1940s, they caused little alarm: "The virilizing action of testosterone has been somewhat of an impediment to its full utilization in women and children," one pediatrician wrote in 1954. "It increases the susceptibility to sexual excitement and causes increased hypertrophy and sensitivity of the clitoris and penis." That testosterone is a sexual stimulant has remained, curiously enough, a relatively unpublicized theme within postwar medicine and has thus contributed little to the drug's public image until recently. It is rather the notoriety of the muscle-building anabolic steroid, the corrupter of sport, that made testosterone a drug that has required public "rehabilitation."

Disapproval of androgenic (male hormone) drugs is not one of our cultural reflexes, because Western societies have never been conditioned to reject testosterone or other hormones as threats to social stability, productive ambition, or general "well-being"—a term that medical authors have frequently used to describe the positive mood effects of testosterone therapy. On the contrary, public enthusiasm for the primitive glandular extracts that became popular during the 1890s persisted as these substances were gradually refined into identifiable and manufacturable hormones during the 1920s and 1930s. Indeed, public interest became strong enough to prompt the Surgical Section of the Medical Society of the State of New York to pass a resolution in 1920 declaring: "The promiscuous use by the laity of preparations of the glands of internal secretion has led to manifest harm." The resolution went on to request that the American Medical Association "take the necessary steps to prevent any endocrine preparation being sold to the public except on a physician's prescription." Two years later a physician in Baltimore commented: "An extravagant use of these products must be hard to resist at a time when almost every layman has had his interest aroused in one way or another in the internal secretions . . . and when consultants are daily besieged by both laymen and physicians with requests to examine a great variety of patients who 'surely must have something wrong with their glands.' " "The laity are becoming versed in the 'wonders' of endocrinology," an Ohio physician observed that same year. "The physician must become informed as to the actual facts." The surgeon L. L. Stanley, who transplanted the testicles of executed prisoners into aging inmates at San Quentin Penitentiary to rejuvenate them, came to the conclusion that ordinary citizens did not share "the bad impression" that "monkey-gland" surgeries and other dubious treatments of the day had made on the medical profession. The public, he wrote in 1922, "clamored for more news about this wonderful and all-absorbing topic, with its mystery and sex-appeal. It became a very interesting topic of conversation among men as well as women in all walks of life."

This conflict between the public's appetite for hormones and the medical profession's resolve to make hormones controlled substances has not been resolved. Nor has the other significant division of opinion, which created pro- and anti-glandular therapy factions among the physicians themselves. One of the early observers described two opposing camps: "the over-conservative group, who assume that the field is merely one of fantastic vagaries," and "the uncritical enthusiasts, who assume a large body of well substantiated fundamental facts that do not exist." "There prevails a widespread feeling," another doctor wrote in 1922, "that many practitioners are making use of endocrine products in therapy in an indiscriminate and haphazard way," administering various substances "merely because advertising matter strongly commends their trial." Medical editorials warned of "pseudoscientific rubbish promulgated by the exploiters of organic extracts." Almost a century later, comparable editorials and warnings in the medical literature bear witness to how ambiguous the medical and social status of sex hormone drugs has remained. While more cautious physicians publish admonitory editorials in medical journals, others accommodate their patients' desires outside the conventional world of insurance company oversight while expressing full confidence in hormone therapies that have been controversial for decades.

The libertarian approach to hormone therapy is rooted in the twentieth-century idea that hormones have mysterious powers. Imagine, for example, a medical universe in which glandular extracts called hormones and glandular surgeries and radiation treatments have made magical effects and transformations the order of the day. Hormones govern psychic processes. Mental diseases are treated with the gonads of lower vertebrates. Animal hormones govern the physiology of plants. Sex gland fluids heal wounds. Testicular transplants rejuvenate old men. Ovary transplants stimulate pregnancy. Sexual identity can be reversed, and homosexuality can be undone. Surgery rescues bisexuals from their ambiguous condition. Sexual desire can be intensified or anesthetized at will. Hormonal changes produce the "vernal crisis," a state of elation that stimulates sexual desire in people in the Northern Hemisphere in the spring. A vegetable aphrodisiac hormone rouses desire. Irradiation of the ovaries cures nymphomania.

This combination of science, fantasy, and speculation defined the early phase of endocrinology during the 1920s and the 1930s. Genuinely valuable hormone therapies had appeared as early as the 1890s, at a time when scientists, physicians, and the public had begun to elaborate a glandular folklore that would take decades to refine into the science of endocrinology. The discovery that thyroid extract could cure myxedema (hypothyroidism) had been made in 1891. That the intravenous injection of adrenal extract caused blood pressure to rise was reported in 1894, and a year later pituitary extract was found to have a similar effect. The success of the thyroid and adrenal therapies lent credibility to a wide range of glandular extract treatments, or organotherapies, that achieved wide popularity in Europe and the United States. As late as 1924 organotherapy was still being defined as "the use of animal glandular extracts to supplement those produced in the body in cases where the activity of the gland is thought deficient." These treatments were based on the principle that various organs produce specific chemicals that are essential to physiological functioning. Physiologists could confirm this theory by removing, let us say, a thyroid gland or a pancreas from an experimental animal and observing the pathological result of the amputation. This early theory of hormone replacement therapy was confirmed when normal functioning was restored by the injection of an extract of the missing organ. The idea that such "chemical messengers" play an important role in regulating physiological processes was revolutionary, because it challenged the nineteenth-century idea that these processes were controlled by the nervous system.

Sex hormone therapy originated just over a century ago in a scientifically naïve yet epochally creative experiment by a distinguished European scientist. On June 1, 1889, the French physiologist Charles-Édouard Brown-Séquard, then seventy-two, told a startled audience at the Société de Biologie in Paris that he had recently succeeded in drastically reversing the effects of his own physical decline over the past quarter century by injecting himself with a liquid extract derived from the testicles of a dog and a guinea pig. Twenty years earlier, Brown-Séquard had proposed injecting the sperm of a healthy animal into the veins of an old man to produce greater vitality. Now he had confirmed the scientific wisdom of this theory by performing the experiment upon himself. The injections had increased his physical strength and intellectual energy and even lengthened the arc of his urine. The result, he claimed, was a "radical change" in both the physiological and psychological function of an aging man. That this "dynamogenic" effect of glandular origin was essentially an unexplained manifestation of biological energy only enhanced its appeal as a therapeutic technique. Extravagant claims about the medical benefits of crude testicular and ovarian extracts circled the globe, creating a therapeutic market that ran far ahead of the efforts of experimental physiologists to confirm their actual effects. Today we know that the extracts Brown-Séquard injected into his patients could not have had the physiological results he imagined. To be sure, it is possible that these injections produced a number of "cures," but their success would have been due to the power of suggestion, the so-called placebo effect. Nevertheless, Brown-Séquard had correctly intuited the existence and some of the functions of sex hormones decades before they were identified and then synthesized during the 1920s and 1930s.

As the progenitor of twentieth-century hormone replacement therapy, the organotherapy movement launched by Brown-Séquard in the early 1890s brought into being a hormone market that has greatly expanded over the past hundred years. Understanding this market requires an analysis of its important features, which have evolved along with the purity and therapeutic effectiveness of drugs that originated as crude and ineffective animal extracts. While the quality of today's hormonal products is vastly superior to what was available in the 1890s, the dynamics of their distribution—that nexus of physicians, consumers, media, and manufacturers that constitutes a market—has changed less than one might expect after the passage of more than a century. Then as now, the medical establishment was divided into credulous and skeptical factions, the public was curious about the possibility of rejuvenating therapies, and unscrupulous entrepreneurs offered dubious products for sale. In its infancy, however, this market naturally differed in some ways from the much larger and more sophisticated markets for hormones that flourished during the 1920s and 1930s and then again after the Second World War.

For one thing, the early campaign on behalf of organotherapy was a medical and not a commercial project. Brown-Séquard and his assistant Arsène d'Arsonval were medical crusaders who distributed their testicular extracts free of charge to interested physicians both in France and abroad. The originators of this treatment thus differed from important factions among their medical contemporaries in three important respects. First, as already noted, their motive was therapeutic rather than economic. Second, they had a concept of medical ethics that distinguished them from opportunistic quacks and reckless medical colleagues. In the United States, Brown-Séquard complained in 1889, "Several physicians or rather the medicasters and charlatans have exploited the ardent desires of a great number of individuals and have made them run the greatest risks, if they have not done much worse." A year later the British medical journal the *Lancet* told its readers about another type of American practitioner:

> There is always a class of medical men who are ready at once to test the value of any new remedy, and during the past month [December 1889] the newspapers have been filled with experiments made in various parts of the country. It is surprising at the first blush to note the different results obtained as reported. In the hands of one experimenter the paralysed immediately walk, the lame throw aside cane and crutches, the deaf hear, and the blind see. The same experiments failed altogether in the practice of another.

In 1893 the *British Medical Journal* noted that "manufacturing chemists" in Britain were making extracts from almost every organ in the body: "We find medical men writing of these ideas and of the cures achieved in the most sanguine strain, and often upon no better evidence than quacks produce for their 'cures.' " Third, Brown-Séquard confronted a skeptical medical establishment whose doubts about organotherapy eventually proved to be both right and wrong, in that his mistaken claims about therapeutic results did not negate his crucial insight into the importance of "internal secretions" as physiological regulators.

All of these late-nineteenth-century issues are relevant to the hormone market of our own era, even as some aspects of the market have changed. Conceptual breakthroughs are now achieved not by the lone investigator who experiments on himself but by competing teams of scientists employed by pharmaceutical firms—a commercial strategy that developed during the 1920s. One consequence of this change is that commercialization has become the premise rather than (as it was in the 1890s) a consequence of drug development. At the same time, the conflict between the medical establishment and its own hormone enthusiasts gets much less attention than it did at the turn of the century, in part because of how the press covers it. Lay publications such as *Newsweek, Vanity Fair,* and *Muscle and Fitness,* which have their own economic incentives to promote hormone therapy as an emerging branch of mainstream medicine, have good reason not to look for quackery in this market. Another factor is the greater institutional self-confidence of modern medicine itself. The medical establishment's campaign against various forms of quackery was more active and conspicuous when scientific medicine had not yet achieved the great prestige it came to enjoy in the course of the twentieth century. The physicians' campaign against a wide variety of glandular nostrums and their promoters was thus part of an ongoing struggle for the scientific respectability that would distinguish them from hucksters. This was a delicate matter at a time when Brown-Séquard was reporting that testicular extracts had been shown to cure, or have some positive effect on, pulmonary tuberculosis, cancer, diabetes, anemia, paralysis, and many other disorders. Small wonder that early organotherapy encountered so much official skepticism, quite apart from the inevitable squeamishness about products that derived from the sex organs of animals. In retrospect, it is clear that the great number of reported "cures" were due to careless observations by physicians or to mood changes experienced by credulous patients who were vulnerable to the power of suggestion. And though these results were being reported by physicians, not by quacks, those who had adopted the methods of the great Brown-Séquard were hardly unbiased. For this reason, distinguishing between the doctor and the charlatan was not the straightforward procedure that the medical profession would have liked it to be.

This medical identity crisis persisted into the 1920s, when the commercialization of gland extracts was becoming a big business. Commentaries from this period refer over and over again to the disagreements and sheer confusion that prevailed among endocrinologists regarding these drugs. "The attempt to estimate the significance of endocrinology to present day medicine presents a difficult task," one researcher wrote in 1921. "To one class of practitioners, endocrinology betokens a mass of extravagant absurdities on a par with phrenology or mesmerism. To another class it betokens a new gospel, the light of which is destined to guide medicine to glorious heights." Caught between these dogmatic extremists, cautious practitioners could not trust the testimony of their own colleagues: "The mere fact that hundreds of physicians and thousands of patients have testified to having profited by the use of this or that endocrine preparation" meant nothing in the circumstances. The uncritical acceptance of glandular remedies by many physicians and patients led in turn to a wide-open hormone market that endangered the reputation of a scientific field that was still struggling toward respectability. "The literature of the day," another endocrinologist wrote in 1924,

> is crowded with articles written by misguided enthusiasts who, having mistaken nebulous theory for scientific fact, argue from false premises toward absurd deductions. As a result both of such writings and of the propaganda of certain of the commercial houses, we see an ever increasing army

of practitioners who are prescribing shot-gun mixtures of glandular extracts, usually and fortunately in too small doses to cause much harm. Such a situation is throwing the whole science of endocrinology into ridicule and disrepute.

Many commentaries in the medical journals of the 1920s make it clear that the medical establishment felt powerless to regulate the behavior of unprincipled pharmaceutical companies. In 1921 the American Medical Association's Council on Pharmacy and Chemistry bluntly noted: "The antagonism of certain pharmaceutical houses is a matter of cold-blood business policy." In 1924 the council took up the matter of "glandular therapy" on account of "the tremendous abuse already evident in the use of preparations of glandular materials promoted by pharmaceutical manufacturers who were willing to exploit such preparations on slight evidence." According to a report from 1922, "commercial interests have seized the vast domain of endocrinology, and nowhere else has the credulity of the public, and, alas, of a large number of physicians been exploited to such an extent as in the United States." One commentator writing in 1925 makes a point of distinguishing between "our best pharmaceutical houses" and "certain so-called pharmaceutical firms engaged in a most fraudulent exploitation of the medical profession." Yet it seems that the real problem was less the existence of unscrupulous firms than the vulnerability of many physicians to their propaganda. What Dr. Leonard G. Rowntree of the Mayo Clinic wanted to see was a "federal investigation of much of the advertising material that comes to our desks," so that naïve doctors would not be "seduced." Effective regulation of this market did not immediately follow the establishment of the Food and Drug Administration in 1928. Even five years later, some of the advertising for endocrine products still reminded one medical observer of the trade in animal products that had prevailed during the seventeenth and eighteenth centuries. Sales of glandular products went into decline during the 1930s only when the commercial production of genuine hormones drove the comparatively primitive extracts off the market.

The commercialization of glandular extracts also raised ethical questions about the relationship between medical research and the profit motive. In 1921 *JAMA* endorsed "the principle that the physician or laboratory investigator in the medical sciences shall not exploit for commercial gain the results of his studies. These principles have long been maintained by the medical profession as a matter of good faith with their patients, to whom they owe protection from exploitation." A year later *JAMA* felt it necessary to raise the conflict-of-interest issue again: "To what extent is the scientific staff of a commercial concern influenced by the commercial atmosphere of competition and dividends in which they do their work?" Today this conflict of interest is firmly embedded in the process whereby pharmaceutical companies carry out clinical trials on their own drugs and then report the results to the FDA. These data are examined, and sometimes challenged, by FDA personnel: they face off against corporate scientists and statisticians who conduct themselves more like lawyers than impartial researchers. A far more dramatic departure from the ethos of the 1920s is the process whereby medical researchers now transform themselves into biotechnology entrepreneurs, thereby institutionalizing conflicts of interest between scientific integrity and financial self-interest.

The glandular products market had always been bound up with claims about the sexual rejuvenation of ailing or aging men, and sexual surgery was another rejuvenating technique that enjoyed a vogue during the 1920s. The vasectomies that the Viennese surgeon Eugen Steinach performed on senile men made him famous around the world. One report from Budapest claimed that "the outer appearance of these subjects became youngish, fresh, their bodily strength increased, the tremor of their hand disappeared, memory and will power returned, and the sexual power was restored." The Paris-based surgeon Serge Voronoff became a wealthy man by means of his "monkey-gland" operations, which involved transplanting slices of testicles removed from apes into the groins of his aging patients. Although these procedures seem bizarre today, the fact that Steinach and Voronoff reported many "cures" before these methods succumbed to medical progress does not necessarily place them among the quacks of their era. On the contrary, their treatments, like those of Brown-Séquard, show how similar the therapeutic results of unconscious error and conscious fraud can be. Even today, uncertainty about the effectiveness of hormone therapy remains one of its defining characteristics.

An important cultural factor that helped to create this promising market for nostrum merchants and physicians alike was the atmosphere of secrecy and shame surrounding the subject of sex. Medical prudery thus left the field wide open to quacks and charlatans who knew how to play on male insecurities: "Sometimes boldly, but often by suggestion and innuendo, they undertake to make all men believe they have symptoms of most serious sexual disorders," as *JAMA* put it in 1921. While this marketing strategy has lost none of its effectiveness, it is important to recognize the difference between the sexual ethos of the early twentieth century and the pervasive sex-consciousness of our own day. That was, after all, a time when many, and perhaps most, physicians were unable to feel comfortable discussing human sexuality with patients who needed their advice about sexual problems. The mail-order business for aphrodisiacs thus served a private market for sexual therapy that many people must have viewed as a desperate last resort. The idea that a sexually useful drug might have an honorable public career as an asset to public health would have caused nervous laughter or ridicule among respectable people. The social respectability achieved by Viagra after 1998 still lay many years in the future.

But the 1920s were also the period during which modern American society became the electrified, motorized, media-saturated, entertainment-obsessed, technology-driven dynamo that it is today. And one ingredient of this new public sensibility was what Julia A. Ericksen has called "an ever expanding public conversation about sex." "The new ideology of sexual pleasure," she writes, "was celebrated in magazines, newspapers, and movies. Advertisers used sexual desire to sell products," and sexual freedom took on the status of a commodity. At the same time, however, the social effects of this new sexual credo were limited by an officially sanctioned emphasis on providing satisfying sex within marriage. Theodore van de Velde's *Ideal Marriage* (1926), a famous early marriage manual that offered advice on sexual technique, exemplifies a sexology that aimed at stabilizing the middle-class home by facilitating domestic sexual satisfaction. The post-1960s idea of sexual gratification as a recreational entitlement for unmarried as well as married people, including senior citizens, thus represents the fulfillment of a sexual ethos that was born during the Roaring Twenties.

Expectations about the sex lives of older people have always played a role in thinking about hormone therapy. Aging has long been associated with declining hormone levels and sexual activity, and the very concept of a substitution therapy presupposes that such a deficiency can be cured by replacing a naturally occurring hormone that is in short supply. The notion of menopause is built on a theory of hormone deficiency and has thus created an enormous market for estrogen replacement therapy, one purpose of which has become to preserve the sexual viability of aging women. Before the Second World War, however, the fundamental question was not how to preserve libido into old age but whether the sexual viability of aging people should be preserved at all.

The absence of concern about preserving sexual functioning past middle age is evident in some of the inquiries physicians addressed to the editors at the American Medical Association during the 1930s. After describing the declining potency of a sixty-year-old man, a California physician comments: "I appreciate that this is not a life and death matter, but it is distinctly annoying and as such merits a doctor's best efforts." This writer is clearly aware of the recent synthesis of testosterone in 1935, since he goes on to ask: "Have the new testis hormones proved of any value and what may be expected of them in patients between the ages of 60 and 70?" In a similarly casual vein, two surgeons writing in 1936 regard the failure of an operation to cure impotence not as a setback but rather as "a blessing in disguise," given the danger presented by increased blood pressure during "the excessive exercise connected with sexual intercourse." Confronted with the dissatisfied wives of impotent patients between the ages of fifty and seventy, another physician asks whether it might be appropriate to point out to these women that the children they had borne were evidence enough of their husbands' sexual success. "Are we to uphold the idea," he asks with some indignation, "that a husband to be really in love with his wife must during his entire life be a potent cave man?"

The proper response to this problem, he suggests, is not therapeutic ambition but an acceptance of the march of time and its consequences for sexual functioning. This lack of interest in prolonging the sex lives of aging patients can be interpreted in two ways. On the one hand, it clearly reflects the social conservatism of the medical profession and the society it served before the Second World War. The sexual candor we now take for granted in the public sphere was then virtually unthinkable. On the other hand, it speaks to the issue of how to regard aging. The idea that aging is a normal process leads to resignation in the face of the inevitable, an attitude that contradicts the progressive dynamic of modern medicine. The alternative view, that aging is pathological, leads naturally to the claim that sex after middle age is a health entitlement that calls for hormone replacement therapy. Today, as the baby boom generation moves into later middle age, it is clear that modern society is embracing the concept that aging is a treatable condition. The demographic engine is driving an expanding market for testosterone products that might boost sexual functioning.

The modern equivalent of the unregulated organotherapy market of the 1920s is the all-but-unregulated market in so-called dietary supplements. These products, which became popular during the late 1990s, include several prohormones that are closely related to the testosterone molecule. Three of these over-the-counter drugs are androstenediol, norandrostenedione, and androstenedione, a substance the body converts into testosterone and estrogens. This last drug achieved fame in August 1998 when it became known that the baseball star Mark McGwire had adopted "Andro" as his performance-enhancing drug of choice. The shock and confusion provoked by the private drug use of an emerging folk hero dramatically demonstrated how far we are from a working consensus on the medical and ethical issues involved in boosting the various capacities of the human organism, whether they be athletic, sexual, or intellectual.

McGwire's use of a legal drug sowed confusion and controversy because it confronted American society with its own conflicted attitude toward performance-enhancing substances. The official position of health authorities, school bureaucrats, sports officials, and the Federal Office of National Drug Control Policy is that all kinds of nonclinical drug use are medically and morally harmful. Yet there is abundant evidence that modern society has a basically tolerant attitude toward numerous pharmacological techniques that aim at improving individuals' "quality of life" and "well-being." In addition to sales of Prozac and Viagra, the burgeoning markets for herbal remedies and supplements reflect a growing demand for an alternative medicine that can boost the human organism as well as heal it.

Such acceptance of pharmacological boosting was evident in the response to McGwire's drug use. The baseball world, including both labor and management, offered him overwhelming support. The commissioner of baseball, Bud Selig, and the head of the players' union, Donald Fehr, issued a joint statement that attempted to dampen interest in an issue that might distract attention from McGwire's home run quest. The Boston Red Sox slugger Mo Vaughn pointed out that he himself was using a muscle-building product called PRO-hGH, an alleged growth-hormone accelerator that is improbably labeled a "food supplement." Vaughn also served as a paid spokesman for MET-Rx Engineered Nutrition, which was then marketing androstenedione, among other products. The prevailing opinion among sportswriters was that the use of Andro was (1) a private matter and (2) irrelevant to the integrity of the game. Public criticism of the drug-taking folk hero was virtually inaudible. Shoppers at Wal-Mart and at Giant Food supermarkets could buy androstenedione right off the shelf. This was curious behavior on the part of a society whose official response to casual drug use was supposed to be the slogan "Just Say No."

A more formal expression of public will came in the form of a law passed by Congress in 1994. The Dietary Supplemental Health and Education Act was intended to protect the supplements industry by preventing the Food and Drug Administration from classifying herbal products and vitamins as drugs that require federal scrutiny. Among the protected products was the hormonal drug androstenedione. Under previous law, supplement manufacturers were required to demonstrate that their products were safe. Now the burden was on the FDA to prove that these substances were harmful. But the absence of research in this area made it virtually impossible for the FDA to regulate supplements under the new regulations. The people's representatives in Congress had dealt a serious blow to the regulatory powers of the FDA, and this weakening has continued. In January 2000 the agency announced that the manufacturers of vitamins, herbs, and dietary supplements would be allowed to market products for "natural states" such as age-related memory loss, menopause, and pregnancy without having to prove their safety or their efficacy. "This is a snake-oil exemption," commented Dr. Sidney M. Wolfe, director of Public Citizen's Health Research Group in Washington. "It's a complete cave-in to the industry."

The FDA's response to such criticism acknowledged the populist wind that was now blowing through the halls of Congress whenever the people's right to medicate themselves came up for a vote. In this spirit the FDA's associate acting commissioner for policy replied to the critics: "What the agency is doing is faithfully carrying out the intent of Congress in passing the law." A lawyer who had once administered the FDA's office that regulates over-the-counter drugs added: "FDA has not done well in this area. Every time they have gone into court to try to limit one of these claims, they have lost. It's because Congress has really changed the paradigm." Populist pharmacology was now the law of the land. In January 2002 the National Institutes of Health (NIH) cosponsored a conference on dietary supplements in partnership with an industry trade group called the Conference for Responsible Nutrition. Only congressional pressure could have forced the NIH into a collaboration with the manufacturers of such dubious products.

This crucial paradigm shift has been facilitated by semantic maneuvers that transform *drugs* into *supplements*. "Everything I've done is natural," McGwire protested after the initial publicity sent Andro sales soaring. But this naïve statement just sums up the terminological confusion from which the supplements industry benefits. While the problem of formulating a workable distinction between nutrients and stimulants bedeviled the doping issue throughout most of the twentieth century, there is no precedent for classifying a hormonal substance either as a nutrient or as a supplement. It is, therefore, misleading to call androstenedione a dietary supplement and market it as if it were protein powder. When the (German-language) *Journal of Physiological Chemistry* reported the synthesis of androstenedione in 1938, the *Index Medicus* classified it as an androgen. A 1939 review article argues that any discussion of nutrients should focus on "special artificial foods intended for consumption immediately before or after athletic performances," such as carbohydrates or glucose. It would not have occurred to its author to label as food the testosterone products that had just come onto the medical market, and there is as little reason to do so today. Hormone therapies are properly designated as substitution or replacement procedures. The drug-testing expert Manfred Donike said years ago that steroids should not become a "popular nutritional supplement" *(Volksnahrungsmittel)*, and that is the responsible position from a public health perspective. But as a testosterone precursor that is legal because it is not quite testosterone itself, androstenedione is a perfect candidate to test societal inhibitions about making sex-hormone boosting a routine, over-the-counter procedure—and that is why the McGwire controversy deserves our careful attention.

Between 1998 and 2004 it became clear that there was no interest group or coalition of interested parties who were both willing and able to control the production, sale, and use of androstenedione. The FDA chose to look the other way as long as the manufacturers did not claim this drug could cure disease. The Drug Enforcement Administration (DEA) could have stopped sales of the drug immediately had it reclassified androstenedione as an anabolic steroid under the 1990 Anabolic Steroids Control Act, but it did not do so. The head of the Office of National Drug Control Policy, General Barry McCaffrey, asked the DEA for such a reclassification in 1998 and got nowhere. The General Nutrition Companies (GNC), which—to the dismay of its retailers—had taken the drug off the shelves of 3,500 stores in 1998, resumed sales in May 1999 on the basis of several dubious studies. By 1997 the supplement market was already worth $12 billion a year, up 50 percent compared with the period before the 1994 law took effect.

FDA action against androstenedione came in March 2004 as a direct result of the "designer steroid" scandal involving baseball stars and other well-known athletes that had erupted in October 2003. "Anyone who takes these products in sufficient quantities to build muscle or improve performance is putting himself or herself at risk for serious long-term and potentially irreversible health consequences," said the FDA commissioner, Dr. Mark McLellan. Why the FDA had waited almost six years to follow through on the early medical warnings about this drug was not explained. By this point, however, the FDA's move against androstenedione, the star "supplement" of the late 1990s, was almost irrelevant. "Andro" had already been replaced by more powerful substances and was now regarded as obsolete: "Several manufacturers said the most revolutionary products (such as Methyldienolone from Gaspari Nutrition) closely resemble powerful—and illegal—oral steroids like Dianabol because they are synthetically modified so the liver can't break them down. The result is a potency and liver toxicity that is believed to be orders of magnitude greater than for androstenedione." The FDA's belated attempt to regulate one hormonal "supplement" now revealed its long-standing failure to track the development of the market for this class of substances.

The key to marketing hormone supplements is to promise the benefits of anabolic steroids while evading regulation by the Anabolic Steroids Control Act. One evasive argument heard during this marketing campaign was to deny that prohormones are closely related to steroids at all. Dr. Scott Connolly, a physician and founder of the supplements retailer MET-Rx, told the New York Times that it was "infantile" to equate hormone precursors with anabolic steroids. "This is complicated stuff and people who don't understand it should stay out of the debate," he said. But expert opinion argued otherwise. "Androstenedione is a steroid, there's no question about it," said Dr. Don Catlin of the UCLA drug-testing laboratory. It shouldn't be available." Dr. Charles Yesalis, a prominent steroid expert, and Dr. Jerrold Leikin, a Chicago physician and toxicologist, each called androstenedione a "sex steroid." The authors of a recent scientific study of three legal prohormones—androstenedione, androstenediol, and norandrostenedione—state unequivocally: "Chemically and pharmacologically, these substances belong to the class of androgenic anabolic steroids." The perennial question, however, is whether expert opinion can ever prevail against what the physicians of the 1920s called the "commercial propaganda" of the drug companies. In this case, scientific opinion failed over a period of almost six years to change a policy originating in Congress that had endorsed the misclassification of certain hormonal drugs.

Defining the risks and benefits of prohormones is another strategy in the public relations contest between manufacturers and regulators. Scott

Connolly of MET-Rx tried to counter medical concerns about the use of androgens by touting the rewards of hormone replacement therapy: "There is this belief that testosterone is bad for you. But there is abundant data that the normalization of testosterone in the body throughout life has many benefits." A chemist at MET-Rx, Patrick Arnold, offered assurances that androstenedione would not do what many consumers clearly desired: "You will not reach superphysiological levels." The purpose of such a public relations effort is to position hormonal products inside the legally protected gray zone between testosterone (a controlled substance) and genuine supplements (e.g., vitamins and minerals). The marketer who promises too much invites unwelcome scrutiny from the FDA. The marketer who promises too little will lose customers to more aggressive competitors. Caught between their commercial ambition and the lingering notoriety of the anabolic steroid, endocrinological entrepreneurs must market so-called steroid alternatives and await regulatory developments.

Although supplement manufacturers have generally refrained from advertising hormonal drugs as aphrodisiacs, sellers on the Internet show no such reluctance. One site promotes a variant of androstenedione called libidione as a "natural Viagra alternative." Another Internet advertisement, for a drug called Pro-Symbio Plus, claims to "wash away the disease of aging" by increasing the level of human growth hormone in the body. Scott Connolly sees aging men as a future market for hormone supplements, and he is not alone. A physician who gave androstenedione to middle-aged men complaining of low sex drive advised GNC: "Let's target the old guys." These are the decisions that perpetuate the idea of a male menopause and a male sexual deficiency that can be repaired with hormones. Nor is belief in such a deficiency confined to aging males. The great irony of the storm of publicity surrounding McGwire's use of Andro was that the media ignored his own self-declared use of the drug as an aphrodisiac: "It's good for your sex life," he said. "I'm serious. You guys think I'm joking, but I'm serious." Casual aphrodisia of this kind could be promoted by testosterone-boosting products such as the chewing gum promised by MET-Rx or the androstenediol tablets (Androstat Poppers) tested by Bodytronics.

The use of androstenedione by professional athletes and others in the United States is actually a legacy of the East German state doping program of the 1980s. East German scientists devised a use for this hormone as a "bridging" drug for athletes who had suspended their intake of anabolic steroids before competitions at which they might be drug-tested.

The German and European patents for an androstenedione nasal spray were applied for on May 6, 1992, by Dr. Rüdiger Häcker, former director of the Research Institute for Physical Culture and Sport (FKS) in Leipzig, and his partner Claudia Mattern. Their claim was that they had invented "a drug for raising the level of testosterone" in the body. Häcker, a key figure in the East German doping program, was once sought by federal prosecutors in Berlin. During the period 1998–99 this team secured the convictions of many former East German coaches and physicians who had given steroids to minors, but Häcker eluded interrogation by taking a job with a pharmaceutical company in Switzerland. In fact, Häcker had not done any of the work described in his patent application; he was simply the first to recognize its market potential. The prominent German biologist and anti-doping activist Werner Franke has called this patent "the first international doping patent" intended to beat drug-testing procedures for elite athletes. Recognized by the U.S. Patent Office in November 1996, it is now owned by the Irish company Arrowdean, most of whose directors are based in tax havens on the Channel and Cayman islands.

The evolution of organotherapy into a market for testosterone and estrogen drugs can be followed throughout the history of the Schering Corporation, a giant pharmaceutical firm with operations in Germany and the United States. Corporate misbehavior in the area of advertising is a frequent theme in the medical literature. During the 1930s, for example, Schering was marketing what it called the "true female sex hormone" under the name of Progynon-B. Schering based its advertising on research by the eminent endocrinologist E. A. Doisy, a future Nobel Prize winner who immediately denounced Schering's misuse of his work. This critique prompted *JAMA* to censure Schering for its "reprehensible advertising policy." In 1940 and 1941 this scenario was repeated in marketing efforts on behalf of the gonadotropic hormone Anteron and the testosterone derivative pregneninolone.

Schering also assisted early research on androgens that proposed a male hormone deficit that might be remedied by hormone treatments. In 1942 the company supplied methyl testosterone tablets to scientists testing the effect of testosterone on the muscular performance of older men. Their speculative conclusion about the prospects for androgen therapy is of historical interest: "An adequate level of male sex-hormone might be important for the maintenance of working capacity. . . . In other words, the reduction of working capacity with age might proceed differently if the sex-hormone concentration could be artificially maintained at a higher level." Male hormone replacement therapy of this kind was the logical treatment for a male menopause syndrome that had been proposed in 1939. And here, too, the terms used in defining a disorder were essential in making it seem to require medication. Describing the observed syndrome as an "exaggerated fatigue in older men" already invited the "artificial" manipulation of testosterone levels to prevent an abnormal level of fatigue. The deeper question was and remains, How do we distinguish between normal and exaggerated fatigue in aging people? Such distinctions are always related to cultural trends, and in free-market societies these trends are both shaped and expressed by advertising. That is why pharmaceutical advertising has disturbed the medical profession for the past hundred years.

Schering tried to promote the idea of male menopause in a film titled *The Male Sex Hormone*, released in 1951. Its descriptions of the anatomy and physiology of the male sex organs served a real purpose at a time when medical training included little if anything about sexual physiology. The film also discusses the clinical uses of testosterone for hypogonadism, which is still a standard procedure, and gynecological disorders, which were poorly served by androgen therapy. Finally, it recommends testosterone for the "male climacteric"—a proposal the American Medical Association called "controversial" and that it refused to endorse. Establishing the male climacteric (or male menopause) as an officially recognized diagnostic category would have benefited Schering by increasing its sales of androgens to the aging male population.

Schering's production of androgens led eventually to unwelcome involvement in the steroid doping of elite athletes. As of 1992 the company was concerned about the public image of testosterone as a doping drug, because it was investigating the potential for a testosterone-based male contraceptive. In 1997 Schering executives had the unpleasant experience of reading about their steroid Primobolan 25 in a magazine article about doping in professional cycling. A year earlier, Schering had acquired a top expert of the former East German doping program, Dr. Michael Oettel, as a developer of hormone products. Once the director of the Central Institute for Microbiology and Experimental Therapy (ZIMET) in Jena, it was Oettel who developed the androstenedione nasal spray patented by his former colleague Rüdiger Häcker. As an employee of Jenapharm, which formerly had produced the East German anabolic steroid Oral-Turinabol, Oettel became an employee of Schering when it acquired Jenapharm in 1996. East German doping expertise was now in the service of a free-market pharmacology looking for mass-market hormone products. At the same time, the acquisition of Jenapharm brought Schering more unfavorable publicity about doping. In October 2002 Schering announced that it would contribute $25,000 to the fund for former East German athletes who had been medically harmed by Jenapharm products.

Today Schering is trying to promote testosterone on the Internet through its former East German subsidiary. Men who find the Jenapharm Web page are invited to answer sixteen questions about the state of their physical and emotional health. Those who find that their symptoms point to a "midlife crisis"—fatigue, hot flashes, a lack of interest in sex—are invited to consult their doctors in order to check for deficient hormone levels. While interactive Web-based medicine of this kind is still constrained by testosterone's status as a controlled substance, such consultations are open invitations to interpret the common symptoms of aging as a syndrome that is amenable to hormone treatment. It is a small step from such an arrangement to looser schemes that might circumvent the law by identifying a pool of cooperative physicians or by redefining the criteria for treatment. The gradual spread of testosterone into the general population, via targeted clinical populations known to benefit from taking hormones (notably hypogonadal and HIV-positive men), can only encourage the expanded use of testosterone as a hormonal tonic for men and women alike.

Testosterone therapy now appears in the American mass media as an accepted procedure for both celebrities and ordinary people. For example, on May 28, 2001, the CBS television show *48 Hours* broadcast a segment on anti-aging therapy. The featured patient in this program was the actor Nick Nolte, who was reported to swallow sixty tablets a day, including the adrenal hormone DHEA, to ward off the aging process. At the end of the segment his physician attached an Androderm testosterone patch to Nolte's chest. On January 13, 2002, the ABC-TV affiliate in Austin, Texas, broadcast a half-hour infomercial produced by a local physician to advertise his "hormone allergy" therapy for fatigue, short-term memory problems, and diminished sex drive. The grateful patient who joined him on this program was a woman in her fifties who was being treated with estrogen, progesterone, DHEA, and testosterone (presumably to intensify her sex drive). The official publication of the American Association of Retired Persons (AARP) has recommended testosterone therapy to its male and female readers on several occasions. "Studies indicate that roughly one in three men over age 65 has low testosterone levels," it reported in 2001. "Yet testosterone levels can be determined with a simple blood test, and, if low, corrected rather easily with injections, a gel (applied to the chest or arm), or a patch."

This is a very casual way to estimate the population of older men who need supplemental testosterone. Such estimates appear because there is no medical consensus on how to define the testosterone level that would warrant supplemental hormone therapy for hypogonadism in older men. But in today's medical market, the absence of a therapeutic criterion for treatment tends to promote rather than restrain the spread of hormone therapy. As three medical researchers noted in 1997: "Whatever the mechanism of hypogonadism, testosterone replacement has been gaining popularity among clinicians for alleviating symptoms and signs of hypogonadism in old age." In other words, medically respectable anti-aging therapy that treats a purported testosterone deficit is now an established practice. The virtual impossibility of distinguishing clinically defined hypogonadism from common symptoms of normal aging—osteoporosis, decreased muscle mass, anemia, mood disturbances, and fatigue—means that a diagnosis of low testosterone gives any willing physician an opportunity to prescribe the hormone for millions of older men who are aging normally. Tying low testosterone levels to premature ejaculation also "leads to the possibility that a large number of men may have chronic hormonal inadequacy" that would require hormone replacement therapy.

An analogous diagnosis could greatly expand the prescription of testosterone for an enormous population of sexually dysfunctional women. The current obstacle to an expansion of this market is the FDA's refusal to recognize in women a testosterone deficiency syndrome that requires medication. While we do not know how long FDA resistance to this form of lifestyle medicine will persist, the developments described above suggest that regulatory opposition will be brief. "Enormous numbers of women will be found to have low testosterone as the underlying basis of their dysfunction," predicts Dr. Irwin Goldstein, a Boston University urologist who treats sexual dysfunction. "Testosterone replacement is the Viagra for women." Yet such facile slogans are invariably misleading. As another pro-testosterone physician has pointed out, "If the administration of testosterone could bring about 'an instant increase in genital sensitivity,' there would probably be a pretty active street market for the drug." This physician argues that testosterone replacement provides not instant sexual desire but rather a sufficient hormonal basis for continued sexual functioning in older women. That rationale for hormone replacement is now driving increased use of testosterone by older men who use products that might eventually benefit their female partners: "The development of transdermal testosterone preparations for men raises the possibility that these delivery systems could be adapted for use in women." Indeed, the growing proportion of sexually functional older men is creating a corresponding demand for sexually functional older women who may benefit from testosterone replacement.

Organized medicine's response to the spread of testosterone therapy within its own ranks has been strikingly muted. It has been a long time since the American Medical Association denounced the "flamboyant exploitation" of the nascent sex hormone market of the late 1930s. That stern reaction was eminently justified by the ignorance, recklessness, and scientific fraud that marked the early marketing of testosterone propionate and other hormone products. Today the recommended doses are much lower, and their effects are better understood. But even more important than the accumulation of knowledge has been the emergence of a perceived right to sexual pleasure and fulfillment for both men and women of all ages. Testosterone therapy for the masses was not possible so long as this right did not exist. The next chapter of this book explains why the best efforts of the pharmaceutical industry to market testosterone could not prevail against physicians whose inhibitions and social conservatism made them both unwilling and unable to deal with their patients' need for sexual satisfaction.

CHAPTER 2

The Aphrodisiac That Failed

Why Testosterone Did Not Become
a Mass Sex Therapy

Synthetic testosterone seemed poised to become a mass therapy for aging men and sexually unresponsive women after the Second World War— but the pharmaceutical advertising of this era could not enlist a critical mass of doctors to join this campaign. Why this drug did not fulfill its apparent destiny of providing rejuvenation and sexual stimulation for the masses is one of the riddles that this book attempts to solve. In 1935, a decade before the publication of Paul de Kruif's highly publicized manifesto *The Male Hormone* (1945), *Time* had celebrated the recent laboratory synthesis of testosterone, declaring that "German and Swiss chemical laboratories are already prepared to manufacture from sheep's wool all the testosterone the world needs to cure homosexuals, [and] revitalize old men." According to *Newsweek* (then called *News-Week*), testosterone was "the secretion that one day might prevent premature sterility and feminine characteristics in men." There is no doubt that many readers of *Time* and *Newsweek* found these prophecies of hormonal salvation entirely credible. As endocrinology, the new science of glands and their secretions, developed during the 1920s, the power of hormones to cure and invigorate the human organism took on a magical aura for ordinary citizens and doctors alike. By the time the laboratory synthesis of testosterone was announced in 1935, it was only natural that ideas about hormone cures and homophobic ambitions to redirect homosexual desire in a more wholesome direction would make their way into the public sphere. "Rub sex chemicals on gums to prevent loss of teeth," the *Science News Letter* told its readers in 1940, and few were prepared to object to this sort of prognostic euphoria.

This optimistic vision has not yet prevailed, as sex hormone therapy has remained instead in a complex state of suspended animation that persists to this day. While synthetic testosterone drugs have received periodic bursts of publicity over the past sixty years, they have not achieved the mainstream status of a comparable (and comparably problematic) drug such as Prozac, which is less effective than members of the public (and some doctors) believe it to be. Understanding why androgens are still in the process of breaking out of the black market serving athletes and bodybuilders requires a historical excursion back to the first modern attempts to conceptualize and treat the sexual disorders of men and women. We must understand how sheer ignorance about human sexuality influenced the thinking and behavior of physicians as well as the anguished patients who sought relief from their intimate forms of suffering. We must appreciate how the sanctity of marriage as a social ideal established unwritten rules of eligibility for access to sex hormone therapy, and how the ideal of heterosexuality has exposed homosexuals to grotesque forms of surgical and hormonal abuse under the guise of therapy. Finally, we must analyze the barrier that separates the internal deliberations of a medical establishment from the wider world of public curiosity and the media that both serve and create its appetites. How does medical information cross this barrier and establish itself in the wider world of public discussion?

Paul de Kruif puzzled over this mystery in 1945 as he promoted testosterone as a mainstream drug for the aging male. By 1939, he says, "the medical grapevine" was spreading the news about what this drug could do for older men, and the result was "a flood of demand." But when a pharmaceutical executive launched an advertising campaign directed at American physicians (see below), it was "remarkable how this hopeful news was kept out of the newspapers, popular magazines and off the airwaves." In fact, there was no conspiracy to keep testosterone a medical secret. As noted in the preface, *The Male Hormone* was excerpted by *Reader's Digest* before it was published, and *Newsweek* devoted a full page to the book when it came out. The failure of testosterone to become the Viagra of its day, catapulted into public consciousness by a media uproar and celebrity endorsements, resulted from the complicated interplay of various interest groups and competing ideas about the role of sexual expression in human life that prevailed at that time.

The social history of testosterone thus encompasses the history of sexual mores and of sexology as a human science. Widely seen as both a medication and a force of nature, testosterone has been used (with varying degrees of success) to treat sex-related conditions in men and women, heterosexuals and homosexuals, young and old. As a "tonic" administered to enhance "well-being," it has symbolized the sexual energy that can do so much to make a human life worth living. At the same time, the use of testosterone has been subject to the powerful social constraints that inhibited the development of all sexual therapies for most of the twentieth century. Much of the history of hormone drugs takes place within this private world of sexual difficulties, of anguish and shame and crippling silences. The history of hormone-based sexology begins during the 1890s, so that is where we shall begin, by acquainting ourselves with a forgotten classic of medical sexology.

WHAT THEY DID TO WOMEN:
THE ORIGINS OF SEX THERAPY

Just over a century ago—at the Fiftieth Annual Meeting of the American Medical Association held in Columbus, Ohio, in 1899—a physician named Denslow Lewis delivered a lecture, as unprecedented as it was unwelcome, titled "The Gynecologic Consideration of the Sexual Act." At this time it was customary for *JAMA* to publish every paper presented at its annual meeting, but in the case of Dr. Lewis this formal recognition was withheld. When the author asked the *Journal*'s editor when it would be published, the latter replied: "I will candidly say that I do not want to publish your paper. . . . There is nothing in it that is not true, and possibly it ought to appear in *The Journal,* but with my personal views in reference to this class of literature, I hardly think so."

This act of censorship was in harmony with the criticism directed at the lecturer immediately following his presentation. "With all due respect to Dr. Lewis," said Dr. Howard A. Kelley of Baltimore, "I am strongly opposed to dwelling on these elementary physiologic facts in a public audience. I am very sorry he has read the paper." The intellectual dishonesty of this response was already evident in the overly casual reference to "elementary physiologic facts" about human sexuality, regarding which, Kelley implied, neither he nor his colleagues required instruction. As a professional courtesy, Lewis had not directly challenged this unfounded presumption of medical competence in sexual matters. But it must have been perfectly clear to his audience that the point of his address was to urge them to acquire a knowledge of human sexuality they did not possess.

Lewis was not the type to take an editorial rebuff lying down. After hearing one official argue that publication would expose the AMA to the charge of sending obscene matter through the mail, he consulted the famous lawyer Clarence Darrow, who years later would do battle on behalf of an embattled Darwinism at the Scopes trial. After listening to Lewis's argument, the great jurist declared that "any physician who did not have the courage to deliver such a paper before an association of scientific men, when he believed it was for the purpose of making people better and happier, and who hesitated for fear that some law might be construed to send him to jail, would not be worthy of the profession to which he belongs." In fact, Lewis had demonstrated uncommon courage in challenging his colleagues' sexual provincialism. But far more interesting to us is what this disturbing lecturer had actually said.

Lewis's paper describes sexual predicaments and related medical procedures that we do not ordinarily associate with people who lived a hundred years ago. Half a century before the Kinsey Reports of 1948 and 1953 forced Americans to look at their own sexual behavior through the unsparing eyes of a fearless zoologist, Lewis asked his fellow physicians to acknowledge the power and dignity of "the instinct that dictates the perpetuation of the species" and to help their patients adapt to its requirements in humane ways. Medical men, he argued, "should not be deterred from its scientific investigation by false modesty or by the fear of being accused of sensationalism." Most dramatically, however, Lewis's progressive scientific outlook was matched by an egalitarian view of marital sex that was distinctly ahead of its time. Both parties, he says, enter into matrimony in a state of sexual ignorance. The husband, having practiced on prostitutes, possesses a sexual knowledge that is "imperfect and often dangerous" as well as a sexual technique that can be downright "brutal." But the most important foundation of the nascent sexual relationship is the principle of reciprocity: "He should understand that he is not the master but the companion of his wife."

This egalitarian principle meant that the wife had a right to sexual pleasure that centuries of tradition had denied her. In A History of Women's Bodies (1982), the historian Edward Shorter makes this point by asking with deliberate provocation: "Did women enjoy sex before 1900?" Years of research, he reports, had persuaded him that "intercourse in the traditional family was brief and brutal, and there is little evidence that women derived much pleasure from it." Shorter's description of premodern sex within marriage is a depressing account of male indifference, wife beating, and the medical horrors of continuous pregnancy and childbirth. It is only during the nineteenth century that "a sort of premarital 'sexual revolution' " takes place; and there are numerous anecdotes even "from around the turn of the century that married women dislike marital relations." Yet the question remains: why was this still the case at the beginning of the twentieth century? If marital sex was failing, not all of this unhappiness could be blamed on the "male torpor" of premodern European and American husbands. To be sure, traditional relations between the sexes lived on within the arrangements of patriarchal family life. But what of the many husbands and wives who, having achieved a degree of mutual affection or even love within this domestic world, could not find happiness in the privacy of their bedrooms?

The solution, Lewis argued in 1899, was the sexual emancipation of the modern wife. This liberation would be made possible by a new understanding of the woman's role in the sexual act itself, and here he entered into that realm of anatomical and physiological specifics that so discomfited much of his audience:

> She should be informed that [intercourse] is a consecration of the marriage vows and a bond of union between her husband and herself. She should be told that it is right and proper for her to experience pleasure in its performance. . . . [I]t is only fair for the girl to understand that there is no immodesty in her active participation, but on the contrary that such action on her part will increase the interest of the event for both her husband and herself.

This interest of husband and wife in their own sex life was of vital significance, because it was essential to the stability of family life. Sexual failure in marriage, Lewis warned, would "bring disaster to many a home and disruption to many of our social institutions."

Modern sex therapy, including the voyeuristic research methods of Alfred C. Kinsey and of William Masters and Virginia Johnson, developed in response to this fear that sexual dissatisfaction could destabilize both the family and the larger society of which it was a microcosm. This statement may sound strange to those who see the relationship between sex and society from a post-1960s perspective, which has emphasized the pursuit of sexual pleasure outside of marriage and has even lauded the politically subversive power of the erotic. Similarly, the modern commercialization of sex and the decline of marriage as a social institution vested with a special respect and prestige have obscured the socially conservative origins of the modern sexology of marriage. The popular sexology that assails us from the covers of today's women's magazines, promising the latest in man-trapping sex tricks, is thus the illegitimate child of a science of marriage that was never intended to serve the needs of sexual freelancers. As we shall see, the earnest pro-marital rhetoric of early sexology lasted well into the twentieth century. Denslow Lewis was a virtually forgotten pioneer of this tradition, and that is why we should understand how his support for the sexual liberation of married women could coexist with what he was willing to do to women in order to turn them into sexually acceptable wives.

A social doctrine dedicated to the preservation of marriage easily accommodated a hostility to "perversions and unnatural practices" in the sexual sphere. The threat here was not "extramarital fornication" by men, which Lewis mentions only in passing, but rather the lesbian relationships that formed between respectable young women who were thereby rendered unfit to have satisfying sex with their husbands. Under the unsuspecting and even approving eyes of their parents, these girls would form deep friendships that progressed from kissing and fondling to the sharing of beds and finally to the "cunnilinguistic practices" a husband's best exertions could not hope to match.

Lewis's response was to treat the lesbianism of these upper-class women as medically remediable, thereby enabling them to move past this temporary deviation on their way to the ultimate goal of marriage. The diagnosis in such cases was "hyperemia of the external genitals," a term that included the hypersensitive clitoris that sexually ignorant husbands of this and future eras were liable to ignore. The treatment for such exquisite genital sensitivity was to deaden it by means of drugs or surgery. A cocaine solution or saline cathartics could be applied to the inflamed organ, or calomel and salines followed by pyrophosphate of iron; or the patient could be drugged with bromides, sometimes along with *Cannabis indica*. Some patients were injected with strychnine. "In one case, the clitoris was hypertrophied and excessively sensitive. As a last resort, I felt justified in performing an amputation, and the ultimate result of this case was gratifying." In fifteen of eighteen patients, Lewis reports, the combination of medical intervention and moral instruction proved to be successful: "The intense reflex excitability subsided. By moral suasion and by intelligent understanding of the duties of the marital relationship, the patients became, in time, proper wives."

The medical techniques of this period could also be applied to intensifying the sexual responses of women who were properly married. One group requiring assistance were women who appeared to be, as Lewis put it, "absolutely devoid of sexual sensation," a female type twentieth-century medical literature would label "frigid." (We shall examine the history of this diagnosis below.) Yet even these apparently intractable problems often yielded to methods Lewis praises even if he does not always describe them: "In many cases, I am happy to say, observation and the intelligent application of a rational therapeusis permit the woman to return to the normal type, and to take her place, where she by right belongs, as the companion of her husband and as his partner in the conjugal embrace." Lewis is more specific regarding forms of "rational therapeusis" that involved operations on or around the clitoris. If this delicate organ adheres to the prepuce, then "a judicious circumcision . . . will often prove successful."

Let it be noted, however, that Lewis's idea of success was almost always defined from a male point of view. Thus he is pleased to report that in a number of cases, "sufficient passion, real or stimulated, was developed to afford the husband a satisfactory sexual life." Unfortunately, it is difficult to ascertain whether "stimulated" actually means "simulated" in this context. That is certainly possible, given that the female strategy of faking orgasm had already been commented on by at least one British gynecologist during the 1880s. It also appears as though Lewis was prepared to carry out sexual surgery on women to meet certain male requirements. "I have known husbands," Lewis told his audience, "to insist on the repair of perineal and vulvar lacerations, and it is perhaps not unreasonable to infer that fear of sepsis was not their only motive." This confession in particular appears to have enraged Dr. Kelly of Baltimore, who in the course of his lengthy denunciation of Lewis's presentation spat out: "I shall never forget the utter disgust which I felt once when a professional friend of mine in Philadelphia told me that he had repaired the perineum of a mistress for the sake of increasing the sexual gratification of her paramour." But what if this operation had served the pleasure not of mistress and paramour, but of husband and wife?— which was, after all, the professional standard Lewis had defended so ably before his audience in Ohio. For Dr. Kelly, even this distinction would not have mattered, given his priggish rejection of sexual pleasure itself. "I do not believe," he declared, that "mutual pleasure in the sexual act has any particular bearing on the happiness of life, that is the lowest possible view of happiness in married life." Here is the historic divide that separates the enlightened Lewis from a colleague who refers to the discussion of sex as "filth."

As a principled advocate of sexual pleasure, Lewis was prepared to apply the most advanced libido-enhancing methods of his era. Accordingly, if a patient's clitoris was abnormally small or "singularly deficient in excitability," Lewis would "endeavor to reproduce the normal physiological state. This is accomplished rarely by electricity, but often by the use of an exhaust pump that may be properly designated a 'congestor.' When this instrument is employed daily for several weeks, it is usual to observe an increase in the size of the clitoris and a development of the normal condition of excitability." Interestingly, the only drugs he recommends as female "aphrodisiacs" are champagne, sherry, port, and whisky, even though primitive testicular and ovarian extracts had become widely available during the 1890s on both sides of the Atlantic.

In summary, the career of this early American sex therapist presents an intriguing demonstration of contemporary techniques and therapeutic goals. The therapeutic armamentarium includes surgical techniques, electricity, a wide range of drugs, and something resembling a vacuum pump to enlarge the underdeveloped clitoris. The physician's objectives include both the elimination and stimulation of sexual excitement, but always in the service of "normal" sex within marriage. Indeed, Lewis was particularly clear on this point: "I believe any deviation from the normal standard in the performance of the sexual act should be carefully investigated." This social conservatism is what separates him from his great successor Alfred Kinsey, for whom polymorphous sexual experience became both a personal adventure and a social crusade.

The sexual therapies Lewis carried out on his female patients were already established procedures in the United States, where aggressive gynecological procedures were especially favored. Clitoridectomy, for example, had been invented by the English gynecologist Isaac Baker Brown in 1858 as a cure for epilepsy and nervous disorders in women, including the imagined results of female masturbation. By 1866 the procedure had provoked a major scandal in the British medical press and was banned as a medical technique. The sense of violation inspired by this procedure was expressed by an American medical editor who sympathized with the British abolitionists and defended the right of women not to be sexually mutilated: "As we view the matter, the ovary bespeaks the sex of the female, the testicle that of the male. Remove either organ, and physiologically, we unsex the individual. To remove the clitoris, then, to allay sexual irritability, is about as unphilosophical as to remove the analogous organ of the male." Yet many American practitioners felt much less constrained about performing sexual surgery on women. "The spate of gynecologic activity in America," one historian reports, "was characterized by flamboyant, drastic, risky, and instant use of the knife." One such enthusiast was Dr. A. J. Bloch, a visiting surgeon at the Charity Hospital of New Orleans and the author of "Sexual Perversion in the Female" (1894). Like many of his contemporaries, Bloch regarded female masturbation as a form of "moral leprosy," and he was willing to act on this conviction. Presented with a masturbating two-and-a-half-year-old girl, who appeared to be afflicted by an undefined nervous disorder, Bloch removed her clitoris and subsequently reported that the child had "grown stouter, more playful, and [had] ceased masturbating entirely."

Clitoridectomy may have been performed in the United States as late as 1925, while the less drastic procedure known as female circumcision, which removes all or part of the "hood" of the clitoris, was being performed as late as 1937. In 1946 *JAMA* published the following query from a physician in North Carolina: "What is the general opinion among gynecologists as to the value of operations on the clitoris for frigidity or reduced libido?" The answer was that such operations were virtually useless, since it had become clear that "in all cases of frigidity there is a large psychic element." A half century after Lewis had operated on women to dampen as well as enhance their sexual responsiveness, medical interest in managing the libidos of heterosexual women was now focused almost entirely on enhancing the responsiveness of American and British wives. By this time, the treatment of what was now called sexual frigidity had become, as we shall see, a cottage industry among gynecologists. Operating within a less overtly patriarchal culture than the one Denslow Lewis had confronted, these men were better prepared than their fin de siècle predecessors to explore the crucial role that "psychic" factors played in the sex lives of their female patients.

A more drastic and dangerous procedure devised as a form of female psychotherapy was the removal of a woman's ovaries. During most of the nineteenth century this operation was performed to remove diseased organs. The removal of nondiseased ovaries for the purpose of altering female behavior was pioneered by Dr. Robert Battey of Rome, Georgia, in 1872, at a time when anesthesia had given surgeons access to large numbers of patients, thereby enabling them to make their reputations by devising new procedures. The pioneering physician Elizabeth Blackwell called this operation "the castration of women"; others called it "spaying." It is interesting to track the euphemisms that were devised over time to designate a mutilating operation that proved to be psychologically ruinous to many women who underwent this form of medical discipline. Female castration was officially known as oophorectomy or ovariotomy, while during the 1920s, 1930s, and 1940s terms such as *surgical menopause, artificial menopause,* and *"medical" castration* established themselves in the medical literature.

The objectives of this operation evolved over time. The initial rationale targeted organic gynecological disorders such as "excessive" menstrual bleeding, "but surgeons soon extended the operation to women who were 'insane,' hysterical, unhappy, difficult for their husbands to control, for example those who were unfaithful to their husbands or disliked running a household. It seemed to them logical and justified to treat these women as abnormal and attempt to make them conform to the 'normality' of obedience, diffidence and running their households in ways that pleased their husbands." Other women who were judged to talk too much were subjected to glossodectomies—the removal of their tongues. In 1893 one male advocate of female castration reported with evident satisfaction what a wholesome effect it had on the typical patient: "She becomes tractable, orderly, industrious, and cleanly." Having been castrated for the "sexual perversion" of masturbation, one woman wrote to her castrator: "My condition is all I could desire. I know and feel that I am well; I never think of self-abuse; it is foreign and distasteful to me." These neutered women were often referred to as genderless "its." The question of whether these strange episodes amounted to therapy or sadism will be examined below.

Surgical discipline of this kind declined during the first decades of the twentieth century in favor of more rational applications. Surgical or X-ray-induced "castration" of female breast cancer patients eventually became an acceptable procedure on the grounds that castration removed the source of the estrogen that stimulated the growth of their tumors. But this therapy came at a heavy price. A medical report from Paris warned in 1922 that in young women "castration entails atrophy of the vulva, uterus and nipples, and the sudden surgical menopause reduces the resisting forces of other organs." Survival of the sex drive after castration was another major issue. "What chance, if any, has a woman castrate of regaining her sexual vigor by the use of theelin and allied substances after castration?" one physician asked in 1939, referring to a commonly used estrogenic drug then on the market. The answer he got confirmed once again the complexity of human sexual biology: "Whereas many women lose their libido after the change of life, a large proportion of them retain their sex desires after the menopause. Furthermore, a few women who were more or less frigid during their reproductive years experience libido after the change of life." (Some postmenopausal women became orgasmic once the fear of becoming pregnant was gone.) The efficacy of estrogenic drugs for castrated women was, not surprisingly, highly problematic.

At the same time, the old temptation to discipline women by extirpating or neutering their ovaries persisted in the minds of some physicians well past the turn of the century. A medical opinion published in 1931 calmly observes that "patients with nymphomania or pathologically increased sex desire are not benefited by bilateral oophorectomy." "What treatment do you advise," one doctor asked the editors of *JAMA* in 1936, "for a woman, aged 43 and physically well, who is a dipsomaniac and also inclined to nymphomania? Would sterilization with irradiation be advisable?" Here is the chastening gynecology of the nineteenth century presented in a twentieth-century idiom that does not even attempt to disguise its patriarchal premise—that castration is a "benefit" if it can rescue a woman from her appetites for sex and drink.

Two alternatives to surgical castration were the destruction of the ovaries by means of X-rays or by the insertion of radium into the uterine cavity. In the 1920s these techniques were considered to be bimodal, in that physicians assumed that irradiation could stimulate "depressed endocrine organs" as well as destroy ovarian functioning. As early as 1932 sexual frigidity was reported to be a frequent result of X-ray treatment to induce artificial menopause. More urgent warnings about the destructive effects of radium and deep X-ray therapy eventually appeared in the *British Medical Journal* after the Second World War: "Not only do hot flushes occur, but severe headaches and intense depressions are in some cases such prominent and distressing features that every gynaecologist should be reluctant to deprive his patient completely, by whatever means, of functionary active ovarian tissue whatever her age may be." Yet in 1950 a British gynecologist reported that the "radium menopause" was "a safe and effective method of treatment" that also destroyed sexual feeling in more than half of the women who underwent the procedure. "It seems an important finding," he notes with apparent concern, "that libido practically disappeared in well over half the patients under review. The cause of sexual anesthesia would appear to be more than a temporary effect of irradiation on the sensory-nerve endings in the genital tract, for that might be expected to resolve in time."

From a modern perspective, the striking feature of such commentaries is the clinician's deadpan reaction to the "sexual anesthesia" with which these women might be living for the rest of their lives. And there were very few departures from this sort of clinical objectivity in the medical literature.

Electrotherapy for male and female sexual problems was another technique that flourished at the turn of the century and persisted in various forms for decades. In the late nineteenth century, men could buy devices to treat their own impotence. Others, suffering from nocturnal emissions (spermatorrhea), could buy an "electric monitor" that administered a strong shock whenever they experienced an erection. The use of electric current to treat male impotence lasted well into the 1930s. For example, in 1936 one specialist recommended electrical "stimulation" to repair the "weakened condition of the sexual muscles." Here is the therapeutic scenario:

> For this purpose the use of the sinusoidal-faradic current of moderate rapidity and as strong as the patient can bear without any pain is most effective. One cable is connected with a rectal electrode and the other with a wet-sponge electrode applied to the perineum and the current is allowed to pass for about ten minutes. Treatments may be given every three or four days. An outdoor life with periods of vacations is distinctly beneficial.

Electric current was also prescribed for female sexual disorders. At the turn of the century electrotherapy was used to cure both frigidity and nymphomania—a methodological paradox that would recur in the use of male sex hormones to treat over- and undersexed women. And here, too, fin de siècle concepts were being translated into treatments for women during the 1940s. For frigidity there was "sensitization of the vaginal mucous membrane" by means of electricity: "The treatment consists in inserting a large vaginal electrode and administering the sinusoidal-galvanic current for about ten minutes." Electric shock treatment for menopausal symptoms was even featured in *Woman's Home Companion* in November 1944: "The most remarkable of these new weapons is electric sleep therapy—a treatment as painless and simple as it is successful. Between 80 and 150 volts of electric current are passed through the brain for one tenth of a second, and that is all there is to it." While I have seen no evidence of attempts to shock sexually overactive women out of their bad habits, there is no reason to believe that doctors would have been unwilling to do it.

By now it should be clear that all of these procedures—surgical, electrical, hormonal, and radiation-based—were embedded in ostensibly therapeutic relationships between male doctors and female patients that are very disturbing from a modern perspective. Our concerns about medical ethics raise at least two questions about the therapists: (1) Were their motives prurient as well as therapeutic? and (2) Were these doctors also misogynists who were uniquely empowered to inflict mental and physical harm on their female victims?

The voyeuristic impulse may well be inseparable from sexual surgery and sex research in general. Indeed, if voyeurism disqualifies the practitioner, then the first sexual healer to be cast out must be Alfred Kinsey, the greatest sexologist of them all. "The beauty of sex research," one of Kinsey's biographers notes, "was that it allowed Kinsey to transform his voyeurism into science," and there can be little doubt that Kinsey's aggressive, participatory voyeurism put him in a class by himself. Lacking Kinsey's fearless gusto for all matters sexual, the gynecological voyeurs who preceded him maintained a sense or pretense of medical objectivity that sometimes took the form of "testing" female sexual responsiveness. Thus in 1903 an American physician named E. H. Smith, eager to find out whether his patients were indulging in masturbation, employed a "mild faradic current" to test them for sexual oversensitivity. During the same period, "clitoridectomists and castrators tested women for indications of the disease of desire by inducing orgasm, manipulating clitoris or breasts." (As Rachel P. Maines has shown, a standard treatment for "hysteria" at this time involved male doctors masturbating their female patients to orgasm. It was in this context that the electric vibrator assumed the role of a labor-saving device for the overtaxed male practitioner.) The electrical test for sexual sensitivity reappears in 1940, when Dr. A. L. Wolbarst of New York used an electric current to confirm the distressing fact that a female patient who was engaged to be married was, indeed, "absolutely anesthetic in those regions." From a modern perspective, such scenarios can seem profoundly ambiguous, leaving unresolved the motives of the therapist.

How did male physicians experience these therapeutic sessions? How many were attracted to, or repelled by, the treatment of female sexual problems? Physicians' attitudes toward these procedures must have varied with the individuals who performed them in what was always a delicate situation. In the late nineteenth century many doctors simply declined to do vaginal examinations, to the dismay of their more conscientious colleagues. As late as 1946 the *British Medical Journal* addressed the delicacy of genital examinations in a way that demonstrated the persistence of the Victorian sensibility. This advisor warned that vaginal examination of a virgin should be avoided if possible. If it had to be done, then it should be carried out under general anesthesia after the patient and her guardian "had been informed of the examiner's intentions," thereby precluding a legal charge of assault. A decade later the same journal cautioned: "Although some women are not sentient in the vagina, in others, if the technique is not careful, erotic feeling will be aroused, and this can cause great offence." Such worries make it clear that such examinations have always been sexually charged situations in which most female patients have felt acutely vulnerable. They have also played a role in the sexual politics of our era, seen by feminists as a prime symbol of the imbalance of power between the sexes in modern medicine.

During the feminist wave of the early 1970s, resentment against medical sexism made the mental state of fin de siècle gynecologists a heated topic among medical historians. While G. J. Barker-Benfield saw (but does not cite) "ample evidence that gynecologists saw their knives' cutting into women's generative tract as a form of sexual intercourse," other historians objected to what they regarded as the demonization of medical men who had done their best in difficult circumstances. "The conspiratorial theory of nineteenth century medicine," one female historian writes, "should be replaced by an explanation that recognizes the paucity of medical knowledge" at that time. Even as acute and intellectually rambunctious a critic of "androcentric" thinking as Rachel P. Maines is inclined to exonerate the early gynecologists: "There are many historical examples of physicians' imposing conceptual frameworks on their clinical evidence that are difficult for modern observers to understand. It is important to recognize that it is not necessary to argue for conspiracy or even misogyny among doctors over time: the evidence suggests that physicians called disease paradigms as they saw them."

The question of misogyny haunts these relationships because so many women suffered terribly at the hands of male doctors whose motives remain unclear. Explaining their behavior does not require us to imagine them rubbing their hands in fiendish anticipation of the intimate damage they will be inflicting on their patients, but their intentions are not the only emotions involved. "Castration," Barker-Benfield writes, "destroyed woman's one remaining thread of identity, her hope for motherhood, in the way critics of the operation described. Many castrated women were left hopeless, sunk into despair on a scale almost beyond imagination." It is likely that this sort of despondency afflicted fewer women in the decades that followed as the quality of their care gradually improved. But imagining the despair and disorientation experienced by women who have undergone such procedures is essential to understanding a medical universe in which men have employed surgery, electricity, radiation, and hormones to reorient the sensibilities of women they regarded as incompetent or in some sense deranged.

Hormone replacement therapy (HRT) is only the most recent chapter in the long history of sexual therapies aimed at improving the lives of women while bringing a measure of relief to the men who must live with their symptoms. The misogynistic potential of such medical practice is addressed in a commentary published in 1949 by a British physician who found himself "appalled" by the use of electroconvulsive therapy to treat unhappily married women. Because the husband usually refused to attend marriage counseling, psychotherapists found themselves talking to the agitated wife—"the more able and worthwhile personality than the one who remains aloof." The absence of the shirking husband ensured that it would be the young wife, filled with "sexual ignorance and childish fantasies," who was subjected to electroshock "therapy." The potential for "devastating" these innocents was always present. While electroconvulsive therapy was useful in some cases, there were too many others where "it ceases to be a scientific procedure and is equivalent to 'Let's shake the nonsense out of her.' " In the nineteenth century the popular diagnosis of "ovariomania" had explained why so much "nonsense" filled women's heads. How long could such primitive thinking about the female temperament survive into the twentieth century?

A penetrating commentary on the psychological origins of modern medical misogyny is Ira Levin's chilling novella *The Stepford Wives* (1972), which appeared just as the feminist movement was gathering momentum in the United States and Europe and not long after the publication of Dr. Robert Wilson's best-selling manifesto *Feminine Forever* (1966). Wilson's book effectively publicized the idea of sex hormone replacement therapy for "menopausal" women who, as the *New Republic* put it, would otherwise "disintegrate into crones." Levin's story describes a successful conspiracy by a group of dissatisfied husbands to replace their all-too-human and imperfect wives with perfectly compliant (and sexually cooperative) biotronic robots, thanks to the "audioanimatronic" technology that had populated the original Disneyland with animated talking creatures. Perhaps the most unsettling aspect of this story is that the murders and re-creations of these women are carried out in a quiet American suburb in order to bring to perfection the conservative arrangement known as monogamous marriage. For this sexual utopia, unlike the free love communes of the 1960s, is one that promises to endure.

While Levin's novella develops the misogynistic logic of male desire to a nightmarish extreme, its numerous realistic touches make most of what happens entirely plausible and connect his science fiction to the gynecological tradition we have been examining. The author drops repeated hints, for example, that the conspiracy against the Stepford wives is motivated by the sexual dissatisfaction of their husbands. "I'm just not interested in sex," the former model Charmaine tells her female companions only days before her abduction and conversion into the ultimate Barbie doll. "Was that any good?" the doomed heroine, Joanna, asks her silent husband after sex. Levin also makes references to the revolution in sex pharmacology that was transforming male-female relationships at this time. In addition to the Pill, there is Bobbie's theory about the mysterious force that is domesticating the women of the town: "Maybe it's some kind of hormone thing; that would explain the fantastic boobs." At the time *The Stepford Wives* appeared, popular women's magazines were filled with articles bearing on the intimate lives of people who could have stepped out of the pages of Levin's novel: "My Husband Was Afraid of Sex" *(Good Housekeeping)*, "Fighting Words: American Women Are Lousy Lovers" *(Vogue)*, "Must Marriage Cheat Today's Young Women?" *(Redbook)*, "All about the New Sex Therapy" *(Newsweek)*, "Why Some Women Respond Sexually and Others Don't" *(McCalls)*. This was the new world of public sexual discussion in which hormone therapies for women found a natural role.

Apart from being a mordant and macabre take on sex in America, Levin's fantasy is a penetrating commentary on the grimmer side of gynecology that can startle even the reader who is already familiar with the masculine preoccupations of the medical literature. For it is impossible to read this dark tale of male privilege without hearing voices from the past. As one historian notes, "Disorderly women were handed over to the gynecologists for castration and other kinds of radical treatment by husbands or fathers unable to enforce their minimum identity guarantee—the submission of woman. The handed-over woman then underwent a period of intense discipline by anesthesia and knife[.]" Levin's story is thus an allegory of an authoritarian gynecology that has produced its own bizarre and sadistic episodes. The leitmotif of these medical events has been not overt cruelty but the satisfaction of male desire.

Denslow Lewis assures his male audience in 1899 that treating wives who were once "indifferent to the conjugal embrace" guaranteed that "sufficient passion, real or stimulated, was developed to afford the husband a satisfactory sexual life." Sexual intercourse after menopause, a physician from Cincinnati told his readers in 1932, can do no harm, "and even if the sexual passion is absent, it need not be refused to a husband." These confident and unself-conscious claims express the mind-set of a profession that has always applied sex hormone therapy to the management of sexual relations in ways that have imposed masculine perspectives on female patients. Although many transparently decent men did their best to relieve the mental and physical anguish of the women who came to them for help, twentieth-century physicians, like their nineteenth-century predecessors, knew too little about sex to practice an authentic sexual science.

SEX BEFORE KINSEY:
WHAT DOCTORS AND PATIENTS DID NOT KNOW

"In hormone therapy," a European scientist said in 1921, "we are adopting Nature's most secret methods." These words, which date from the dawn of modern endocrinology, acknowledged the dramatic successes of recent hormone therapies as well as biological mysteries that might not be solved for generations. For even as medical scientists learned more and more about the chemical structures and biological functions of the "internal secretions" that were coming to be known as hormones, physicians and laypeople alike were conspicuously deficient in basic knowledge of the psychology and physiology of human sexuality.

This ignorance has had two related sources during the past century: scientific and social impediments to carrying out research on sexual functioning, on the one hand, and a deeply rooted folklore about sex that influenced both popular opinion and medical doctrine, on the other. Quite apart from difficulties caused by the complexity of biological systems, societal inhibitions about public discussions of sex delayed the acquisition of medically useful knowledge by discouraging the funding of research. The sudden interest in sex research catalyzed by the Viagra boom of 1998 demonstrated how long this sort of work has been suppressed by old taboos and the timidity of potential sponsors. Medical neglect of sexual matters was also encouraged by physicians' disgust at the quacks and charlatans who had been offering the public sexual nostrums and devices from time immemorial. Disapproving reports of these fraudulent therapies were a regular feature of *JAMA,* the public bulletin board of American medicine, for decades after the turn of the century. The carnival atmosphere surrounding the marketing of such products was already evident in their brand names: Gold Medal Brand Sexual Pills (1921); New Life Gland Capsules (1932); Bulltone, a Sexual and Nerve Tonic for Men (1937); the Giant Developer, a mechanical masturbator of a type the postal service had repeatedly barred from the mails (1938); Nu-Gland Tablets for "loss of vitality in men" (1939); and the Famous Dr. Lorenz Electro Body Battery (1940). At the same time, the proliferation of such products embarrassed physicians by reminding them of how little they could do about most of the sexual problems experienced by their patients, since quackery rushed in where physicians feared to tread. Yet another source of confusion was the hormone therapy propaganda emanating from the lay press and the drug companies, which persuaded many physicians to prescribe these drugs despite the warnings against them that were constantly appearing in the medical journals. The medical profession as well as the public, one prominent endocrinologist complained in 1934, had "lost all sense of proportion, direction and balance whenever the subject of endocrinology is touched on."

Physicians' naïveté about sexual biochemistry was matched by the inability of many practitioners to talk about sex with their patients comfortably and knowledgeably. Medical education before the Second World War included almost nothing about human sexuality, a deficiency that persisted and was still being lamented in *JAMA* as late as 1988, as physicians confronted a ballooning AIDS epidemic that was being driven by sexual behaviors. One physician wrote in 1966:

> By and large, neither medical schools nor other sources of sexual knowledge available to the physician have prepared him adequately to assume these responsibilities. The physician's own sexual experience, however amusing and remarkable when recounted in cocktail lounges, may equip him but little for his counseling tasks. . . . His own problems in this sphere may intrude into the counseling process. He may become so uncomfortable and embarrassed that he makes the patient equally uncomfortable, so that they both then seek the cool relief of changing the subject. Or he may permit himself vicarious pleasure which the patient soon detects, and the patient flees from this "too nosey" doctor.

This unhappy situation had prevailed throughout the century, causing many physicians to evade sexual issues whenever they could. One technique was to refer women with sexual problems to the relatively few female physicians available. Another was to tell young people about to be married to "leave all that to nature." The family doctor, the pioneering sex researcher Robert Latou Dickinson wrote in 1941, "does not sense that among present day youth 'the frankness is amazing, the ignorance appalling.' Too young, he dare not be thought to show too detailed an interest lest he be thought saturated in sex. Unmarried, the medical man is supposed by our convention to be blankminded on sex technics and the medical woman to be sexless unless married." Dealing with patients at the other end of the life cycle, as noted earlier, physicians showed little interest in preserving or reviving the sex lives of older people. Impotence, for example, "should hardly be of any great concern" to married people in their sixties, one doctor commented in 1957. Given the uselessness of "aphrodisiac medication," the best solution was celibacy. This dismissive reference to sex hormones was by no means representative of medical opinion about their efficacy. But it does suggest how easily these drugs could serve both physicians and patients as a convenient and evasive alternative to the kind of marriage counseling that might confront people with the causes rather than the symptoms of their marital problems.

Practitioners confronted a standard repertory of dilemmas for which hormonal treatment might be indicated. What, for example, should a doctor do about a wife's sexual demands on an aging husband? In the words of the exasperated physician in Maine already cited in chapter 1, "Are we to uphold the idea that a husband to be really in love with his wife must during his entire life be a potent cave man?" While many physicians would have prescribed testosterone, there was also a feeling that the loss of a man's sexual powers was simply part of growing old. A decade later, in 1946, a doctor in Missouri encountered women of fifty-nine and seventy who were having "sex dreams with orgasm" but were miserable because they had no sexual partners with whom to find satisfaction. "Fortunately," *JAMA* comments, "the exaggeration or reawakening of the libido long after the menopause is rare. Treatment is difficult. There is no specific remedy to decrease sex desire." So what should an aging and oversexed woman do? "Reading interesting books without romance, such as books on travel or history, may help. For some women cold baths and for others warm baths just before retiring are useful to insure restful sleep. If such simple methods do not help, such a patient should consult a psychiatrist."

At a time when surgeons were removing uteruses and ovaries from many younger women, doctors encountered postoperative surges in sex drive in patients who had already undergone hysterectomies or the artificial menopause long before middle age. One thirty-five-year-old woman had experienced an intensification of libido "to the extent that she is afraid of herself." Another woman of the same age had become afraid of "losing her mind." Medical men did not understand and could not treat these symptoms. "Occasionally androgens will decrease this disturbing phenomenon," one commentator suggested in 1949, but this remark just illustrates the haphazard approach to the clinical use of sex hormones that was so widespread at the time. (It is now apparent that doses of testosterone drugs can stimulate sexual desire in many women.) The libido-depressing (anaphrodisiac) drugs discussed in the medical literature did not play a role in these cases, but were either the subject of rumors (saltpeter in the food to cool off girls at private schools) or were prescribed to dampen the libidos of sex criminals. For the standard menopausal symptoms like hot flashes, many physicians prescribed sex hormones: commercial estrogenic preparations such as theelin, amniotin, Menformon, or progynon, which had been developed by the future Nazi war criminal Dr. Carl Clauberg to treat infertility. For overstimulated women, however, there was only the soothing advice of the attending physician: "avoidance of coffee, nervous sedatives and life outdoors are helpful." Or: "Treatment should consist of the avoidance of all sex stimulants, such as suggestive literature, motion pictures and theatrical performances. The patient should sleep in a room by herself as frequently as is necessary. She should exercise as much as possible in order to use up physical energy, and she should keep her mind well occupied." Both of these therapeutic strategies date from 1932. Almost two decades later the case of a forty-five-year-old woman in Oklahoma afflicted by increased libido at menopause elicits the same sort of advice: "Are the talk of other women and her reading habits healthy? Psychotherapy plus small doses of phenobarbital and a busy schedule can frequently be combined to subdue the disturbing problem."

Perhaps the most interesting aspect of these cases is the treatment of sexual feeling as a problem rather than as a blessing in the lives of women who have survived the removal of their reproductive organs. Today, when longer lives and better drugs have made geriatric sex positively fashionable, the renunciation of sexual activity by older people is likely to appear as an unnecessary and incomprehensible sacrifice. That these women experienced increased libido not as a welcomed opportunity but as an emotional burden shows us the extent to which the sexual mores of an earlier era affected how people imagined the role of sex in their lives. We should also keep in mind that these reports relate their experiences as seen by medical men whose conservative outlook did not encourage the enhancement of female sexuality outside marriage and childbearing. It was this sort of cultural conservatism (see below) that prompted these men to offer women pacifying advice about keeping up a busy schedule and avoiding sexual stimulation at the movies.

Conversely, women who were distressed by loss of sexual desire after menopause often encountered resignation on the part of their physicians. "If a woman broods over this or over the change of life in general," one commented in 1936, "a few intimate conversations concerning a more optimistic view on life may prove helpful." Such responses were prompted by a combination of prudishness and a sense that available medical techniques were of little use in this area. While some doctors prescribed testosterone drugs in the hope of rekindling sexual relationships within marriage, others undoubtedly consciously chose not to do so, either because they did not believe in the efficacy of hormone therapy or because they believed that sexual stimulation was better avoided than encouraged, especially in people who were already into or beyond middle age.

This cautionary approach was doubly important when female sexual appetite seemed to be out of control and a threat to social decorum. A report from 1938, for example, shows how these emergencies could inspire physicians to adopt therapeutic strategies ranging from the ridiculous to the perverse: "For the severer types of the condition, called nymphomania, every possible therapeutic method, including castration, roentgen therapy of the ovaries, hypnotism and even marriage to a male suffering from a similar condition (satyriasis), has been tried with absolutely no effect." Testosterone, too, was enlisted in the therapeutic assault on nymphomania. In 1940 the *American Journal of Psychiatry* reported the use of testosterone propionate on five "morbidly oversexed females," only one of whom had engaged in "overt antisocial behavior." Injected with 25 milligrams of the drug, this promiscuous eccentric admitted that her sexual appetite had been reduced "but complained bitterly that she was being de-sexed." The assumption that a "male" hormone would neutralize female desire was, in fact, untenable; the result of this therapy, as reported by the patient, may have been due to a placebo effect.

British and American physicians' knowledge of sex and sex hormones during the twentieth century can be inferred from the questions they submitted to medical journals of record such as the *British Medical Journal* and *JAMA*. Would a virgin go through menopause earlier than a married woman? Would the sex instinct survive menopause? Would castrating a male counteract a compulsion to commit "sex crimes" against children or "sex maniac crimes" against adults? Could sex crimes be caused by eating hormone-treated meat or poultry? Could lack of sexual excitement affect the nervous system of a normal woman? Could circumcising a woman cure her frigidity? Was there a drug to suppress the sex urge in men with frigid wives? Why did prostitutes never become pregnant? Was a post-childbirth distaste for sex a recognized syndrome? Was there a safe aphrodisiac for such women?

Other questions addressed the reputed powers of sex hormones. Was there a "sex-gland treatment" to increase the size of the penis? Was there a hormone therapy to increase the size of a woman's breasts? Could sex hormone injections increase fertility in husband and wife? These and other inquiries demonstrate how the expectations of many physicians had been raised by the commercial propaganda of the pharmaceutical manufacturers or by reports of clinical success with these drugs. And in their offices these practitioners encountered patients whose heads were filled with traditional, essentially folkloric, ideas about human sexuality and the hormone drugs that might regulate or enhance it.

Medical folklore expresses fears and wishes about physiological processes that are believed to be beyond the control of medical science. Given the special social and biological hazards that have been associated with being a woman, from the consequences of spinsterhood to the perils of childbirth, it is only natural that a folklore about the physical aspects of female sexuality took root and was passed down through generations. Women have feared and believed, for example, that the removal of their ovaries or any other operation that was performed to sterilize them would lead inevitably to the loss of sexual desire. "They have been told by some neighbor, friend or mother," one Texas physician wrote in 1946, "that once they have their female organs removed they will become fat, lazy, disinterested, and develop a negative libido." Their inclination to succumb to this gloomy prognosis will only increase, he said, when the doctor begins to give them sex hormones, thereby precipitating an emotional crisis that may well require psychiatric treatment. (These women seem to have taken the unusual position of regarding hormone replacement as a stigma—a mark of their anatomical deficiency—rather than as a therapy that might restore them to sexual wholeness.) A British woman without sexual experience whose ovaries were removed was told by her friends that she would never be capable of having sexual intercourse. Most medical folklore concerning sexuality expresses this sort of fatalism, implying that men and women are condemned to endure the loss of sexual identity and satisfaction as their bodies undergo surgery or suffer the ravages of the aging process.

Fear and hope combined in a primitive contraceptive technique based on the traditional belief that a woman could not conceive without orgasm. An American physician wrote in 1933:

> All know that on many women the fear of pregnancy acts as a terrifying specter. It hangs over their heads as a sword of Damocles and prevents them from normally enjoying the sex act. Many of them are laboring under the impression that if they restrain themselves, if they do not let themselves go, the danger of pregnancy will be greatly lessened. Some even think that pregnancy is impossible if they do not participate and do not permit themselves to reach an orgasm. I have known many women who were considered frigid and who had never enjoyed the sex act until after their menopause.

This gnawing fear of pregnancy and the loss of emotional fulfillment it has inflicted on countless women are never mentioned by those cultural conservatives who point to the birth control pill as one of the causes of degeneracy in the modern world. One historian observes, "The sad reality of a Victorian married woman's sex-life which modern prejudice has created, of joyless inhibition and ignorance, is quite unhistorical, but it must give way to a reality which may sometimes have been sadder: of women fearing and regretting sexual pleasure because they above all wished to avoid having another child." The belief that joyless sex prevents pregnancy, which may well persist in some societies to this day, may vary by social class. In 1951 a female physician in Britain reported that "this pathetic hope" was widely held among "uneducated women." In a similar vein, she observed that women's fear of menopause is likely to be more intense in "the culturally restricted woman."

Male sexual folklore is similarly anxiety-ridden and demoralizing. Fears that youthful masturbation or frequent sexual contacts can cause impotence are remnants of nineteenth-century sexual mythology. The idea that impotence is virtually inevitable has also been reinforced by cultural phobias about sexual activity in older people. We have already seen how many physicians virtually promoted the development of impotence in older men by treating sexual decline as an inevitable sequel of the aging process.

Other fears and insecurities have afflicted younger men. Many people, a stereotype-busting British psychiatrist noted in 1950, "still equate virility and potency. The most virile type of athlete, say a champion boxer, may be congenitally impotent, and is frequently, in fact, feebly sexed; and it is common for a vigorous type of intellect, of the type which by analogy we call 'virile,' to be compatible with complete celibacy and absence of erotic interest." The belief that the size of the genitals is an index of virility and sexual vigor is equally false; indeed, he says, men of meager physique are likely to be more sexually active than heartier types. A related stereotype holds that men who work in "physical" occupations are more sexually active than those in "sedentary" positions. While the tenacity of these male stereotypes derives in part from nineteenth-century notions about the survival of the fittest, they have been fed more recently by the anabolic steroid epidemic that has paralleled the use of androgens in clinical medicine. By making possible the bodybuilding subculture that emerged during the second half of the twentieth century, testosterone drugs created a new and medically dangerous myth conjoining hypermuscularity and sexual athleticism that has turned male action figures such as Sylvester Stallone into iconic figures around the world.

The popular appeal of hormonal drugs can be seen elsewhere in the medical folklore of the twentieth century. A striking number of sexually related wish-fulfillment fantasies of both men and women appearing in the medical literature from the 1930s through the 1950s are based on a belief in the powers of sex hormones. Some assumed that sex hormone injections could cure female sterility. During the 1950s and 1960s an analogous idea that testosterone injections can boost male fertility by means of a "rebound" effect was taken seriously by medical scientists. A British physician noted in 1946 that a male patient had been "impressed by the idea of taking a glandular preparation." Similarly, an American physician mentioned in 1952 "the type of placebo that minor surgery and hormone therapy symbolize to the ordinary layman." In 1966 a man asked another American doctor for "a fancied magical pill" to cure his impotence or his wife's frigidity. These and many other episodes reported in the medical journals make it clear that ideas about potent hormone therapies belonged to a medical vernacular that was shared by doctors and their patients during most of the century.

HORMONES AND THE STATE:
SEX AND MARITAL STABILITY

The medical sexology of the twentieth century traditionally endorsed the principle that monogamous marriage is the foundation of a stable society. This claim will surprise many people, for it is common to identify sex research with sexual nonconformity, promiscuity, and subversion of the home, but the apparent paradox is inseparable from the inquiries into human sexuality that rank as some of the best-known scientific enterprises of the modern era. Such projects require influential supporters and reliable funding; in the case of pioneering sex research, it is of particular interest to see which social interests were willing to stand behind this kind of work during its initial stages.

While the sex research that originated in the 1920s in the United States had both federal and private support, private interests took the initiative and public responsibility. It was John D. Rockefeller, Jr., who established the Bureau of Social Hygiene in 1911 to investigate the white slave trade in New York, and this concern about the social plague of prostitution eventually extended to include more general studies of sexual behavior. At the same time, worries about the state of the American family led to the formation in 1922 of the National Research Council (NRC) Committee for Research on Sex Problems, at a time when the divorce rate and sales of marriage manuals were rising together and fueling anxieties about the future of marriage as a social institution. Sponsorship of this initiative by the NRC, which had originally been founded by Congress in 1916 to coordinate research during the First World War, signaled an indirect acknowledgment by the federal government that sex research could serve the common good. It also demonstrated a realization on the part of the American academic elite that the private sphere of sexual intimacy would have to be treated as a public policy issue if scientific expertise was going to help preserve the American family. The first research grants funded a variety of studies, ranging from investigations of the sexual physiology of animals and humans to sexual behavior surveys of college and medical students; they too were funded by Rockefeller or his foundation.

Early-twentieth-century activities related to sex research in the United States included both moralistic campaigns that encouraged sexual self-discipline and what one historian has called "underground fact-finding research, much less moralistic, which was not published and probably could not be published at that time." This handful of "underground" sex researchers consisted of anything but sexual anarchists. On the contrary, the most important of these dissidents, the obstetrician-gynecologist Robert Latou Dickinson, who would later become an invaluable supporter of the pro-marriage sexual radical Alfred Kinsey, "was a Christian gentleman and a habitual do-gooder who sprinkled his conversations with the acclamation 'Glory to God,' " a "resolute Victorian who . . . was completely devoted to the preservation and promotion of marriage in a changing world." The crucial difference between Dickinson and other physicians was his profound conviction that sexual ignorance caused great suffering, and his belief that it was a physician's obligation to educate his or her patients. The courage of these convictions prompted Dickinson to publish "The Average Sex Life of American Women" (1925) and his "Medical Analysis of a Thousand Marriages" (1931) in the flagship publication *JAMA* at a time when few physicians would have dared to submit this sort of material to any medical journal. The purpose of this work, he pointed out, was "to foster successful and stable unions" within which sex should be enjoyed to the fullest possible extent. In retrospect it is clear that the sexual enlightenment for which Dickinson and Kinsey crusaded will take even longer than they might have imagined. "If we can utilize scientific research to stabilize even a few apparently unsuccessful marriages," *JAMA* editorialized in 1966, "some good has been served." The angry responses that greeted the reader-response sex surveys published by Shere Hite in 1976 and 1981 are more recent evidence that the challenge of integrating sex into marriage still ranks as one of the major social problems of the modern age.

In the 1920s public discussion of sexual relations within marriage could not approach the level of clinical candor that was eventually made possible by the Kinsey and Hite reports, and the same inhibitions were at work inside the privacy of the physician's office. Situated between the public campaigns for chastity and the handful of intrepid physicians in pursuit of underground sexual knowledge were the vast majority of doctors, whose sexual conservatism and ignorance resonated with and reinforced the fears and inhibitions of their patients. "Our present beliefs concerning normal sex life and average experience and practice," Dickinson wrote in 1925, "have the status of surmises standing on foundations no more secure than general impressions and scattering personal histories." It was time, he argued, for physicians to begin collecting tens of thousands of sexual histories that would elucidate human sexual behavior and physiology. Dickinson himself translated principle into practice by gathering thousands of case histories and by observing the vaginal walls and cervixes of women who masturbated to orgasm as he peered into them through a hollow glass phallus.

Medical ignorance about sex did not, however, translate into intellectual modesty about sex among most physicians. The knowledge vacuum was filled instead by a patriarchal ideology and a sexual conservatism that embodied the gender biases of contemporary society. Normal sex was intercourse between men and women who were both married and young enough not to have gone through female menopause or the "male climacteric" we shall examine later on. This rather narrow age range accounts, as we shall see, for the ambivalence doctors expressed in the 1940s about using sex hormones to reinvigorate aging men and women, a rehabilitative project some saw as pointless or even medically dangerous. This normative sexual ideal also explains why doctors used sex hormones and other medical procedures, as early as the 1920s and for decades thereafter, to "cure" homosexuals of their sexual orientation (see below). The primacy of heterosexual marriage also imposed itself through a medical vocabulary that left no room for doubt about where sex belonged: intercourse was "the marriage act" (1930) that took place in "the conjugal bedroom" (1952). The medical profession thus played an important role in preserving the ideal of monogamous marriage in the face of rising divorce rates and the unprecedented mobilization of women into wartime industrial production after 1940.

Restoring the traditional patriarchal family became a major priority in Britain and the United States after the social dislocations caused by the Second World War. In Britain the issue of sexual fulfillment within marriage came under the purview of the Marriage Guidance Council (established in 1937), a voluntary body that received funds from the government as it began the construction of the postwar welfare state. The methodology of lovemaking thus became a societal priority in a way that oddly anticipated the mass initiatives of Mao Zedong: "Techniques had to be learned and worked at. The Council's first booklet *How to Treat a Young Wife,* in line with other manuals of the time, stressed the importance of the husband developing the full sexual potentialities of the wife." The Christian secretary of the council solemnly declared that "good sex adjustment means satisfying orgasms for both. Simultaneous orgasm is a desirable ideal." A sexual performance principle that seemed to imitate (or parody) the tyrannical conventions of *Brave New World* was now the officially sanctioned policy of a state intent on consolidating an ideal of the family that had literally nauseated the citizens of Aldous Huxley's emotionally barren dystopia. An additional irony was that a sworn enemy of organized religion, the heathen sexual libertarian Dr. Kinsey, had created a sexology that was now making it possible to bring the joys of physical intimacy into proper Christian homes.

The participation of the medical establishment in this project emphasized the rhetoric of social cohesion rather than sexual expertise. This uneven contribution to the campaign to support the nuclear family can be tracked in the pages of the *British Medical Journal,* which offered a steady stream of commentary on the national reconstruction of marital relationships. "Now that the country is becoming alive to the importance of the family unit," one correspondent noted a year before the end of the European war, "it is time that the medical profession concerned itself more positively with the prevention of marital disharmony" and the "social disruption" it brought in its wake. Sexual failure and "the appalling breakdown rate of marriages" involved "the welfare of the nation" and were thus presented as a kind of threat to national security. Perhaps because a great war had just been fought and won, the traditional objective of nationalistically minded obstetricians and gynecologists—increasing the birth rate to build the armies of the future—played a very minor role in this campaign, and it, too, was played off the issue of women's sexual gratification. Every married woman should be aware, one doctor asserted, that "the acme of her sex life and the source of the most intense and lasting pleasure are not to be looked for in coital activity but in the birth of her baby." This dissent from the pro-orgasm propaganda of that era anticipates later objections to the demands of a sexual performance principle based on orgasmic frequency. The performance approach to sexual success was now spreading through Western societies as a consequence of Kinsey's quantitative approach to sexual "outlet."

Today it is clear that this British discussion of sexual problems was skewed by an unconscious masculine bias. For while the campaign promoting socially beneficial sexual gratification tended to focus on the alleged sexual deficiencies of troubled wives, letters to the *Journal* tell another story that received little attention then or afterward. "I have been consulted lately by several men, all about the age of 45," one doctor writes in 1946, "who after service abroad for some three or more years return home to their wives to find themselves completely, or almost completely, impotent. Instead of happy reunion after so many years apart, the marriage is in danger." Other letters tell the same story in more veiled terms. "Soldiers abroad idealize their wives and homes," another physician wrote at this time, "and the wives contemplate a heaven on earth when their husbands return. It does not work out that way. For a time all is thrilling; then the 'honeymoon' is over, there are troublesome problems of home and work and children, and disillusion takes place." "Soldier's impotence," one psychiatrist reported, was in fact common among demobilized military men and former prisoners of war. Britain's sexual deficit was more evenly shared by the two sexes than it appeared. At the same time, it is not surprising that British medical men did not make a point of spreading this sort of news about the nation's returning heroes.

Medical interest in the use of drugs to treat these postwar sexual problems is not much evident in the published record, even though various drugs, including Benzedrine and codeine-laced Veganin tablets, had been promoted to the public during the war in order to increase human efficiency and productivity on behalf of national survival. And those drugs that were prescribed do not seem to have done much good. The unspecified "tonics and stimulants" given to a returning soldier and his wife by one physician had not helped them solve their sexual problems. The testosterone drugs advertised in medical journals were thought to be effective for impotence (in fact, they are not), but they do not seem to have been widely used. "Is there any safe aphrodisiac I can give" a thirty-six-year-old woman without a sex drive, one doctor asks in 1947. "Drugs reputed to have an aphrodisiac action are rarely of any value, and the same is true of hormones except where there is gonad deficiency," came the discouraging and apparently uninformed reply. Yet the sexually stimulating effect of applying testosterone ointment to the clitoris had been reported in the *Lancet* in 1939. Reports about the libido-boosting effects of testosterone in women had been appearing in the American medical literature since 1941. Whether this practitioner had not been reading the professional literature, or had been filtering it through the lens of his own sexual inhibitions, is an open question.

Why British physicians did not respond more enthusiastically to the opportunity to use androgens to revive sex in marriage is not entirely clear. What we do know is that British interest in sex hormone therapy stressed estrogenic drugs rather than androgens, and that clinical reports of aphrodisiac effects that had usually been associated with quacks were received skeptically. At the same time, the stimulating effect of androgens did not always encourage physicians to continue using them. Some women who got androgens for breast cancer and then felt a sudden and unexpected surge of sexual appetite found this a distressing rather than a pleasurable experience. An agitated woman's reporting this sensation would not have prompted the physician to try androgens in other patients who might become similarly upset. If, on the other hand, a woman chose, perhaps out of embarrassment, not to report the aphrodisiac effect at all, then the doctor would remain unaware of testosterone's potential to boost libido. More generally, the sexual conservatism of the medical profession, which was still inclined to believe that women were naturally less interested in sex than were men, would have provided doctors with little motivation to spread the news about a sexual stimulant beyond the clinics that served the troubled married women they were treating as best they could.

While scientific skepticism and cultural conservatism surely inhibited the acceptance of these drugs, the tepid response to androgens at a time when the Marriage Guidance Council and leading citizens were clamoring for more orgasms in British bedrooms remains puzzling. For the ethos of sexual success within marriage was so strong that it was inflicting a new kind emotional stress on women. As one British writer recalled:

> At the center of that religion of marriage was a cult every bit as hallowed as that of the Virgin: the cult of the orgasm, mutual and simultaneous. It descended to the young people of my generation from both Lawrence and Freud as the Inner Mystery, something they all aspired to, a sign of grace. Because of it I had impossible expectations of my marriage, my sex life, myself. I was an absolutist of the orgasm before I had had enough experience to ensure even sexual competence.

And the curse that lay upon those who failed to achieve this holy grail was called frigidity.

PATRIARCHAL SEX THERAPY: CURING "FRIGIDITY" WITH HORMONES

The practice of stigmatizing only sexually unresponsive women as frigid is a relatively recent innovation of the English language that happens to coincide with the rise of gynecology as a male-dominated medical discipline. In 1660 in England a marriage could be dissolved if "either party" were "frigid." A dictionary published in 1700 applies the term to "a weak disabled Husband." As late as 1893 we find "a man of physically frigid temperament." W. M. Gallichan's *Sexual Apathy* (1927) finally shifts the burden of "frigidity" to the wife, and that is where it has remained ever since. Gender bias has also shaped how the respective sexual disorders of men and women have been presented to lay and medical audiences. While female "frigidity" and male "impotence" are treated in the medical literature as analogous disorders, there has always been a disproportionate emphasis on female sex problems as the source of marital disharmony. In fact, the history of frigidity is best understood as an important battleground in the gender wars that reshaped relationships between men and women during the twentieth century.

This gender bias has also been evident in the popular media that report medical research findings and opinions to the public. Take, for example, an article on "cold" women that *Reader's Digest* condensed and reprinted from the popular American men's magazine *Argosy* not long after the first Kinsey Report was published in January 1948. Here, as in Britain, frigidity was presented as a kind of public health crisis that threatened the well-being of an entire society. "There is no greater personal tragedy," this (male) writer intoned, "than that of a normally ardent man married to a woman who is cold and unresponsive. This situation has contributed heavily to the alarming increase in divorces and broken homes, to alcoholism, and to innumerable psychological crack-ups." From this perspective, the physiological ease with which male orgasm is achieved exempts the "ardent" husband from responsibility for his sexual predicament. He is both the reliable spouse and the emotionally injured party who must endure tragic suffering on account of his wife's unfortunate defect.

A comparison of this article with another popular treatment of this subject makes clear the sheer confusion that Kinsey's work could generate in some of the less sophisticated writers that were reporting his findings to the general public. *Argosy* had told its masculine audience that "the mind plays a tremendous part in regulating sex life" in a woman, and that "sex is not as serious for a man as for a woman." But it was also possible to construe the new sex research in an entirely different way, in accordance with more traditional ideas about female sexuality. In August 1956, for example, the editors of *Popular Science* magazine offered the husbands in their large and technologically minded audience some practical instruction regarding the psychosexual management of their wives. Citing Kinsey as his authority, this author depicts men and women as if they were different kinds of household appliances. Because he is endowed with more elaborate circuitry, it is the husband who must take the initiative, while it is the wife who exists in a sexually somnolent state and needs, figuratively speaking, to be turned on. "Scientists," he reports, "have evidence that the brain plays a tremendous part in the male sex drive. But it has very little direct connection with female sex behavior." For example, the scent of perfume can trigger a series of powerful feelings in a man because he is equipped with "a wide array of such push-button associations that are almost completely absent in a woman's thinking." Confined within this sexually mindless state, few women even have erotic daydreams. "Sooner or later the majority of healthy males discover that sex just isn't as urgent or interesting to their wives as it is to them." Given these different thresholds of sexual arousal, the author explains, it was no wonder that so many men saw their wives as "frigid."

The progressive contribution of these popular sex commentaries was to point out to husbands that their wives, too, were entitled to sexual pleasure, and that husbands would benefit from thinking about the emotional lives of their partners. Exercising this responsibility required the insights into human sexuality that modern sexologists like Kinsey were finally making available to ordinary people. Embracing this knowledge, however, was to prove difficult for many lay readers as well as doctors —particularly for one group of medical men, who regarded Kinsey and all his works as nothing less than an abomination.

The medical term *frigidity* has been applied to a variety of female sexual disorders, including painful intercourse (dyspareunia), an inability to achieve orgasm, and other disturbances associated with sexual experience. This broad and elastic definition of the disorder made it easily applicable to large numbers of women who could now be stigmatized as the principal source of America's domestic sexual crisis. Men too, of course, had sexual problems that were frequently discussed in the medical literature. But neither the disrupted sexual relations caused by male impotence nor the fatigue and depression of the male climacteric were presented as threats to the stability of the American home.

The theme of frigidity was further politicized by psychoanalysts whose dogmatic approach to female sexuality was suffused by a misogyny directed at women they labeled neurotic or too self-assertive in their opinions or behavior. Freudian doctrine held that female maturation required a woman to give up the clitoris as her principal erotogenic zone and to adopt the vagina as her major source of sexual gratification. Frigidity was thus defined as a failure to move beyond the "infantile" clitoral phase into the genuine female adulthood represented by the "vaginal orgasm."

Kinsey infuriated many psychoanalysts by denying the existence of the vaginal orgasm and by insisting that the clitoris was the center of women's erotic stimulation. The vaginal walls, he said, are not richly endowed with nerve endings and are therefore relatively insensitive to stimulation. Female masturbation, he noted, involved stimulation of the clitoris far more often than vaginal penetration. He then proceeded to rub salt in the wound by arguing that their fixation on vaginal orgasm had caused psychoanalysts and other therapists to waste a great deal of their patients' time and money. "This question is one of considerable importance," Kinsey and his colleagues wrote, "because much of the literature and many of the clinicians, including psychoanalysts and some of the clinical psychologists and marriage counselors, have expended considerable effort trying to teach their patients to transfer 'clitoral' responses into 'vaginal responses.' Some hundreds of the women in our own study and many thousands of the patients of certain clinicians have consequently been much disturbed by their failure to accomplish this biologic impossibility." Several years after Kinsey's death, Masters and Johnson's classic study *Human Sexual Response* (1966) demonstrated that the great sexologist had been right about the clitoris all along.

Kinsey's sympathetic and tolerant attitude toward human sexual behavior in its great variety contrasted sharply with the doctrinaire and censorious style of his principal antagonist, the psychoanalyst Edmund Bergler, who is plausibly described by one of Kinsey's biographers as "an irascible New York analyst." Bergler's psychoanalytic theory of frigidity was published in 1944 and consists of the following claims: (1) frigidity is the absence of vaginal orgasm and nothing else; (2) most women are, therefore, frigid; (3) frigidity produces a plethora of neurotic and unattractive women; (4) healthy female sexuality is passive; (5) men are not to blame for frigidity; and (6) there is no therapy for frigidity apart from a protracted course of psychoanalysis.

Bergler's misogyny is evident in the deeply felt and gratuitously unflattering descriptions of the frigid women he has treated. Here we meet the "beautiful, coquettish woman" endowed with "artificial charm" and a "brilliant façade," the woman with the "housewife" complex who exudes "a remarkably nonsexual atmosphere," and the hysterical type who is constantly in search of "the imaginary Casanova." In 1950 the psychoanalysts William S. Kroger and S. Charles Freed extended the frigid population to include the "gold-digger," the prostitute, and the nymphomaniac, as well as "homosexuals, aggressive old maids, agitative female 'champions' in constant competition with men, narcissistic women and violent espousers of virginity." Female self-assertiveness virtually guaranteed sexual failure, since women had to accept "the passive rôle or suffer automatically from frigidity." Or as Kroger and Freed put it: "The 'normal' woman, during the sex act, should be passive and receptive of the penis."

This analysis of frigidity expressed both the patriarchal and professional interests of its promoters. The vaginal doctrine decreed that as many as 75 percent of women were frigid—as opposed to Kinsey's estimate of 10 percent. Female orgasms achieved outside of marriage were proof not of orgasmic capacity but of neurosis—a bit of pro-marital prudery the pro-marriage Kinsey could only deride. Female satisfaction was dependent on passive acceptance of penetration by the penis—a male conceit Kinsey mocked in *Sexual Behavior in the Human Female*. Husbands bore no responsibility for sexual failure within marriage—a claim that ignored much commentary in the medical literature. And psychoanalysts had a monopoly on the only "cure."

This doctrine of frigidity was a prescription for continued suffering and inaction. Indeed, a striking feature of the strict Freudian position was how little hope there was to offer the frigid women of the world— so many potential patients, so few analysts, so little time to cure them. Frigidity, Bergler wrote in 1954, "is so widespread in our culture that it is the emotional plague," and his office on Central Park West was one of the few venues on earth where resistance to this pestilence was even possible. "As a mass problem," he had declared in 1944, "the question of frigidity is, unfortunately, not to be solved." The only effective treatment was protracted psychoanalytic treatment of the unconscious, since it was "wrong to imagine that frigidity can be cured by mobilizing the conscious forces."

Mobilizing these forces could require nothing more than offering the unhappy couple some practical advice. As one physician from West Virginia put it: "I have repeatedly seen many normal, well balanced, adult married women whose complaints of lack of sexual pleasure and orgasm in intercourse were remedied by showing them or their husbands the position of the clitoris." To call such people frigid, he added, was "a flagrant distortion of fact." But psychoanalysts had good reason to indulge in such distortions, since monopolizing the definition of frigidity enabled them to dismiss more economical and successful treatments that were based on what the conscious mind could do. The sexual instruction offered to couples by Masters and Johnson in the 1960s exemplified the alternative to Freudian pessimism about frigidity, and soon the clitoral/vaginal debate was being politicized by people for whom "consciousness-raising" was a battle cry. *Ramparts* magazine took up the Great Orgasm Debate in 1968, declaring that the doctrine of the vaginal orgasm "was a part of keeping women down, of making them sexually as well as economically, socially and politically subservient." By 1975 *Ms.* magazine had declared life without orgasms a state of oppression against which women should revolt. In prefeminist days, women without orgasms had been left in anguished isolation from their fellow sufferers. "But now there are groups where non-orgasmic women can come out from behind closed doors. From the young divorcée to the woman who's been married for 20 years, women who've never had an orgasm are getting together to share pent-up feelings, undo crippling myths, and learn skills which give them more pleasure." Feminists must have been pleased to hear that some participants in group therapy for non-orgasmic women found their male partners intimidated by their new sexual assertiveness.

From the 1920s through the 1940s medical reports estimated that frigidity afflicted anywhere from 25 percent to 75 percent of American women. By 1940 this mass diagnosis of impaired female libido had coincided with two new developments in the use of androgens. The first was the pharmaceutical houses' campaign to persuade American physicians that the new testosterone drugs they were marketing would energize middle-aged men suffering from the new disorder some physicians were calling the male climacteric. This syndrome, which was seen as analogous to menopause, prominently included a flagging libido. The second event was the inadvertent discovery that testosterone was a female aphrodisiac.

Testosterone's effect on the female sex drive was first observed in women who were being treated with androgens for various gynecological disorders or for metastatic breast cancer. The first recorded case involved a woman whose ovaries had been removed and who was suffering from "the menopause syndrome." During her treatment with androgens she informed her physician that for the first time in ten years she had experienced a surge of sexual desire. The same physician also noted that he had treated "several elderly women who found the resurgence of libido distressing." Another physician later described a similar scenario. Following her hysterectomy a patient had been given androgens to control uterine bleeding, a practice that was "the fashion of the day" during the 1940s, and she too had experienced a resurgence of sexual desire. "Her physicians were amazed that testosterone, the so-called male hormone, could accentuate libido in the female to the degree experienced." Indeed, the aphrodisiac effect was so pronounced that when she returned for further evaluation, her physicians decided that "it would be better to discontinue it in order to reverse her libidinous tendency." The eruption of sudden and unexpected sexual desire could also take on a tragic aspect in the cases of women who were undergoing androgen therapy for metastatic breast cancer:

> It is not unusual for these women, despite the fact that they are being almost destroyed by the ravages of their disease, to show a considerable increase in sexual desire. This may be of such an extent that a problem is created. The husband, being aware of the basic disease, has lost much of his desire for sexual contact with his wife, so that the wife's increased sexual desire may therefore create a serious crisis.

Androgen therapy could also cause problems for couples in good health, "since if administered in excess to women with normal libido it may cause abnormal intensification of desire and may lead to marital complications."

These episodes were significant in that they demonstrated an aphrodisiac effect that neither the doctors nor the patients had anticipated, thereby ruling out the possibility that these sexual feelings had resulted from the power of suggestion, the so-called placebo effect. For this reason these events can be seen as inadvertent approximations to the double-blind clinical trials that attempt to objectively measure the effects of drugs, taking pains that neither the researchers nor the experimental subjects know whether a given subject has been given the drug or has received the inactive placebo. In fact, the early androgen episodes were even less suggestive than the standard double-blind protocol in that none of the participants conceived of the therapeutic procedure as an experiment meant to test the effect of a drug. That some of the affected women found the aphrodisiac effect distressing would seem to rule out the possibility that the eroticism they experienced represented the fulfillment of a wish. Similarly, the doctors' astonishment that a "male" hormone could stimulate female libido suggests that their comments and behaviors did not contribute to the effects they observed in their clinics. "Theoretically," JAMA's editors commented in 1946, "androgen might be considered a counteracting agent, but actually it stimulates the sex urge in women."

The medical assault on frigidity also employed or considered a variety of more exotic techniques. In 1922 a German physician warned against the use of X-rays to stimulate the female sex drive. Alcohol and wheat germ oil, supposedly rich in "the reproductive vitamin" E, were recommended as cures for frigidity. An excellent and painless treatment for the insensitive vaginal membranes that could cause frigidity, according to one New York physician, consisted in "inserting a large vaginal electrode into the vagina, connecting it with the negative pole, while the positive pole is connected with a wet abdominal electrode." Running sinusoidal-galvanic current through the woman's pelvis for ten or twenty minutes, he wrote in 1942, produced "excellent" results. It is worth noting that psychotherapy (including hypnotherapy) or psychoanalysis were recommended in the medical literature less often than more tangible interventions such as drugs and electrodes.

Some physicians, in conformity with the popular belief that any sex hormone was also a sex stimulant, also believed that estrogenic substances could intensify female libido. A report in 1941 claimed that applying an estrogenic substance to the clitoris had cured frigidity in several women. The aphrodisiac powers of the estrogenic drug known as theelin were so feared by one practitioner that he warned it could produce "psychosexual panic, frank insanity or suicide" in emotionally fragile women. Here, too, we encounter a physician who is apprehensive about the potentially harmful consequences of a woman's being overwhelmed by a sudden and unexpected surge of sexual stimulation.

Testosterone drugs were the favored pharmacological technique of the 1940s for treating frigidity. Testosterone propionate ointment could be applied to the vulva or clitoris to increase genital sensitivity. Testosterone could be injected or pellets implanted under the skin to intensify libido: "Many married women volunteered the information that the loss of sexual desire led to marital discord. Following pellet implantation there was a return of coital pleasure, which often terminated in orgasm. A reawakened interest on the part of the husband usually followed and husband and wife once more fell in love." By 1943 testosterone propionate was reported to be in widespread use to treat women with sexual and other endocrine disorders. In 1947 a team of authors noted that over the previous decade "the effect of androgens in increasing libido in women has been an almost universal observation." It appeared that androgens influenced libido in three ways, "causing, a) a heightened susceptibility to psychic stimulation; b) increased sensitivity of the external genitalia, particularly of the clitoris and c) a greater intensity of sexual gratification." Perhaps the most interesting point about these scientifically primitive observations is that they have been repeatedly confirmed by later investigators.

Nevertheless, that such outcomes were observed does not mean that all claims about the effects of testosterone drugs were (or are) valid.

Demonstrating the psychological or even physiological effects of drugs on human beings is extremely difficult and sometimes impossible. The problems associated with establishing aphrodisiac effects are even more vexing because of the powerful preconceptions and wishes associated with human sexuality, which are likely to create self-fulfilling prophecies of heightened pleasure. Observations of such effects might also be skewed by clinicians' feelings about the people to whom these drugs are given, by the confidence medical men can have in their own therapeutic powers, or by their therapeutic ambition to control sexual behavior.

The medical profession's interest in controlling sexual appetite was evident when women labeled nymphomaniacs were treated with sex hormones. Although they appeared to be the polar opposites of their frigid counterparts, these contrasting deviants turned out to have more in common than one might have expected. One physician, for example, distinguished in 1959 between two categories of oversexed women: those who did not and those who did experience orgasm. To achieve the desired reductions in sexual activity, he prescribed "male" and female" hormones, respectively. The first (frigid) group received testosterone so they could finally experience the orgasms that would end their desperate quest for satisfaction. The second group received progesterone to lower their sex drives. In both cases the practitioner looked back on his therapeutic efforts with satisfaction, since the cause of social stability had been served. But there was an even more notorious group of sexual deviants whom society saw as a threat and who presented the sex hormone therapists with a far more difficult challenge.

REORIENTING MALE DESIRE:
CURING HOMOSEXUALS WITH SEX HORMONES

Medical ambitions to "cure" homosexuals originated in the early endocrinology of a hundred years ago and persisted in various forms throughout the twentieth century. Because sexual "inversion" has long been regarded as a single disorder or perversion, this therapeutic project has always included the dream of eradicating homosexuality from the face of the earth, since a treatment for one should be a treatment for all. The idea that homosexuality does not require treatment, on the grounds that no sexual orientation can be classified as a disease, is of very recent origin. Until 1987 the American Psychiatric Association (APA) recognized homosexuality as a treatable condition so long as the patient sought medical assistance: "Treatment for homosexuality is appropriate only when a patient is uncomfortable with his or her sexual orientation" (ego-dystonic homosexuality). This definition, formulated in 1973, was a further improvement on the APA's famous eighty-one-word definition of sexual deviance that described homosexuality as a disease. In May 1987, after years of lobbying by gay activists, the APA removed the diagnosis of ego-dystonic homosexuality from the third edition of its official inventory of mental disorders (the *Diagnostic and Statistical Manual of Mental Disorders,* or *DSM*-III). Henceforth, any distress about sexual orientation was to be categorized as a "sexual disorder not otherwise specified." This reform turned tradition upside down by asserting that the actual disorder was the *distress* caused by sexual orientation rather than the orientation itself. The reclassification of homosexuality was a stunning act of reform on the part of a medical establishment that had long regarded homosexuals as diseased and had subjected them to a variety of "therapies" that often seemed more like punishments.

Medical "treatments" meant to undo homosexuality have been notable for their use of pain and suffering. To be sure, the illusory cures achieved by surgeons' knives during and after the First World War marked something of a humane advance over the tortures and executions traditionally inflicted on homosexuals. Yet it is a curious fact that most such medical treatments carried out in modern times have continued to employ various types of suffering to bring about "therapeutic" reversals of sexual orientation. We shall see, for example, that even the sex hormones administered during these procedures often caused physiological and psychological misery, or were prescribed to offer an alternative to aversion therapy centered on inducing nausea in the "patient."

The sadistic aura of this therapeutic style demonstrates the ease with which physicians can absorb and act on cultural prejudices that remain unaffected by their medical training. The despised status of the male homosexual among medical men is evident in a flurry of letters that appeared in the *British Medical Journal* just after the Second World War. These commentaries, which coincided with the campaign to reconstitute the nuclear family in Britain, were provoked in part by British law: a man arrested for private homosexual activity could be sentenced to years in prison. It was clear that the medicalization of homosexuality that had begun at the turn of the century was still confronting a powerful impulse to punish rather than treat sexual deviance. One of the more enlightened correspondents deplored, for example, "the enormity of the retributive sentences being passed upon patients who should be given all the benefits that psychology has to offer." In fact, the *Journal* itself had encouraged medical ignorance by refusing to discuss homosexuality in its pages.

But resistance to the cruelties being inflicted on these outcasts did not necessarily translate into according them an equal measure of human status or dignity. The power of the disease model was evident in this doctor's plea on behalf of those "unfortunate inverts . . . who owing to causes that are quite beyond their own control, being abnormal in their endocrine make-up or unhappy in the environment of their early childhood, are deprived by Nature and by society of the reasonable satisfaction of instincts which are the foundation of human happiness." These people were exiles, even if it was not their fault that their instincts had been "diverted up a biological blind alley."

For other physicians, as one of their number put it, homosexuality was quite simply "a dirty, unaesthetic, and abnormal practice at best" that constituted "too dangerous a threat to civilization to be handled with kid gloves." From this point of view, the main concern in dealing with homosexuals was to ensure with absolute certainty that pedophiles in particular would be prevented from preying on boys and vulnerable adolescents. Less punitive proposals included a recommendation for more schools for maladjusted boys where "effeminate mannerisms" could be educated out of existence. More specific forms of treatment, including drugs, are virtually absent from the discussion. Indeed, several years earlier (in 1942) one physician had sarcastically dismissed a colleague's claim that "repulsively feminized boys" could be changed into "normal virile adolescents" by means of "a few hormonic injections." Almost forgotten in this debate was the question of whether homosexuals wanted to be treated at all. For as one medical man pointed out: "It would be rash to assume that all homosexuals are to be pitied. Many are untreatable by psychological methods because they disdain treatment or seek it only when faced by unwelcome social implications." And unwelcome social sanctions had long been standard fare for "sexual inverts." In 1730 the Court of Holland had resolved "to exterminate this vice to the bottom" and followed up by putting seventy-five men to death. Two centuries later, officially sponsored violence against homosexuals took the form of treatment by compulsion. Now it is time to see why some physicians believed that homosexuality could be treated at all.

The medical rehabilitation of homosexuals required an understanding, or at least a theory, of their disorder. At the end of the nineteenth century, physicians saw homosexuality as a consequence of the "degeneration" of the central nervous system that could express itself as a number of malformations of mind or body, which also included alcoholism, tuberculosis, cleft lips, and misshapen ears. In his *Psychopathia sexualis* (1886), the pioneering sexologist Richard von Krafft-Ebing declared that every expression of the sexual instinct that did not serve "the purpose of nature—*i.e.,* propagation—must be regarded as perverse," a diagnosis that conformed to the sexual mores of the Victorian era. The common explanation of this disorder was that the homosexual was a deficient or counterfeit man. In his *Die conträre Sexualempfindung* (1891, translated into English as *Perversions of the Sex Instinct*), for example, the German physician Albert Moll claimed that the homosexual was "in reality nothing else but a woman" who tended to be attracted to the most virile of men. Still, this observation begged the question of why the sexual instinct in some men was "inverted" in such a way as to result in same-sex attraction. Scientific curiosity could not be satisfied by a vague degeneration model that pretended to account for everything from a twisted mouth to pedophilia. A medical explanation would have to address the organic basis of sexual dimorphism itself—the biological origins of male and female sexuality.

The theory of gonadal "internal secretions" launched by Charles-Édouard Brown-Séquard in 1889 provided a framework for conceptualizing the operation of male and female biological forces operating within the human organism. This theory also justified the therapeutic injections to boost male and female functioning that came into practice during the 1890s, long before scientists and physicians had acquired any real understanding of reproductive physiology. The administration of organ extracts included both testicular and ovarian substances, even if the former were far more widely used—in men, women, and even infants—than their ovarian counterparts. Still, Brown-Séquard noted that an American physician then practicing in Paris, one Mrs. Augusta Brown, had "with great courage" injected animal ovarian extracts into many women, with "extremely interesting" results. He assumed that injecting a fluid derived from the fresh ovaries of young animals into old women would energize them, just as testicular extracts seemed to revive old men. Given the enthusiasm with which he promoted the "dynamogenic" effects of testicular extracts, it is not surprising that Brown-Séquard maintained that testicular extract was more powerful than ovarian extract. Indeed, to have argued otherwise would have challenged the biological foundations of male supremacy. The important point here is that the theory of internal secretions upheld the model of sexual dimorphism by postulating both male and female principles that could be translated into the rudimentary physiological concepts of the day.

The observed consequences of removing the sexual organs supported the same model. The effects of male castration on sexual functioning and physical strength were well known, while the atrophy of the uterus following the removal of the ovaries was confirmed during the 1870s when oophorectomy came into fashion as a treatment for menstrual and emotional disorders. By 1907 the British scientist Edward Schäfer was hypothesizing that "internal secretions containing special hormones" were the messenger substances that allowed the testicles and ovaries to influence the development of secondary sex characteristics. Testing the potency of sex gland extracts on castrated animals would not be possible until about 1920, but a therapeutic principle had been born. The concept of the internal secretion opened up the possibility of a replacement therapy that could compensate for the debilitating consequences of male and female castration and, perhaps, for the mysterious deficiency disease known as homosexuality. (The 1912 edition of *Psychopathia sexualis* makes what appears to be the first published connection between internal secretions and homosexuality.) For the time being, however, because physicians lacked empirically effective sex gland extracts, gland grafting became the therapeutic procedure of choice for repairing physically damaged heterosexuals and sexually aberrant homosexuals.

Between 1890 and 1910 the Viennese physiologist Eugen Steinach performed transplantation experiments on animals demonstrating that sexual development was dependent on secretions from the sexual glands. One observer of these successful operations was the Viennese urologist Robert Lichtenstern. In 1915, while serving as a military physician during the Great War, Lichtenstern was called on to treat a man whose testicles had been destroyed by enemy fire. Having become disillusioned with the traditional reparative methods, he decided instead to apply the surgical technique that had so impressed him in Steinach's laboratory. In June 1920 he told the Berlin Urological Society that even after the passage of five years, the result of this operation remained a "complete success." By this time Lichtenstern had performed eighteen such operations, transplanting both normal and undescended testicles into men suffering from castration, eunuchoidism, and homosexuality. Again he reported remarkable recoveries, including the appearance of the "energetic and manly aspect" that would later be ascribed to testosterone injections during and after the 1940s. As for the origin of the homosexual impulse, Steinach had traced the behavior of his "homosexual animals" to the influence of a "hermaphroditic sex gland," and Lichtenstern assumed that the same applied to human subjects. Both men were further persuaded by Steinach's (eventually discredited) finding of abnormal tissue in the testicles of homosexuals. So the reversal of sexual inversion in the clinic appeared to be real.

But doubts about the efficacy of these operations surfaced repeatedly during the early 1920s. Attempts to replicate the procedure that had succeeded in Vienna produced mixed results. The surgeon Richard Mühsam reported initial success in reversing homosexuality, but by 1926 he had become completely disillusioned. Perhaps the most scientifically interesting case was the observed sexual transformation of a homosexual who received a piece of testicle without his knowledge during an operation to repair a hernia, thereby ruling out the role of suggestion in his sexual reorientation. In retrospect, however, it is clear that none of these purported sexual transformations were what their creators believed and reported them to be. Indeed, the same sequence of announced success followed by disillusion would be repeated during the 1920s in the case of the "monkey-gland" transplants carried out by Serge Voronoff for the purpose of restoring virility to worn-out men. We may assume that placebo effects, wishful thinking, and spontaneous psychosexual adjustments all played a role in persuading even accomplished scientists and doctors that their techniques had achieved astonishing cures. The next stage in the medical campaign to save homosexuals from their misdirected libidos would follow much the same pattern.

The availability of synthetic androgens by the late 1930s transformed the practice of clinical endocrinology by rescuing male sex hormone therapy from the pseudoscience of human gland grafting. During the 1940s these heavily advertised drugs were prescribed for a wide range of disorders with a lack of inhibition that, with the benefit of hindsight, now appears both absurd and medically irresponsible. Given that the medical view of homosexuality had not substantially changed between 1920 and 1940, attempts to use injectable testosterone propionate to reverse homosexual orientation were entirely predictable. As one physician put it in 1940: "If homosexuality is merely the result of an endocrine disturbance, the prospect for its cure must be excellent today." The following passage from a marriage manual published that year suggests how little speculation about the origins of homosexuality had changed since the turn of the century: "Perhaps when we understand more of the mysteries of the glands of internal secretion and of the chemicals of the body known as 'hormones' we shall gain a better physiological and chemical insight into the nature of homosexuality. When that day dawns—it is now somewhat in the future—we may be able to treat it more effectively and to restore individuals of unusual chemical endowment to normal." The principal difference between this tolerant clergyman and some of his scientific contemporaries was that they felt they now had laboratory methods that enabled them to reformulate the older theory of endocrine imbalance in more precise biochemical terms.

The idea that the bodies of homosexuals contained less male hormone and more female hormone than those of heterosexuals first appeared in 1935. By 1940 a number of investigators were confident enough in their ability to assay hormone levels to claim that homosexuality was rooted in abnormal sex hormone ratios rather than the psychological complexes hypothesized by Freud and others. Given "such highly suggestive hormonal differences," one research team wrote, "one may assume that such data point to a definite biologic mechanism in homosexuality. Of course it is not possible at this time to evaluate the true significance of the difference, but it seems that the constitutional homosexual has a different sex hormone chemistry than the normal male." This theory was also endorsed by a trade journal distributed by the Parke, Davis pharmaceutical company, which may have spied a potential market niche for synthetic testosterone. In fact, the Dutch drug company Organon had shown an interest in developing a drug to treat homosexuals as early as 1935.

The endocrine theory of homosexuality was attractive because it promised a cure by means of drugs that were already on the market. The genetic explanation, by contrast, postulated "an abnormality of the chromosomal structure with a subsequent sexual differentiation of certain cerebral functions"—a condition which appeared to be beyond correction. Half a century later, as we shall see, ideas about sexual differentiation of the brain have survived scientific scrutiny in a way that ideas about sex hormone imbalance have not.

The endocrine imbalance theory promulgated during 1940 had already run into trouble by January 1941. This report described the sex-hormone medication of "a negro of passive homosexual type" who, over a period of six months, was subjected to the following regimen, thanks to donations from five drug companies: Stilboestrol, the potent synthetic estrogen, by mouth; an implanted 150-milligram tablet of testosterone; intramuscular injections of a gonadotropic preparation derived from pregnant-mare serum; desiccated thyroid by mouth; injections of Pituitary Gonadotropic and testosterone propionate; and more estrogenic preparations, namely, Emmenin and Estriol. The result of this trial was that apart from nausea, "none of the drugs of the entire series gave rise to any detectable change of behavior or attitude."

A more damaging critique of the endocrine imbalance theory came from the nascent sexologist Alfred Kinsey, who pointed to methodological problems in the measurement of androgen and estrogen levels and challenged the very concept of homosexuality itself: "More basic than any error brought out in the analysis of the above data," he wrote in 1941, "is the assumption that homosexuality and heterosexuality are two mutually exclusive phenomena emanating from fundamentally and, at least in some cases, inherently different types of individuals." Drawing on the 1,600 sex histories he and a colleague had collected by this time, Kinsey argued that distinguishing between these two types of sexual orientation was meaningless when at least a third of all men had had one or more homosexual experiences, and the great majority of "homosexuals" had had some (or even a lot of) heterosexual experience. In the last analysis, there were no clearly defined types of sexual orientation with which even reliably measured hormone levels could be matched. From this perspective, the psychiatrists who were treating homosexuality as an organic endocrine disease were profoundly misguided. In addition, Kinsey's doubts about the hormone assays of this era were well founded. Twenty years later the sexologist John Money would offer the following assessment: "It is impossible at the present stage of scientific knowledge to identify the full variety of related forms of the sex hormones that are functionally active in the body, or to estimate their quantity."

The attractiveness of the androgen-estrogen hypothesis can only have made it easier for endocrinologists to believe in their own analytic methods, and as a result the sex hormone treatment of homosexuals continued. "Organotherapy by compulsion," initiated by a court order or by parental decree, was reported in 1944. The problem was that testosterone propionate combined with chorionic gonadotropin was not curing homosexuals, even in studies that encouraged belief in the drug and did not compare its effects with those of a placebo. In fact, it was becoming increasingly clear that androgens did not reverse but actually intensified homosexual libido, so that "sometimes instead of helping one gets a worsening of the condition."

Medical naïveté about homosexuality was exemplified in a 1944 endorsement of androgen therapy by Louis A. Lurie, M.D., the director of the Child Guidance Home of the Jewish Hospital in Cincinnati, Ohio. Lurie's portrait of the homosexual as a poorly adjusted and potentially criminal delinquent was poles apart from Kinsey's way of thinking about the same individual. Yet Lurie used Kinsey's data to bolster the idea that homosexuality was a progressive disease of civilization that did not occur among primitive peoples. Given this alarmist view of sexual inversion, it is no wonder that Lurie was prepared to believe that testosterone propionate could save many young men from the ruin and waste of a homosexual future.

Lurie's therapeutic successes were achieved in the treatment of four adolescent boys whose personal histories and disorders he describes in some detail. All are depicted as immature, effeminate, physically underdeveloped, and presenting some form of endocrine disorder: hypogonadism, adiposogenital dystrophy, eunuchoid skeletal development, and female skeletal development, respectively. There are frequent references to "effeminate" mannerisms of speech and gait and to symptoms of deficient virility. Or as Lurie succinctly puts it: "The 'fairy' is easily recognized." Still, for all their sissified traits, Lurie has no choice but to call these subjects "innate" homosexuals for the straightforward reason that only one of them had ever had an overtly homosexual experience. Lurie's use of the effeminate model showed that he had disregarded Kinsey's crucial caveat about the popular folklore of sexual types: "There are popular and even clinical concepts of physical stigmata which are attached to the homosexual; and although there are some 'homosexuals' which show what are popularly considered to be 'effeminate' characteristics, there are others that are physically as robust and as athletically active as the most 'masculine' of men"—something the bisexual and physically robust Kinsey knew well from his own experience. Lurie, however, believed that the reality of innate homosexuality, like the mass of the proverbial iceberg, could be inferred from what was visible above the surface: "The homosexual trends and drives of the other 3 [boys] were obvious and unmistakable. Obvious also was the fact that their innate homosexual drives were due to endocrine dysfunctions. As a result of disturbed gonadal secretion, the boys failed to develop normally both structurally and functionally. Their resultant behavior was such that it stamped them as sexual deviates of the homosexual type."

The circularity of this argument is evident: the "fairy" type defined by Lurie is the "homosexual" type that society-at-large had already "stamped" as a sexual deviate. Lurie's typology is sexual folklore dressed up as endocrinology: the only difference between his criteria for homosexuality and the "popular physical stigmata" deplored by Kinsey is the endocrine theory of the "sissy" and his glandular deficiencies.

What remains to be explained is what the injections of testosterone propionate actually did to these boys. The reported transformation of Lurie's first subject is representative of all four cases: "The results were startling. . . . His voice became deep. . . . Coincident with these structural changes, there was a marked change in his personality. Instead of a fearful, highly emotional and demonstrative effeminate boy, he became a pleasing type of the aggressive male." Two joined the armed forces, a third got married, and the fourth "began to feel a thrill when standing next to a girl." In sum, "The latent homosexual trends were gradually converted into normal heterosexual equivalents."

The physical and psychological changes in these boys were in all likelihood real. It was no secret at this time that testosterone propionate could promote secondary sexual development, increase sexual appetite, and produce self-assertive drive in androgen-deficient males. The real question, however, is whether androgen therapy changed anyone's sexual orientation. As two contemporary observers pointed out, the "adynamic hyposexual male" could undoubtedly benefit from androgen therapy that promoted maturation. What is more, they appear to endorse Lurie's claim that he had reversed sexual orientation, on the grounds that "hypogonadal subjects are more vulnerable to homosexual influence than normal males." The problem, however, is that "innate" homosexuality is not the same thing as being "vulnerable to homosexual influence" from others. The sexual confusion of these hyposexual male adolescents was not homosexual orientation. Indeed, with the benefit of hindsight, one might say that the observed effects of the testosterone propionate make this clear. At the time, however, androgen replacement therapy appeared to be converting one psychosexual type into another.

The demise of the endocrine theory and the repeated failures of psychotherapy to cure homosexuality gave new impetus to various forms of "aversion therapy." These techniques aim at building conditioned reflexes meant to wean subjects away from homosexual desire by forcing them to associate homosexual experiences with unpleasant sensations. Such methods are often coupled with subsequent attempts to awake heterosexual feelings. Electric shock was first used to treat alcoholism in 1925. Ten years later it was used for the first time to treat a homosexual who was told to indulge in sexual fantasies while receiving shocks. The following procedure carried out in 1963 represents the basic scenario: "A patient was made to stand in a 9-ft-square room in which the floor was covered with an electric grid. He was shown slides of a nude man while current was passed through the floor to his bare feet. The authors report successful adaptation from homosexuality to bisexuality after 4000 trials." A variation on this treatment shocked the patient while he read out loud descriptions of homosexual behavior, a procedure that was repeated more than a thousand times.

Another treatment used in the 1960s substituted nausea induced by apomorphine injections for the pain of electric shock, in order to create an aversion to males whom the patient found sexually attractive. The basic strategy was to associate the misery of nausea with photographs of naked men. This procedure could be augmented by an audiotape offering the kind of insights usually acquired during talking therapy: "This began with an explanation of his homosexual attraction along the lines of father-deprivation occurring at a time when awareness of homosexual attraction was not abnormal. . . . The adverse effect of this pattern on him and its consequent social repercussions was then described in slow and graphic terms ending with words such as 'sickening,' 'nauseating,' etc. followed by the noise of [some]one vomiting." The next phase of the treatment was to give the patient photographs of sexually attractive young women and stimulate feelings of sexual excitement with androgens and mood-enhancing techniques that reveal more than anything the sheer naïveté of the therapists: "Each morning he was given an injection of testosterone propionate and told to retire to his room when he felt any sexual excitement. He was provided with a record-player and records of a female vocalist whose performance is generally recognized as 'sexy.' " A 1987 review of aversion therapies describes these techniques as still being in the experimental stage, neither proven nor discredited.

More radical treatments to prevent homosexual behavior and orientation appeared in Germany during the 1970s. West German surgeons reported they had performed stereotaxic neurosurgery on homosexuals involving the destruction of certain regions of the hypothalamus area of the brain. The logic of this surgery was that targeting the part of the brain assumed to control female sexual behavior would somehow reverse pedophilic homosexuality. The surgeons called this operation successful on the grounds that it had eliminated all homosexual activity and even given these patients more insight into their deviant behavior. The sexually deadening effects of this treatment were described as equivalent to the effects of "antiandrogen" drugs, such as ethynyl oestradiol and cyproterone acetate, that have also been used to treat male sexual deviants.

Almost entirely absent from the biomedical campaign against homosexuality has been any concern about converting lesbians into heterosexual women, a disparity that points to the cultural prestige of the male heterosexual role, to the cultural forces that influence the research agenda, and to the traditional invisibility of the lesbian, whose sexual orientation is seldom recorded in her medical file. A rare exception to this rule is a speculative proposal to prevent female homosexuality in rats by the controversial East German endocrinologist Günter Dörner, whose real interest has been to find a hormone therapy that would prevent the birth of human homosexual male infants. Dörner's proposal was to administer prenatal androgen therapy to pregnant, androgen-deficient women so that the fetal hypothalamus would not experience a low androgen level during the fourth and seventh months of pregnancy, thereby averting "a predominantly female brain organization" in a male infant. This hypothetical treatment was based on his observation that male rats castrated at infancy and given androgens as adults displayed what he described as female sexual behavior, allowing themselves to be mounted by normal males, a posture called lordosis. This receptive posture, Dörner says, constitutes "homosexual" behavior in male rats. Eugen Steinach, too, believed that he had created "homosexual" animals by means of gonadal transplantations.

Dörner's analogy between the sexual postures adopted by "female-like" male rodents and the sexual behaviors practiced by human homosexuals has been severely criticized on both scientific and ethical grounds. As one skeptic bluntly asked: "When does the male homosexual display the equivalent of lordosis? Is it when he is being the (passive) insertee in anal intercourse? Is he less of a homosexual if he is the (active) insertor?" Forced analogies of this kind often point to the influence of nonscientific agendas on the presentation of scientific claims. Dörner's objective is "a preventive therapy of sexual differentiation disturbances" whose logical outcome would be fewer homosexuals and eventually, perhaps, no homosexuals at all—a homo-cide achieved by hormone therapy. It is not surprising that this sort of eugenic ambition provoked criticism in a society whose medical establishment had once volunteered its services to the Nazis' program of racial hygiene.

One group of West German critics, noting with concern the widespread public interest created by coverage of Dörner's work, claimed that his ultimate goal was the "endocrinological euthanasia of homosexuality," a therapeutic project based on the increasingly disputed idea that homosexuality is a disease rather than a sexual way of being. For if homosexuality is "a personality structure" rather than a symptom of disease, then removing it is not healing but rather a form of psychic murder. This is implicit, of course, in the 1987 revision of the APA manual that removed homosexuality from its list of disorders, a redefinition that would seem to equate any "treatment" of homosexuality with medical malpractice. Dörner lashed back at his critics, calling them character assassins and claiming that his work had ended the prosecution of homosexual acts in East Germany by 1968. His real intention, he maintained, was to prevent disordered brain development that eventually resulted in mental disabilities. But this defense of Dörner's research seems disingenuous given the deviant status of homosexuality in a world full of therapeutic schemes. "As long as society has not made its own peace with the homosexuals," wrote one critic, "research into the possible causes are potentially a public danger for them."

The irony of the Dörner controversy is that his theory of a "homosexualized" hypothalamus has been resurrected by a scientist who is himself a homosexual. Based on his studies of brain anatomy, Simon LeVay, like Dörner, has suggested that different androgen levels in the womb during a critical developmental period could account for the genesis of "gay" and "straight" fetuses. The crucial difference between these research projects is that LeVay's biological theory of homosexuality, for the first time in medical history, neither promises nor welcomes the prospect of a cure.

APHRODISIA FOR THE MASSES?
THE SECRET LIFE OF TESTOSTERONE THERAPY

From the late 1930s to the late 1940s, synthetic testosterone drugs seemed to be on the verge of becoming a mass therapy for both men and women. The idea of a male climacteric analogous to female menopause was launched in *JAMA* in 1939, and there appeared to be a huge potential market of aging males in need of a rejuvenating androgen therapy. "The male hormone," Paul de Kruif declared in 1945, "is now ready for the possible power to extend the prime of life of men." Many physicians during this period also believed, as we have seen, that testosterone was a performance-enhancing drug for equally large numbers of sexually unresponsive women. Pharmaceutical companies aggressively promoted their sex hormone products in medical journals. That mass marketing did not follow the availability of synthetic androgens as de Kruif had anticipated appears in retrospect as an interesting promotional failure on the part of the drug companies. Given that they had already created a thriving market for estrogens, why did androgens turn out to be a harder sell? The principal reason, as we have seen, was sexual conservatism. The advertising for androgens that appears in medical journals during the 1940s focused on treating the physiological and mental decline of aging men. The idea of improving their sex lives was a subtext that doctors and patients were free to infer from these messages; but the explicit promotion of sexual viability for aging men that we now associate with Viagra and Levitra was absent, as were proposals to improve the sex lives of women by using these drugs. This emphasis on male symptoms certainly reflects the gender hierarchy of this period. Yet at the same time, the discretion and ambivalence with which physicians have treated the use of androgens to stimulate sexual response in both sexes over the past half century makes for an interesting case study in the sociology of medical knowledge. That is why we shall end this chapter by looking closely at physicians' doubts about testosterone. But first we must gauge the early demand for the androgens that became available for clinical experimentation from 1937 onward, see how the medical profession judged their value as therapeutic drugs, and examine the social and professional inhibitions that prevented the development of the mass market for androgens that de Kruif and others had envisioned.

The popular demand for androgens in the mid–twentieth century or at any other time has never been easy to estimate, mainly because physicians have always viewed these drugs as controversial; their limited knowledge and emotional reactions have helped to relegate androgens to a relatively obscure corner of the pharmacopoeia. At the same time, however, the general public has long shown great interest in these drugs, creating a demand on which physicians have recently begun to act. The intensity of that interest is revealed in a forgotten episode in the history of the androgens market that dates from 1939.

Our story begins in Oss, Holland, the home of Organon, a pharmaceutical company that put itself on the commercial map by marketing large quantities of female hormone drugs during and after the 1920s. In 1931 Organon put on the European market the first biologically standardized male sex hormone (Hombreol), its declared clinical purpose being to treat enlarged prostate glands. Associating the advanced age of prostate sufferers with their lower hormone levels, Organon scientists concluded that these patients needed more of the male hormone. Today this therapeutic strategy looks absurd, since testosterone is known to promote growth in existing cancers of the prostate. But the commercial failure of Hombreol was caused by other factors. The lingering notoriety of Brown-Séquard's rejuvenation claims, along with the recent craze for transplanting "monkey glands" into aging men, gave an odor of impropriety to even the latest versions of the male hormone. The fact that the synthesis and production of pure testosterone was not possible until several years later was of lesser moment.

An encounter that might have ignited popular demand for testosterone in the United States occurred in New York in 1939, when two synthetic forms of the drug (testosterone propionate and methyl testosterone) had been on the market for about two years. The principals at this business meeting were the president of the Organon Company, Saul van Zwanenberg, and Elmer Bobst, head of the Roche-Nutley pharmaceutical company. Having discussed the role of hormones in modern medicine, the two executives agreed to set up a joint subsidiary of the American firm to be called Roche-Organon, which would receive bulk shipments of hormones from its Dutch partner and market them in the United States. The first product to be put on the market was testosterone propionate, which was to be sold as Neo-Hombreol.

The promotional material sent to physicians was composed by Bobst, who found himself in something of a quandary as he pondered what to say about his new drug, whose effects were largely unknown. "It occurred to me," he wrote many years later, "that as a man ages there usually is a certain diminishment of his most prominent masculine traits; muscle tone often slackens and sexual interests wane." Armed with this insight into the physiology of aging, the inspired copywriter produced an open letter to physicians, romantically titled "The Land of Bimini," that invoked the quest of Ponce de León while arguing that "proper administration of testosterone propionate can play the same role in man as does estrogen therapy in the menopause, the female climacteric." "We suggest," he continued, "the experimental use of *Neo-Hombreol* for combating the annoying symptoms of the male climacteric." Injections were to be followed by the application of Neo-Hombreol ointment "for maintenance purposes." Free samples of the ointment were offered to every physician willing to return an enclosed card.

The response from the physicians, some of whom were apparently intent on healing themselves, was, in the words of the promoter, "almost incredible. We received more requests for free samples of Neo-Hombreol than for any pharmaceutical we have ever introduced." Bobst professes surprise that some of these doctors had somehow "picked up the idea from my letter that the [ointment] would have a regenerative value in cases of impotency. A surprising number of the physicians, in fact, indicated that they intended to try the medication on themselves, in the interests of scientific inquiry, of course. But some of the medical people chided me for being just a bit too enthusiastic on behalf of my product." The most prominent of these critics was Bobst's "close friend" Morris Fishbein, editor of *JAMA*. In a strongly worded editorial, Fishbein scolded Bobst for trying to take advantage of physicians whose "extraordinary degree of ignorance" about hormones Bobst apparently took for granted. "Today," the editorial began, "the desks of physicians are being flooded again with fantastic advertising claims for sex hormones" whose legitimate medical applications would only be delayed by this sort of hormonal hucksterism. Bobst seems to have regarded the contretemps as a game in which all was fair in love and commerce, and he gleefully claims that the effect of the *JAMA* editorial was to double sales of Neo-Hombreol. Yet this entire episode ended in a curiously muted anticlimax. Bobst denied manufacturing licenses to other American drug firms, including Parke, Davis and Abbott Laboratories, on the grounds that these companies would be in a position to undersell Roche-Organon because they had incurred no development costs. Faced with prosecution under the Sherman Antitrust Act, Bobst refused to obey a court order to sell the licenses, accepted a consent decree, paid a $3,000 fine, and stopped selling testosterone.

The touchiness of the American Medical Association about the appearance of hormone quackery was no doubt exacerbated by the public's interest in sex hormones. "Within the past few months," the AMA's Council on Pharmacy and Chemistry reported in May 1939, "extravagant claims for the action of the male sex hormone testosterone have appeared in professional and lay publications. The naturally popular appeal of this substance has aroused wide interest with the aid of ample newspaper publicity." Lacking both endocrinological and sexological expertise, the great majority of American doctors cannot have welcomed this public interest in a hormonal aphrodisiac, and it is not surprising that they did not encourage research into its clinical applications beyond disorders such as breast cancer, prostate hypertrophy, and testicular deficiency. Some worried about a sex-driven steroid epidemic analogous to the one that would later spread throughout the elite sports world: "A substance which may be exceedingly useful in the hands of physicians could gain ill repute from untoward effects following its promiscuous, ill advised and unwise use in self medication by the layman," *JAMA* warned in May 1940. In retrospect, this admonition was a sensible public health advisory, since even the clinical use of testosterone at this time tended to be incautious and often unwise. Today we know that the administration of androgens to patients with enlarged prostates, acne, and gynecomastia could not have made less medical sense, but such were the actions of some physicians in a clinical environment characterized by ignorance and the near-total absence of protests against reckless prescribing and overdosing.

Androgens were also promoted by the pharmaceutical companies whose continuing interest in the testosterone trade was confirmed in *JAMA* in 1942: "Recently many reports have appeared in medical journals claiming that a climacteric occurs in middle aged men. Brochures circulated by pharmaceutic manufacturers depict the woeful course of aging man. None too subtly these brochures recommend that male hormone substance, like a veritable elixir of youth, may prevent or compensate for the otherwise inevitable decline." In fact, the male climacteric syndrome did not emerge in the medical literature until synthetic androgens became available in the late 1930s. Today the commercial prospects for an expanded androgen market are still linked to the idea of a male menopause that has yet to be fully accepted by mainstream medicine.

While promotional campaigns by the pharmaceutical companies did not turn the entire medical profession into adherents of mass androgen therapy, some doctors were interested in learning whether these medications could relieve their patients' sexual disorders. "What treatment would you suggest for a partial loss of power of erection in a 60 year old man?" one physician from Virginia asks *JAMA* in 1942. Would testosterone propionate make a difference? No, came the rather melancholy reply: "The common cause of loss of power of erection in a man of 60 years is age, and this patient may be older for his years than he should be."

The conservatism of this diagnosis lies in its view of advancing age as one of life's natural stages rather than as a condition that might be treatable with hormones. Indeed, this sort of medical fatalism clearly played a role in discouraging the wider use of testosterone to treat aging males. The same attitude was evident in *JAMA*'s reply in 1957 to a doctor in New York who wrote: "A 64-year-old patient has become depressed because he is unable to maintain an erection. A brief trial with testosterone injections was futile." What could be done for this patient? "Impotence," *JAMA* replied, "is often a normal development in a person 64 years of age, and it should hardly be of any great concern to him or his wife, if she is of a similar age. It is usually not helped by any aphrodisiac medication." While this response was technically correct, in that impotence is a vascular rather than a hormonal disorder, it missed a larger point about sexual dysfunction that had not escaped the attention of wiser physicians. For as another *JAMA* commentary had pointed out in 1953: "The effect of impotency on the patient psychologically far, far outweighs the physical harm. Failure to recognize the possibility of impotence and its later development undoubtedly wrecks many marriages. A man will put up with the illness of his wife 'for better or worse,' but a woman is not inclined to overlook impotency when it develops in her husband, even though there have been children and middle life has been reached." Other physicians, however, seem to have felt that the sexual lives of even middle-aged people were not worth salvaging if the cost became too heavy for society to bear. When, for example, a U.S. Army physician reported in 1944 that he had cured the impotence of a forty-year-old man by injecting him with testosterone, *JAMA*'s comment was again less than humane though technically accurate. Androgens, the commentator stated, were not recommended in cases of impotence, a viewpoint that holds today unless the therapeutic goal is to create a placebo effect to boost the patient's self-confidence. Yet quite apart from the question of whether the drug worked, he continued, "It is probably not worth while economically or socially to attempt such a vigorous stimulation of this individual as is implied by the promiscuity referred to. [The anxious patient had attempted intercourse with several women.] The goal of treatment of patients with the climacteric is preferably autonomic and psychologic comfort rather than restoration of potency." In other words, the sex life of a forty-year-old man was not worth the high price of testosterone propionate, especially if he sought normal sexual functioning in the arms of more than one woman.

Public awareness of sex hormones prompted some patients to ask their doctors for sexually stimulating drugs. In 1941 a New Jersey physician wanted to know what might be available for a twenty-seven-year-old woman who complained that she had never felt sexual desire: "She wants to know if there isn't something she can take to increase her libido," he reported. "Unfortunately," came the reply, "there is no drug that can be safely relied on to increase libido in women"—a therapeutic pessimism that some other physicians at this time did not share. When a doctor from Oklahoma wrote in 1949, "I have had requests from middle-aged men for injections of testosterone," *JAMA* replied that testosterone "is of value in aiding erections and easing the mental attitude during the male climacteric." This categorically optimistic appraisal of the drug's effects cannot have been based on anything more substantial than clinical impressions and hearsay.

Diagnosing the conditions that testosterone might relieve was further complicated by the dubious status of the male climacteric as a treatable disorder. What kind of symptoms warranted androgen therapy? It is not surprising that some male physicians seem to have felt considerable empathy for other middle-aged and older men who found themselves struggling with sagging spirits and flagging libidos. A physician from Indiana, for example, reported in 1945 that he had been injecting testosterone propionate into "a vigorous man in his middle seventies who complained of inadequate energy, impaired memory for recent events and general letdown." The patient had responded so well to this treatment that now he was pressing for a larger dosage. Would this be medically unwise? *JAMA*'s answer reveals interesting attitudes both toward the symptoms and toward the use of the drug. The commentator accepts the existence of the male "climacteric" and even claims that in the absence of prostate enlargement or cancer, "one might be justified in increasing the dosage of testosterone propionate to 50 mg. three times weekly without fear of harm to the patient"—yet another clinical assessment that was unsupported by scientific evidence. At the same time, this *JAMA* advisor's feckless approach to doubling the dosage of a powerful androgen was matched by his willingness to prescribe it for a vague malaise that appears to have been unrelated to any organic disorder whatsoever. Given that "inadequate energy" was a symptom one might have expected to find in almost any septuagenarian, why was this patient given a drug at all? One is tempted to answer: Because synthetic testosterone was available to enhance the quality of an old man's life.

Testosterone was thus seen as a socially beneficial, performance-enhancing drug for the male climacteric whose effects reached far beyond the sphere of personal satisfaction. As early as 1939, Dr. Charles W. Dunn of Philadelphia was reporting that testosterone increased both mental and physical energy, thereby enabling older men to fulfill their "social and economic responsibilities." The male climacteric, he stated in 1945, "is an important syndrome because it occurs chiefly in men with important responsibilities, men who require sustained energy, physical and mental, throughout the day to perform competently their assigned responsibilities." Productive citizenship originated in a man's performance-enhancing hormones. But testosterone for busy executives did not take off, in part because a half century would pass before baby boom demographics and various new treatments to combat aging combined to create a mainstream medical ethos that could accommodate "cosmetic" medical procedures on an unprecedented scale.

What is interesting, in retrospect, is that medical interest in testosterone as an energy-boosting "tonic" did not become more widespread than it did, given the public interest noted by physicians and the frequent reports of its effectiveness in the medical literature during the 1940s and 1950s. "Androgens," a *JAMA* editorial declared in 1942, "exert a tonic and stimulating action, associated perhaps with their metabolic effects," and "are active also in normal middle aged men beset by aging processes" unrelated to testicular dysfunction—a potential patient population numbering in the millions. Nor did the doubtful status of the male climacteric as a clinical entity dissuade a significant number of physicians from prescribing androgens for aging men. Testosterone propionate was thus presented in 1942 as an appropriate treatment for men between fifty and sixty-five "when they complain of vague and often apparently unrelated symptoms." "An adequate level of male-sex hormone," another team of authors suggested in 1944, "might be important for the maintenance of working capacity. . . . In other words, the reduction of working capacity with age might proceed differently if the sex-hormone concentration could be artificially maintained at a high level"—in effect, mass hormone doping to boost the efficiency of adult male workers. As already noted, in *The Male Hormone* (1945) Paul de Kruif promised an even more comprehensive hormonal rejuvenation . . . for men.

By then, the sexual problems of American women were being discussed in the popular press with a candor that, while restrained by today's wide-open standards, represented an advance beyond the strict decorum of the previous generation. Before the First World War, popular magazines had addressed marital problems with cautious indirection. The *Atlantic* had asked "Why Marriages Fail" (1907). *Good Housekeeping* had inquired into "Why So Many Married People Are Discontented" (1912). The *Ladies Home Journal* had told its readers about "Things Women Keep Quiet About" (1913). By the 1940s the popular magazine *Hygeia* was publishing such articles as "The Psychology of Sex" (1940) alongside a recipe for "Broccoli with Hollandaise Sauce," "Sex Education for the Woman at Menopause" (1941), and "Marital Frustration in Women" (1943). The *Woman's Home Companion* offered "Marriage as a Doctor Sees It" (1942); the *Reader's Digest,* as already mentioned, examined the unhappy lives of "cold women" (1948).

By 1950 the potential size of this sexually troubled female market was estimated to be in the millions: "Gynecologists and psychiatrists, especially, are aware that perhaps 75 per cent of all women derive little or no pleasure from the sexual act. Many women not only experience no pleasure, but actually suffer pain and revulsion." But what could physicians do for women for whom sex was a burden? The need for an effective and affordable drug seemed obvious: "Because of the enormous number of patients with frigidity being seen by the all too meager number of competent psychotherapists, a more efficacious and rapid form of therapy is indicated." Following this clarion call for a mass remedy, these authors offer an appraisal of testosterone therapy marked by the ambivalence that appears frequently in the medical literature after 1945: "Current treatment involving androgen, even if successful, is only substitutional." Nowhere, however, do these physicians explain why they object to the "substitutional" character of a therapy that had been "successful" in treating some female patients.

Indeed, over the previous two decades substitutional estrogenic therapy for women had become a familiar part of American medicine. As one contributor to *Hygeia* pointed out in 1941, menopausal symptoms were "readily amenable to substitution therapy, namely the administration of ovarian hormones, now available in the chemically pure state. . . . Why not take advantage of those palliative remedies that have been provided through the instrumentality of scientific research?" he asks encouragingly. This confident nonchalance about hormone replacement therapy anticipates the acceptance of HRT that has firmly established itself in modern medicine. But we should keep in mind that embracing HRT did not come naturally to all physicians during the 1940s and 1950s. "One of the greatest sins of the medical profession today," the chief gynecologist at Johns Hopkins Hospital wrote in 1954, "is unnecessary treatment with hormones when these women are free or practically free from symptoms. Another sin that is committed by many physicians is the administering of hormones to almost all women over 40 who have vague complaints, perhaps of a psychosomatic nature." Strikingly absent from this critique is any interest in hormone therapy as routine prophylaxis or even as the "palliative remedy" recommended more than a decade earlier in *Hygeia*. This principled disagreement about the role of hormone therapy has taken various forms over the past sixty years and continues to shape the debate about the roles synthetic hormones should play in the lives of normal people who do not suffer from the medical conditions that require specialized treatments.

The effectiveness of testosterone in intensifying female sexual response was reported throughout the 1940s and 1950s. Numerous observations of this effect were made, as we have seen, after the drug had been administered for other therapeutic purposes. What was more, the drug seemed to affect healthy women not afflicted with endocrine disorders. "It has been demonstrated," *JAMA* announced in 1945, "that testosterone compounds may increase the sexual desire of many women even with normal menstrual cycles, probably through the enlargement of the clitoris, since this organ responds to androgens." Dissemination of this information to the general public appears to have been the exception rather than the rule. In *The Sexual Responsibility of Woman* (1956), the popular author Maxine Davis noted rather vaguely that "certain chemicals in responsible medical use for a good many years are helpful in that they increase a woman's ability to enjoy her marital relations. . . . And, curiously, male hormones have also been found advantageous for increasing desire in women who assumed they were victims of a frigid temperament." The tone conveyed by the words used in this passage—"certain" chemicals in "responsible" medical use—bespeaks a discretion about sex hormones that the author may have picked up from her physician-informants. Whatever its source, the implied consensus discouraging widespread discussion of the role of "certain chemicals" in providing sexual stimulation for women has remained intact to a degree that is quite remarkable, given modern society's well-known appetite for news about sex.

That consensus grew out of the medical doubts and sexual conservatism felt by many physicians regarding testosterone during the 1940s and 1950s. Indeed, in the same year that *The Sexual Responsibility of Woman* was revealing the good news about testosterone to its readership, all that *The Complete Medical Guide* was telling its readers was that testosterone injections masculinized female animals. The virilizing effects of androgens on female patients did, in fact, exert a sobering influence on the physicians who first used them during the early 1940s. The growth of hair where it did not belong, mannish husky voices, and swollen clitorises dissuaded many doctors from prescribing androgens for women.

Still, the deterrent influence of these side effects should not be overemphasized. Grotesque megadoses of androgens were given to many women on the basis of guesswork, as clinicians groped their way toward rational dosing of these powerful drugs. The only serious exchange of views on this topic I found appeared in 1942 in the *Journal of Clinical*

Endocrinology, where E. C. Hamblen of the Duke University Hospital warned that the misuse of androgens was producing a "contrasexual mutilation of the woman." In one case, a physician had given a fifteen-year-old girl with muscular dystrophy 2,500 milligrams of testosterone propionate—more than twice the annual dose of a doped female East German sprinter—over ten months because he had been told that androgens promoted the growth of skeletal muscles. Unfortunately, even this dosage did not relieve the girl's paralysis. Hamblen noted that even though clinical studies had failed to trace a single female disorder to androgen deficiency, many doctors were still giving androgens to women. Was it possible, he asked, that physicians were "unable to resist the commercial solicitations of pharmaceutical chemists who, having male hormones to sell, but embarrassed by such a limited field in andrologic practice, insist that these be used in gynecology?"

This broadside was answered by Robert B. Greenblatt of the University of Georgia School of Medicine, an avid proponent of androgen therapy for women. Greenblatt argued that while overdosing was medically hazardous, doses of testosterone "far below the virilizing level" were effective for treating disorders such as uterine bleeding, breast pain, pelvic discomfort, and dysmenorrhea. Last but not least: "Testosterone propionate will restore libido in women who once have known libido but have lost it." In the end, Greenblatt's equanimity prevailed over Hamblen's alarm, as concern about deforming side effects led to lower doses and fewer disfiguring incidents. But doubts remained about the safety and efficacy of androgens in males. "One out of every five men over 50 years of age has carcinoma of the prostate," a group of physicians wrote to *JAMA* in 1954. "The growth of carcinoma of the prostate is stimulated by testosterone. Does more need to be said?" The power of this syllogism seems not to have registered at the pharmaceutical companies, which continued to bombard doctors with promotional literature touting testosterone as the cure-all for "a rather vague group of conditions in older men," as these doctors phrased it.

But prostate cancer was not the only area of concern. One gerontologist feared that adding testosterone to the systems of older men would result in elevated androgen levels that could "aggravate and accelerate some processes of aging." This theory was unusual in that it reversed the conventional folklore about rejuvenation through testosterone that continued to alienate many physicians. *The Complete Medical Guide* (1956), for example, echoed many years of medical distaste for the idea that testosterone could bring about the "rejuvenation" of old men, a repugnance that played its own role in limiting the use of androgenic drugs.

Other observers pointed cannily to the psychosomatic complexities of human sexual response and debunked the simplistic notion that libido was equivalent to hormones. For example, two clinicians who gave androgens to one male patient in 1949 reported what might seem like a paradoxical result: "The drug itself produced obvious genital stimulation with erections, nocturnal emissions, and erotic dreams, but still there was no significant urge to the sexual act." This split between tumescence and desire will baffle those who equate sex with arousal, but it was real enough to the physicians who were trying to establish a connection between this man's feelings and his sexual organs. Giving him androgens was useful only in that now he could no longer blame an assumed androgen deficiency for his lack of interest in sexual relationships. Deprived of this alibi, "the patient recognized that the treatment was not fundamentally attacking his problem." The lesson for his physicians was that "giving the drug alone does not serve any useful function." Five years later another commentator agreed that giving androgenic support to a younger adult "may only help prolong the vicious cycle involving sexual inadequacy and fear of sexual inadequacy in which the patient already finds himself." Like the previous patient, such people were psychologically troubled rather than hormone deficient. Low hormone levels generally occurred in older people who, for that reason, were more appropriate candidates for hormone therapy.

The sexual conservatism of American physicians also played a role in limiting the clinical use of testosterone, and their terminology sometimes expressed their disapproval of excessive sexual appetite. One reads of "pathologically increased sex desire" (1931), a "pathologic increase in libido" following estrogen therapy (1935), or "abnormal intensification of desire" following androgen therapy (1943), and such language is used of both men and women. This cautious approach to sexual desire seems to have been motivated less by prudishness than by a reluctance to stimulate appetite in the absence of sufficient opportunity to gratify it. "In the case of the sex hormones," one researcher wrote, "special attention must be paid to finding compounds or doses which do not stimulate the sex libido or function, an undesirable effect in old age." Androgens administered to women endowed with normal sexual desire might cause "marital complications." "Fortunately," *JAMA* declared in 1946, "the exaggeration or reawakening of the libido long after the menopause is rare. Treatment is difficult. There is no specific remedy to decrease sex

desire." Androgen therapy that increased libido "without normal channels for satisfaction" could lead to "psychic trauma." According to Dr.
August A. Werner, one of the inventors of the male climacteric, it was
preferable "not to stimulate tissues which are incapable of response."

The medical assessment of testosterone therapy for men and women
was both divided and ambivalent. Some physicians clearly believed in its
efficacy and others did not. A third faction discussed testosterone with
a curious degree of ambivalence, suggesting the presence of strongly
mixed feelings not meant for public display. Interestingly, this ambivalent faction included two of the most famous sexologists of modern
times, Alfred C. Kinsey and William H. Masters. The following passage
from Kinsey's *Sexual Behavior in the Human Female* (1953) offers a fas-
cinating insider's look at how the therapeutic value of sex hormones had
been inflated by various interest groups:

> A general knowledge of the hormones has become widespread in the pop-
> ulation as a whole, but in regard to certain critical matters this knowledge
> is quite incorrect. Journalistic accounts of scientific research, over-
> enthusiastic advertising by some of the drug companies, over-optimistic re-
> ports from clinicians who have found a lucrative business in the adminis-
> tration of sex hormones, and some of the discussions among state
> legislators and public administrators who hope that hormone injections
> will provide one-package cure-alls for various social ills, have led the pub-
> lic to believe that endocrine organs are *the* glands of personality, and that
> there is such an exact knowledge of the way in which they control human
> behavior that properly qualified technicians should, at least in the near fu-
> ture, be able to control any and all aspects of human sexual behavior.

This myth of the sex hormone had flourished since the 1920s, evolving along with the succession of glandular extracts and purified hormones that came onto the market and stimulated the imaginations of laymen and scientists alike. But the troublesome complication for Kinsey
and other thoughtful participants in the sex hormone drama was that the
myth was partly true. The evidence presented in his book makes it clear
that testosterone had been found to be a sexual stimulant for normal
men and women. What is more, Kinsey hints broadly that the administration of testosterone to normal males in the privacy of doctors' offices
was more common than one might have inferred from reading the medical literature. At the same time, Kinsey attempts to soften the effect of
these revelations by rejecting the notion that "the hormone plays a prime
part in controlling sexual behavior" and by declaring at the very end of

the same chapter that while "the levels of sexual response may be modified by reducing or increasing the amount of available hormone, there seems to be no reason for believing that the patterns of sexual behavior may be modified by hormonal therapy." This rhetorical balancing act suggests that even the uninhibited Kinsey may have worried about making cheap androgens available to a population whose sexual problems he knew better than anyone.

Kinsey's famous successor took a curiously asexual approach to hormone therapy. "One of the most controversial subjects in medicine today," Masters wrote in 1956, "is that of sex-steroid replacement in the aging individual." Masters's lugubrious and little-known meditation on hormone replacement for the geriatric set is one of the most peculiar texts of modern sexology. "I am completely convinced," he asserts, "that a third sex exists and is rapidly multiplying in our society today. The basic components of this third sex or 'neuter gender' are presently considered to consist of former males and females who have reached the age of approximately sixty years." A decade before *Human Sexual Response* (1966) made Masters and Johnson household names by emphasizing lifelong sexual potential, the former was describing older people as neutered creatures whose physiological maintenance depended on a hormone replacement regimen Masters saw as a kind of tonic:

> Steroid replacement technics in no sense represent a panacea for the problem of aging. There is no evidence of increased longevity for those patients under combined steroid influence. However, in the majority of treated patients there is significant physical and mental resurgence of power potential. . . . Many patients have demonstrated conclusively that they are better adjusted and equipped to face the exigencies of the physiologic aging process, as well as infinitely better psychologically oriented, when treated as individual members of the third sex during the concluding years of their normal aging process.

Ten years later, Masters and Johnson were treating the sexual lives of women over sixty as a natural phase of human development that was properly assisted by combinations of estrogen and progesterone: "There is no reason why the milestone of the menopause should be expected to blunt the human female's sexual capacity, performance, or drive. The healthy aging woman has sex drives that demand resolution," the authors declare. As for aging men: "If he is in adequate health, little is needed to support adequacy of sexual performance in a 70- or even 80-year-old male other than some physiologic outlet or psychologic reason for a reactivated sexual interest." Testosterone, whether for men or women, is never mentioned. In *Heterosexuality* (1994), Masters and Johnson damn testosterone therapy with faint praise by stressing its usefulness to the limited number of androgen-deficient patients who had been identified a half century earlier. One gets the impression that the positive results reported by Kinsey and later authors had never existed.

Modern medicine did not reach a consensus on the use of testosterone drugs after the Second World War, and it has not achieved a consensus more than fifty years later. In retrospect, it is not inconceivable that a more aggressive campaign by the pharmaceutical companies and some influential physicians might have created a critical mass of medical opinion in favor of making the male climacteric a standard diagnosis. Such a coalition would have opened the door to androgen therapy for millions of people. It is less conceivable that androgen-based sexual stimulation for (married) women could have been more widely practiced than was already the case. We have examined the medical and moral reservations that then set effective limits on this kind of experimentation. A scenario in which scientific and cultural factors will promote the use of androgens far beyond the current medical and black markets is much more conceivable today. But before moving on to the cultural and economic dynamics of today's hormone market, let us ponder a question sent in to *JAMA* in 1953 by a doctor in Arkansas: "What are the contraindications to the use of testosterone in small (10 mg.) daily doses? Are there any harmful results in the prolonged use in men when it seems to produce a sense of well-being and greater activity? Is this imaginary or real improvement? What daily dose is recommended?" The sobering fact is that while endocrinologists today do not have definitive answers to any of these questions, there is a growing and unregulated hormone market out in cyberspace that thinks it does.

CHAPTER 3

The Mainstreaming of Testosterone

CELEBRATING TESTOSTERONE

"If there is such a thing as a bodily substance more fabled than blood," *Time* magazine declared in April 2000, "it's testosterone, the hormone that we understand and misunderstand as the essence of manhood." For several weeks during what was greeted as the first spring of the new millennium, media interest in the male hormone seemed to be everywhere. At the beginning of May, *NBC Nightly News* presented two sequential segments that described the alleged benefits and medical hazards of synthetic testosterone drugs. The second installment, "Turning Back the Clock," might have been mistaken for a promotional video produced by a pharmaceutical company. The obligatory medical caveats about testosterone faded into the background as a Typical Aging Patient, pumping iron and striding on a treadmill, took center stage. Asked whether he had any reservations about testosterone, this hale and upbeat clergyman replied with a laugh: "I'm seventy-two years old! What do I have to lose?" A question about the sexual stimulation often attributed to the drug was gracefully deflected by a vague but suggestive reference to what every man can observe about his own body as his hormones ebb and flow during the course of a night.

The media event that seemed to catalyze this sudden Testosterone Boom was an article in the *New York Times Magazine* by the gay writer

Andrew Sullivan. As an HIV-positive man, Sullivan had begun a series of testosterone injections to restore the subnormal hormone level caused by his viral infection. The reactions of his mind and body to these injections generated an enthusiasm that makes his personal testimony a paean to the powers of what Sullivan calls "a syringe full of manhood." He writes, "My appetite in every sense of that word expanded beyond measure." But the sudden prominence of testosterone was not due to the drug-induced epiphany of one man. The real cause of testosterone's sudden emergence into the limelight was the imminent release onto the market of AndroGel, a testosterone-based ointment for testosterone-deficient (or "hypogonadal") men that required a doctor's prescription to obtain.

A curious aspect of the initial publicity surrounding AndroGel was the discrepancy between the modest size of its eligible target population and the enormous numbers of men who, judging from the media coverage, seemed poised to use it as a recreational drug. While four to five million American men were estimated to qualify as hypogonadal, only about a quarter million among this group were currently being treated with testosterone. This leaves a considerable market untapped, and it was clear that the excitement provoked by the prospect of an easy-to-apply testosterone ointment was not emanating from the relatively limited number of men who would be legally entitled to use it. Suddenly, it seemed as though the laws governing prescription drugs had been suspended by a magical wish of a public seeking to fulfill a pharmacological fantasy without recourse to mundane legal mechanisms and official medical opinions. The idea of being able to apply a powerful hormone as if it were suntan lotion was presented as the fulfillment of a deep popular longing for unlimited access to a drug associated with the enhancement of energy and sexual pleasure.

Public demand for various forms of alternative medicine, including hormone therapies, was already challenging the medical establishment's traditional monopoly on therapeutic procedures as well as the definition of health itself. The growing respectability of alternative therapies further encouraged the idea that hormone therapy could be made available to a greatly expanded number of potential clients. Newspaper advertisements recruiting older subjects for clinical trials offered the same exciting vista of rejuvenated minds and bodies. A medical clinic in Austin, Texas, for example, announced at this time that it had "received permission to begin clinical trials to replace Human Growth Hormone that normally decreases with aging." This advertisement featured a fit, middle-aged couple in bathing suits at the beach who were experiencing "normal" aging, thereby making it clear that hormone therapy was now a procedure for the healthy, not for the sick. Such an inversion of a medication's conventional role makes growth hormone more of a lifestyle drug than a therapeutic one. And a similar refashioning of testosterone therapy for healthy people was taking place in popular publications during the spring of 2000.

Another striking feature of the intense publicity then surrounding testosterone was the tentativeness with which the media claimed that use of the drug was actually expanding. Sullivan declared vaguely that testosterone was "becom[ing] increasingly available" and that "recreational demand may soar." The NBC Nightly News referred without further comment to "the growing popularity of testosterone." "Testosterone can make a difference in bed and at the gym," Time announced. "And soon you'll be able to get it as a gel." In December 2002 the manufacturer of AndroGel placed an advertisement in Business Week that read: "Fatigued? Depressed mood? Low sex drive? Could be your testosterone is running on empty." This ad was addressed to the "estimated 4.5 million men [who] have a medical condition called hypogonadism." As this advertisement points out, only about 5 percent of American men would have legal access to testosterone in any form, be it a gel, a skin patch, or an injection. Time's assurance to its readers that they would have access to AndroGel was therefore sensationalism; but it was also an implicit endorsement of the populist pharmacology that seemed to be asserting itself in a brave new world of freely circulating hormones.

The problem for journalists was that testosterone's conversion into a recreational drug was an ongoing process rather than an accomplished fact, and the uncertainties this implied required a hedging of bets on the eventual outcome of the AndroGel story. The unresolved question was whether "we're verging on a moment when testosterone will be treated as one more renewable resource," as Time put it. Making testosterone into a nutritional supplement would normalize the status of the drug and promote its wider distribution. But journalists had done little to determine exactly how and how much testosterone was actually spreading through the body politic. Much of the buzz about testosterone was thus an anticipation of its eventual migration out of the approved clinical population into a much larger pleasure-seeking clientele. And the drama of this waiting game was intensified by the excitement that attends the imminent violation of a taboo.

The gradual erosion of this taboo was made possible by the recognition of hormone deficiency disorders in men and women during the course of the twentieth century. These disorders are alleged to occur in two very large groups of people: (1) adults of any age who are supposedly handicapped by deficient sexual appetites (sexual dysfunction), and (2) older men and women who are affected by menopausal symptoms that include low sexual desire within the context of a larger syndrome characterized by deficient energy, willpower, and "well-being."

Sexual dysfunction has been inflated into a full-blown syndrome that is said to affect millions of people. Sometimes these disorders are such unstable media creations that they can disappear from public view and then reappear years later under a new rubric before vanishing from the media radar screen once again. In February 2000, for example, one journalist announced the appearance of "a new phylum of illness, female sexual dysfunction, which will soon cycle through the same paces as 'erectile dysfunction.' " (We have already seen that medical literature has discussed—and prescribed testosterone for—female sexual dysfunction since the 1940s.) Nor was this topic confined to the medical journals. While *Health* magazine had published an article on hypoactive sexual desire (HSD) in 1990, the formal definition of this "new phylum of illness" went back farther than that. Janice M. Irvine has described how inhibited sexual desire (ISD) came to prominence during the 1970s and 1980s, when sex therapists found themselves faced with an apparent epidemic of disinterest in sex. In the course of responding to this new public health crisis, they

> turned the armamentarium of clinical medicine on sexual boredom and indifference and (1) made it a disease, (2) conducted massive biomedical research into its etiology and treatment, (3) developed new treatment programs that proved to be significantly longer-term than earlier programs, and (4) implemented the use of drug treatment in certain cases. Thus, a widespread human problem of flagging sexual interest within marriage had been medicalized, enabling sexologists to tap a potentially unlimited market.

The disorganized and sometimes amnesiac process that has allowed sexual dissatisfaction to mutate into a succession of vaguely defined disorders recalls a 1926 *JAMA* editorial on the treatment of impotence: "The so-called aphrodisiacs sometimes accomplish something. Iron, arsenic and mainly large doses of strychnine may give results. . . . Alcohol is indispensable in frigidity and premature ejaculation. . . . Ultraviolet rays are sometimes useful and psychotherapy is never to be neglected." The comic-therapeutic promiscuity of this recitation reminds us that medical diagnoses and therapies can be responses to other medical events. The late-twentieth-century diagnosis of female sexual dysfunction, for example, did not appear until Viagra had entered public consciousness as a sensational, all-purpose aphrodisiac that was imagined to increase blood flow to the female genitalia. Once again, the availability of a "treatment" catalyzed a diagnosis that appeared to justify the therapy. Similarly, the emergence of ISD just happened to coincide with the dynamic growth of the sex therapy profession, suggesting that the availability of a treatment may have had something to do with the rapidly increasing supply of sexually distressed patients and the therapists who treat them.

Sex hormone therapy has always had a role in the treatment of sexual dysfunction disorders that involved true hormone deficiencies. But the more interesting persistent question has been whether hormones are an appropriate therapy for the much larger numbers of physiologically normal people, young and old, who may experience loss of desire. "Despite lack of supporting evidence," Irvine writes, "laboratory research is dominated by a search for hormonal determinants. And, logically, this perspective has led to the development of pharmacologic agents to turn desire back on." The antidepressant Wellbutrin enjoyed a vogue as an aphrodisiac that ended when it was found to trigger seizures. Testosterone therapy has continued despite what Irvine called in 1990 "the lack of empirical evidence for its effectiveness"—a characterization I would contest, even as I endorse her analysis of the social process that produces dubious diagnoses. The more important issue, however, is not the efficacy of any particular drug but the entire pharmacological approach to normal people's loss of desire, which is misleadingly referred to as sexual dysfunction.

What is sexual dysfunction? The clinical definition of hypoactive sexual desire, Daniel Goleman wrote in 1990, "is engaging in sexual activity (including masturbation) or having sexual thoughts, fantasies or urges less than twice a month." But this clinical definition becomes irrelevant as soon as we look at the sex lives of large numbers of people. A professor emeritus of psychiatry reveals, for example, that fully half of the HSD couples he sees are suffering from a problem he calls "marital dissatisfaction," noting: "Many of these clients discover in therapy that they have lost not their sexual feeling but their feeling for their spouses." "In many cases of HSD," Goleman adds, "a person's sex drive may be muffled by stress or depression, then altogether squelched by a major life change." In a similar vein, married people who exhaust themselves in work and child care "may not have true HSD, but their anhedonic, all-work-and-no-play lifestyle may be just as destructive to their libidos." It is the sheer complexity of such marital problems that tempts some doctors and patients to look for salvation in higher levels of testosterone, the so-called hormone of desire. While those experiencing low sexual desire may be adults of any age, the well-defined market for hormone replacement therapy consists of "menopausal" or "postmenopausal" men and women.

HORMONE THERAPY AND THE DISCOVERY OF
SEXUAL DEFICIENCY

The mainstreaming of hormone therapy for older people is one consequence of the recent shift toward cosmetic medicine and its promises of personal fulfillment. As the medical historian David Morris points out, "A postmodern revision of aging that began in the 1970s has begun to promote a positive vision of the elderly as 'healthy, sexually active, engaged, productive, and self-reliant.' There is now a rich market of elderly consumers, whom advertisers court with commercials that show vigorous white-haired couples at play in their retirement years." These gamboling senior citizens represent, in addition to their good health, a prosperity associated with wealth, class, and professional achievement. The handsome, silver-haired male partners featured in these ads have not spent their working lives as doormen or dishwashers. Such "successful aging" is inseparable from the media advertising that sustains the ideal and from the medical entrepreneurs who meet the needs created by rising expectations about the "quality of life" to which older people are said to be entitled.

Media images that conflate health, wealth, and personal fulfillment into a myth of successful aging make their own contribution to how we imagine the aging process and how we might eliminate, delay, or mitigate its effects on our lives. At the daring end of this advertising spectrum are the Viagra ads done by former U.S. senator Bob Dole, confirming Morris's observation that postmodern illness "has become a quasi-public performance played out before an audience of support groups, e-mail lists, and paramedical legions." Such groups have played an important role in eroding the authority of establishment medicine. In addition, all of these activities, like those of AIDS activists, feed back in one way or another into the thoughts and feelings of people who feel ill or who must contemplate the possibility of illness. The public presentation of illness and its medical adversaries can also encourage flagging spirits to seek hormone therapy or some other kind of treatment.

The entire process of initial self-diagnosis, searching for help, and post-therapeutic self-assessment has been infiltrated by media-driven norms pertaining to illness that frame the experience for the patient. Where, for example, is the threshold of discomfort beyond which one is ill? How should one feel as one ages? How much sex makes one a "normal" member of one's cohort? Do aging people answer such questions in their own autonomous voices, or do they adopt the idiom of a youth-obsessed society that has imposed what Morris calls "a culturewide hypochondria that takes the form of health worship"? "The fate of the elderly," he notes, "depends to a large degree on what dominant narratives a culture constructs about the last years of life. In the industrial West, aging has been deeply influenced by the omnivorous cultural narrative of medicalization, especially in the field of gerontology, as people increasingly view their lives from birth to death as a sequence of medical events."

Today the construction of narratives about old age has unprecedented significance, because the number of older people and the medical market that serves them are of unprecedented size and will be expanding for the foreseeable future. This market will continue to sponsor the kind of advertising that creates and manipulates hopes, anxieties, and expectations about intimate relationships and experiences that might be enhanced by drugs. Also unprecedented is the amount of information contained in this advertising, which can empower or can disorient its audience of aging people. How, for example, can an advertisement help us to distinguish between genuine disease and the normal effects of aging? Does pharmaceutical advertising have the authority to make this distinction? Is it ever intended to make such a distinction? Or is its purpose to make normal symptoms look like disease states that require treatment? Let us now examine the theory that the medical-pharmaceutical complex constructs diseases in order to create markets for the products that treat them.

Marketing campaigns that promote drugs seem to be the outgrowth of corporate advertising rather than clinical medicine. Such commercial ambitions raise questions about the origins and reliability of the diagnoses that define the disorders that create lucrative markets for drug companies. This tension between marketing and medicine makes certain disorders vulnerable to the chicken-and-the-egg dilemma. Does the disease exist before there is a drug to treat it? Or does the treatment make it possible for the disease to exist in the first place? One way out of the quandary is to recognize that a disease exists on two levels: as a biological process located inside the individual and as a social event that situates the individual inside a nexus of relationships that should promote his or her treatment. This distinction suggests that the biological dimension of some diseases is irrelevant until it is defined as a problem by medical professionals—those who have the authority to make a disease a social event that unfolds in a clinic or a hospital setting. In the meantime, the commercial ambitions of the pharmaceutical companies have already entered the scene by deluging physicians with advertisements in medical journals. Reinforcing this propaganda barrage are the sales representatives who lobby for novel (off-label) uses of drugs to treat conditions that hitherto may not have been considered treatable.

Thus, when synthetic hormones find markets we find ourselves asking, Are treatable disorders simply defined into existence so as to create demand for new hormone products? But such a question is too simplistic to encompass the complex process that makes a disorder a clinical and social reality. Navigating this complexity requires, among other things, a capacity to appreciate the therapeutic effects of drugs even while recognizing the commercial motives that prompt manufacturers to produce misleading advertisements. A major pharmaceutical company is, after all, both a benefactor of humanity and an amoral money machine, and tolerating this ambiguity is a prerequisite for making sound judgments about its claims regarding what is normal and what is pathological. The same tolerance for ambiguity should enable us to analyze the strategies employed by pharmaceutical advertising without assuming that the marketing of hormones is always just a cynical plot to entrap customers.

The social construction of a medical disorder such as loss of sexual desire involves not the sheer invention of symptoms but rather a particular interpretation of symptoms that exist in a significant number of people. A subcategory of this interpretive process is what one might call the clinical or pragmatic construction of a disease that does not exist, at least within the nexus of doctor-patient relationships, until physicians believe it can be treated with drugs or surgery. "Unless you have a treatment, you don't have a condition," says Dr. Irwin Goldstein, a Boston University urologist and sex therapist. "If there is nothing for me to say except, 'See a psychiatrist,' then what is the rush to accurately describe and research your condition?" One corollary of such medical pragmatism is the assumption that a medical condition is a biological state and not a psychological one, a supposition that can exclude important psychosomatic factors from the diagnosis. This complicated relationship between physical symptoms and mental states is at the heart of the "menopausal" conditions that have been associated with aging men and women for the past sixty years.

The diagnosis of low sexual desire, like the early accounts of the male menopause, takes an extreme disorder affecting a limited number of people and extrapolates it into a mass diagnosis that now applies to millions who seem to require help. The biomedical foundation of the alleged disorder has dissolved into a hopelessly vague set of conditions—labeled marital dissatisfaction, stress, and anhedonic lifestyle—whose origins could be anywhere and everywhere. How can the origins of marital dissatisfaction or a major life change be defined, let alone quantified, in a scientifically adequate way that would call for hormone therapy rather then marriage counseling? Even a somewhat better defined syndrome such as ISD or HSD loses its coherence as soon as it is applied to a larger number of people. "The syndrome of ISD," Irvine points out, "suffers from the same conceptual murkiness as premature ejaculation: how fast is too fast, how low is too low? What, specifically, is low sexual interest? Is it based on quantity of sexual activity or quality? Who decides normal frequency?" Constructing the difference between the normal and the pathological can, in fact, be a highly arbitrary exercise. For what are the criteria that would enable us to declare where subnormal sexual interest begins on the vast spectrum of human sexual experience? The point here is not that ISD does not exist as a meaningful condition for some people, but that it becomes socially significant—media-driven and a potential boon to hormone manufacturers—only when the threshold of pathology approaches a range that is characteristic of large numbers of potential "patients." It then seems more practical to offer hormone replacement for a waning sex drive than to address the psychosocial context of sex, such as the state of a marriage.

Such anxieties about physical or psychological problems can escalate into treatable syndromes given the right circumstances. This process requires a corporate strategy of "marketing diseases," which often relies on a few people who seek out treatment and then advertise its beneficial effects by word of mouth. The marketing of antidepressants has followed the corporate model. Dr. Joseph McMullen, a Harvard University psychiatrist, calls this practice "a trend toward pathologizing daily life" and points to the inflation of a rare disorder called social phobia into a mass-marketable syndrome. "Over the last few years," he said in 2000, "psychiatrists have been inundated with drug-company mailings that cite 'experts' renaming 'social phobia' as 'social anxiety disorder.' The Food and Drug Administration recently approved Paxil to treat social phobia. But the mass media report this to the public as a treatment for shyness!" The surgery that creates the "designer vagina" originated in the practice of a Los Angeles plastic surgeon whose enthusiastic patients went on to tell other women about the enhancement of their sexual pleasure. Over time such word-of-mouth testimonials can create a new market for cosmetic medicine. "I worry absolutely that this will be the next thing they'll tell women is wrong with them," a professor of plastic surgery commented. Cosmetic vaginal surgery, too, was at first a therapeutic procedure to correct an uncommon condition, such as a vagina made misshapen by childbirth, but eventually it also became an operation to enhance sex. Rationalizing this type of surgery is made easier by the difficulty, here as elsewhere, of defining the boundary between repairing and enhancing the human organism.

Part of the problem of identifying real disorders is that people apply media-driven criteria of illness as they diagnose themselves. Imagine, for example, the worried male who has been left to distinguish between erectile dysfunction and normal functioning in various situations that may or may not have sexually stimulated him. The performance anxiety that affects many men who do not consistently experience arousal has two major sources: the popular idea that the male is always ready for sex and the familiar image of the male sexual organs as a hormonal-hydraulic apparatus that functions like a machine, independent of the emotions. Men who imagine sexual responsiveness in these terms may not understand that sex is primarily an emotional rather than a physical experience, and they will tend to overestimate the significance of physical symptoms that appear to deviate from the imagined healthy norm. "If you don't get a night or waking erection almost every day, then your testosterone level is too low—even if you are in your seventies!" So reads an article promoting the use of the anabolic steroid androstenedione that appears in a pseudo-medical publication sponsored by the Gero Vita Laboratories of Toronto. Performance pressure of this kind is, as we shall see, an inevitable result of the campaign to promote hormone therapy for large numbers of men.

The marketing of hormones serves the newly privileged beneficiary of postmodern medicine known as the empowered patient. The postmodern medical scenario, according to David Morris, "implies a shift, incomplete and ongoing, in which the patient, no longer merely a bundle of symptoms reported by an unreliable, subjective ego, emerges at moments as a valued participant in the medical process of diagnosis and treatment." Pharmaceutical advertising and countless Internet sites provide many patients with unprecedented amounts of medical information, which they then bring to their appointments with physicians who may be uninformed about new drugs or procedures. The empowered patient enjoys a sense of entitlement to the benefits of the newly respectable field of cosmetic medicine: laser eye surgery, plastic surgery, Botox injections for wrinkles, laser hair removal. Lifestyle medicine of this kind changes the ethos of medical practice by shifting the emphasis from the preservation of health to the aesthetics of the body. Once dependent on their doctors, some patients are now clients whose tastes come first. (This is the medical culture that offers the "designer vagina" to enhance sexual performance.) The patient's sense of entitlement changes the definition of a medical disorder, because he or she refuses to accept conditions that were considered normal before therapies aimed at their correction emerged. This aesthetic or restorative medical activity is driven by two powerful interest groups: a generation of patients dissatisfied with the physical consequences of the aging process and a medical profession paid handsomely by patients for these services, without interference from health maintenance organizations. The demands of these patients are also served by a Congress whose antiregulatory bias has encouraged less than stringent regulation of health-related products, including controversial drugs such as ephedrine and androstenedione.

But the postmodern, empowered patient is also the potential dupe of what Morris calls "the confusing welter of self-help programs, group therapies, alternative healers, and experimental drugs" that make up the new therapeutic cornucopia. The myth of the hormone-driven personality that dates from the 1920s continues to attract clients to hormone clinics and other establishments that make unfounded claims about the efficacy of their treatments. Synthetic human growth hormone, for example, "has captured the fancy of many people who, in quest of greater muscle strength and vitality, appear to have little difficulty obtaining hormone from entrepreneurial physicians, notwithstanding the failure of the scientific literature to support these uses." Such judgments from the world of academic medicine are directed against an expanding "alternative" medical culture that is built on anecdotal evidence and the kind of pseudoscience about hormones that is constantly appearing in bodybuilding magazines. Moreover, this ongoing competition between peer-reviewed medicine and tabloid medicine is one-sided, as the tabloids enjoy most of the advantages. Stories about successful hormone cures will inevitably have more popular appeal than reports of standard clinical trials that rarely offer dramatic evidence of the power of drugs.

PRESERVING THE FEMININE ESSENCE:
ESTROGEN AND MENOPAUSE

The popularizing of estrogen as a treatment for the female menopause exemplifies a cure aimed at a disorder whose social construction has depended on the interpretation of physical and emotional symptoms by doctors, by female patients and their husbands, and by the society that assigns roles to aging women. Its marketing has involved a complex interaction among the doctors who prescribe the drugs, the patients who have often demanded the drugs, and the companies that produce the drugs. Nevertheless, it is important to recognize the imbalances of power in these relationships, and in particular the vulnerability of the millions of women who have been candidates for modern estrogen therapy since the 1960s. Faced with having to make difficult choices on the basis of inadequate and often conflicting information, some women have concluded that estrogen therapy for menopausal or postmenopausal symptoms is primarily a marketing scheme at their expense. Trudy Bush, an epidemiologist at the University of Maryland, pointed out in 1997 that "there is a perception on the part of some women who are activists that there is a conspiracy to force women to buy these hormones and force doctors to prescribe them. Instead of the military-industrial complex, it would be the A.M.A.-pharmaceutical complex. But things aren't so simple."

Since the 1930s, estrogen therapy has been both a marketing scheme and a mass therapy that was widely assumed to offer substantial benefits to large numbers of women. In this sense, the AMA-pharmaceutical complex unquestionably exists, since thousands of physicians have written millions of prescriptions for hormone products they regarded as beneficial to their patients. This alliance has also taken legal action to promote estrogen replacement therapy (ERT) in the face of warnings about its possible hazards. In 1977, for example, the Pharmaceutical Manufacturing Association, the American College of Obstetricians and Gynecologists, the National Association of Chain Drug Stores, and the American Society of Internal Medicine, along with a number of state and county medical societies, filed suit in a federal district court to block the

FDA's authority to warn consumers about a possible link between ERT and cancer. A *JAMA* editorial likewise complained in 1980 about "the public anxiety created by the Food and Drug Administration and concerned persons" regarding the health hazards of ERT—a public face-off between the ERT lobby and federal regulators. This medical-pharmaceutical coalition has also been opposed by a feminist campaign bent on refuting the idea that menopause is a disease. "According to feminists," one sympathetic scholar writes, "the menstrual and menopausal myths are a form of social control. If women are perceived as physically and emotionally handicapped by menstruation and menopause, they cannot and may not compete with men." This struggle for control of how menopause is presented to the wider world has cast the debate over whether menopause is a real or a socially constructed disease squarely into the arena of gender politics. One type of feminist critique impugns the motives and thus the competence of a "male-dominated, profit-oriented U.S. medical system" and the "men who control research and drug companies." The challenge, however, is to determine how male dominance of the medical-pharmaceutical complex may have influenced the diagnoses of female disorders that can be treated with drugs.

Early critiques of hormone replacement therapy (HRT) recognized that it had achieved the status of a dogma. As noted in the previous chapter, a physician in 1954 complained bitterly about "unnecessary treatment with hormones when these women are free or practically free from symptoms," as well as "the administering of hormones to almost all women over 40 who have vague complaints, perhaps of a psychosomatic nature." Yet this practitioner also maintained that "there is a real need for the use of estrogenic hormones in those women who have severe menopausal symptoms." This early commentary on the practice of ERT already points to the role of gender-based ideology in the menopause debate. Physicians who prescribed powerful hormone drugs to women who did not present symptoms, or to middle-aged women as a group, presumed that hormone deficiency is a biological universal among older women, thereby disregarding both physiological and sociological differences among women that indicate otherwise. (For example, better-educated women are less resigned to physical decline than are their less-educated counterparts.) Such essentialist thinking based on inadequate data points to nonscientific motives that originate in the emotional complexes of men and in societal folklore about the emotional instability of women.

Another skeptical view of ERT was presented at the 1965 meeting of the American College of Surgeons. On this occasion a panel of five gynecologists offered an implicit rebuke to the contemporary ERT fad being led by Dr. Robert A. Wilson of New York (see below). They argued that distinguishing between the use and abuse of estrogen was difficult, and that menopausal women were not a medically homogeneous population. Dr. Somers H. Sturgis of Harvard conceded the palliative value of estrogen during the menopausal and postmenopausal years, but he also pointed to the marital context in which many women developed their symptoms: The typical patient, he suggested, "probably has a paunchy husband, at the top of his career, who pays little attention to her. Her children are grown and gone away," and estrogens cannot solve these problems. Yet another factor was the demand for estrogen from women who had heard reports about its rejuvenating powers. "The menopausal woman is suffering from more than an endocrine deficiency," said Dr. M. Edward Davis of the University of Chicago. "Increasingly, they are asking their physicians, 'How can I stay young?' " "A central fallacy to clear up," said Dr. John H. Morton of Loma Linda University, "is that estrogen can make a 'sporty' ovary from an atrophic one," a fantasy indulged in by women who hoped to "regain their youth" by means of estrogen therapy. But where had this fantasy come from? And who might have encouraged it? Although these gynecologists had to be aware of the influence of their colleague Robert Wilson and of the many popular articles about his work, they chose not to mention his role in the ERT boom of the early 1960s. This act of professional courtesy required these physicians to shift the responsibility for excess demand for estrogen to the female patients who had been most vulnerable to Wilson's estrogen crusade. The solidarity of the guild prevailed over a more candid approach to women's health.

Feminist resistance to estrogen replacement has employed social construction theory to invalidate the disease model of menopause. One such argument is that hormone therapy preceded the identification of the disorders it might cure. "Estrogen therapy is a treatment in search of a disease," as the sociologist Alice Rossi put it in 1992. Two years later, in her pioneering social history of estrogen drugs, the medical historian Nelly Oudshoorn echoes Rossi as she describes the matchmaking process whereby, back in the 1930s, a drug was introduced to a disease it might cure. "Sex hormones may best be portrayed as drugs looking for diseases," she says. "Before the actual process of marketing could begin, the pharmaceutical company had first to create its audiences." Oudshoorn presents us with an inside history of the Organon company of Holland, an early hormone manufacturer that began building its business on fe-male sex hormones in 1923. Organon "could succeed in creating a mar-ket only if it linked up with the needs of the medical profession: the com-pany had to create arrangements with the medical community in order to find diseases that could be treated with its new products." Oudshoorn shows how Organon marketed hormones in a mercenary and reckless fashion, constantly adding to the list of disorders for which they were the recommended treatment.

Nevertheless, what ultimately counts is not how the drugs found ther-apeutic roles but whether they helped the patients who used them. It is well known, for example, that Pfizer was developing Viagra for one pur-pose when its scientists found that it could better serve another. Social construction theory therefore goes astray when its assessment of a drug's value is based entirely on distrust of the manufacturer's crass motives. The whole point of this rhetorical maneuver, after all, is to impugn the value of the drug. The feminist version of social construction theory can also overlook the fact that women—even feminists—may use or promote hormone therapy without necessarily succumbing to the ERT propa-ganda that surrounds them. Additional surprises include Robert Wilson's unsparing criticism of a male-dominated medical profession that had long neglected the suffering of menopausal women. The most prominent ERT crusader of his era deplored the patriarchal attitudes of his col-leagues, in part because "most medical opinion was hardened against the very concept of hormone therapy" that Wilson saw as deliverance for aging women. Wilson's observation also suggests there was no medical-pharmaceutical plot to put hormones into women.

So does female menopause exist today as a disease? While some fem-inist observers would argue that a male-dominated medical establish-ment has succeeded in turning menopause into a deficiency disease, there is no consensus view. "Menopause is not the onset of disease," *Harvard Women's Health Watch* stated in 1996, "but a biological marker that sig-nals the end of one's reproductive years and the beginning of a new de-velopmental stage of life. It has been associated with psychological changes, particularly depression; but there is little evidence that these are the result of declining estrogen levels or that they can be influenced by hormone supplementation." Such a formulation shows that menopause can be regarded as a biological phenomenon without treating it as a pathological one. Indeed, this proclamation from the heart of the med-ical establishment expresses a feminist doctrine of self-determination. "Instead of pondering hormone choices," it continues, "your energies may be better spent considering who you want to be in your post-reproductive years." Here feminist thinking has trumped expert opinion and dealt a blow to the standard biomedical model that prescribes ERT. Indeed, feminists have an obligation to participate in the construction of menopause, precisely because its interpretation will remain a social process that is rooted in gender politics as well as medical science.

Why has promotion of the female menopause advanced ahead of the recognition and treatment of its male counterpart? Why did hormone therapy for women develop into a thriving business as early as the 1920s and 1930s while comparable therapies for men were failing to take hold? One technical factor that helped to account for this discrepancy was the earlier availability of female hormones: synthetic testosterone was not available in commercial quantities until the late 1930s. It is most unlikely, however, that an issue as emotionally charged as male and female aging can be understood primarily as a matter of pharmacological progress here and stagnation there. We should rather assume that differing assessments of the male and female organisms have encouraged the idea that men and women require different kinds of medical attention. One result of this dual approach to male and female health—which originated in traditional ideas about the relative weakness of the female organism and in the vulnerability of women as a subordinate group—was the early development of hormone therapy for women. As the medical historian Roy Porter points out, "It is no accident in what remains a man's world, with a medical profession still male-dominated, that it is mainly 'women's complaints' which have become medicalized." During the earlier part of the twentieth century this imbalance of power made women more vulnerable than men to careless diagnoses of dubious disorders that could be treated with hormone products. The most sweeping diagnosis of this kind, based on what Oudshoorn calls "the image of the hormonal woman," ascribed female inferiority to female hormones. "Throughout her entire life," a Dutch physician wrote in 1940, "the woman is controlled by the rhythmic function of her ovaries, and the changing hormonal content of her blood causes a major psychological and bodily lability. For men such a problem does not exist. This is the reason why women are handicapped in their struggle for equality with men."

The biological fragility and instability of the female sex was supposedly evident in female conditions such as menstruation and menopause, and in a sex drive that did not possess the force of its male counterpart. The female sex hormone industry of the 1920s thus set out to repair these deficiencies with or without clinical trials of the drugs that went on the market. For menstrual disorders the Organon company began marketing Ovarnon in 1925, and from that point on the advertised uses for synthetic estrogens multiplied dramatically. Later drugs such as Menformon and theelin were recommended for menopause as well as for schizophrenia, melancholia, epilepsy, and a motley collection of other disorders. "This wide range of applications," Oudshoorn notes, "illustrates how, since the 1920s, female sex hormones developed from a treatment specifically indicated in cases of well-defined menstrual disorders to a more universal medicine applicable for a wide variety of conditions in female patients, all attributed to dysfunction of the ovaries." In other words, the medically vulnerable condition of the female organism originated in a sex organ that could be treated with sex hormones. Being female was now associated with a permanent (but treatable) state of hormone deficiency.

The medical sexism of some hormone doctors became apparent when the feminism of the 1960s and 1970s began to challenge male authority in Western societies. *JAMA* announced the first tremors of this social earthquake in a 1963 news item titled "Submissive Women Arise—and Marriages Fall," in which a psychiatrist ascribes this housewives' revolt to arrested emotional development in both husbands and their female partners—a diagnosis that ignored the social equity issue altogether. The gender ideology of the ERT advocate Robert A. Wilson, presented in his best seller *Feminine Forever* (1966), offers a more heartfelt analysis of the female predicament that also manages to preserve traditional ideas about what a woman should be. Wilson was a charmer whose passionate sincerity embraced both the distress of his menopausal patients and a romantic worship of the feminine essence that hormones could preserve. Menopause without estrogen therapy, he says, is a catastrophic deficiency disease, and "no woman can be sure of escaping the horror of this living decay." He continues, "I have seen untreated women who had shriveled into caricatures of their former selves."

Wilson saw all women as vulnerable to menopause and in dire need of the hormone therapy that could mitigate its horrors. This extremism seems to have originated in very strong feelings about female disfigurement that also prompt the worship of feminine beauty that is so evident in his book. "There is hardly anything lovelier to sight and touch," he says, "than the skin of a young woman of about twenty—so smooth, pliant, and delicate." This is the feminine essence that estrogen therapy can preserve in older women, as well: "The outward signs of this age-defying youthfulness are a straight-backed posture, supple breast contours, taut, smooth skin on face and neck, firm muscle tone, and that particular vigor and grace typical of a healthy female." To this female aesthetic Wilson added a maternal imperative: "Women who have plenty of sex but no children somehow strike me as vaguely tense and unfulfilled."

Despite his cultural conservatism, Wilson was also a progressive gynecologist who criticized male physicians for their "lack of basic sympathy for women," debunked the stereotype of "frigid" women, and demystified the fashionable, media-driven fixation on the female orgasm as a criterion of sexual health. This combination of the traditional and the emancipatory is not as paradoxical as it might seem. Wilson's career as a paternalistic-progressive crusader for hormone replacement reminds us that a dedication to "the emotional liberation of women" and their sexual fulfillment does not presuppose a feminist analysis of gender relations. The more enlightened defenders of traditional marriage have always wanted to enhance sexual relations between husbands and wives. Indeed, Wilson's "conservative" activism coincided with a growing awareness that the traditional family arrangement was becoming increasingly unstable, and an important goal of estrogen therapy was to "prolong the happiness of millions of families whose marital foundations might otherwise have eroded under the usual psycho-sexual stress of middle life." In retrospect, one difference between Wilson's hormone agenda and our own is our growing willingness to believe that "menopausal negativism" afflicts large numbers of hormone-deficient men as well as women.

The antifeminist, even misogynistic feelings displayed by certain estrogen enthusiasts raise serious questions about the motivations behind the campaign for ERT that triumphed during the 1960s and 1970s. For all of Wilson's good intentions, there is something unbalanced and disturbing about his fixation on supple bodies and the confessional impulse that prompts him to proclaim his "lifelong penchant for the more magic attributes of love." Self-revelations of this kind point to a male self-absorption that could not accommodate the equality of the sexes, let alone the dignity of the wrinkled crones who appalled him. Indeed, the connoisseur of the female essence has every reason to oppose women's rights in the modern sense, since it is the contrasting essences of the sexes that provide the spice of life.

A more straightforward example of this sort of pro-estrogen misogyny was displayed at the 1973 meeting of the Gerontological Society in

Puerto Rico. As the seventy-one-year-old president of the American Geriatrics Society, Dr. Francis P. Rhoades, described the grim toll of menopause—hypertension, osteoporosis, sickly skin, flabby breasts, ailing genitalia, nervous disorders, and more—one could hear "a constant undertone of hissing from some 200 scientists, more than half of them women, who represented the various disciplines that make up gerontology." Speaking as a member of an all-male panel, Rhoades told the women in attendance that the "rather sudden, catastrophic change" of menopause would make them "functionally castrated" for the last twenty or thirty years of their lives, unless they submitted to "adequate supplemental estrogen and progestogen therapy." And he, like Wilson, warned that women age differently than men: "The male experiences only a gradual decline in his gonadal output of hormones, and thus he remains essentially a man until his death. With the woman the situation is entirely different." Small wonder a participant described this tension-filled meeting as "the Battle of San Juan."

The sheer dogmatism about gender difference displayed by this ranking physician should have raised questions about his insistence on prescribing hormones for all "postmenopausal, hypogonadal women regardless of age," and we may assume that his zealotry had this effect on some of those present. Yet male physicians' attitudes toward their menopausal patients did not become an issue in the 1960s, even as they were administering estrogenic drugs to millions of women. "There is no convincing proof that estrogen has ever induced cancer in the human being," Wilson wrote in 1962. "It would seem advisable to keep women endocrine rich and, consequently, cancer poor throughout their lives. A consequence of this would be the elimination of the menopause." Today, with the benefit of hindsight, we know that he was underestimating the carcinogenic dangers of estrogen. As early as 1975 ERT had been linked to endometrial cancer; and on July 15, 1977, the commissioner of the Food and Drug Administration announced new regulations requiring that all patients be warned about the dangers of estrogen use. The FDA's action prompted an angry accusation in the pages of *JAMA* that the commissioner had "officially expressed his distrust of the medical profession." This protest against federal regulation concluded with a statement that is breathtaking in its naïve credulity regarding the relationship between drug companies and the physicians whose cooperation they solicit: "As in the case of virtually all pharmaceuticals, the medical profession and the pharmaceutical industry can be expected to move toward more beneficial and relatively safer estrogen therapy programs. The ethics of the profession and the profit motive provide the driving forces. Only government interference can freeze progress."

These contentious episodes make it clear that female HRT had become a part of the gender politics of this era, with conflicts raging on several fronts. In one corner of this arena the FDA confronted the medical-pharmaceutical alliance that was bent on resisting government regulation. ERT advocates such as Wilson played to a large male constituency by telling harried husbands that "estrogen makes women adaptable, even-tempered, and generally easy to live with." Another gynecologist, Dr. Robert W. Kistner, agreed that ERT helped to preserve the domestic tranquillity of many American homes. One consequence of a sharply lower estrogen level, he said, "is that intercourse becomes painful. This leads to marital difficulties and is a factor in many cases of philandering by husbands." Wilson also argued that the female change of life impaired social efficiency far beyond the marital bedroom. "The menopausal syndrome," he wrote, "is based on an erratic disorientation of the woman's entire frame of mind, a combination of fixed ideas and unpredictable caprice. In a business situation, this plays havoc not merely with the morale of the woman's subordinates, but it may also lead to serious errors of executive judgement. With more and more women entrusted with decision-making posts in business, government, and in various institutions, the effects of menopause present a new type of management problem that has yet to be fully understood by the experts of corporate administration." It is no wonder that Wilson called his work "one of the greatest biological revolutions in the history of civilization."

The medical community itself was split into opposing factions on the use of ERT. Research scientists began to realize that some of the physicians targeting menopause were exaggerating the scope or the severity of its symptoms, and that physicians' allegiance to a certain feminine ideal was influencing therapeutic goals. "There is no persuasive evidence to justify routine use of conjugated or any other kind of estrogen in the treatment of anxiety, depression, or other emotional symptoms in menopausal women," one publication declared in 1973. Yet these were the very symptoms from which estrogen was supposed to rescue female menopause–afflicted husbands. The implication that such mental disturbances were inherent only in aging women reinforced the traditional gendered caste system in which men were presumed to be emotionally stable while women were not. In this sense, universal ERT aimed less at alleviating symptoms than at redeeming the female sex from a presumed innate deficiency that could be repaired with hormones.

The prominence of the female menopause as a medical and social issue for most of the twentieth century contrasts starkly with the relative obscurity of its male counterpart. Even today "some of the normal things that occur with aging are being attributed to hormonal changes in women, whereas the same symptoms in men are not." It would be interesting to know how many men have wondered about this discrepancy, given their own frequent complaints about age-related discomforts and dysfunctions. After enthusiastically reviewing the benefits of ERT for women, one physician commented in 1971: "A number of husbands have asked me, 'Why on earth can't we men have something like this?' " He continued, "Perhaps this will be worked out in time." In the meantime, this practitioner was administering male hormone therapy on an ad hoc basis to his male patients. In some cases of unsatisfactory sexual performance, he observed, "an injection of male hormone may be of value if only as a psychotherapeutic effort." To judge from the medical literature, many such conversations and injections have occurred in physicians' offices since the 1940s. But the disorders of aging men did not coalesce into a menopausal syndrome that became part of our gender folklore. The hot flashes reported by male patients did not take on the symbolic significance accorded hot flashes in women. This differential treatment of aging men and women suggests that the bifurcated development of the popular myth of the hormone-driven personality during the 1920s and 1930s reflected the unequal social status of men and women. The biological rationale for distinguishing sharply between male and female menopause was that ovarian hormone production shut down abruptly while male hormone levels declined gradually. Yet this physiological difference was only part of the story. The first description of male menopause published in 1939 had pointed out that the "climacteric symptoms" shared by men and women included "intense subjective nervousness, definite emotional instability characterized by irritability, sudden changes in mood . . . and depression and crying"—a collection of symptoms most people would still identify as "female." Gender stereotyping was still filtering out reports of emotionally unstable men and emphasizing the sudden mood changes of their menopausal wives.

Gender stereotyping of this kind was still being promoted a generation later by the estrogen enthusiast Robert Wilson, whose cultural conservatism held that men do not experience catastrophic aging: "A man remains male as long as he lives. Age does not rob him of his sexual appetite nor of the means of satisfying it. . . . No abrupt crisis has to be faced. A man's life proceeds in smooth continuity. His feeling of self remains unbroken." This blanket exemption from the degenerative effects of aging was a remarkable claim for an experienced physician to make. It may well be that Wilson's own robust health and a practice that was limited to women reinforced the culturally sanctioned bias that emphasized female rather than male decline. At the same time, he did acknowledge that by the age of sixty-five a man "may require medical assistance if he wishes to continue a fully sexed life. In principle, the same therapy applies to him as to women. The gradually diminishing sex hormones must be supplied through medication. Excellent male steroids are now available by injection, implantation of pellets, or as tablets for this form of therapy."

One feminist critique of HRT for women focuses on the cultural bias that reserves dignified aging for men. "Males in western culture," E. Ann Kaplan writes, "have constructed things so that they do not have an analogous so-called change of life, and they are seen to continue to be productive as they age. There is no specific marking of aging for them, no symbolic change from 'useful' to 'no-longer useful.' " "The fact is," a feminist colleague adds, "that, even as a commerce in male aging grows, until recently men have managed to keep their own midlife problems and their own fears of aging relatively secret."

Today, however, the belief that men are exempt from serious midlife problems related to physical decline and sexual functioning has been effectively demolished by the massive advertising campaign on behalf of Viagra. Husky, smiling, and radiating a newly restored self-confidence, the men who populate these magazine and television advertisements demonstrate once again the power of market-driven images to reshape societal attitudes. In this case, advertising a product that restores male self-confidence simultaneously erodes a traditional stereotype of male invulnerability. This exposure of male secrets fulfills a prediction that feminist commentators were making even before the drug was launched in 1998. "Midlife men," one of them pointed out in 1997, "are becoming more vulnerable in their own aging: the same medical/commercial forces that have been bringing women their public menopause are on the verge of bringing same-age men their public climacteric or their 'midlife crisis.' Men too will be told their biology is their disease; they'll be pressured to become anxious, to buy cosmetic surgery and rejuvenation drugs and other prepackaged remedies. Some of this is already happening." In fact, the campaign to reinvent a public climacteric for men had been unfolding throughout the 1990s.

DOES THE MALE MENOPAUSE EXIST?

The social construction of male menopause as a recognizable syndrome was made possible by its female counterpart. Both the female and male menopause syndromes emerged along with glandular products that were used to treat them. Crude ovarian preparations were prescribed for female menopausal complaints as early as a century ago. When these drugs proved to be unsatisfactory, the stage was set for another marketing initiative with a more advanced product. "In the late 1930s," Oudshoorn notes, "Organon promoted the treatment of menopause as one of the major indications for female sex hormone therapy. In 1938 the board of directors of Organon decided to choose menopause as the major medical indication in the yearly advertisement campaign for female sex hormone preparations." Similarly, the male menopause did not emerge as a medical diagnosis in 1939 until synthetic testosterone had been tested in clinics and was available to treat it. Diagnosing the male climacteric thus became heavily dependent on the effects of the drug that appeared to alleviate such symptoms as depression and fatigue: if the drug worked, the disorder was real (see below). This linkage between syndrome and hormone was of great commercial significance, since administering the drug to a given number of lethargic middle-aged or elderly men would inevitably suggest the existence of a hormone deficiency in some of these people, who would then become purchasers of testosterone.

The early diagnosis of the male menopause was as vague as that of its female counterpart. Uncertainty about how to define this syndrome pervades the formulation of the concept. "It seems reasonable to believe," an early proponent of the diagnosis wrote in 1939, "that many if not all men pass through a climacteric period somewhat similar to that of women, usually in a less severe but perhaps more prolonged form." Even for a clinician who accepted its existence, "the typical climacteric syndrome" was a matter of reasonable belief rather than of scientific certainty. "The male climacteric," two physicians wrote in 1942, "presents one of the complex problems of aging. Its etiology is confused and undetermined. Its symptomatology is involved, tremendously varied, and rarely brought to the attention of the physician in all its diversity." Here is a description of a postmodern illness that antedates the vocabulary of postmodernism. If postmodern illness includes "a crucial element of ambiguity about whether the disorder really exists," then the male climacteric was postmodern illness before its time.

The male and female menopause syndromes described in medical and popular sources were also similar in that symptoms observed in women served as the basis for diagnosing a similar condition in men. "The climacteric symptoms in men," August A. Werner declares in 1939, "may be classified as in women as nervous, circulatory and general in distribution. Among the more prominent symptoms may be mentioned intense subjective nervousness, definite emotional instability characterized by irritability, sudden changes in mood, decreased memory and ability for mental concentration, decreased interest in the usual activities, a desire to be left alone, and depression and crying." The idea that at least some pillars of the community were fated to become weepy depressives given to typically "female" mood swings contradicted a popular image of male strength and stability that was still intact as Werner made his case. This does not mean that the male menopause diagnosis necessarily marked a step in the direction of gender equality; its gender politics have evolved along with gender relations as a whole and with the pharmacological mores of our society. Diagnosing and treating menopausal men in the prime of life once seemed to be important because their productivity and responsibilities were of a different order than those of women. Today, however, the same diagnosis and treatment may be framed quite differently, as a lifestyle entitlement that serves pleasure (one's quality of life) rather than productivity. Now many men are prepared to admit to hormone deficiencies they believe require treatment. And for the contemporary lifestyle consumer of hormones, dependence on pharmaceuticals has become more common than it was in the 1940s.

Today the popular image of the male and the female menopause makes this syndrome a stage of life through which all must pass. This simplistic model of human aging has long served the pharmaceutical industry and the physicians who offer "anti-aging" therapies, but the popular conception of a life "passage" through the purgatory of hormone deficiency has for just as long ignored contrary data that have appeared in the medical literature. While August A. Werner found it "reasonable to believe [in 1939] that many if not all men pass through a climactic period somewhat similar to that of women," Carl G. Heller and Gordon B. Myers maintained in 1944 that the male climacteric was "a relatively rare syndrome, probably affecting only a small proportion of men who live into old age." A decade later *JAMA* agreed that "the so-called male climacteric is a rare condition, especially when the diagnosis is limited to persons who manifest objective disturbances analogous to those observed in women and in whom certain well-defined abnormalities can be demonstrated by objective laboratory procedures." This was a diplomatic way of saying that once subjective complaints about lethargy and libido were excluded, the number of verifiable cases of male climacteric would turn out to be a very small fraction of the male population. "It is difficult to make a diagnosis of the male climacteric," this editorialist concluded, "precisely because well-established diagnostic criteria have not been instituted."

The diagnostic criterion that could be subjected to an objective laboratory procedure was a measured testosterone deficiency. Yet the number of such testosterone-deficient (hypogonadal) men was quite small, in that even "most elderly men exhibit no signs of testicular failure," as Heller and Myers reported. Dr. Julius Bauer agreed that the term *male climacteric* was a misnomer and that the disorder would be better called "testicular insufficiency." But how many men belonged in this category? A half century later, in 1994, William H. Masters and Virginia E. Johnson offered the following estimate: "In our experience, about 5 percent of men over age 60 have a condition that can legitimately be described as a male climacteric. These men have clear-cut testosterone deficiencies (not simply low-normal levels of testosterone) and characteristically complain of listlessness, weight loss or poor appetite or both, low sex drive, usually accompanied by impotence, a weakness or easy fatigability." In other words, neither the diagnosis nor the clinical incidence of true testosterone deficiency (hypogonadism) had changed over the course of fifty years. What had changed was the society in which men now experienced the social construction of aging as a disease even as they were offered treatments that were alleged to slow it down. Demographic factors promoting the male menopause now included "an aging population, an abundance of researchers, an oversupply of clinicians and an aggressive medical-industrial complex, among others," all of which had an interest in making the male climacteric a standard diagnosis. "I don't believe in the male mid-life crisis," the epidemiologist Dr. John B. McKinlay said in 1992. "But even though in my perspective there is no epidemiological, physiological or clinical evidence for such a syndrome, I think by the year 2000 the syndrome will exist. There's very strong interest in treating aging men for a profit, just as there is for menopausal women."

Even before Viagra suddenly changed the sexual health paradigm for aging men, the sex hormone market was gradually becoming a unisex menopause market. Now, men too were being forced to confront the newly fashionable idea that aging was a treatable, and therefore avoidable, condition. "Is Her Majesty's government going to make hormonal-replacement therapy available to men?" a hopeful member of the British House of Lords asked in 1989. (Prime Minister Thatcher's government did not.) "It's becoming popular to blame 'male menopause' for the strange behavior of some middle-aged men during their so-called 'midlife crisis,' " *JAMA* reported in 1992. "Some researchers are suggesting that what they call 'andropause' can be treated with supplemental testosterone." A year later the popular journalist Gail Sheehy called male menopause "the unspeakable passage" that most men refused to acknowledge because it was so threatening to their sense of potency. "The emphasis on performance," she wrote, "is the single greatest enemy of a satisfactory sexual life." Inevitably, however, one effect of creating a public climacteric for both sexes was to increase uncertainty and performance anxiety among older people unsure whether their sex lives were satisfactory by contemporary standards. Accompanying the new opportunities presumably conferred by hormone therapy was a new obligation to maintain a quality of life that matched that of one's peers. For if menopause was a treatable condition, then the prospect of therapy meant new opportunities that implied new challenges and new kinds of failures for those who could not keep up. As early as 1965, *Newsweek* was reporting "older couples fearful that their sex life falls short of some cultural ideal."

Marketing menopause to men and women means promoting the promise of better sexual performance as the principal therapeutic benefit of hormone therapy, and this promotional campaign has had both useful and harmful effects. "Nowhere in the course of history have we lived as long and expected as much from intimate relationships," observes David Schnarch, Ph.D., director of the Marriage and Family Health Center in Evergreen, Colorado. "It's a crime that we live in a society that compares the love lives of 60-year-olds with those of 20-year-olds, but the older population really has the better deal. This is a time when people have the best sex in their lives, and it all has to do with maturity." However inappropriate the comparison between adolescents and their grandparents, the resulting pressure to extend the sex lives of aging people has also undercut harmful stereotypes about the sexless elderly. "One commonly recognized belief among younger persons in our society," two physicians wrote in 1960, "is that older persons, especially grandparents, have no sexual feelings. . . . Thus, it is common for the physician to see in his daily practice older persons who feel guilty about having sexual feelings; often these feelings are not acceptable to the older person, to the physician, or to other people in the environment in which the older person is living." Forty years later such inhibitions continue to affect many lives and medical relationships. McKinlay has pointed out that even today "many patients and doctors have a 'don't ask, don't tell' policy" when it comes to sexual problems.

Unfortunately, the public life of this issue has been dominated by performance ideals rather than by an emphasis on the sexual benefits that come with maturity. "We used to treat older people as though sex was not possible," one medical expert notes, "but now we've flip-flopped and transmitted the message that everyone is supposed to be having fantastic sex forever. Over age 50, the quality of sex depends much more on the overall quality of a relationship than it does for young couples." Sex research itself creates pressures to "improve" sexual performance by publicizing ideas about latent sexual capacities. "Somehow," Janice Irvine wrote in 1990, "the popular media have transformed 'women are sexual and can have multiple orgasms' into 'real women must be hypersexual and must have multiple orgasms.' " Emulating the remorseless logic of high-performance sport, the potential sexual athleticism of the human organism becomes a mandatory athleticism in the service of a pleasure-seeking competition. Normal sexuality becomes outmoded; hypersexuality becomes the norm. This homogenizing approach to human sexuality originates in the quantification of orgasmic sexual experience introduced by Alfred Kinsey and in the proselytizing zeal of the human potential movement. Lost in the process is the variability of human sexual expression that Kinsey emphasized along with his quantitative methods.

A German businessman in his fifties visits his doctor with a familiar set of complaints. He has been feeling listless and is frequently sick, trudging his way apathetically through a life without purpose. The thought of sex just deepens his sense of fatigue. His family doctor listens to this unhappy recitation, shrugs his shoulders, and replies: "That's just the way it is. You're getting older." Eventually this sufferer finds his way to Dr. Gerald Müller, who, along with a urologist and a gynecologist, runs an anti-aging clinic in Hamburg that specializes in hormone replacement. Here patients receive testosterone, human growth hormone, estrogen, progesterone, the adrenal hormone DHEA, melatonin, and thyroid and thymus hormones in the form of pills, injections, ointments, vaginal insertions, and implants. After a year of 250-milligram testosterone injections every two weeks, the once apathetic patient now feels "like a man of thirty-five, fit and full of energy, the depressions are gone, and sex is fine again." It would seem that modern medicine had scored another victory on behalf of "successful aging."

Readers of American newsmagazine features on hormone therapy will recognize this story as one of the signature medical fables of our time. Indeed, Americans ought to find this scenario familiar, given that the founder of the Hamburg clinic had consciously adopted a "California" mode of healing—an example of cultural fashion driving medical globalization. If there is something un-American about the tale, it is the patient's claim that "hormone treatments for men are still looked down on here," as if to confirm America's global leadership in this as in other futuristic endeavors. What all these exemplary patients have in common is the atomized manner in which they are presented to a public wishing to believe that such treatments work. The standard narrative almost always omits their personal histories, the actual life circumstances from which they emerged to seek help from the hormone doctors. This is human biology severed from every context (other than sexual appetite) that gives meaning to most modern lives. The point of removing marital, family, and professional histories from these vignettes is to demonstrate a cause-and-effect relationship between hormone replacement and the almost magical transformation from misery to happiness that these people claim to have experienced. Extracting the troubled individual from the social nexus in which his problems developed therefore conveys the powerful but misleading impression that all of the variables apart from hormone levels have been controlled for and are finally irrelevant to the patient's health. Such case histories amount to a theater of illusion whose techniques are finally indistinguishable from those of advertising. Rarely does one read of a treatment that has failed to restore the demoralized client. Such redemption through hormones satisfies a taste for medical melodrama whose classic precedents are the miracle cures of the New Testament.

The complexities that are excluded from this hormone melodrama include biological as well as cultural information about the exemplary patient who supposedly is transformed by hormone therapy. How, for example, can his health status be evaluated without knowing something about his overall medical history? What were his testosterone and other hormone levels when he arrived at the clinic? Is this a genuinely hormone-deficient person, or is it someone afflicted by a malaise that does not register in the laboratory tests that are supposed to distinguish between the normal and the pathological? How have his sexual relationships affected his attitude toward sexual experience? Marital status is highly significant in that sexual activity in older people is correlated with the availability of a steady partner. Impotence is more common in older single men, who also live fewer years on average than their married counterparts. Meaningful work and professional status have a profound effect on feelings of well-being and thus on interest in sexual self-expression. Older people may also ask themselves why they should be having sex at all. Many older women, for example, feel that they have finally earned a respite from the sexual demands of their husbands, and there are undoubtedly husbands who feel the same way about their wives. Every older couple must negotiate a mutually agreeable sexual arrangement that can, in fact, be threatened by any therapy that intensifies the sexual demands of one partner. That is why Viagra has disrupted as well as repaired relationships between older people who had adapted to a less active sexual modus vivendi. These are some of the factors that influence the sexual psychology of older people, some of whom may require testosterone replacement to restore libido. At the same time, sexual self-expression is not a simple generic phenomenon that can be reduced to its hormone substrate.

Those who do decide to undergo anti-aging therapies will find many physicians ready to accommodate them. Some physicians are even willing to break the law to deliver these services to eager patients. As of February 2003, for example, cosmetic dermatologists were injecting patients with Restylane, a synthetic, collagen-like skin filler, in defiance of FDA regulations and federal law, and thereby "putting themselves at risk for malpractice suits, professional rebuke and, in extreme circumstances, revocation of their medical licenses[.]" The actual risk run by these providers of cosmetic treatments is relatively low. Patients in search of rejuvenation are unlikely to file malpractice suits, and condemnation from professional colleagues would require clear evidence of negligence, incompetence, or substandard care. Even the government agencies responsible for regulating medical procedures appear to be uninterested in disciplining this kind of medical lawbreaker.

Half a century ago, "outlaw" medicine—procedures that scandalized or discomfited the medical establishment—meant plain and simple quackery. The idea of medicating or injecting people into a "supernormal" state was an exotic fantasy rather than an imminent threat to a stable notion of what is normal for human beings. Today, however, outlaw medicine is better defined not as the fraudulent but as the experimental and controversial: the brave new world of fertility clinics, cosmetic surgeries, prenatal eugenics, and hormone clinics for all and sundry. In this sense, it is becoming increasingly difficult to distinguish between today's outlaw medical practices and the future of medicine itself, which already offers a growing number of therapeutic procedures to normal people. The future roles of testosterone drugs will evolve within the contest between this wide-open medical ethos and our traditional sense that a well-lived life follows a natural trajectory from birth to death and that aging is a fate, not a disease.

CHAPTER 4

"Outlaw" Biomedical Innovations

Hormone Therapy and Beyond

HORMONE THERAPY AND COSMETIC PROCEDURES: THE NEW MEDICAL ETHOS

The commercial promotion of various hormone therapies is only one symptom of a profound ethical disorientation within medicine that is gradually changing our sense of what medical science is and what it should be. This uncertainty about the norms that should regulate both medical research and clinical practice results in part from the recently achieved sequencing of the human genome and what this knowledge portends for our understanding of human biology and our ability to guide its evolution in the direction of enhanced health and human capacities. In a similar vein, the announcement in 1997 of the successful cloning of a sheep triggered a global controversy about the proper limits of genetic engineering and its permissible applications to the creation of human beings. There is a widespread sense that human wisdom is trailing well behind human ingenuity, as physicians, ethicists, politicians, and ordinary citizens grapple with questions about how society will deal with medicine's greater powers. In the foreseeable future, doctors will be able to predict and intervene in the disease process in unprecedented ways. The molecular fine-tuning of drugs will give our already problematic relationship to pharmacology a new urgency and intimacy. Medical technicians will be able to make fertile more of those who were once sterile, while surgeons and other specialists will be able to further alter minds and bodies in conformity with the wishes of people whose status as patients will include the power to command their own aesthetic transformations or to bring forth progeny Nature did not intend for them to have. The resulting disorientation can leave even sophisticated clinicians at a loss for words. Dr. Mark V. Sauer, a fertility specialist at Columbia-Presbyterian Medical Center in New York, put it as follows: "Sometimes I wonder: What have I done? You don't always know, from where you start, where you may end up."

Confusion about the proper limits of medical intervention is the result of two mutually reinforcing trends, one economic and the other cultural, that preceded the recent breakthroughs in genetic engineering. Many physicians who feel underpaid by health maintenance organizations (HMOs)—including ophthalmologists, dermatologists, dentists, and obstetrician-gynecologists—are supplementing their incomes by offering a variety of cosmetic procedures to their patients: laser eye surgery, Botox or Restylane injections for wrinkles, super-whitening techniques on teeth, liposuction for the aging or obese. This trend is profoundly changing the ethos of medicine by dissolving the traditional distinction between therapeutic procedures and physical enhancements that seem to be superficial repairs rather than corrections of deformities. The loss of this distinction between the healing and the aesthetic diminishes the ethical status of the physician by commercializing his or her motives, since cosmetic medicine cannot possess the ethical gravitas of a practice that strives to rescue patients from the loss of their faculties, or from suffering, or from death. Some of these physicians will end up colluding with the narcissistic or even delusional impulses of their patients simply because they want to be paid for services rendered. Even granting the therapeutic effects of some cosmetic surgeries, the fact remains that physicians who cater to patients' demands that are motivated by vanity or social fashion diminish the stature of practitioners by making them as much beauticians as healers.

Cosmetic medicine can also make doctors less available to patients who have more serious problems and less disposable income. According to one health care management consultant, "The result is a tiering effect, where the best doctors are doing the private stuff and doctors unable to succeed in those things will provide the public service care. We have created an incentive for everyone who can to get out of low-margin businesses, and that could have enormous policy implications."

The commercialization of medicine can also take on the trappings of unabashed merchandising. Physicians who sell nonprescription nutritional supplements, vitamins, anti-aging creams, and weight-reduction remedies right out of their offices, not to mention mops and magazine subscriptions, cease in effect to be doctors, because of the conflict between the welfare of the patient and their own financial ambition. "It creates a financial conflict of interest," says Dr. Donald E. Saunders, Jr., a professor of medicine and a bioethicist at the University of South Carolina, "and it wounds the trust bond between the physician and the patient. Doctors always have an unfair advantage in dealing with patients. Fundamental to medical ethics is to curb that power and work against our own interests if that's what it takes to put the patient first."

The erosion of such self-discipline is due in part to the soaring prestige of the entrepreneurial ethos and the triumph of the capitalist model in the post–cold war world. The public service model, which discourages financial ambition, is incompatible with entrepreneurial medicine and is thus in decline. The substitution of a medical market for the preentrepreneurial medical culture familiar to earlier generations makes many patients into empowered consumers whose personal wishes gain unprecedented influence within the doctor-patient relationship. Patients who, for example, are "educated" by the Web sites and direct-to-consumer advertising sponsored by pharmaceutical companies will demand drugs from their doctors with a new self-confidence. Fearful of losing their patients, many doctors will comply. The new breed of patient thus liberalizes the prescribing policies of many physicians and legitimizes forms of alternative therapies, such as herbal remedies, acupuncture, and the use of various supplements, that have forced their way into modern medicine by popular demand. A growing population of empowered patients beset by aging processes has created new markets by demanding rejuvenating treatments that further erode the distinction between therapy and enhancement, aging and disease, life itself and perpetual medication.

OFFSHORE ENTREPRENEURIAL MEDICINE: FROM EMBRYOS TO CLONING

The commercialization of medicine is most dramatically illustrated by the new reproductive services market. "The United States," Rebecca Mead has noted, "is the only country in the world in which the rules of the marketplace govern the trade in gametes and genes." Robert Jansen, an Australian fertility specialist, has described the American egg trade as "a thoroughly commercial activity" that no longer has anything to do with altruistic motives on the part of the donor. "Personally," he says, "I am frightened by it." An odor of eugenic ambition hangs over the entire enterprise, as competing agencies recruit the young, the beautiful, and the physically well endowed as egg donors. There are egg auctions that sell to the highest bidders, and there are clinics that sell embryos made for "adoption." "Is there something chilling about the idea of making embryos on speculation and selecting egg and sperm donors according to their looks, education and ethnicity?" one journalist asked in 1997. Her rhetorical question has an answer: at this point in history, most people will find this procedure discomfiting. What is more interesting is the widespread assumption that these inhibitions will eventually give way to a general acceptance of genetic engineering. As a *Nature* editorialist put it in 1996, UNESCO's International Bioethics Committee should be "examining scenarios in which 'improvements' to the genome that are currently regarded as out of bounds have become practicable and, to some, eminently desirable." Addressing the outcry against human cloning in December 2002, Robin Marantz Henig noted that "it's eerie how many of the arguments made today against cloning echo the arguments that were made against in-vitro fertilization," indicating that such arguments will also fail to stop the cloning of human beings. "At least some of this new century's most far-fetched techniques may eventually become so commonplace as to offer no apparent need for deliberation or debate."

The market for exotic reproductive services is not limited to the United States. Indeed, one of the medical consequences of globalization has been the emergence of transnational markets in drugs and fertility procedures that circumvent the restrictions enacted by lawmakers or medical associations—an "offshore" medicine that escapes one society's medical standards for the less restrictive mores of another. When, for example, doctors in London refused in 1993 to implant donated eggs into one wealthy woman on the grounds that she was too old for motherhood, she simply left England and had the procedure done at a private fertility clinic in Rome. Seven years later, an Italian couple confronted a storm of controversy provoked by their attempt to have their embryo implanted in the womb of a surrogate mother. They eventually decided to leave Italy, presumably for England or one of the seven states in the United States that permit surrogate motherhood. "There was so much negative pressure from the church, Catholic politicians and the medical establishment," said their doctor, Pasquale Bilotta, "they decided to go abroad."

When the Italian infertility specialist Severino Antinori announced in 1998 his plan to create the first human clone, he said he would weigh the possibility of leaving Italy for a country where he could conduct the first phase of animal research in a more congenial legal climate. A less credible would-be cloner, the maverick American physicist Richard Seed, achieved much notoriety the same year when he announced that he was going to clone himself, and that he had received invitations from two foreign countries to move his operation to their territory. That this eccentric amateur was taken seriously as a human embryologist only underlined the element of hysteria helping to feed the public debate. The grotesque flavor of Seed's exhibitionism, and the clear absence of any sane motive, seemed to cry out for a prohibition on this unwholesome practitioner, his abominable experiment, and any similar enterprises. Some observers, however, recalled the unintended consequences of other prohibitions. "Outlaw the exploration of human cloning," the historian of science Daniel Kevles wrote in 1997, "and it will surely go offshore, only to turn into bootleg science that will find its way back to our borders simply because people want it."

Another strategy is to head for the ethical vacuum of cyberspace or the legal immunity of the high seas. A transnational plan for providing nonprofit abortion services to women on a ship located in international waters off the coast of Malta provoked outrage in the island nation whose state religion is Roman Catholicism. Leading Maltese Catholic bishops called the plan a "monstrosity." "Such a move tries to defy the laws of the country and the values of the society being targeted," said a government spokesman. The irony, of course, is that a floating clinic in the year 2000 is a decidedly low-tech vehicle for the delivery of controversial medical services or substances. Ships can be boarded, searched, and confiscated, but regulating the Internet market for lifestyle drugs such as Viagra and testosterone is much more difficult.

The struggle between cutting-edge reproductive medicine and both social and medical tradition has been particularly intense in Italy, where advanced fertility specialists have been opposed by the Roman Catholic Church, conservative political groups, and the Italian Medical Association, whose 1995 code of ethics prohibits surrogate motherhood. As late as 1995 Italy was the only country in Europe that exercised no legal or administrative controls over more than one hundred private fertility clinics. Politicians who opposed Italy's new role as the Wild West of assisted reproduction charged that foreign women were coming to Italy for "pro-creative tourism." This unregulated environment was the unintended re-sult of a directive handed down by a Christian Democratic health min-ister in 1985, which advised public hospitals to allow fertilization procedures only if married couples provided the sperm and the egg. By 1992 there were 120 private clinics operating beyond the control of the Italian Register for Medically Assisted Procreation. As of June 2002 Italy still had no law governing artificial fertility.

While only a small number of people participate in these experiments, such exotic and expensive procedures have a disproportionate and charis-matic effect on public opinion that changes our sense of what can and should be done to human beings on medical grounds. Those who undergo such procedures are widely seen as the advance scouts of future genera-tions of patients for whom such benefits will be routine. In the meantime, modern societies are faced with difficult policy decisions as they attempt to balance the anticipated benefits of medical research against traditional ideas about the need to preserve human nature as we know it. Francis Fukuyama has emphasized the importance of a shared sense of what human nature is, since "much of our political world rests on the existence of a stable human 'essence' with which we are endowed by nature, or rather, on the fact that we believe such an essence exists." This belief is nothing less than "a safe harbor that allows us to connect, potentially, with all other human beings." Its other essential role is to "put limits on the kinds of self-modification that have hitherto been possible."

What are the prospects for regulating outlaw biomedical research and procedures that can be practiced in (or migrate to) just about any place on earth? To some extent the answer to this question depends on the technology that is a candidate for regulation. A hierarchy that orders such technologies according to their potential threats to human identity would rank human cloning and artificial reproduction toward the top of our scale of concern; hormone therapies would rank lower, because they do not affect the germ line or the nature of procreation. We may there-fore assume that the more threatening procedures will provoke more ur-gent calls for regulation than other therapies, and that has indeed been the case. Still, our culturally acquired inhibitions about innovative bio-medicine apply to all procedures, up and down the hierarchy, that seem to threaten our sense of what a human being is and should be.

Regulating biomedical research depends on establishing a consensus that specific limits on the manipulation of the human organism must be respected. This consensus must in turn be built on a durable system of values. But the public debate over human cloning that took place during 1997 offers a sobering look at how unstable and ultimately changeable these culturally acquired inhibitions can be. Press commentaries initially reported a general revulsion against cloning human beings. "Overwhelmingly," the *Boston Globe* reported in June of that year, "Americans say they are appalled by the idea of a human clone, a test-tube baby created by a single human cell without benefit of sexual reproduction and genetically a twin to the donor. For many, cloning is morally objectionable, personally reprehensible, and the sickest form of human narcissism." This general revulsion against the abuse of biotechnology was supposedly rooted in the instinctive ability of ordinary people to define and defend Nature itself.

The *Economist,* for example, assumed that "most people" objected to human cloning because of "a gut feeling that in the matter of bringing new people into the world it cannot be good to offend so egregiously against the natural order, especially when the point of doing so is still hard to see." A *New York Times* editorial assessed the public mood as follows: "The mere thought of cloning provokes a revulsion in many people who see it as arrogant tinkering with Mother Nature." None of these gauges of public opinion offered anything resembling survey data or hard evidence bearing on the public's mood. Journalists simply intuited in the general public a deeply rooted understanding of Mother Nature's plan. "How drastically," one reporter asked, "is the natural order being tweaked?" "I certainly understand a desire for progeny," said the prominent bioethicist Willard Gaylin after a sixty-three-year-old woman gave birth that year, "but I do feel we have a responsibility to the symmetry of life and to some of the rules of nature." "Human cloning means bypassing nature," said a representative of the Vatican's Pontifical Council for the Family a year later. Seldom had an ideal of Nature inspired such an ecumenical harmony of views.

In a passionate and carefully reasoned critique of human cloning, the social philosopher Leon Kass articulated a model that combined certainty about public opinion with certainty that the public's intuition of Nature's design is correct. Kass equates human cloning with human degradation: "To pollution and perversion, the fitting response can only be horror and revulsion; and conversely, generalized horror and revulsion are prima facie evidence of foulness and violation. The burden of moral argument must fall entirely on those who want to declare the widespread repugnances of mankind to be mere timidity or superstition." On the contrary, he asserts, such feelings constitute a bulwark against the blurring of "once-given natural boundaries . . . by techno-logical change." And he, too, invokes the wisdom of "the man or woman in the street."

While Kass is confident in the merits of his argument, he is not at all sure that it will prevail in a world "whose moral boundaries are seem-ingly up for grabs." Given his belief in the general public's intuitive sense of Nature's limits, the violators of moral boundaries are by definition the elites and opinion leaders who shape public discussion of medical issues. Kass is particularly hard on the field of bioethics, which has succumbed to "the accommodationist pattern of rubber-stamping all technical in-novation." He maintains that the moral laxity and utilitarianism of the bioethicists have contributed disproportionately to our ethical disorien-tation and have weakened our sense of natural law: "Today, one must even apologize for voicing opinions that twenty-five years ago were nearly universally regarded as the core of our culture's wisdom on these matters." Dismembering our sense of Nature, he argues, has dismem-bered our sense of ourselves.

The cloning debate of 1997 brought to the fore these fears about the endangered status of Nature and the limits it had designed. In March President Clinton warned against the temptation "to play God," im-posed a ban on federally funded human cloning research, and asked sci-entists with private funding to cease work on cloning until a national bioethics commission had reviewed the issue. "Each human life," he said, "is unique, born of a miracle that reaches beyond laboratory sci-ence. . . . Any discovery that touches upon human creation is not simply a matter of scientific inquiry. It is a matter of morality and spirituality as well." In retrospect, however, the president's religious rhetoric was more ornamental than principled. For the government's interest in promoting "laboratory science" had up to that point always exceeded its interest in regulating it.

Kass's invocation of "the deep ethical norms and intuitions of the human community" accorded well with ornamental presidential rheto-ric and the moral absolutism of the Vatican, but it did not resonate with all of his fellow intellectuals. Some commentators proved to be far more interested in the potential utility of cloning than in the idea of its funda-mental obscenity. "For now," wrote the historian of science Daniel J. Kevles, "cloning should rightly be confined to animals. But as the tech-nology evolves to invite human experimentation, it would be better to watch and regulate rather than prohibit."

The constitutional scholar Laurence H. Tribe rejected the sort of cultural conservatism that posits natural law as the fundamental principle of bioethics. His concern, he said, was that "the very decision to use the law to condemn, and then outlaw, patterns of human reproduction—especially by invoking vague notions of what is 'natural'—is at least as dangerous as the technologies such a decision might be used to control." A ban on cloning would cast unwarranted aspersions on other unorthodox reproductive practices that deserved legal protection. "To ban cloning as the technological apotheosis of what some see as culturally distressing trends may, in the end, lend credence to strikingly similar objections to surrogate motherhood or gay marriage and gay adoption." What is more, a ban on cloning would make cloned people into "a class of potential outcasts—people whose very existence society will have chosen to label as a misfortune and, in essence, to condemn." Finally, a ban on cloning would unacceptably stunt the growth of human knowledge, since "a society that bans acts of human creation for no better reason than that their particular form defies nature and tradition is a society that risks cutting itself off from vital experimentation, thus losing a significant part of its capacity to grow."

Tribe's rejection of a cloning ban is quintessentially secular and liberal. He opposes censorship that is based on moral judgments, he extends protection to people who are regarded as deviants, he endorses the defiance of "nature and tradition," and he insists on an uninterrupted accumulation of knowledge into the indefinite future. This is how the secular worldview responds to those who would put "the deep ethical norms and intuitions of the human community" above the progress of science. By the end of 1997 Lori Andrews, an expert on the legal aspects of reproduction, reported that the initial fears about cloning had given way to acceptance: "I absolutely think the tenor has changed. I see a total shift in the burden of proof to saying that unless you can prove there is actually going to be harm, then we should allow it."

Given that human cloning would threaten long-established ideas about family relationships and even our sense of human identity, it is reasonable to argue that society has a stake in the formulation of policy pertaining to the creation of such human beings. But which persons or institutions might be able to regulate this type of biotechnology? "The biotech revolution raises big moral issues that scream out for international governance," the social theorist Francis Fukuyama said as he imagined babies being designed offshore in the Cayman Islands for customers around the world. Since global regulation is nowhere in sight, however, what about national or even continental governance? The problem here is that globalization has made national regulations impractical or even obsolete. In Britain, human cloning is opposed by the Human Fertilisation and Embryology Authority, but it cannot prevent the migration of scientists to unregulated laboratories abroad. While the European Union enacted an ordinance in July 2000 to ban "processes that would change the genetic identity of human organisms," in the global context this is a local ordinance that may prove difficult to enforce even within the Union. Two months later, the European Parliament called on the British government to give up its increasingly positive attitude toward the cloning of human embryos. In December 2000, however, the British Parliament voted to liberalize the existing rules on embryo research, allowing stem cells to be removed from human embryos at a very early stage in their development. This vote was interpreted by opponents of human cloning as a step favoring the eventual application of this technique to human beings.

As *Nature* pointed out in March 1996: "When issues of international scientific and commercial competitiveness are at stake, national regulations on research and its implications may present only a flimsy barrier." As of 2002, for example, the Chinese government had made stem cell research a matter of national prestige. The acceptance of such research, which involves the destruction of tiny embryos, is facilitated by the routine abortions ordered by local officials and by the idea, shared by many Chinese, that the fetus does not have a soul. The government of Singapore is pursuing the same strategy, having designated medicine, pharmaceuticals, and biotechnology as one of four "industrial pillars" on which it will build a "knowledge economy." "By turning itself into a 'regulatory haven' for stem-cell research," the *Economist* noted, the government "hopes to attract disaffected scientists who feel their freedom to investigate is compromised elsewhere." Such a policy makes it clear that the race to the bottom that globalization theorists usually associate with corporations' demands for cheap labor can also take the form of demands for deregulated research environments.

Deregulation makes possible a medical market that, in the absence of controls, could turn into an entrepreneur-driven eugenics industry. Such an enterprise might even give rise to what the philosopher of science David Papineau has called "a class of genetically well-endowed self-cloners." "Human cloning isn't inevitable, but the possibility is likely," said Dr. Ezekiel Emanuel, a medical ethicist at Harvard Medical School, in January 1997. "So I will put my faith in Congress rather than turning a blind eye to the artificial-reproduction community, which doesn't have a stellar history of voluntary compliance, and which I trust even less." A year later, on February 12, 1998, the Senate defeated Republican legislation to ban human cloning, because of concerns that such a measure might inhibit scientific research. Senator Christopher S. Bond attributed the defeat of this bill to the influence of biotechnology and pharmaceutical companies. "The big drug companies and other special interests," he said, "want to reserve the right to make huge profits off of unethical procedures." By the end of 1997, only the state of California, not the U.S. Congress, had passed a law to make cloning illegal. (At that time, human cloning research had been banned in England, France, and Germany.) Two years later the *New Republic* commented: "We are much closer to cloning humans than most people realize, and our elected representatives have not even begun a serious debate on how to respond." In November 2002 a German observer warned that human cloning experiments were under way in "many Asian laboratories" and that ethical restraints were being dismantled around the world. "If a global ban on the cloning of human beings is not achieved as soon as possible," she wrote, "the manufacturers of human beings will have won. The global market will open the moment the first adorable baby is born."

Another government body that might regulate human cloning in the United States is the Food and Drug Administration (FDA). In January 1998, provoked by the publicity surrounding Richard Seed, the FDA announced that anyone planning to work on human cloning would require its permission to proceed. Dr. Michael Friedman, acting commissioner of food and drugs, warned that the agency was "prepared to move" against Seed or anyone else who undertook unauthorized research of this kind. In retrospect, it is clear that this official response was expressing what might be called the Frankenstein reflex—an instinctive but often transitory recoiling from biomedical experimentation that threatens ordinary people's sense of the natural order. "It's been a public and media assumption that there is nothing on the books that would even slow or stop Dr. Seed," observed a spokesman for the Biotechnology Industry Organization, and the FDA seemed to be acting on the premise that this regulatory vacuum needed to be filled. As anti-cloning bills flooded state legislatures, it was easy to believe that the American public was demanding the regulation of cloning research as a matter of principle. Yet the FDA's claim of jurisdiction was based not on principle but on practical reasons of safety. As the bioethicist Arthur L. Caplan pointed out, it was by no means clear "whether a regulatory body charged with insuring the safety of drugs and medical devices intended for commercial sale has the standing to say anything about human cloning." He added, "Even if the regulatory net of the F.D.A. is extended to human cloning, the way to debate the pros and cons and fine points of the subject is not through the filter of a bureaucracy whose mandate does not include metaphysics."

The regulation of cloning was again the focus of national debate in early 2003. A proposal to ban therapeutic cloning for medical research drew the opposition of the National Academy of Sciences and forty Nobel laureates. On February 27, 2003, a deeply divided U.S. House of Representatives voted to ban both types of human-cloning experiments. The majority clearly regarded therapeutic cloning as a slippery slope into nightmarish experiments on embryos. "These researchers are not crazed Dr. Frankensteins," protested Representative Rush D. Holt, a New Jersey Democrat. "They are people like your neighbors, highly ethical, who are working hard to relieve suffering, to improve quality of life. Let's not make them criminals." The Senate did not follow suit, and as of March 2003 the goal of a universal ban on the reproductive cloning of human beings remained unachieved. At the end of 2003, the United Nations was weighing how to deal with the issue of human cloning.

The cloning debate has demonstrated that there is still no authority or institution with the standing, or with sufficient motivation, to regulate the most controversial biomedical research of the era. "Where is Washington in all of this?" Rebecca L. Skloot asked in February 2003. "Since the advent of reproductive medicine more than 30 years ago, the federal government has had almost no role in overseeing the technology or guaranteeing its safety." The *New York Times* similarly noted in 1997, "The Federal Government, which could have controlled research through targeted funding, has steered clear of the field since the early 1970's, leaving researchers to grapple with the marketplace." In fact, letting the marketplace regulate biotechnology was a strategy the *Times* had once endorsed. A 1992 editorial noted approvingly, "Just a few years ago the rapidly advancing field of biotechnology aroused fears that scientists might inadvertently create monstrous life forms or unleash devastating new germs on an unprotected world. The nation has gained experience and the fears have largely subsided. Now, biotechnology is viewed as the next high-tech industry that can bring new energy to the economy, and the regulatory mood has rightly shifted from containment toward encouragement." Five years later the cloning of Dolly the sheep made the regulatory mood at the paper somewhat more cautious. "Like most technologies," read one editorial, "cloning is bound to have both virtues and vices. But before these advances get too far ahead of us, society will need to sort through what is acceptable and what is the nightmare beyond."

What this sensible recommendation omitted was any notion of how "society" was going to make these crucial distinctions and fateful decisions. This commentary also failed to point out that such judgments are made not by society as a whole but by experts and journalists and politicians, whose combined efforts produce a frame of mind that is often confused with "public opinion." But how are we to assess the collective opinions of a public whose only direct forms of self-expression about social issues are sporadic polling data and infrequent referenda?

Some contributors to the cloning debate solved this problem by taking very small (but presumably representative) samples of lay opinion. The social ethicist Jean Bethke Elshtain advised her readers to "listen to the radio call-in shows" and heed the words of ordinary folks. "Talk to the man and woman on the street and you hear murmurs and rumblings and dark portents of the 'end-of-times' and 'now we've gone too far.' The airwaves and the street win this one hands down," she says, and presumably at the expense of more sophisticated people whose instinctive feelings about cloning are less sound than those of the common man. Leon Kass, like Elshtain a professor at the University of Chicago, pointed to "opinion polls showing overwhelming opposition to cloning human beings," and he, too, invoked "the man or woman in the street" as witnesses against this abomination.

MEDICAL POPULISM AND OUTLAW MEDICINE:
FERTILITY TECHNIQUES AND MEDICAL MARIJUANA

But what does the public think about outlaw medical procedures? The fact is that public opinion is the silent protagonist of this drama: frequently invoked, infrequently consulted, and routinely taken for granted. In addition, public opinion is appealed to by those who favor controversial biomedical procedures as well as by those who oppose them; some of the most interesting anecdotal evidence concerns public opinion about infertility techniques in countries with large Catholic populations, such as Italy and Poland. "We have no law[,] which means that everything is imaginable," the president of the Italian Committee on Bioethics, Francesco D'Agostino, said in 1995. Yet the public response to this medical anarchy has not been alarm. "There is widespread acceptance of fertility assistance. The case of [the test-tube baby] Elisabetta, for instance, was viewed by the public as a great curiosity, not as a scandal. Public opinion did not say, 'No.' Most people said, 'Why not?' " This evidence of popular support for unorthodox fertility procedures left Italian politicians in a difficult position, caught between popular acceptance or even demand and the hostile attitude of the Catholic Church and its conservative allies. As D'Agostino pointed out, "Politicians are not sure what the public opinion is, and they have a fear of losing consensus." Fertility treatments are likely to be a particularly difficult target for politicians because people's feelings about mothers and their right to have babies are deeply rooted. Conversely, these sentiments work to the advantage of an entrepreneurial medical populist like Dr. Severino Antinori. "What I want to see," he says, "is a law that controls the centers, and not the wishes of the people."

Medical populism of this kind also appeared in Poland in 1995. A young, childless couple from a small farming village, both devout Catholics, journeyed to a fertility clinic in Warsaw that offered advanced in vitro fertilization techniques. When the woman discovered that she was pregnant with triplets, she was overjoyed: "I went to church to thank God for letting me have these children," she said. This innocent and effortless conflation of science and religion was not, however, the position of the church or the politicians it was counseling. State officials found the procedure that gave this woman her children to be in violation of a strict antiabortion law passed in 1993, and they announced plans to close the clinic. The couple's parish priest, who fully endorsed their unorthodox pregnancy, said that many of his parishioners found it hard to understand why the "medical miracle" that had blessed this couple with children was contrary to church teachings. "Maybe it is a problem for the authorities in Warsaw," he said, "but people here see it differently."

The conflict between regulatory authority and "the wishes of the people" is the hidden fault line in today's pharmacological landscape. Part of the problem is that what the people wish for cannot always come true, and these unmet needs can fuel a level of dissatisfaction that has political consequences. It is, after all, the prospect of "medical miracles" that prompts the most determined foes of regulation, such as the Competitive Enterprise Institute, to call for the abolition of the FDA and its alleged restrictions on the development of new wonder drugs. While it is doubtful that public opinion would endorse this sort of radical deregulation, we should also acknowledge that we really do not know much about what the public thinks about regulating useful (as opposed to merely recreational) drugs. Indeed, widespread support for the legalization of medical marijuana in California and Arizona suggests that the public can support therapeutic drug use even if this means legalizing a controversial substance like marijuana for medical purposes.

In November 1996, California voters, by a margin of 56 percent to 44 percent, passed Proposition 215, the Compassionate Use Act of 1996, which requires only a "doctor's recommendation" for marijuana use by patients with AIDS, cancer, glaucoma, "or any other illness for which marijuana provides relief." Voters in Arizona passed a similar measure, Proposition 200, by a margin of 65 to 35 percent. (By May 2000, half a dozen states and the District of Columbia had approved marijuana as a medicinal substance.) The results of these referenda created what the director of the National Institutes of Health, Dr. Harold Varmus, called "a public health dilemma" that had to be resolved. One solution he did not endorse was putting it up for a public vote. "I don't think anyone wants to settle issues like this by plebiscite," he commented, echoing the position of the Clinton administration. Three years later the medical director of the National Center on Addiction and Substance Abuse, Dr. Herbert D. Kleber, reiterated this argument shortly before the voters of Alaska were scheduled to decide whether to legalize marijuana for private use: "Marijuana for medicinal purposes should not be decided by referendum. Would you have had a referendum on penicillin for pneumonia? You don't decide these things by popular vote. You decide them by the science."

As a general proposition, the idea of practicing medicine by referendum is indeed absurd. But should the public have no role whatsoever in formulating policy regarding drugs? One difference between those physicians who favor and those who oppose the use of medical marijuana can be found in their responses to the idea of sharing the decision-making process with the general public—and their estimates of the public's intelligence and probity. The physician who distrusts the collective common sense of the lay public will be more disposed to fear the approval of marijuana as the first step on a slippery slope leading to a more drug-dependent society. The physician who trusts the public will be less inclined to fear a vast, latent appetite for mood-altering drugs that only strict regulation has managed to hold in check.

AIDS activists of the late 1980s and the 1990s succeeded in challenging the exclusive authority of the medical establishment to regulate the distribution of therapeutic drugs during a medical emergency. The idea that sound public health policy means choosing "science" over the "popular vote" proved to be mistaken, because public health by definition requires social science perspectives that medical scientists may overlook, as public policy regarding AIDS clearly demonstrated. Activism on behalf of medical marijuana has succeeded in bringing another, if less dramatic, emergency to public attention, though in this case the principal target has been federal regulators, since physicians appear to be deeply divided on the issue.

Opponents of medical marijuana have ignored the results of a medical referendum that demonstrated significant support for the medical use of marijuana. A survey of two thousand oncologists carried out by Harvard Medical School in 1991 showed that 44 percent of them had recommended marijuana to their cancer patients. In 1999 the Institute of Medicine, a branch of the National Academy of Sciences, summed up two years of research and interviews as follows: "Marijuana's active components are potentially effective in treating pain, nausea, the anorexia of AIDS wasting and other symptoms, and should be tested rigorously in clinical trials." This was not a simple case of science versus the will of an ignorant public. The clinical experiences of many physicians had already persuaded them of the drug's value, and their tacit professional endorsement may have found its way into lay thinking about how marijuana can reduce human suffering. "Doctors have long recognized marijuana's value in reducing pain and aiding in the treatment of cancer and AIDS, among other diseases," the New York Times editorialized in February 2003.

Opposition to referenda involving medical issues is rooted in the unrealistic assumption that medical science always speaks with a unified and authoritative voice that will prevail on the basis of its own verifiable merits. In fact, the results of clinical trials are rarely conclusive. Their value is especially uncertain when the clinical trial is supposed to measure subjective responses such as pain relief. As one prominent physician pointed out in regard to marijuana, the demand for "evidence of therapeutic efficacy" was inappropriate because it ignored medical reality: "The noxious sensations that patients experience are extremely difficult to quantify in controlled experiments. What really counts for a therapy with this kind of safety margin is whether a seriously ill patient feels relief as a result of the intervention, not whether a controlled trial 'proves' its efficacy." In this scenario, the authority of the patient outweighs that of the researcher.

The referenda endorsing "medical marijuana" alarmed federal authorities who were engaged in prosecuting the "war on drugs" on behalf of the American public. On December 30, 1996, the chief federal official on drug policy, General Barry R. McCaffrey, fired back at the medical marijuana movement. Accompanied by Attorney General Janet Reno, Secretary of Health and Human Services Donna Shalala, and an official from the Drug Enforcement Administration, McCaffrey threatened the doctors of California with the loss of their federally issued licenses to prescribe drugs if they recommended marijuana to their patients—a sanction that would effectively prevent them from practicing medicine. Lacking constitutional authority to amend the California criminal code, federal officials chose instead to intimidate physicians. In response, a group of doctors and patients filed a class-action lawsuit in federal district court in San Francisco, claiming that such interference in the doctor-patient relationship unlawfully violated the First Amendment. On July 17, 2000, U.S. District Judge Charles R. Breyer ruled that medical marijuana should be legally available to patients who could demonstrate that they needed it for medical purposes, such as the relief of AIDS-related wasting disease or for alleviating the nausea caused by chemotherapy in cancer patients. In September 2000, another federal judge in the Northern District of California, William Alsup, ruled that the government could not sanction doctors who recommended marijuana to their patients. In short, federal officials had failed to persuade either the lay public or the federal judiciary that the campaign against medical marijuana was in the public interest. Responding to the votes in California and Arizona, General McCaffrey argued that the public had been duped; that Proposition 215, the California referendum that had legalized medical marijuana in 1996, was "not a medical proposition"; that "compassionate use" legislation was, in effect, "a stalking horse for legalization" that would eventually harm society as a whole.

The public has been a spectator rather than an articulate partner in the debate over medical marijuana. Both supporters and opponents of "compassionate use" saw the public as benefiting from their respective campaigns. Federal officials saw the results of these plebiscites as threatening to bring about an even greater drug emergency than American society was already facing. Compassionate use activists, on the other hand, could point to the one-third of California voters who told pollsters "they personally knew someone who used marijuana for medical reasons." Small wonder that federal officials saw the specter of a new kind of populist pharmacology looming on the horizon, and their draconian approach to disciplining doctors seemed to reflect their sense of panic. It is also worth noting that prior to the California referendum, elected officials, such as Governor Gray Davis and Senator Dianne Feinstein, aligned themselves with Washington rather than with their own voters. A long tradition of societal disapproval of marijuana intimidated politicians and prevented them from riding this version of populist pharmacology to greater popularity.

The medical marijuana controversy intensified during the conservative administration of President George W. Bush. In January 2003 a federal jury in San Francisco convicted a medical marijuana activist, Ed Rosenthal, on three federal counts of cultivation and conspiracy. This prosecution marked the most serious of the clashes between federal authority and California law, which had continued in the courts. In 2001 the U.S. Supreme Court ruled that under federal law "medical necessity is not a defense to manufacturing and distributing marijuana." In July 2002 the California Supreme Court ruled that Proposition 215 accorded medical consumers of marijuana "limited immunity from prosecution" under state law. In October 2002 a federal appeals court in San Francisco ruled that the federal government could not revoke the licenses of doctors who recommended marijuana to their patients; in October 2003, the U.S. Supreme Court would let that ruling stand. Now, the same Judge Breyer who had ruled in favor of medical marijuana in July 2000 barred Rosenthal's defense lawyers from informing the jury that California state law had allowed the growing of marijuana for medicinal purposes since 1996. Once they realized that the defendant had been empowered by Oakland's medical marijuana ordinance to act as "an officer of the city," five of the jurors who had convicted him demanded a retrial. They were joined by the San Francisco district attorney and two members of the San Francisco Board of Supervisors. The *New York Times* declared that the five-year minimum sentence handed down by Judge Breyer "shows that the misguided federal war on medicinal marijuana has now escalated out of control."

The major public health question raised by the medical marijuana debate concerns the public's right to weigh in on the social status of a controversial drug. The repeal of Prohibition in 1933 is, of course, the great precedent in this regard. Propositions 215 and 200 represented more refined judgments, in that they aimed at serving a medically needy minority rather than a pleasure-seeking majority that wanted to regain access to a recreational drug. Yet here, too, federal officials looked on with some fear and trembling as the public delivered its unwelcome verdict in the form of referenda that had originated outside the political establishment. Sympathizing with the public in this contest of wills was Dr.

Jerome P. Kassirer, editor of the prestigious *New England Journal of Medicine.* "Whatever their reasons," he wrote in a signed editorial, "federal officials are out of step with the public. Dozens of states have passed laws that ease restrictions on the prescribing of marijuana by physicians, and polls consistently show that the public favors the use of marijuana for such purposes. Federal authorities should rescind their prohibition of the medical use of marijuana for seriously ill patients and allow physicians to decide which patients to treat." This position paper amounted to far more than a veteran physician's response to the horrors of "intractable nausea, vomiting, or pain." It was also a resounding endorsement of the public's intelligence at the expense of "the absolute power of bureaucrats whose decisions are based more on reflexive ideology and political correctness than on compassion." Kassirer also rejected the slippery slope argument that underpinned the government's case against this drug: "I believe that such a change in policy would have no adverse effects. The argument that it would be a signal to the young that 'marijuana is OK' is, I believe, specious."

That a prominent physician was acting as an intermediary between the people and their government pointed to the public's lack of engagement in this debate. Public opinion about drug policy expresses itself through periodic referenda and through the purchasing power exercised when it is legal to buy the drugs in question. The importance of the medical marijuana controversy was that it did something to redress the onesidedness of this relationship between the people and their representatives. "California's experiment with medical marijuana," Michael Pollan noted in 1997, "could well turn out to be a turning point in the drug war, if for no other reason than it is rapidly transforming what has long been a simplistic monologue about drugs—Just say no—into a complex conversation between the people and their Government." Given "the peculiar new landscape created by legalized medical marijuana," he observed, we are now "on a kind of frontier, a decidedly gray area where the old rules of engagement in the drug war have been suspended (sort of), but where the new rules are still being worked out, sometimes painfully."

The medical marijuana story interests us for three reasons. First, the legal twilight zone in which medical marijuana exists has been produced by the political ineptitude of the federal authorities who regulate controversial drugs. The government's threat to revoke the federal prescription licenses of doctors who recommended marijuana to their patients "inflamed public opinion" and then failed to survive the scrutiny of federal courts. The widening gap between federal policy and grassroots opinion portends similar policy crises in the future concerning other drugs, possibly including hormone replacement therapies. As of October 2000, the voters of California, Alaska, Washington, Oregon, Arizona, Maine, Hawaii, and the District of Columbia had passed referenda endorsing medical marijuana. Government attempts to restrict the drug's use succeeded only in provoking a backlash. The results of these and later referenda display a striking degree of pharmacological libertarianism in a population subjected for years to a relentless, federally sponsored war on drugs that has targeted marijuana as a socially dangerous substance.

Second, the medical marijuana issue presents us with an opportunity to see whether "a complex conversation between the people and their Government" about drugs is even possible. The government's position, after all, was that "the proper way to determine the safety and efficacy of any potential medicine is through the FDA's scientific review process—not through a public vote." Most significant conversations about pharmacological innovations occur between drug companies and the FDA or between doctors and patients who are bombarded by drug company advertising. Their huge advertising expenditures indicate that drug companies now view their "conversations" with medical consumers as at least as important as the sales pitches that are presented in print or in person to doctors. Campaigns on behalf of drugs that promise desirable alterations in mood epitomize this direct appeal to people for whom medical consultation may now seem irrelevant. "What is a symptom?" asks Peter D. Kramer in an essay on a drug—"Prozac in drag"—that is marketed to women as a remedy for the mood swings and irritability of premenstrual syndrome. "How bad must symptoms be to warrant medicating them and risking a drug's side effects? Who gets to decide, doctor or patient?" Today the balance of power in these decisions is shifting in the direction of patients, who are encouraged to make their own decisions about cosmetic medical procedures that may improve mood, appearance, or vitality. But this vibrant medical market does not involve any sort of conversation between the people and their government.

Third, the travails of medical marijuana are interesting because the emerging male hormone market is going through a similarly awkward transitional period. Here, too, federal authorities have threatened physicians who want to prescribe anabolic steroids, in this case to elderly patients who cannot be construed as recreational drug users. The common problem is that these small patient populations are dwarfed by the much larger populations of recreational users who alarm federal authorities. The key question in both cases, then, is whether therapeutic drugs should be denied to some patients because their medicinal use might encourage larger numbers of nonpatients to use them for what the government and most doctors would call nontherapeutic purposes. Federal prosecutors can make outlaws out of those physicians who are willing to risk sanctions because they believe these drugs will relieve suffering.

The social and medical status of anabolic steroids resembles that of marijuana in that the government has contested the therapeutic value of both substances and put doctors willing to prescribe them at legal risk. Commentators on both drugs have used the term *gray area* to describe their still-unresolved status as medicinal substances. As one legal observer has noted, court decisions have left "a gray area of uncertainty for physicians wishing to prescribe anabolic steroids for conditions of advanced age." Fifty years ago, as we have seen, male hormone therapy for the elderly was neither controversial nor legally hazardous for the physicians who endorsed it. "Certain steroid hormones," two physicians wrote in 1951, "are now recognized as therapeutic agents of established value in many geriatric conditions." Today, however, the question for the Department of Justice "is whether to prosecute physicians who knowingly prescribe steroids for viable, yet unapproved, treatments."

The stigmatizing of steroids over the past generation has made it difficult for physicians to use them for the legitimate purpose of combating wasting disease in both geriatric and AIDS patients. In 1993 the founder of Anabolics for AIDS said:

> With the failure of AZT, anabolic steroids may be the very best hope of extending and improving the quality of lives of HIV/AIDS patients, yet many doctors refuse to even consider the treatment. Anabolic steroids have been under a government-promoted cloud of suspicion for nearly a decade. The legislative reclassification of the drugs, federal prosecution of physicians who prescribe the medication and adverse publicity have combined to create an aura of fear that few physicians are willing to face.

Geriatric hormone therapy was similarly affected. "This threat of prosecution," one observer wrote in 1997, "has virtually eliminated all research and development as well as application of steroid treatments for aging conditions. . . . In the face of possible criminal prosecution, and with the prospect of losing defense insurance and indemnification, it may very well be a fool who administers steroids for anything that is not a recognized medical condition under the [Anabolic Steroids Control] Act."

HORMONE THERAPISTS AND HORMONE EVANGELISTS

The dramatic change in the legal status of anabolic steroids resulted directly from the drugs' abuse by bodybuilders and athletes, which became notorious during the 1980s. The transformation in the social status of anabolic steroids can be followed throughout this period in the pages of *JAMA*, where coverage of androgen abuse has focused primarily on athletes. It took time before steroid abuse came to be perceived to be a threat to society, however. What is more, the threat is seen to pertain only to certain social venues. Steroid use by professional football players, for example, has been tacitly accepted for decades, whereas steroid use by adolescents and Olympic athletes presents a threat to the ideal of drug-free living for the general population.

The increase in the social visibility of steroid abuse was gradual. An early survey of athletic doping published in 1972 treats steroid abuse as an afterthought to doping with more familiar stimulants such as amphetamines. A physician writes, "It has been stated that 80% of weight lifters, shotputters, discus throwers, and javelin throwers are using" steroids, but at this early date there is no sense of alarm. "Use of anabolic steroids is nearly universal among competitive body builders," other researchers reported five years later. But bodybuilding then was still a marginal subculture; it would not be absorbed into the American mainstream until the 1990s. By 1984 steroid use was said to be "extending down to the junior high school level," and there was a growing awareness of the black market operating within athletic circles, through mail order schemes, and in Mexico, where drugs could be purchased without a prescription. "It is apparent that androgenic anabolic steroid drug abuse has reached alarming proportions in noncompetitive athletes," three doctors in Chicago reported that year. "Every professional football player I know takes them," a U.S. Army steroid expert said in 1987, with the exception of quarterbacks and placekickers, who did not need brute strength.

The presumed use of steroids by these professional athletes has never caused a major doping scandal because sportswriters, with few exceptions, have chosen (or have been told) not to write about it. By 1988 the Council on Scientific Affairs of the American Medical Association had issued a report on the abuse of anabolic steroids and synthetic human growth hormone (HGH) by both athletes and the general population. Then, in September of that year, the Ben Johnson doping scandal at the 1988 Seoul Olympic Games inflicted on the anabolic steroid a global notoriety from which it is only slowly recovering. By that time medical observers of the steroid market were tracking the use of these drugs by both athletes and the much larger nonathletic population. Only days before the scandal erupted in Seoul, one study showed that 7 percent of American high school seniors had used steroids. The Anabolic Steroids Control Act of 1990 was passed by a U.S. Congress bent on deterring steroid abuse inside as well as outside the sports stadium. The American Medical Association protested the act's rescheduling of anabolic steroids, on the grounds that making unapproved medical use subject to criminal penalties would deprive patients of appropriate therapies. This argument failed to sway legislators, because the demonized image of the anabolic steroid now far outweighed its value as a therapeutic drug.

The emerging hormone replacement market for aging people has avoided this stigma. Hormones for aging nonathletes can be rationalized as therapeutic drugs, and doses are lower than those taken by many athletes and bodybuilders. This sort of hormone use appears legitimate, because it does not threaten the norms of sportsmanship or medical safety. Enhancing the "performances" of the aging or the elderly can, after all, be seen as a legitimate goal of geriatric medicine. But as large numbers of doctors migrate into what is now known as anti-aging medicine, hormone replacement is ripe for exploitation by practitioners whose ethical standards have been distorted by a marketing approach to medicine. These are the people who call aging a disease and declare that hormone therapy can turn back the physiological clock. Such entrepreneurial physicians exemplify the ethical disorientation of American medicine at a time when HMO reimbursement schemes are stampeding a large number of doctors into marketing tactics that would have been held in contempt not very long ago. The American Academy of Anti-Aging Medicine, founded in 1993 by a dozen doctors, recruited 4,300 new members within five years; as of February 2004, the Academy was claiming a membership of 11,500 doctors and scientists in sixty-five countries.

My own encounter with this style of anti-aging medicine came at a free "seminar" held on September 21, 2000, at a hospital in Austin, Texas. The speaker was a plastic surgeon—a well-turned-out, silver-haired fellow of about sixty-five, wearing a dark suit and a pleasant, shiny pinkish face that had cost him $17,000 to reconstruct. His own surgery, he told us, had been inspired by a challenge from a patient. If this procedure is good for me, he asked the doctor, then why haven't you had it done to yourself? To the usual repertory of surgical procedures, he and his colleagues had added human growth hormone replacement as an anti-aging technique. Their newspaper advertisement announced that they were carrying out an "FDA reviewed clinical protocol" on the rejuvenating effects of this drug.

We in his audience were a somber group of about a dozen people, including some who appeared to be likely candidates for face-lifts. Most of the presentation concerned various plastic surgery procedures, and these were mostly for women. There were plenty of before-and-after color photos projected on a screen, with lots of breasts and some full-frontal nudity. The speaker showed us before-and-after photos of his two twenty-something daughters and as much as told us that their plastic surgeries had turned their lives around. Before surgery they were unmarried, childless, and lacked college degrees. Following surgery, they had graduated from college, had married (one a doctor, the other an MBA), and were blessed with two and four children, respectively. Mr. Right had finally come into the life of another female patient, age thirty-four, following her surgery, and we were treated to a wedding photo.

This plastic surgeon told us that he had been injecting himself with growth hormone for five months. He was also taking the adrenal hormone DHEA and was applying testosterone topically, his goal being to get his hormone levels back to where they were when he was twenty. I asked about anticipated side effects. Occasional carpal tunnel syndrome, he said. People with cancer and some other conditions were excluded. Growth hormone therapy, he declared, was "at the forefront of medicine," even if he could not predict long-term side effects. His basic message was that cosmetic medicine is a path to personal success that all can take for a price.

One topic the speaker did not address was how the medical establishment deals with physicians who, like this plastic surgeon, inject themselves with growth hormone and get into trouble. The Massachusetts Medical Society, for example, "has intervened in several cases in which physicians have taken growth hormone to increase their sense of well-being and physical performance." Given the benefits of growth hormone reported by these physicians, it is only natural to ask why their actions would come to the attention of medical authorities in the first place. In fact, these self-medicating physicians rarely refer themselves for treatment as drug abusers. One doctor told me, "Usually the referral comes from peers or supervisors, e.g., department chiefs, who are concerned about aberrant behavior. The physicians in trouble usually do not see anything 'wrong' in what they are doing, expressing the belief that they are simply 'enhancing' their performance, allowing them to work longer hours with less fatigue." In other words, they talk just like professional cyclists who make it through their exhausting days on drugs.

This discrepancy between how self-injecting doctors feel and how their colleagues may see them points to the risks of an evangelizing medical style that has become increasingly visible as the hormone therapy market has expanded. These practitioners have attracted media coverage that offers the public sensationalistic accounts of hormone cures accompanied by fragments of the unresolved debate between the hormone promoters and their medical critics. A corollary of such hormone evangelism is a self-revelatory style that makes the physician a charismatic role model for patients who complain of chronic fatigue, listlessness, a fading libido, or depression.

One member of this avant-garde is Dr. Adrienne Denese, whose office is located on the fashionable Upper East Side of Manhattan. The *New York Times* reported: "A series of injections of human growth hormone, or hGH, at her clinic, she maintains, gives patients glowing skin, increased muscle mass, elevated sex drive, a lighter mood, sharper mental acuity and the whiz-bang metabolism of an 18-year-old." Such claims of comprehensive benefits for patients typify the proselytizing that may originate in the physician's own sense of having been rejuvenated by hormones. "My patients who used to take antidepressants don't take them anymore," she says. "They take hGH and it makes their mood lighter. Even I take it, and I'm more animated, I feel good and I don't take Prozac anymore." But why had she been taking Prozac? Was she clinically depressed or just looking for a mood swing? Her approach to hormone treatments suggests that this distinction has ceased to matter: the whole concept of medical therapy has become elastic enough to encompass a broad spectrum of disorders, all the way from psychiatric emergencies to episodic bad moods.

Another rejuvenation specialist is Dr. Alan P. Mintz, whose Cenegenics Anti-Aging Center has migrated from Las Vegas to Austin. "Our goal," he says, "is to bring the endocrine system back to where it was at age 30. I've been taking hGH for three and a half years, and I've never felt better or stronger." Back in New York is Dr. Bruce J. Nadler, a plastic surgeon and competitive body builder, whose office features "a picture of him clad only in a bikini-brief bathing suit, posing next to his silver BMW Z3 convertible." He and his wife inject themselves with growth hormone. "It made my body function in a much younger way," he says. "I'm one of the baby boomers. We're the generation that never wants to get old."

The hormone self-injectors who run clinics (and are willing to be pro-filed in the press) seem to have narcissistic needs that most physicians do not. It is safe to say that this penchant for self-display is incompatible with the professional self-restraint we associate with the physician's code of conduct. We should also recognize that the physician's urge to inject his or her own story into this medical narrative is a logical consequence of the idea that aging is a disease rather than a natural process. A nor-mal medical consultation involves a patient who suffers from a condition the physician does not share. The asymmetry of this relationship rein-forces the physician's self-shielding reserve and the authority this reserve is meant to protect. But the aging process is the "disease" that every physician shares with every patient, and thus doctor and patient can take the "cure" together if the physician is so inclined. Doctors who recruit patients into their own hormonal regime replace the asymmetrical rela-tionship with a more egalitarian approach that reveals their own "human needs" in an unconventional way. Such candor raises questions about the appropriate role of self-revelatory behavior on the part of the physician. It is, after all, the patient's needs that are supposed to be served by the consultation, not those of the doctor. For this reason, the patient may have good reason to wonder, either immediately or after-ward, about the motives that prompted the doctor to talk about him- or herself in the first place. To be sure, such camaraderie "democratizes" the doctor-patient relationship and may help to recruit patients. This arrangement is problematic, however. First, hormone therapy remains a medically riskier proposition than its evangelists make it out to be. Sec-ond, hormone evangelism encourages the patient to share the physician's anxieties or coping strategies for dealing with the aging process. Such an invitation from the physician to share his or her own narcissistic values is difficult to reconcile with a medical ethic that protects the well-being of patients.

While hormone evangelists are the most conspicuous advocates of testosterone therapy for aging men, there are also more cautious clini-cians who use testosterone to treat symptoms such as fatigue, low libido, and depression. One of these practitioners is Dr. Gerd Ludwig, a pro-fessor of urology and director of the Frankfurt-Hoechst Municipal Clinic in Germany. Dr. Ludwig does not believe that a male climacteric exists or that the aging process is a disease, and for that reason he believes that only a minority of aging men should be treated with testosterone. He does not know how to determine the "normal" testosterone level for men older than fifty, and he is careful to enumerate the possible side effects of male hormone therapy: heart attacks, liver damage, blood clots, and, especially, prostate cancer. But he feels these are calculable risks worth taking, since some men with low testosterone levels experience "a dramatic improvement in their sense of well-being"—a clinical judgment that has accompanied the use of testosterone over the past sixty years. He estimates that about 30 percent of men older than sixty have testosterone levels that cause problems, and that only 5 percent of older men actually require hormone replacement therapy. He is also aware that public demand for testosterone will not wait for the results of long-range clinical trials, and that some doctors will accommodate patients who want hormones. "We urologists make a point of not making false promises to our patients," he said in September 2000. "Whether all other physicians behave that responsibly, I cannot say."

So who among the hormone therapists is practicing outlaw medicine? The answer to this question depends, of course, on how one defines unethical behavior by physicians. Still, certain behaviors would seem to be clearly unacceptable. For example, some offshore physicians on the Internet are paid only if they prescribe the drug being promoted by their employer. The result is likely to be a financially coerced diagnosis whose real purpose is to justify the prescription. Physicians who prescribe hormones as a form of cosmetic pharmacology occupy a more ambiguous position, because the significance of a cosmetic procedure is not always clear. Indeed, the word *cosmetic* itself can mean either "superficial" or "reparative." Surgeries on faces or breasts that rescue people from chronic misery are cosmetic in name only. Less urgent surgeries intended to enhance appearance may serve the medically sanctioned purpose of promoting a patient's well-being. The legitimacy of the procedure will depend in part on the informed consent of a patient—who may be unduly influenced by pressure from the physician. The larger problem, however, is that patient well-being is a highly elastic concept that can be invoked to justify any therapy once the physician has determined that it will be served. For example, if well-being is equated with slowing down the aging process, then any anti-aging therapy, including hormone replacement, can be defined as legitimate medicine. The legitimizing of well-being as a medical goal invites the use of testosterone or human growth hormone in many patients.

Indeed, it was an expanding definition of well-being for aging people that opened up the male hormone market during the 1990s. This cosmetic pharmacology is impossible to regulate, because every cosmetic procedure is potentially a reparative procedure. Monitoring the elusive distinctions between (mere) "enhancements" and (more profoundly) beneficial "therapies" is simply beyond the capacity of medical societies or the federal government. A permissive therapeutic ethos and the impossibility of surveillance combine to create a medical landscape in which ethical disorientation becomes less the exception than the norm. As Dr. Ludwig puts it, how other physicians dispense hormones is beyond his control and, by implication, beyond the control of the medical societies that are supposed to regulate the conduct of their members.

A different and more humane sort of outlaw physician risks federal sanctions by prescribing testosterone drugs to seriously ill or debilitated patients who may be expected to benefit from androgen therapy, including the elderly and those suffering from AIDS-related wasting disease. This sort of medical practice prescribes genuinely therapeutic procedures that preserve or restore function rather than serve narcissistic ambitions. But while this does not appear to be entrepreneurial medicine, it too can also have unintended effects on the larger society. Take, for example,

> the practice by some doctors with large AIDS practices in the urban centers of prescribing testosterone and anabolic steroids for patients who are not wasting or have no other symptoms associated with low testosterone. These doctors believe that the steroids can be used as a preventive or prophylaxis for people with AIDS, including those who may be quite healthy and whose BIA [bioelectric impedance analysis] tests and other indicators of wasting are normal; they believe that building up the body acts in this case as a sort of insurance against wasting, should it ever occur.

The social side effect of prophylactic androgen therapy is that it promotes the use of androgens in HIV-negative gay men, who often admire the steroid-boosted physiques of their HIV-positive friends. The physician who prescribes androgens for a prophylactic purpose thus faces the same dilemma confronted by the physician who prescribes medical marijuana, since use of the drug to relieve suffering may promote more permissive attitudes toward the use of the drug by much larger numbers of people. Those who favor a law-and-order approach to recreational drug use are likely to see the "compassionate" prescribing of androgens as a form of outlaw medicine comparable to recommending marijuana for pain relief.

The hormone therapy market exemplifies the ethical perplexity of modern medicine in both its conceptual and practical dimensions. The conceptual confusion derives, as we have seen, from the ease with which the ideas of therapy and well-being can be stretched to fit the requirements of any medical imagination. The practical issues pertain to the enforcement of professional standards of ethics that change in response to factors that may be quite independent of the research findings reported in the medical literature. When, for example, does entrepreneurial medicine become the exploitation of one's patients? When has a physician allowed a pharmaceutical company to set the therapeutic agenda? What can medical regulators do when the very concept of therapy is stretched to the breaking point to accommodate the requirements of cosmetic medicine? While these problems are occasionally discussed in medical journals, they have by now proliferated far beyond the control of the medical establishment and federal regulators.

The entrepreneurial hormone market thus embodies the vexing uncertainties about the meaning and legitimacy of therapeutic ambitions that serve a demanding and expanding clientele. At the present it is impossible to predict the eventual outcome of this contest between medication and regulation, even if the clear trend is toward an expanding use of male hormone drugs. One way to forecast developments in the area of hormone replacement is to look for an analogous subculture that models the emerging hormone market. Ideally, we should be able to study human behavior within this subculture over many years. The prime example of such a medical subculture is the hormone-doping community that has existed within the world of high-performance sport for the past thirty years. Here are all the essential protagonists: ambitious patients, accommodating physicians, beleaguered regulators, and a vast public whose feelings about the non-medical use of hormones are increasingly ambivalent. Here, in short, is a global experiment in libertarian pharmacology that has flourished even in the face of a long-standing campaign to put it out of business. To this day, the ultimate fate of the anti-doping effort itself remains uncertain.

Over the past century, sports medicine has evolved alongside general medicine as a kind of parallel medical universe in which unsanctioned experimentation has become a common and often shadowy practice. The gradual convergence of cosmetic medicine and elite sports medicine grants ordinary people the physiological status and medical prerogatives of athletes for whom various forms of "replacement" therapy have become routine. The sports world and its drug culture can thus be seen as a social laboratory that can offer insights into the larger male hormone market, which will continue to expand as the definitions of therapy evolve. In the next chapters of this book, I argue that the parallel universe of athletic doping tells us much of what we need to know about the role of hormone therapy in the lives of those who will come after us.

CHAPTER 5

Hormone Therapy for Athletes

Doping as Social Transgression

Athletic doping is comparable in important ways to the use of drugs in the larger society. This chapter and those that follow show how examining the doping subculture in sport can illuminate the larger pharmacological landscape in which ordinary people use drugs. How realistic, for example, are campaigns to produce "drug-free" athletes and citizens? A review of doping before the age of steroids shows how nostalgic fantasies about drug-free athletes falsify history and mislead those who would rid sport (or society) of illicit drug use. The idea that the sports world was pure and honorable before anabolic steroids spread across the world remains an influential misconception. In fact, a long series of attempts to boost athletic performance with various drugs, ultraviolet rays, oxygen tents, and other devices has been under way since the 1890s. Sports officials whose rhetoric and policies might benefit from some historical perspective seem to be unaware that any of these interventions ever happened. A better grasp of the nature of athletic ambition and its inevitable consequences in modern societies that worship "performance" would help these officials to address doping issues in a more informed and realistic manner. Such a perspective would acknowledge the extreme physiological demands of the competitions they stage and the need for intense medical surveillance of certain athletic competitions whose physical requirements invite doping by athletes.

High-performance sports medicine also presents an opportunity to examine the implications of "client-centered" relationships (or alliances) between patients and physicians. This chapter shows how athlete-doctor relationships have anticipated the increasing client demand for restorative or enhancing medical services among ordinary people, who often expect hormone therapy to improve or extend their lives. This trend raises basic questions about the purpose of medical treatment. For example, should physicians treat ordinary patients like athletes, whose first priority may be performance rather than health? Conversely, should physicians treat athletes like ordinary people or clients whose special needs may include hormone treatments? "Sports is simply one segment of society and athletes should not have an exemption to use drugs," a prominent sports physician once said. But many other physicians have disagreed with this view, which may not take into consideration the medical needs of the older athlete who is entitled to be treated as a patient. As one steroid expert has put it: "Should you penalize an aging athlete who needs replacement dosages because he competes? Shouldn't we just give them enough to return them to a normal level?" Such cases demonstrate that recreational as well as elite sport creates medical dilemmas for an aging (and, one hopes, exercising) population.

The chapter on public responses to athletic doping explores how modern people think about the potentially controversial uses of drugs. An examination of public opinion and behavior vis-à-vis sports doping incidents shows that "the public" does not always reject the use of controversial drugs for certain purposes. For this reason, authorities who issue urgent and categorical proclamations against "drugs" will do little to convince an audience that has learned to be more discriminating about using and judging pharmacological products. The tacit acceptance of drugs by certain athletic communities can be compared to similar attitudes that appear within other large groups of drug users outside the sports subculture. Even a hallowed social institution like Major League Baseball may refuse to prohibit a controversial drug despite the prevailing condemnation of drugs. What is more, Major League Baseball's refusal to ban the anabolic steroid androstenedione appears to have caused little public reaction, even as sports commentators and legislators become increasingly vocal in their disapproval. As one drug-testing expert commented in 2000, "Either the public hasn't figured out what's going on or it doesn't care that so many athletes are on performance-enhancing drugs." But knowing what the public does care about is essential to effective policy making. Understanding how most people feel about drug use is important, because disrespected laws may discredit the rule of law itself. For example, that segment of the sporting public that accepts athletic doping as a form of pain relief has its counterpart in the voters who approve of medical marijuana despite the hostility of the U.S. government to its "compassionate use" for this purpose. Similarly, pressure to dope to boost athletic performance has its counterpart in the pressure to enhance sexual or professional performance.

Chapter 7 compares the two "wars" on drugs that have been waged on behalf of creating drug-free athletes and citizens. Until very recently, sports officials around the world wrestled ineffectually, and often dishonestly, with the problem of how performance-enhancing drugs should be regulated. The Olympic anti-doping campaign and the War on Drugs initiated by President Richard Nixon both began in 1968, and these deeply flawed initiatives have resembled and sometimes influenced each other ever since. While the two anti-drug crusades differ in certain ways, both have been presented as important, and even essential, projects in public hygiene, medical as well as moral. Both take for granted the importance of role-modeling effects in dissuading children and others from using drugs. Both have relied heavily on moralizing rhetoric to prevent cheating or a slide into drug-induced degeneracy. The crucial difference between these campaigns is that they target different forms of excess. While the anti-doping campaign is supposed to aim at producing drug-free performances that stay within natural limits, the so-called war on drugs aims at producing better social and workplace performances by encouraging sobriety. The anti-doping campaign in sport can thus be seen as a kind of popular referendum on enhancements: Given the choice, does the public prefer to watch drug-free athletes or winning athletes? The war on drugs, in turn, is a kind of popular referendum on intoxicants: Given the choice, does the public prefer to retain or surrender its access to various kinds of inebriating experiences? The crucial similarity that links these crusades is an emphasis on self-control that is portrayed as serving a larger community.

The anti-doping campaign in sport has long been subverted from within by its simultaneous demands for higher performance and self-restraint. This internal contradiction between achievement and sportsmanship is the engine of the doping problem that even the most recent reforms are unlikely to halt. The unacknowledged secret of the anti-doping campaign is that the inevitable demands for higher performance create new forms of "legitimate" doping, even as officially sponsored doping controls are strictly enforced. In the war on drugs, the fundamental objective of increasing productivity is itself unacknowledged, hidden behind moralizing rhetoric. Moreover, the campaign refuses to recognize that the selective indignation that condemns some substances while tolerating various other forms of lifestyle doping will not dissuade people from using drugs. In each case, the demand for higher performance determines the outcome of the regulatory process. In the sports world, the outcome is persistent and innovative doping practices that may be accompanied by drug-testing procedures. In the larger society, the outcome is a continuing crusade against those drugs that symbolize diminished productivity and personal degeneration, and that appear to threaten the work ethic, while lifestyle drugs that are intended to enhance the various performances of an aging population are celebrated and allowed to establish themselves in the pharmacological marketplace.

In the last analysis, the problems arise in regulating controversial drugs because of the belief that people are entitled to use pharmacological substances that can improve their lives. Why, one might ask, should people renounce the use of such drugs at all? The anti-doping campaign and the war on drugs can be understood as mutually reinforcing attempts to persuade modern people that drugs are both corrupting and unnecessary to lead a good life. Yet it was not always so. The widespread acceptance of the idea that doping is a kind of perversion is relatively recent. Indeed, it was the testosterone derivatives known as anabolic steroids that transformed modern feelings about the doping of elite athletes. Doping as we know it is therefore a cultural construct whose origins we need to understand in order to comprehend our own disapproval of it.

DOPING BEFORE STEROIDS: CLEAN AMATEURS AND DOPED PROFESSIONALS

Objections to performance-enhancing drugs have long been couched in language traditionally reserved for narcotics and the depravity that was assumed to accompany drug addiction. "A drug addict," the *Lancet* commented in 1937, "suggests to many a vicious and rather disgusting person who, however wretched his condition may be, has brought it upon his own head." The conflation of athletic cheating and self-destructive moral depravity has been a permanent feature of the age of doping. Condemnations of doping during the past century have typically relied on a combination of ethical and medical arguments—drugs are both unfair and medically dangerous—that was inherently unstable, because it implied that doping drugs violated both norms. This definition introduced instability into the definition of doping in two ways. First, a performance-enhancing drug without harmful side effects would meet the criteria for medical safety and should therefore escape censure; similarly, an agreement among competing athletes to use the same drug would appear to make its use fair. In fact, uncertainty about the immorality of performance-enhancing drugs was evident during the 1950s, as we shall soon see. The controversy of the late 1950s regarding athletes' use of amphetamines thus served as a precursor to the doping controversies that would eventually engulf Olympic sport. In 1958, for example, it was reported that one of the "shallowly sensational" clichés making the rounds about amphetamines was an implicit indictment of the elite milers of this era: "They definitely do stimulate—the four-minute mile would not have been possible without them."

The 1950s were in some ways an age of innocence that had not yet encountered the consequences of effective performance-enhancing drugs. The doping practices of the professional cyclists who competed in France were often ignored in the early British discussions of doping, because those competitors belonged to a different social world. A cultural apartheid separated drug-free amateurs from professional athletes, whose right to use drugs was taken for granted. Revelations about amateur athletes' use of amphetamines therefore provoked real consternation. Well-informed people understood that a significant number of professional athletes, both human and equine, were using drugs to boost their performances, but they also assumed that professional athletes enjoyed a tacit exemption from the ethical standards that applied to amateurs. How distinct these worlds were is evident from the utter silence in the Anglo-American controversy about the behavior of amateur runners regarding the long-established doping practices of European professional cyclists.

These separate worlds of "clean" amateurs and "dirty" professionals also presented different levels of medical hazard to the two types of athletes, and it was the professionals who were safer. Indeed, the world did not turn its attention to doped cyclists until the death of the Danish amateur Knud Enemark Jensen at the 1960 Rome Olympic Games. Before the 100-kilometer team road race, the Danish trainer had given Jensen and three others a stimulant called roniacol to promote the circulation of their blood—an experiment that ended tragically when Jensen collapsed as (according to his handlers) a result of "heat stroke." As an American sportswriter pointed out at the time, "Deaths are rare, and occur mostly in amateur races. Professionals are experienced in such matters and use drugs only within prescribed limits." The coach of the French cycling team in Rome confirmed the sharp divide between the athletes: "Many pros are drugged, of course, but we don't drug amateurs."

The irony of such drug deaths was that amateurs were supposed to be immune to the financial pressures that caused professionals to dope themselves. It became disturbingly clear that some athletes—perhaps many athletes—even in the absence of financial incentives might use drugs to satisfy other kinds of ambitions. Drug use by Olympic athletes posed a threat to the distinction between moral amateurs and amoral professionals that was then still culturally significant. We should also note that doping was associated with medical harm, an assumption that was important because it reinforced the ideal of self-restraint. For an honorable amateur like Roger Bannister, the rejection of drugs originated in a refusal to despoil the glory of sport by violating ethical standards that were seen as a part of the amateur tradition. The idea that doping was medically dangerous contained its own kind of moral admonition, as if Nature were bent on punishing those who sought to violate the limits that had been imposed upon the human body.

We know surprisingly little about how amateur athletes thought about drugs in the 1950s. In 1955 the British sports physician Adolphe Abrahams reported "a persistent belief among athletes that there must be something [drugs or medicine] that would create energy or postpone fatigue," and his point was that they would have had no objection to taking it. Abrahams himself emphasized medical caution and consistently refused to adopt a moralistic position on athletes' use of drugs. The stimulants that concerned him as a physician were "those drugs which by inhibiting or paralysing the protective mechanisms that normally guard against over-exhaustion could contribute to a greater physical output." He was not the first to argue that such drugs were potentially dangerous to those who took them, and he was confident that "no reputable practitioner in this country" would encourage their use.

At this point, however, Abrahams reverses field and asks his readers to consider, "for the sake of argument," a scenario featuring a drug "capable of conferring enhanced athletic efficiency" that posed no medical hazard whatsoever and that was "universally available," thereby eliminating the problem of limited access for a favored few. "What objection could be raised against its use?" he asks. "Only that—to use the question-begging term—it would be unsporting to enable athletes to surpass records achieved by the giants of the past, who lacked that advantage. I do not think the conscience of the sporting world would or need be disturbed." Here in 1953 is the first occasion on which Abrahams opens the door to the legitimate use of performance-enhancing drugs by athletes.

Two years later he emphasized the uselessness of drugs in sport and the power of the placebo effect, once again condemning any "drugs that could stimulate the body to exertion beyond its normal limits of fatigue." Here was another contribution to the public discussion of amphetamine use by athletes. "Should Athletes Take 'Pep' Drugs?" appeared in the *Sunday Times* of June 16, 1957, and reiterated Abrahams's basic themes, including the warning against narcotics that "remove the inhibitions that ensure self-preservation" and the idea that any power that drugs possessed was due to the power of suggestion. Here, too, he argued that distinguishing between the legitimate and illegitimate medication of athletes was anything but a straightforward exercise. It is not easy, he noted, "to draw the line where legitimate stimulation ends and reprehensible 'doping' begins; the distinction is largely a matter of opinion and conscience. Was it, for example, 'unsporting' to use oxygen in ascending Everest? . . . Are we to refrain from 'drugs' that sharpen the appetite, improve the digestion and so contribute to physical well-being?" The widespread contention that "drugs" were "unsporting" presented the thoughtful observer with what he called "a debatable situation." Such open skepticism toward the ethic of sportsmanship must have disturbed many of his readers. Abrahams turned again to the example of oxygen a year later in a lecture to the Society for the Study of Addiction: "If it were practicable to construct a tunnel with oxygen-enriched atmosphere in which runners competed, record performances would be accomplished. But would this be approved? If amphetamine and cortisone can directly release another reserve of energy, are they not to be accepted as contributing to normal physiological well-being?" Once again, he had chosen to open the Pandora's box that lurks in any honest discussion of human enhancements— the problem of defining normal human functioning and the intolerable deviations from this norm.

As one British commentator put it in 1953, society was now confronting the question "Where would sporting competition end?" in a world of drug-enhanced athletics. "Either sporting competitions would be between bio-chemists of the future, or they would go down by involving all competitors in a problem of personal honour versus chemical enterprise." At the same time, we must keep in mind that this discussion was occurring at an early phase of the modern doping debate.

British sports officials were intent on banning drugs whose objectionable nature they could not yet define. Britain's most prominent sports physician (Abrahams) was telling his audiences that doping was "largely a matter of opinion and of conscience." His own objections to drugs were that they were ineffective and potentially dangerous, not that they constituted an offense against the amateur ethos. (At the time, no one knew whether drugs really could stimulate athletes.) Indeed, Abrahams's evident interest in the oxygen priming of athletes was a clear challenge to the amateur ethic of self-restraint.

As amateurs gradually acquired professional-style ambitions to perform at the highest levels, a deeper divide separated those who saw athletic performance as a suitable area for scientific interventions and those who did not. One scientifically curious trainer who was active during the 1950s was the Australian swimming coach Forbes Carlile. Eventually elected to his sport's international Hall of Fame, Carlile became a tireless campaigner during the 1990s against elite swimmers' use of drugs and high-tech bodysuits. In the 1950s, however, his attitude toward performance-enhancing techniques had been far more accommodating. When swimmers took aspirin before competitions to improve their performances, he had no reason to object. To his own athletes he recommended Fizzy Phosphates (potassium biphosphate). "In the 1950s," he told me half a century later, "I became interested in the use of hypnosis to aid performance—but after a time abandoned it as too time-consuming and possibly ineffective with champion athletes." Although he does not believe that Australian athletes were using amphetamines, that is not the point. The crucial factor, as he observes, was the guilt-free mentality of those who were trying to reach and exceed human limits: "This was a different, and in most parts of the world, an innocent era when anti-doping laws had not been thought of." It simply did not occur to him that the use of performance aids might be unethical. When the *New York Times* called an Australian Olympic swimmer named Judy Joy Davies in the midst of the amphetamine controversy of 1957, she cheerfully replied: "Some of our champion swimmers fearlessly admit they take pep pills to help them shatter records." Here, in all of its exuberant naïveté, is the romantic doctrine of athletic heroism before the discovery that doping was sin. The uncertainty over whether this young woman's "pep pills" were actually amphetamines is, once again, essentially irrelevant. What counts is a mind-set of entitlement: athletes and their handlers feel that they are allowed to push back the limits of human performance however they can, since there are no ethical norms to say they should not do so.

We still do not know how many of the elite athletes of this era felt entitled to pursue higher performance by any means possible. The Canadian runner Bruce Kidd recalls what a fellow Olympian told him about Vladimir Kuts, the great Soviet runner who won gold medals in both the 5,000- and 10,000-meter races at the 1956 Melbourne Olympic Games. "What I most remember is someone—I think it was actually Gordon Pirie—telling me that Kuts was doped in the 1956 Olympics, and that he noticed an arm lined with needle marks when they stood on the podium." Five years later Pirie commented publicly on doping among runners: "Sudden staggering performances quite out of keeping with known form can only be explained by the use of drugs."

In 1954 a Soviet team doctor had admitted to an American counter-part that Soviet weightlifters were boosting their performances with testosterone. And two years before that, at the 1952 Oslo Olympic Games, "there were reports of used hypodermic needles and empty am-pules found in the locker rooms." Reports then emanating from Europe make it clear that an underground pharmacology of high-performance sport had already taken root.

A striking characteristic of that era was the general absence of mor-alizing about drug use by elite athletes. Even traditional athletes who cat-egorically refused to take drugs could be curiously nonjudgmental about performance-enhancing techniques. Russell Mockridge, a great Aus-tralian amateur cyclist and a deeply religious man who had once studied to be a priest, refused to condemn his peers on ethical grounds. "If I could not win a race without artificial stimulation, I would retire from cycling tomorrow," he wrote. Yet he also emphasized that the peril to his doping colleagues was medical rather than moral. Taking a drug might simply be practical—an argument that favored doping, since descending a mountain at 60 miles per hour without first taking a stimulant could cost a rider his life. Stimulants should be "used wisely," he observed, since "examinations by the doctor will have taken place . . . and the trainer will have found just what sort of stimulant will most benefit the rider." Medically supervised doping made good sense to this former sem-inarian. What he deplored was the "bomb" and its "hideous" ingredi-ents—"amphetamine and its derivatives, and caffeine, digitalis, corti-sone, hormones, intravenous camphor, picritoxin, leptazol and many others." In short, drugs were dangerous because they corrupted the body, not the soul.

Mockridge also pointed out that the professional riders who used stimulants under medical supervision were not so different from certain other consumers: "Recent reports of university students in France and America who used benzedrine (amphetamine) type drugs during examination time told of these stimulants being available to anyone who cared to call at the local chemist's shop." Another observer of this double standard was a president of the American College of Sports Medicine, Albert Salisbury Hyman. In 1960 he noted that while educators continued to single out the athlete as a drug-free role model, most American college students had simply come to accept the use of drugs to boost both intellectual and athletic achievement. This physician pointed to

> the more or less paradoxical attitude of many educators; whereas stimulating drugs like caffeine and amphetamine are accepted by common usage as permissible in cramming for intellectual examination and mental competition, these same substances have not found similar acceptability in athletic competition. The undergraduate does not readily recognize such subtle distinctions; the concept on the campus is that what is accepted for his mental development is equally acceptable for his physical development.

Medically supervised doping was already a part of professional cycling by the 1950s. "Certainly, if approached scientifically," Mockridge wrote, "with the aid of doctors specializing in their use, and administered by faithful trainers, the strong stimulant can be used, and is used, by leading European champions, several times a year." The anti-drug champion took note of this sports medical subculture with a matter-of-factness that grew out of his intimate knowledge of the stress and pain endured by the riders who took drugs. Situated between the needs of his fellow riders and the indifference of the larger society that took their suffering for granted, Mockridge seems to have viewed this type of medical relationship as a sensible arrangement that protected the riders from self-inflicted medical harm. Such tolerance was not, however, socially acceptable outside the cycling subculture. The Danish doctor accused of recommending the stimulant that apparently killed Knud Enemark Jensen denied any role in the affair. It was Jensen's trainer who admitted that he, like many other professional trainers, had served as the medical proxy who actually gave his rider the stimulant. Today the role of medical expertise in the maintenance of elite athletes, as we shall soon see, continues to raise questions about the ethical legitimacy of performance-enhancing sports medicine.

Most fundamentally, the discussion of amphetamines in the 1950s revealed deep splits between amateurs and professionals, purists and experimentalists, moralists and pragmatists that were dividing a sports world already confronting the dilemmas of pharmacological performance enhancement. An instructive episode from this era occurred in 1950 at a board meeting of the Danish Sports Association (Danmarks Idræts-Forbund, or DIF), where the sports physician Ove Bøje charged that a Dr. Mathiesen had administered unspecified "hormone pills" to Danish rowers at a competition in Milan. This statement unleashed a bitter debate whose basic themes have recurred in every major doping controversy over the past fifty years.

While Dr. Mathiesen admitted that he had given these pills to the athletes, he denounced Bøje's comment as "a low blow. I am myself an opponent of doping, but the minor treatment I prescribed for the rowers is not doping, it does not involve an artificial stimulant, but is rather a supplement that restores natural requirements." This was by no means the first attempt to distinguish between nutrients and stimulants as performance-enabling and performance-enhancing substances. It is, however, the earliest report concerning the alleged hormone doping of athletes I have ever seen—so early that Mathiesen could call a hormone supplement for athletes an innocuous medication without giving the matter a second thought. An official of the Danish Athletics Association invoked the specter of original sin, declaring: "A serpent has slithered its way into Paradise, and it is called doping." The chairman of the DIF's medical committee argued that the rowers had not been doped, because the doses they took were too small to make a difference. The chairman of the Danish Rowing Association denounced Bøje for making public charges that amounted to "a malicious attack on Danish rowing." The chairman of the DIF warned that passing an anti-doping resolution would only confirm suspicions that a DIF doctor had done something improper. Out of this heated debate spilled all of the modern doping themes: doping as evil, doping as a matter of milligrams rather than motives, doping as a threat to national honor, doping as a public relations problem. But for the journalist who covered the debate, one aspect of this meeting stood out—"It felt like being at a medical conference." The slithering serpent was dressed up as a doctor.

THE ENTREPRENEURIAL PHYSICIAN

The physician who seeks to enhance the performances of elite athletes with drugs stands at a threshold between two medical worlds. On one side is the healing art that aims to restore and maintain health, a project that includes a respect for the limits of human anatomy and physiology. On the other side lies a realm of experimentation, a medical and ethical gray zone in which athletes and their doctors repeatedly cross the lines between what is legal and what is illegal, between what is medically ethical and what is not. This ethically ambiguous medical style makes the high-performance sports physician an interesting precursor of the entrepreneurial physicians who advertise their techniques for enhancing human capacities.

The entrepreneurial physician who administers hormones as rejuvenation therapy resembles, as we have seen, a type of healer who once provoked controversy. The purveyors of glandular remedies during the 1920s and 1930s—manufacturing Gold Medal Brand Sexual Pills, Sex-Co Restorative Tablets, and Master Hormones, among other products—served the sexual distress market that still drives so much of the hormone and supplement business today. The important difference between these quacks and their modern counterparts is that the latter use real hormones that have physiological effects on patients. From this standpoint quacks are uninteresting, because they cannot tempt or threaten us with the prospect of real biomedical innovations; they cannot lure us into new relationships to our bodies or our minds. But these two generations of entrepreneurs also display significant similarities. Both claim to offer cutting-edge therapies, both rely heavily on placebo effects, and both share a disdain for the peer-reviewed science that stigmatizes their methods as dubious or fraudulent. So, too, did the more ambitious high-performance sports physicians, long before entrepreneurial hormone therapists came to public attention during the 1990s.

There are sports physicians who now cater to both elite and recreational athletes wishing to enhance their performances. Providing hormones for this reason violates American law and anti-doping statutes, but these rules do not deter the widespread use of hormones for what the law calls nonmedical purposes. The *American Journal of Sports Medicine* acknowledged in 1990 that "many physicians collaborate in steroid abuse through the inappropriate supplying of steroid prescriptions to athletes." The pro-doping lobby within the ranks of physicians is international in scope. "I am well aware that some of our physicians are prescribing doping substances," the German anti-doping official Hans Evers commented in 1995. Indeed, the doping subculture in Germany was so entrenched that some athletes were avoiding those Olympic training centers where they could not get drugs. Yet the roles that physicians have played in the doping subculture have never gotten the attention they deserve. Let us begin by looking at the relationship between high-performance sports medicine and medical ethics.

MEDICAL ETHICS

A declaration concerning the ethical principles that should regulate sports medicine was passed in October 1981 at the thirty-fourth general assembly of the World Medical Association in Lisbon. This document includes the following statement of principle: "The physician must oppose all methods which are not in accord with medical ethics or which have injurious consequences for the athlete who uses them; this applies, in particular, to procedures which alter the composition of the blood or biochemical processes." More specifically, the declaration prohibits "the use of medications or other substances, irrespective of their type or the manner in which they are introduced into the body, including stimulants or sedatives that affect the central nervous system, or procedures that alter the reflexes in an artificial manner." Also prohibited are techniques that reduce pain or other self-protective reflexes, "induced alterations of the will or of the general mental state," and "artificial altering of age- or sex-related characteristics." This was a utopian document that appears even more naïve today than it did twenty years ago. Apart from the belated work of the World Anti-Doping Agency (which began operating only in 2000; see chapter 7) and of a small number of European state prosecutors, every current trend within the world of high-performance sport contradicts the spirit and purpose of this declaration. In 1984 the German Sports Physicians Association issued a similar statement of principle: "Every type of prohibited performance enhancement in sport," it declared, is to be condemned. If future developments present the danger of a "crossing of the boundary" from therapy into the realm of doping, then an expert commission should intervene. That the boundary had already been crossed seems to have escaped the attention of those who formulated this document. At a time when some physicians regarded steroids as ineffective, it was still possible to imagine that the most urgent problems for medical ethics lay many years in the future.

By the 1980s better-informed sports physicians understood that the urgent ethical issues were already demanding attention, though their responses often differed. One fundamental problem facing the sports physician was that the limits to certain kinds of athletic performances appeared to have been reached. In 1986, for example, the chief physician for the West German summer Olympic team, the controversial Joseph Keul, stated that within a few years record-setting performances would be virtually impossible. In 1984 the president of the World Federation of Sports Physicians, the West German scientist Wildor Hollmann, had stated: "We have reached the maximum; the athletes have entered the biological border zone." A year later this prominent physician declared that high-performance sport had passed these biological limits, thereby forcing sports physicians into an ethical dilemma. He warned, "Sports medicine must seriously consider whether it is going to collaborate with or oppose this development." His own view was that sports medicine was obligated to refuse to aid the development of superathletes. "We cannot serve as the repair shop for the victims of performance mania," he argued. "We have much more socially relevant obligations to the physically active population."

This rhetorical response to the ethical crisis of sports medicine continued during the 1980s. In an age of commercialized Olympic sport, Hollmann said in 1985, the physician "adapts to pressures that have very little to do with health, ethics and morality in the classical sense." "I said eleven years ago," he declared in 1989, "that the time would come when we would have to say good-bye to sport and its traditional values. In some sports that time has come." He even proposed the creation of a "fifth category" of athletic event, a "sports show that has nothing to do with traditional definitions of sport"—in effect, a freak show that would provide an outlet for athletes determined to take drugs.

This pessimistic view, and his belief in the sports physician's obligation to the physically active population, did not prompt this medical man to become a conscientious objector to high-performance sports medicine. Hollmann justified his decision to persevere in four different ways. First, he said, some sports were not as severely affected by doping as others, so the physician could still work with elite athletes who did not use drugs. A second argument was that the physician was a watchdog: "Sports medicine takes the pulse of high-performance sport. Our assignment is to look at the professional issues in the widest context and call questionable developments by their proper names." A third and more interesting claim was that the physician's basic obligation to his athlete-patients made conscientious objection untenable. "The question arises as to whether we physicians can continue to be a part of this," Hollmann observed in 1985. His answer was that withdrawal from the high-performance sports scene was "wholly incompatible with our professional code. As physicians, we are obligated to give help to anyone who requests it." But what did *help* mean in this context? Was it conventional healing, or was it performance enhancement? Was it even possible to distinguish between aiding recovery and enhancing performance? Hollmann apparently thought not, pointing out that ethical objections to steroid use "do not change the fact that it is clearly possible to improve recovery in specific situations that occur only at the limits of human ability." Finally, Hollmann suggested that high-performance sport and the will to set records expressed a dynamism that was part of being human. "The drive toward performance is inherent in man," he said, and it was the nobility of this elemental force that made doping more a tragedy than a crime, as primal ambition clashed with fated limits. Thus, in the last analysis, Germany's foremost anti-doping moralist could not bring himself to close the door on performance-boosting sports medical procedures.

The West German sports physician Heinz Liesen, a onetime medical advisor to the national soccer team and a consultant to many other elite athletes, displayed no such conflicts. Over the past twenty years Liesen has consistently taken a libertarian and performance-oriented position, arguing that anti-doping activism is an irrational response to the physiological experiences of elite athletes. "Elite sport," he said in 1988, "has now reached the limits of human performance where extreme physiological events occur. The body of a high-performance athlete is no longer comparable to the body of a normal person." The appropriate response to such extreme physiological events is to repair their injurious effects. "Anabolic steroids can be used for the therapeutic purpose of restoring fitness. It is easy to do it in such a way that it doesn't show up in a drug test. But I'm not allowed to." In addition to promulgating this doctrine of therapeutic realism, Liesen has repeatedly dismissed ethical concerns about high-performance sports medicine. "We are, indeed, moral theologians when it comes to sport," he commented acerbically in 1985, and his position has not changed over the intervening years. "I regard it as better to leave the dishonest doping discussion behind and worry instead about the health of the athlete," he declared in 1999. "There are many people who talk about doping and don't have a clue."

Such libertarian attitudes toward the use of hormonal drugs have been opposed by most sports physicians and officials who speak publicly about doping. "It is well known that there are doctors who participate in doping," one German Olympic official said in 1986. "Their technique is to hide behind the cloak of a physician's obligation to preserve confidentiality." "Anyone who, like Mr. Liesen, administers hundreds of injections on the basis of unproven theories violates medical ethics," scolded the prominent West German sports physician Herbert Reindell in 1987. "Such behavior is irresponsible. It is at the very least an attempt to affect performance in a way that is not permitted." A year later Manfred Steinbach, an important West German sports official, accused Liesen of promoting "a doping mentality" that contradicted the spirit, if not the letter, of the anti-doping regulations. This conflict between the hormone replacement advocate and his critics was not as straightforward as it appeared to be, however. A couple of years later, as a high official of the West German Track and Field Federation, Steinbach participated in the recruitment of East German coaches with doping experience. "I want to drink deeply out of the East German bottle," he said in 1990, as news about doping poured out of the former GDR, and he was as good as his word. Such lack of scruples on the part of some powerful officials is an important aspect of the "dishonest doping discussion" of which Liesen complained some years later. Many sports officials who have publicly signed on to the anti-doping crusade have demonstrated similar hypocrisy, which can include a lack of interest in vetting the physicians who tend to elite athletes. The contest between regulation and deregulation of steroids thus occurs on two levels. The public debate features the beleaguered medical renegade, locked in verbal combat with his more numerous critics who loudly subscribe to the sports world's war on drugs. The real subversion of the anti-doping campaign occurs out of public view and takes the form of quiet cover-ups, bureaucratic foot-dragging, and "educational" campaigns directed at athletes who do not take such moralizing propaganda seriously. On the contrary, many ambitious athletes are more likely to seek the counsel of a physician whose attitude toward drugs and performance is strictly practical.

THE DOCTOR-ATHLETE RELATIONSHIP

One of the most interesting aspects of hormone doping as a form of social behavior is the tacit consensus it creates in members of athletic subcultures who want to take hormones to enhance performance. That this tacit agreement violates official codes of conduct and certain laws is seen as a practical rather than as an ethical obstacle—an attitude that sustains recreational drug subcultures, as well. This consensus—the mutual solidarity of the dopers and their medical counselors—is consistently ignored by journalists and sports officials, who prefer to see doping as a result of individual weakness. The widespread refusal to think about the deeper implications of doping-by-consensus has enabled sports officials to define doping as an individual transgression rather than as a collective project resulting inevitably from an insistence on ever higher levels of performance, which is the inherent logic of high-performance sport. The social and economic interests that benefit from doping thus escape the kind of scrutiny that is focused on the athletes who are caught using drugs.

One aspect of doping-by-consensus is the doctor-client relationship that unites athletes with those physicians who regard anti-doping regulations as a violation of the athlete's right to privacy and of his or her opportunity to achieve maximum performance. Such private compacts between doctors and athlete-clients, hidden from the prying eyes of the Food and Drug Administration and other authorities who would regulate hormone consumption, differ in no essential way from similar relationships between nonathletic patients seeking hormones and the doctors who are willing to write the prescriptions for them. (Major League Baseball still rejects serious steroid testing on privacy grounds.) An examination of such doctor-athlete collaborations can therefore provide us with insights into the motives behind and some possible consequences of unregulated hormone replacement therapy in the general society.

Official strictures against doping, like most condemnations of drug abuse, present the wrongdoing as a failure of citizenship. By using drugs, the athlete is seen as betraying both "clean" opponents and the larger society that has an interest in honest competitions. The hormone-prescribing sports physician who discards such idealistic notions about sport and its traditional values effectively abolishes this ethically regulated community by regarding each athlete as a patient who has an absolute right to privacy and to the treatment of his or her choice. The controversial West German sports physician Armin Klümper, for example, spoke of "the private domain of the individual athlete" whose right to treatment must be fiercely defended against meddling sports officials. "Everything that helps is permitted," he said in 1984, and over time this viewpoint has only gained ground among elite athletes and the medical personnel who support them. "As a physician," Heinz Liesen said in 1999, "the only thing that concerns me is the health of the athlete and nothing else." By treating the athlete as a patient who possesses an absolute right to treatment, the physician effectively removes him or her from the community of athletes that anti-doping rules are supposed to serve. Because this athletic community is widely seen to represent the larger national community, politicians have little choice but to endorse anti-doping rules to promote personal virtue and public health.

"The limits of human performance must be respected and they may not be violated," the German interior minister, Wolfgang Schäuble, declared in 1989. During the 1970s, however, Schäuble's sportive nationalism had prompted him to adopt a more accommodating attitude toward anabolic steroids for West German athletes (see below). But by the end of the 1980s, following the Ben Johnson scandal at the 1988 Seoul Olympic Games, the stigma attached to these drugs made it impossible for any politician to call for medically supervised steroid use. How long political support for this strict anti-doping position will last remains an open question, but we can assume that erosion of the political consensus against doping would only increase the influence of the libertarian sports physicians who became prominent during the 1980s and 1990s. It is worth noting that ambitious and controversial German sports physicians such as Heinz Liesen, Joseph Keul, Armin Klümper, and Hans-Wilhelm Müller-Wohlfarth retained their important official positions in (West) German sport even as the anti-doping campaign intensified in Germany. That their careers flourished during the endless German doping crises of the 1990s points to the profound ambivalence toward performance-enhancing techniques that pervades modern societies that regard international athletic success as a significant aspect of their national identity.

However charismatic many athletes may have found some of these physicians, it is important to keep in mind that medically supervised hormone doping results from a collaboration between a cooperative physician and an athlete-patient who wants to use the drugs. There is a crucial difference between the East German physicians who gave male hormones to children and the physicians who write hormone prescriptions for the older athletes who seek them out. While the first group practiced a form of criminal medicine, the second practices a form of medicine that would be legal were it used to address problems of aging, not to enhance the performance of young athletes. But apart from physicians' obligations to the law, what are their obligations to the athlete-patients who share their libertarian attitude toward the use of hormones? The anti-doping campaigns of the past decade have paid little attention to how elite athletes actually feel about drugs. As in any other group of ambitious people, there are diverse opinions. Individual temperaments and the specific demands of the athletic disciplines in question do much to determine whether athletes accept or reject pharmacological performance enhancement. Because the social stigma attached to doping makes open discussion about drugs among athletes almost impossible, the general public has no real way of knowing what they are thinking; athletes have been unable to explain why so many of them feel that using drugs is acceptable. In fact, many years of doping crises had to pass before elite athletes began to accept drug testing as a necessary evil—a change of heart that professional cyclists, among others, have not embraced. At the 1964 Tokyo Olympic Games, four years before Olympic drug testing was introduced, many athletes refused to cooperate with the IOC Medical Commission when it attempted to do some spot-checks for drugs. A doctor in Mississippi was surprised to hear in 1984 from a pair of steroid-consuming athletes that "they really did not consider themselves to be taking a drug." Nor is this kind of libertarian attitude toward hormone consumption by athletes particularly unusual. A 1985 study of anabolic steroid use by female athletes, for example, reported that the participants justified their use of these drugs on the grounds that "it was within their individual rights to use anabolic steroids if they wished"—a view of drug use that many people outside the sports world would share.

The problem, of course, is that many athletes are public figures, and as such they are routinely denied the medical autonomy of private patients. The tension between a growing societal acceptance of hormone replacement for ordinary people and the continuing campaign against hormones in the sports world is the deeper doping crisis sports officials do not seem—or cannot afford—to acknowledge. In this sense, athletes who are caught using hormones are disciplined for acting out a medical scenario that is becoming increasingly common among nonathletes. It appears that on one level a doping penalty is a form of scapegoating inflicted by a society that feels deeply ambivalent about performance-enhancing drugs. The more aggressive high-performance sports physicians resent this double standard, blaming it on the ignorance and hypocrisy of medical colleagues who should know better than to cave in to alarmist views about steroids.

High-performance sports physicians serve clients who, like so many modern consumers of alternative medicine, want fast results they can feel. As Heinz Liesen once put it: "It is my duty to help athletes with long seasons and a short recovery period to achieve their best performances." This drive for an efficient sports medicine effectively excludes the ethical concerns that anti-doping initiatives are supposed to represent. "If what is being done is allowed, then it's OK," as one biathlete said in 1988. The elite athlete's urgent need to feel well legitimates anything that works, perhaps even the much-castigated methods of the East German sports medical establishment. Before the East German state collapsed, some West German athletes envied East German athletes their medical care. One of them, Sabine Evers, mused in 1989: "The doped East German athletes were better taken care of than we are. If I can assume their doctors are not totally unscrupulous, then they are much better protected from doping than we are, since here everything happens in a gray zone." Another West German track-and-field athlete threatened to end his career unless he were given access to East German doping secrets. This demand for enhancement by any means necessary reaches far beyond the world of sport. The enormous market for alternative medicine and for the vast array of over-the-counter "supplements" bears eloquent testimony to the expanding medical ambitions of our era. So here, too, the athlete who tests the limits of what is permitted acts out a drama of medical salvation that has become increasingly common in the general population. The difference is that the athlete's medical ambitions are regulated on behalf of a social consensus about drugs—even as the public is becoming less and less sympathetic to regulating the therapeutic hormone use of the ordinary citizen.

The ultimate strategy of hormone-prescribing sports physicians is to legitimate their practices by establishing hormone replacement as a therapeutic norm. Why, they ask, should athlete-clients not have the same right to hormone therapy as anyone else? Such a question necessarily challenges the fundamental ideas represented by the official anti-doping consensus. A well-known exponent of this heretical position was the late Dr. Robert Kerr, a California physician who talked openly about administering steroids to several thousand athletes, bodybuilders, and policemen during the 1970s and 1980s. As a practitioner of his own brand of libertarian pharmacology before the enactment of the Anabolic Steroids Control Act of 1990, Kerr left behind a frequently cited manifesto that attempts to normalize pharmacological enhancement and to define athletic doping as sound medical practice.

"I think you will agree," the doctor wrote in 1982, "that if the 'alteration from normal' is neither a true hazard for the patient, or others, and if the patient derives a certain amount of happiness or satisfaction from it, then perhaps it isn't so bad after all." This sentence contains three principles that challenge traditional medical ethics and the ethos of current anti-doping doctrine: (1) the alteration of human physiology for non-therapeutic purposes is permissible, (2) any medically harmless procedure is permissible, and (3) personal satisfaction legitimates medical treatment. Twenty years later, a society that has demonstrated a prodigious appetite for mood and memory and energy enhancers would be hard put to disagree with these three propositions. Moreover, Kerr specifically addresses the use of performance-enhancing drugs by athletes:

> To my way of thinking "doping" is a term for the use of medicinal agents that will cause the athlete to act or think in a highly abnormal manner. A drug that energizes the athlete by causing him to feel "high" or hyperactive, or to perform in an abnormal way before and during an athletic event, is not proper. A "natural high" should suffice, but something that causes the sensorium to function in an abnormal manner should not be used.

Here the doctor shows his solidarity with the society that is waging a war on drugs by opposing psychoactive substances that impair athletic performance and that are disdained by virtually all of the athletes he knows. The tone of this steroid manifesto—unlike that of the prickly Liesen—is calm, patient, and deliberately reasonable. At times the author gives the impression of being a simple naïf for whom social conventions do not exist. Yet a careful examination of Kerr's proposals reveals an agenda that cannily anticipated the enormous demand for performance-enhancing lifestyle drugs that we have witnessed in recent years. The results he saw in his thousands of patients were more than enough to persuade the doctor that steroids were humane drugs. "Body building," he declares, "has taken literally thousands of short, small and shy men out of their doldrums, and produced a new generation of well-built men with a sound sense of pride and self-confidence." Here, at last, was the male hormone therapy for the masses of which Paul de Kruif had dreamed back in 1945.

The obstacle to mainstreaming steroids was the medical consensus that warned of dangers to the liver, the heart, and the reproductive system. Kerr reported that he rarely saw side effects, and that he had never seen a side effect he could not treat by adjusting the dosage. The real problem, he believed, was one of image and public relations: "Anabolic steroids will never be viewed by the public and athletic officials as anything but a hazard to the athlete's health until the drugs are strictly controlled by physicians. Only with adequate, safe controls can the anabolic steroids be viewed in the same light as antibiotics, anti-asthmatics, and other medications used in daily life." Medical supervision would remove the stigma from doping by making androgens safe. The next step would be the introduction of androgenic drugs into the everyday lives of ordinary people.

High-performance sports physicians and other steroid advocates have long maintained that the medical hazards of testosterone and its derivatives remain uncertain. As one Swedish coach commented in 1984: "They have been used, and sometimes abused, by 20 million people since 1960, and I am wondering: Where is the damage?" This skepticism is shared by a significant number of physicians. In 1987, for example, the president of the American Academy of Sports Physicians told a *New York Times* reporter, "I think it [the anabolic steroid] is a vastly abused substance. It obviously isn't terribly lethal, but it does have the side effects and it does probably cause significant health hazards to some people who take it." Such half-hearted condemnations do not make for compelling anti-doping arguments. They reveal instead the ambivalence toward performance-enhancing drugs that many doctors share. As the reporter commented, "Some physicians see no profound objections to the use of drugs that improve performance if they are prescribed and used in a responsible fashion." In other words, the medically supervised doping once advocated by the notorious Dr. Kerr had become acceptable to some of his medical colleagues.

The idea of safe, low-dosage steroid doping also harmonizes with the "lesser harm" argument that a number of sports physicians have propounded over the past two decades. "Athletes are going to take anabolic steroids," Robert Kerr said in 1983. "But the vast majority of athletes in this country are not taking drugs under anyone's supervision." An essential role of the physician, from this perspective, is to protect the athlete from his or her own self-destructive urges to overtrain or overdose— to commit suicide, as some West German doctors once put it. In the absence of strict and genuinely effective doping controls, Dr. Wilfried Kindermann argued in 1988, "anabolic steroids must be removed from the list of banned substances. If steroids were legalized, then at least we physicians would have an opportunity to talk with the athletes about responsible doses." Accommodating the doping practices of one's athlete-clients is not quite the same thing as promoting them, but one result of this collaboration is to certify the medical acceptability of drugs that have earned the physician's seal of approval.

Why do so many physicians fail to exhibit anti-steroid militancy? We should keep in mind that from the time of their introduction around 1940, testosterone drugs were described by medical authors as essentially benign, until athletic doping made the anabolic steroids notorious during the 1980s. It was well known that androgens could masculinize women, and that they might promote the growth of prostate cancers in men, but these side effects did not cause physicians to stigmatize the drugs. Anti-doping campaigners constructing an ethical argument have always put far more stress on the dangers of steroids than has the medical literature. The assessment of two scientists in 1980 is typical: "It is true that pharmacologic administration of testosterone esters to normal men results in little in the way of side effects of any kind." The one side effect of note was a decrease in the production of sperm that might eventually provide contraceptive opportunities for men. Whereas androgens did pose health threats to women, there was "no real contraindication to their administration to men."

Indeed, published assessments of testosterone-based male contraceptives have consistently emphasized the relative safety of these drugs. A World Health Organization study reported in 1990 that weekly injections of testosterone enanthate had maintained "safe, stable, effective, and reversible contraception for at least 12 months." Nor was this result surprising, since the "overall safety of testosterone enanthate administration ha[d] already been well established during decades of widespread clinical use." The caveat was that "long-term theoretical hazards from the use of androgens," including possible prostate and cardiovascular disease, remained uncertain. Six years later the long-term safety issue regarding men with normal testosterone levels remained unresolved: "The safety of androgens, used as long-term physiological replacement therapy in hypogonadal men over the last 40 years, has been well documented. However, there is a dearth of systematic information on the use of androgenic steroids in eugonadal [i.e., normal] men, especially after more prolonged (over 12 months) exposure." Unencumbered by the moral campaign against drug use by athletes, contraceptive researchers could focus on the task of producing a "balanced assessment of the risks and benefits of androgen-based contraceptive regimens." They did not feel obligated to cast these drugs in a doping drama or to expound on the social responsibilities of the people who might use them.

The uncertainty about side effects has encouraged speculation about what constitutes safe doses for athletes who want to use androgens. The Olympic champion speed skater Erhard Keller, a dentist who holds a degree in sports medicine, proposed to regulate doses on the grounds that drug use by athletes is simply inevitable. "The doping problem will not be eliminated," he said in 1989. "For that reason I am calling for the legalization of anabolic steroids within certain limits. Doses of up to 20 milligrams a day, such as are used after surgical operations, are not harmful." In a similar vein, the former West German shot-putter Ralf Reichenbach called steroids "medically defensible" under a doctor's supervision. "I've been taking steroids for years and I feel fine," he said. In March 1998 Reichenbach dropped dead. A year and a half later, the Olympic champion Florence Griffith Joyner died suddenly for unknown reasons while on an airplane. For almost two decades, the 100-meter and 200-meter records she set in 1988 have not even been approached by the world's fastest women. But neither these deaths nor rumors about doping-related death lists could persuade most elite athletes that steroids were truly hazardous drugs. This uncertainty about the risks and benefits of testosterone-based drugs has played a major role in sustaining the appeal of the anabolic steroids among athletes, bodybuilders, and those seeking rejuvenation or aphrodisiac effects.

The concept of substitution therapy has enabled entrepreneurial physicians both inside and outside the sports world to legitimate hormone replacement procedures. The steroid expert James Wright has pointed out that some athletes, as well as some physicians, see steroid use as a kind of replacement therapy: "These are drugs that help the body recover from physical and emotional stress, and if the hormone levels are reduced because of stress, then I suppose the argument could be made that it is a replacement dose." The sports physician Heinz Liesen has offered a classic version of this argument that emphasizes both the safety and medical common sense of male hormone replacement:

> The world-famous hormone researcher Adlerkreutz from Finland says at every conference that giving testosterone to a man is much less dangerous than giving birth control pills to a woman. Why do we make such a drama out of this? If a body cannot regenerate itself by producing a sufficient amount of hormone, then it is certainly appropriate to help it out, just as one would give vitamin C, B-1 or B-2 or stimulate its immune system, so that it can recuperate rather than remain sick.

Why modern society has made such a drama out of doping is perhaps the deepest question that this book attempts to explore. Why would a civilization bent on maximizing performances of various kinds require certain performers to exercise self-restraint? I have argued that an undeclared (and unconscious) purpose of this demand for self-restraint has been to provide symbolic confirmation of the unchanging essence of human nature at a time when that very idea has been radically destabilized by the prospect of genetic manipulation. While the cloning spectacle of the past several years has most dramatically demonstrated this anguish over the mutability of human identity, the anguish over doping can be seen as a comparable episode in the larger biomedical drama about human limits. From this perspective, doping scandals are symbolic demonstrations of our unwillingness to succumb to unbridled experimentation on the human organism. These shows of resolve are, in fact, eminently practical in that they target a small number of performances that provide mere entertainment rather than the more tangible forms of productivity necessary to sustain postindustrial civilization. In this sense, athletes are expendable role models; their performances are subjected to ritual tests of self-restraint (doping tests) even as armies of more essential workers are encouraged to be productive without limit. Here is one reason for the sports physician Heinz Liesen's denunciation of what he calls "the dishonest doping discussion" of recent years.

The East Germans avoided a Western-style drama by making doping routine and by suppressing public debate of the entire issue. Five years after the collapse of the GDR, the effects of this pharmacological indoctrination were still evident. The former East German shot-putter Grit Hammer exemplifies the mind-set of many athletes who literally grew up with doping. Indeed, the indoctrination had been so effective that she still could not think of any reason to object to it; after all, with so many people getting off on one drug or another, what distinguished her former drug regimen from the current drug habits of so many of her contemporaries in the open society of the West? The only reason to stop using steroids was that the anti-doping regulations of the reunified German sports establishment prohibited them. This unregenerate view of doping is instructive because it forces us to confront a frequently overlooked aspect of the phenomenon. It reminds us that our sense of what constitutes doping is socially conditioned and that restricting the idea of doping to athletes is sociologically indefensible, since many other people pursue enhancements through drugs. That we routinely exclude these points from our public discussion of doping should prompt an examination of our motives for doing so. Is it possible, for example, that our vociferous attacks on East German doping have served to distract us from certain unsettling similarities between that country's value system and our own? The architects of the East German program who cultivated the doping mentality in young people were unique in that a tyrannical government had granted them the resources to engage in the hormonal manipulation of thousands of human subjects with no ethical restraints. At the same time, these personnel were well aware that many of their Western counterparts shared both their ambitions and their willingness to use hormones to develop athletes. As one East German sports scientist, Hermann Buhl, pointed out in 1990: "We are not the ones who came up with the idea of substitution. That one came from your side, after you suddenly found yourselves in a bind and were wondering how to justify the use of such drugs. Then somebody hit on the idea of declaring them to be therapeutic in nature."

This analysis of West German ambitions and motives was essentially accurate. The Federal Institute of Sports Sciences, operating under the authority of the Federal Interior Ministry in Bonn, had carried out testosterone experiments on athletes during the 1980s. While this represented a minuscule project in comparison with the East German State Plan 14.25, it remains an instructive example of how research on a doping substance could be rationalized by physicians as a search for therapeutic effects. According to the research leaders, the point of this work was to determine "whether the administration of small doses of testosterone that compensate for a deficit improves regeneration and thus makes an essential contribution to stabilizing the health of elite athletes" and "accelerating restoration of a normal state of health." Indeed, the principals argued, their objective had been to persuade their athletes that testosterone was useless as a doping substance. That these researchers sponsored by the government had been sports physicians with pro-steroid reputations—namely, Joseph Keul and Heinz Liesen—made this project all the more problematic in the eyes of many parliamentary representatives, who wanted to know why it had been undertaken in the first place. Looming in the background was the frustrated sportive nationalism of a West German sports establishment that had been losing badly to doped East Germans. But the larger issue, we see once again, is the difficulty of assessing the medical value and social acceptability of hormone therapy administered to athletes for whom any sort of therapy has an ambiguous meaning. For who could distinguish between restoring their health and enhancing their performances? While the East Germans had solved this problem by cynically equating good health and good performances, their West German colleagues were under greater pressure to submit to the requirements of the Hippocratic oath in a public forum.

The hypocrisy of Buhl's accusation against the West Germans lay in his disingenuous claim that East German doping personnel did not employ the substitution argument themselves. Buhl himself maintained that he had given steroids to athletes not only to boost their performances but "out of concern for the athlete whose organism we have more or less ruined due to the stress of training." This alibi was promptly labeled a "fraud" by Buhl's colleague Lothar Pickenhain. The real purpose of the research, he said, was to perfect a less androgenic steroid that would result in fewer masculine side effects in female athletes. Indeed, one of the few compensatory pleasures the East German hormone experts derived from the collapse of the GDR was the opportunity to crow about the superiority of their doping techniques. Alluding to the horrible, doping-induced death of the West German heptathlete Birgit Dressel in 1987, Manfred Höppner sneered: "In our country there was no Dressel case, because we did not leave the field to medical charlatans." The point here is that once their doping secrets were revealed to the world, the East Germans felt obliged to articulate "humane" rationales for administering hormones to athletes. If East German medical scientists like Höppner felt they had nothing to apologize for, it was in part because they knew that many in the West had long shared their interest in experimental hormone therapies aimed at boosting athletic performance.

A number of Buhl's East German colleagues were already using the substitution concept to rationalize steroid therapy as they reached out to their West German colleagues at a conference on anabolic steroids held in May 1990 at the Research Institute for Physical Culture and Sport (Forschungsinstitut für Körperkultur und Sport, or FKS) in Leipzig. Like some of the East German coaches then being hired in large numbers by West German sports federations, these East German scientists were unable to conceal their enthusiasm about the use of "hormonal regulation." "Anabolic steroids," two of them wrote, "intervene in informational processes and affect adaptation [to stress] in this way. We have thoroughly investigated their effects on the various functional systems dependent on training regimens while studying problems of hormonal regulation. The results suggest that high-performance training offers medical opportunities which are scientifically well-founded and enable us to prescribe doses without side effects." To legitimize these "medical opportunities," the authors make a point of proclaiming the sanctity of the human genome: "The probing and extension of human capacities in sport are neither unphysiological in a fundamental sense nor reprehensible, so long as this is achieved in the context of the human genetic endowment." These conference proceedings are full of such rhetorical cunning aimed at rehabilitating the compromised reputations of the authors, as they courted the approval of well-placed West German colleagues who might find them jobs at universities or pharmaceutical companies.

These overtures from east to west were based on an awareness that many scientists, doctors, and athletes on both sides of the Berlin Wall accepted the legitimacy of hormone therapy for the purpose of boosting athletic performance. Their shared perspective included a purely functional view of medical care that rendered the Hippocratic oath irrelevant. One East German pediatrician who had known about hormone experiments on young girls put it as follows: "A sports physician is the only physician who, from the very first day, can act in a manner that is contrary to the best interests of his patient." Five years after the collapse of the East German state, the former East German sports physician Alexander Stohr found himself unwanted at a (West) German Olympic training center, after "it was made quite clear to me that my view that health took priority over athletic success was unacceptable." The essential point here is that the grotesque aspects of the East German doping program have obscured the numerous similarities that connect its doctors to the less scrupulous among the entrepreneurial hormone therapists and sports physicians of the post-Communist age. We should also keep in mind that some of the East German doctor-athlete relationships were no less collaborative than comparable relationships in Western societies that involve hormone-seeking patients and hormone-prescribing physicians. Like their East German counterparts, these doctors are willing to risk their clients' health in the search for rejuvenation and sexual stimulation.

Following the revelations about their doping practices in the GDR, East German doping scientists justified what they had done by invoking exactly the same ideas as their pro-steroid Western colleagues. First, the drugs were safe: "We haven't given the athletes anything we would have regarded as dangerous to ourselves or our families," said Rüdiger Häcker of the FKS. "It would be much more honest to call for a controlled legalization of steroids," said Manfred Höppner, the former director of the East German Sports Medical Service (SMD), "even if doctors who have nothing to do with elite sport would gladly crucify me for expressing this opinion." Second, he said, sports physicians had an obligation to supervise potentially dangerous self-medication: "If we hold back, then the athletes will treat themselves, or we will simply leave the field to medical charlatans," Höppner stated in 1990. Third, the physician should have discretion as a medical professional to promote "quick recovery and improved stress tolerance" with "pharmacologically appropriate doses" of steroids. In July 2000 Höppner was convicted of being an accessory to causing bodily harm to athletes, including children. At the same time, his vision of hormone replacement was becoming the norm in a growing number of hormone clinics and plastic surgeons' offices that serve those who are willing to pay for it.

One goal of such treatments has always been the stimulation of sexual appetite, and here too the illicit steroid culture of the sports world can serve as a social laboratory in which we can study how people have reacted to the availability of testosterone drugs. For example, East German trainers who gave steroids to female athletes as young as thirteen knew perfectly well that they were stimulating precocious sexual appetites and creating sexual opportunities for themselves. But higher-ranking officials viewed sexual stimulation as a nuisance. As early as 1977 Manfred Höppner had observed the inadvertent aphrodisiac effects of giving steroids to women: "The effect on the sexual drive was relatively strong in some women. This resulted in special problems, particularly in training camps where the 'official' male partners of these women were not present." In the early 1940s, as noted in chapter 2, American physicians had observed disturbingly intense libidos develop in breast cancer patients who had received megadoses of testosterone propionate. Forty years later a different kind of steroid regimen was producing the same unintended result. According to the researchers, "The increase in libido was so severe and unbearable for some women that they requested cessation of the hormone treatment and release from participation in elite sports." Lacking a market for sex drugs or any other practical purpose for hormone therapy, East German researchers regarded intensified libido as an impediment to winning sports medals. In the sexual therapy market of the West, the same stimulating effect was marketable as a form of therapy.

Inside the sports world the stimulating effect of testosterone has occasionally been seen as a therapeutic benefit for athletes with sexual problems. Given testosterone's long history of such use, it was inevitable that its legitimate (therapeutic) and illegitimate (performance-enhancing) roles would eventually coincide in the context of particular athletic careers when questions were asked about the use of an officially banned substance. This overlap was already evident at a hearing on anabolic steroids that was held in the West German Parliament (Bundestag) on

September 28, 1977. Among those offering testimony was Christian Gehrmann, a specialist in the training of women for throwing events who would eventually become notorious for doping his female athletes. "Among some [male] athletes who train very hard," he testified, "I have observed a decline in potency. So they go to doctors and I assume they are treated with steroids. Their health improves, and their potency is restored." One purpose of this hearing was to examine the possible use of steroids to develop athletes who could improve West Germany's stature in the world by winning international competitions. Promoting the sexual therapeutic value of the male hormone to the Bundestag was no doubt intended to normalize its use for other ends as well. Gehrmann's highly successful (and government-sponsored) career as a steroid enthusiast reflected his view of androgens as multipurpose drugs, and he was allowed to operate for years before German sports officials finally reined him in.

This purported need for testosterone sex therapy has served as one of many explanations offered by athletes to account for prohibited levels of testosterone or steroids in their bodies. The conflict between any person's presumed right to therapy and sports federations' recently acquired right to monitor the hormone levels of elite athletes raises once again some fundamental questions about the medical status of the elite athlete in the modern world. In 1994, for example, the German distance runner Martin Bremer claimed that his use of testosterone esters had been prompted by sexual difficulties, a claim that was contested on scientific grounds by the biologist and anti-doping activist Werner Franke. In 1999 the professional cyclist Christian Henn, a former German champion, was caught with a sky-high testosterone level that he attributed to a fertility potion provided to him by an Italian midwife. He also claimed that this mysterious substance had enabled him and his wife to have children. A fifty-eight-year-old Japanese billiards player once defended his use of methyl testosterone on the grounds that "my wife had a right to be [sexually] satisfied." Such cases make clear an essential difference between the hormone subculture in sport and hormone therapy in the wider world, where the right to medical benefits and privacy still prevails. To ensure that high-performance athletes are drug-free model citizens, their blood or urine must be carefully monitored as a deterrent to drug use. These drug tests produce a physiological transparency that effectively cancels the right to medical (and sometimes sexual) privacy. Public knowledge of female athletes' use of birth control pills, for example, has become a routine consequence of drug-testing procedures, since those drugs affect hormone levels. In this way, the athlete who is assigned the role of model citizen may eventually wind up being a citizen whose medical privacy is constantly being violated.

The promise of hormone sex therapy can thus attract both athletes and nonathletes who are in search of cures for their problems. But not everyone can act on that attraction; for this reason, ready access to testosterone drugs can be associated with the power and privilege of an elite accustomed to their intimate needs being satisfied. There have even been a few cases of politically powerful men availing themselves of drugs intended for athletes. Steroids were administered to some members of the East German leadership, though it is most unlikely that they derived any benefit from using them. The same issue of access can arise when the drug therapy does not involve hormones. In 1992, for example, Erich Schaible, a division chief in the German interior ministry with responsibility for federal sports policy, had his knee injected with the famous Klümper-Cocktail of drugs by the controversial sports physician after whom this treatment is named. In this case the therapeutic benefit to the patient was overshadowed by the political signal sent. Taking advantage of his status as a celebrity, the government official was treated like an elite athlete by a renegade sports physician the government had prosecuted for using banned drugs. Accepting the controversial treatment suggested official approval of an "outlaw" therapy that appealed to "patients" outside the circle of the doctor's loyal athletic clientele.

The appearance of privileged access to drugs in the sports world points to speculations about powerful men elsewhere who are alleged to be bent on keeping the treatments available despite all efforts to control them. A columnist for one muscle magazine, for example, once alleged that "neither the DEA [Drug Enforcement Administration] nor the Food and Drug Administration (FDA) dare touch testosterone, even though it is listed under the [Anabolic Steroids Control] Act. Too many influential folk are using it—including aging senators, congressmen, state attorneys and senior policemen." Viagra, too, encouraged the idea that there is a tacit pro-sex drug agenda controlled by a powerful male establishment. Comparing Viagra to steroids, a member of a research group on drug policy predicted that the anti-impotence drug would never be regulated beyond requiring a doctor's prescription: "Historically, the Federal motivation for controlling drugs has been sociological rather than pharmacological. Viagra has obvious appeal to rich and powerful men. And you can be certain that they're not going to jail."

The more important point is that Viagra is a relatively safe and effective drug that has found a market extending far beyond a powerful elite. This enormous clientele includes an unknown number of men, unaffected by erectile dysfunction, whose use of the drug in hopes of enhancing their pleasure makes it virtually impossible to distinguish between "recreational" and "performance-enhancing" pharmacology. In other words, sexual therapy for the masses is both safe and legal. This development points in turn to the growing similarity of athletes and ordinary people as patients in search of various kinds of higher performance.

THE PATIENT AS ATHLETE, THE ATHLETE AS PATIENT

The gradual convergence of the athlete and the patient as medical clients results from the rise of performance as a cultural ideal for many people. Together with a cultivation of the self, our culture's emphasis on individual development has created a need for tests and ordeals that can demonstrate success, showing that personal growth has been achieved. If successful performances are seen as validating the lives of the performers, then people may view medical care as an enhancing technology that goes beyond mere healing to create a higher level of ordinary functioning or even a state of supernormal health.

The vocabulary of performance has become essential to our descriptions of the tensions and stresses of a modern lifestyle that embraces performance as its fundamental principle. Physicians, too, must cope with the demands made on their patients by a performance-oriented society; they frequently must make decisions about giving drugs to people under stress whose lifestyles can be hard to distinguish from the disorders of which they complain. A physician who sometimes prescribes the stimulant Ritalin for female patients puts it this way: "The biggest problem with the women is that they set the bar too high. Nobody could realistically accomplish all these things without taking a performance enhancer."

It is interesting that the physician who describes this predicament employs the language of sport. The woman under pressure is, metaphorically speaking, a high jumper who demands of herself an impossible performance. What is more, she will need to drug herself to perform adequately. The physician also points out that this predicament is shared by "nearly everyone else—all the citizens of our hard-working, stress-fueled society. Can low doses of stimulants help anyone—children or adults, ADD [attention deficit disorder] diagnosis or not—concentrate better on boring tasks? If it does work this way, why shouldn't anyone try Ritalin? Can it help a person improve his or her performance when some career-related circumstance has raised the bar dramatically?"

Do physicians collaborate in such acts of doping to boost performance? Often they do, and this points once again to the unsettling comparisons that can be made between legitimate drug therapy for patients and the illegitimate doping of athletes. For why should these performances be subject to different degrees of regulation? Why should some performances be off-limits to pharmacological enhancement while others are not? One way to approach this problem is to separate performers into juvenile and adult factions. The parent who asks the physician to prescribe Ritalin to improve a child's academic or athletic performance erases what may appear to be an artificial distinction between legitimate and illegitimate performance enhancement. For how can one separate performance from development in a child whose development is nurtured by his or her performances in school or on the athletic field or at the piano?

Performances in the medical context do not always involve pharmacological, surgical, or psychological enhancement. The more zealous advocates of natural childbirth, for example, "see labor as a kind of performance, for which a woman can and should rehearse, and in which she can comport herself more or less admirably. They see it, in other words, as an opportunity to define the self." And the role model for this act of self-definition is the athlete: "Maybe they hold fast to this ideal for the same reason people climb Everest or paraglide in the Andes. They regard labor as an extreme sport—an ennobling physical challenge that we pampered First Worlders are supposed to courageously endure and savor. Spurning the palliatives of modern medicine is part of the drill, an emblem of virtue." In this competition, as in sports, the challenge is to put on a drug-free performance that is also a peak experience to be cherished for the rest of one's life. Here the role of the physician is to facilitate the performance by leaving the stage to the patient-athlete. In other cases, the physician will have to intervene with drug or surgical or psychotherapeutic enhancements. But performance, not the technique that facilitates it, is the primary objective, and that is why athleticism is the most powerful metaphor for expressing this quest for self-transcendence. For athleticism is human dynamism rendered visible in its most accessible and dramatic form.

The idea that the good life requires peak performances comparable to those of athletes originated in the human potential movement of the 1960s and 1970s. What connects the 1960s and the 1990s is the mandate to achieve self-actualization and generally to expand human potential. What separates these two campaigns on behalf of human potential is cultural context and how that context values or devalues specific human capacities. In its earlier phase, the idea of human potential was shaped by countercultural ideals that rejected the technological ethos and its dehumanizing emphasis on productivity and efficiency. Human potential therapists used techniques such as "encounter groups, sensory awareness enhancement, meditation, bioenergetics, and bodywork massage" to release the emotions and energies supposedly repressed by a technological civilization. Influenced by the ideas of the radical psychoanalyst Wilhelm Reich, the humanistic psychologists of the human potential movement saw sexual release as a catalyst of sociopolitical transformation. Sexual intimacy and social action were thereby combined into a progressive lifestyle that scorned competition in favor of cooperation.

The more recent movement has embraced the technological ethos spurned by the anti-modernist counterculture. In 1962, for example, the founders of the Association of Humanistic Psychology pronounced themselves "opposed to thinking about human beings in mechanistic and reductionistic terms." Today, however, when the technological ideals of productivity and efficiency shape the ethos of peak performance, the fulfillment of self-actualization often takes the form of quantifiable norms: virtual miles on running machines, orgasms and erections achieved in bed, items recalled via "memory drugs," wrinkles erased by laser and knife. The iconic drugs of these two cultures also underscore their difference. LSD, peyote, and marijuana were regarded as mind-expanding substances that subverted competitive ambition, whereas mass-market drugs such as Prozac, Ritalin, and Viagra are embraced as enhancers of performance. (In Ireland, Viagra has been fed to racing greyhounds.) Even a so-called mind-expanding drug like Ecstasy prolongs physical endurance on the dance floor. This emphasis on quantifiable performance can be thought of as an athleticizing of the search for an authentic self.

Patients and athletes can thus seek personal authenticity not through self-examination but through performances that express self-assertion. Patients and athletes are also similar in that both groups require medical care. To an increasing degree, high-performance athletes are patients who are plagued by stress and the resulting physiological deficits that require constant monitoring and various substitution therapies. Even as such physiological deficits have led directly to the long-standing doping practices of professional cyclists, the media have seldom explained this connection in covering the doping scandals that have plagued the sport in recent years. During the 2001 Tour de France, few people were aware that the doctors who tended to the riders had official permission to transport and use up to three hundred drugs and other substances. Whether or not to call such use doping was at the discretion of International Cycling Union officials, who elected not to list the drugs on their colorful Web site (www.uci.ch).

Their decision to leave the list of these substances unpublished continued a tradition of concealing from the public the kind of medical support that riders need to surmount their exhaustion and make it to the finish line. One result of this secrecy has been persistent confusion among journalists and the public about what doping is and what sports doctors are allowed to do to boost the athletic performance of their cyclist patients. The truth of the matter is that they have been allowed to do a great deal, thanks to the connivance of cycling officials and an ignorant or complaisant press corps. These are the respectable and responsible parties who are supposed to inform the public that consumes the sporting spectacle as both ritual and entertainment. That this enormous, amorphous, and essentially voiceless constituency will unquestioningly accept what is served up to them is taken for granted.

CHAPTER 6

"Let Them Take Drugs"

Public Responses to Doping

The question of how ordinary people feel about the doping practices of elite athletes is significant because it indirectly addresses the status of all pharmacological enhancements in the modern world. When and why people condemn athletic doping (if they do) should tell us something about when and why they might decline to use enhancing drugs themselves. Such abstinence would suggest that they wish to preserve rather than augment the selves they already have. It would also suggest that ordinary people expect athletes to respect the same limits they do. Alternatively, many ordinary citizens might assign athletes a special status that allows them to pursue pharmacological enhancement, because they are regarded as special beings whose potential should be realized by any means that is available to them. A tolerance for doping athletes might also derive from compassion for suffering worker-athletes, professional cyclists in particular, who are conceded a right to pain relief while they are going through their ordeals.

The very idea that public tolerance of or sympathy for doping actually exists has rarely appeared in the media that cover the use of illicit drugs in sport. After three decades of anti-doping campaigns sponsored by national and international sporting federations, as well as the constant dissemination of anti-doping messages in the media, the doped athlete is typically presented as a fallen creature. If this is the public's perspective, then it would presumably abandon elite sport were it ever to become convinced that institutionalized doping was the norm. "If the American public ever thought our athletes all used drugs to compete, [the Olympic movement] would die overnight," the executive director of the United States Olympic Committee said in 1999. Similarly dire warnings about how doping threatens the very future of sport became common after the 1988 Seoul Olympic Games. Manfred Donike, the scientist whose drug-detection instruments had found traces of an anabolic steroid in Ben Johnson's urine after the runner set a world record in the 100-meter sprint, declared in 1990 that nothing less than "the credibility of sport" was at stake. The same year a German sports official solemnly observed that doping raised the question of whether sport was "going to be accepted in this society." A year later, an authoritative American publication called "the scourge of drugs" a "devastating public relations nightmare" for the sport of track and field. Apocalyptic pronouncements of this kind took on a life of their own during the 1990s, and the Tour de France doping scandal of 1998 led to yet another wave of highly publicized doubts about whether high-performance athletes would ever be capable of meeting the ethical standards that were constantly being invoked in the media.

These assessments and prognostications took public opinion for granted, as though it were a homogenous cloud of disapproval that hung over athletic venues and cycling routes like a sword of Damocles. Journalistic opinion frequently cited public opinion without presenting any evidence of what the public was actually thinking. "The public is disappointed again and again when new offenders are caught," the *Frankfurter Allgemeine Zeitung* told its readers in 1990. Doping, Richard Williams of the *Guardian* told his public in 1998, is "generally felt to be the worst of sporting crimes." A well-informed medical sociologist similarly stated in 2000 that "the public response to the use of drugs in sport is both more forceful and more emotive than the public response to most other forms of cheating." While active athletes tend not to comment in this vein, the desperate state of professional cycling in 2001 induced Germany's leading professional cyclist, the 1997 Tour de France champion Jan Ullrich, to join the chorus. "I am just as disturbed about this as the public is," he told the press after a small army of Italian police raided the riders' hotel rooms during the 2001 Giro d'Italia in search of doping products. The irony of this statement, whatever its sincerity, was that professional riders, as we shall see, had long been better placed than others to pose some awkward questions about the actual state of public opinion about doping.

The evidence presented in this chapter demonstrates that uniform public condemnation of athletic doping does not exist. Significant numbers of sports fans have demonstrated sympathy with doped athletes in a variety of ways, whether celebrating them in public, attending their performances without protest, or expressing their views in the (very few) opinion surveys that have tested what is conventionally called public opinion. As we examine this evidence, it also becomes clear that the term *public opinion* is itself profoundly misleading, because it conceals the existence of factions that hold differing opinions about this as well as most other issues that warrant media attention. Indeed, given the demands that politicians, sports officials, and corporate sponsors make on elite athletes, the tolerance of doping by segments of the general population should come as no surprise. The widespread idea that athletes express the vitality of a nation promotes the toleration of doping by making athletic success appear to be a matter of national security. The tabloid press in some countries exacerbates this syndrome by making it an exercise in national pride to defend doped athletes. The result of such campaigns is to stimulate public demand for athletic performances that may not be possible without doping.

That the doping of athletes might be required to satisfy such a public demand was evident long before the anabolic steroid epidemic began during the 1960s. As early as 1939, before doping was being recognized as a societal problem, a Danish exercise physiologist was reporting that the use of stimulants by athletes was fuelling "the record-breaking craze and the desire to satisfy an exacting public." Exactly half a century later the president of the German Track and Field Federation, Helmut Meyer, asserted the importance of his mandate to produce successful athletes for the nation: "The public demands it, and that's the way it should be."

Such comments about what the public wants simply underscore that public opinion has no authoritative voice of its own. From time to time surveys about doping are carried out, but here too public opinion is mediated through the journalists who report on the data. For the most part, public opinion about doping exists only to the extent that journalists, politicians, and sports bureaucrats define and appropriate it for their own purposes. We have already seen that there are two kinds of public opinion that these public actors express: either a demand for drug-free sport or the traditional demand for athletic heroes that fails to reckon with the issue of drugs. These opposing views share two characteristics: they depend on the media for their existence, and claims about their authenticity are almost invariably exempted from the scrutiny one usually expects from professional journalists.

Autonomous public opinion about doping exists only in the form of spontaneous demonstrations by the crowds who attend sporting events in stadiums or who line the roads during cycling races. Many of these episodes have been reported in newspapers and magazines, and almost all of them seem to demonstrate indifference to the doping practices of athletes. This apparent unanimity of opinion does not in itself give these manifestations the status of a valid plebiscite, let alone that of a scientific survey. For one thing, any stadium crowd is a self-selected sample of the general population that may be unrepresentative in a variety of ways. It is also impossible to know how many people cheer a doped athlete while other spectators display indifference or disapproval by sitting in stony silence. Such informal demonstrations may also have less to do with the ethics of athletes than with the sheer charisma and notoriety of celebrities whom the public appreciates for their defiance, irrespective of whether they are sports figures or rock stars. Still, while these demonstrations may be difficult to interpret, they call into question the received wisdom about public attitudes toward the doping of athletes.

Consider a series of four events that occurred in three countries—Italy, Germany, and Canada—over the past decade. In each case the sporting public was presented with an opportunity to embrace, reject, or ignore a celebrated athlete who was known to have committed a doping offense.

It is April 22, 2001, a spring Sunday in Rome, and the final whistle of the soccer match between Lazio Rome and Vincenza Calcio has just sounded. The home team has been victorious, and at this moment Lazio's Portuguese star, Fernando Couto, runs to the northern end of the stadium, tears off his shirt and flings it into the stands. The crowd erupts into an ovation, and everyone present understands the significance of this affectionate exchange between the player and his fans. For Couto has recently tested positive for the anabolic steroid nandrolone, and he is facing a sixteen-month exile that could mean the end of his career. "I was really moved by the public," Couto says later. "This is a delicate moment for me." In the meantime, his club is making strenuous efforts to present Couto as a victim of incompetent laboratory technicians and unscrupulous pharmaceutical companies that contaminate their dietary supplements with the steroid for which Couto had tested positive. Eventually, Couto was suspended for only four months.

It is January 2001, and the German wrestler Alexander Leipold appears at a match in Schifferstadt, a town nestled in the Rhine Valley west of Heidelberg. Following his Olympic championship performance at the 2000 Sydney Games, Leipold had tested positive for nandrolone and was stripped of his gold medal. Upon returning to competition after a four-month ban, Leipold is greeted by 1,600 fans whose applause for the compromised champion goes on for minutes.

It is August 1999, and the German long jumper Konstantin Krause is reflecting on the return to competition of the American sprinter Dennis Mitchell. Having tested positive for elevated testosterone, Mitchell convinced a disciplinary panel that the high level had been caused by the consumption of a large quantity of beer and repeated sexual intercourse with his wife in the course of a single night. Krause is disillusioned not because of the success of Mitchell's humiliating alibi but because the stadium crowd celebrates his performance:

> Because nobody really cares whether the good Dennis was doped or not. What's important is that he is fast. I've been amazed at his appearances this year. He won the 100 meters in Linz and was wildly cheered by the spectators. Naïve people would ask: "Why are the people cheering like that, since he's only running that fast because he's doped?" The public has its own answer: They want to see the ultimate performance regardless of where it comes from. Doped is an unpleasant and marginal piece of information the people in the stadium ignore.

Now it is January 18, 1991, and Ben Johnson is about to run the 50-meter dash at the Hamilton Spectator Indoor Games in Canada. During his prerace introduction he receives a 30-second standing ovation from the sellout crowd of 17,050. It is, *Sports Illustrated* notes, "a startlingly affectionate reception." One banner in the crowd reads: HE WAS FRAMED. Two months earlier, meet promoters had been pursuing him avidly, and he was holding more than a million dollars' worth of endorsement contracts. Two years earlier, only months after Johnson's disgrace in Seoul, 76 percent of a German television audience had taken the position that the visibly doped Johnson should not have been disqualified and should have been allowed to keep his gold medal. Presented with this demonstration of public opinion, a top official of the German Sports Association announced that he was "totally shocked."

These and other reports make it clear that the audiences that assemble to watch elite athletes in modern societies have often shown themselves to be indifferent to doping convictions. We shall also see that sporting publics have at times refused to condemn prominent athletes who trafficked in doping products or who used recreational drugs. While the emotional embrace extended to such compromised athletes is not necessarily an endorsement of doping, it does mark a refusal to stigmatize an athlete who has used a banned drug to enhance his or her performance. And the most significant example of a sporting public that refuses to turn its back on doped athletes are the millions of people who follow professional cycling in Europe.

The Tour de France has offered many examples of public indifference to doping. Even as a catastrophic scandal was overwhelming the 1998 Tour, its director, Jean-Marie Leblanc, remained confident that the event would retain public support: "In ten days there will be just as many spectators in the Pyrenees as there ever were. The wonderful performances and stage victories outweigh everything else." "The Tour must remain clean," he intoned with Orwellian mendacity, as if the burgeoning scandal was simply the result of a recent aberration. Leblanc had been a cycling journalist before taking over the management of the Tour, and he must have known about the drug subculture that a code of silence had effectively concealed from outsiders.

The weight of the evidence suggests that Leblanc's appraisal of public opinion was essentially correct. While here, too, we must acknowledge that journalistic speculation outweighs systematic evidence of public opinion, the speculations that have appeared in print point to little in the way of grassroots opposition to doping. Two weeks after Leblanc made his comment, a German sports journalist introduced his readers to the major protagonists in the ongoing doping drama:

> On one side are the journalists, the sociologists, the analysts. On the other side are the athletes and the managers. Over here are the organizers and the sponsors. Over there the state prosecutors. And there in the middle is the public that is, as usual, lining the roads. The detailed scandal reports appear to have changed little in France, aside from the fact that many fans are mourning the exclusion of the [doping-compromised] Festina team while others are mocking them.

And how did consumers treat the corporate sponsor? Within a few months of the scandal, Festina actually reported "that the scandal had a positive effect on sales of its watches and that it would pay the team's $5 million expenses next year." Three years later, it was still being reported that the company had experienced a significant rise in name recognition and sales. Despite the notoriety of the athletes it had sponsored, the public was now buying greater numbers of its watches, not fewer.

The 1999 "Tour of Redemption" provoked similar assessments of public opinion from professional observers of the professional cycling scene. "Despite negative publicity," a British journalist wrote, "Le Tour still fascinates a French public that has long accepted the inevitability of doping in cycling." The focal point of interest for French cycling fans and state prosecutors alike was Richard Virenque, the one member of the disgraced Festina team who had not admitted to doping following the revelations of 1998. Virenque's eventual confession in October 2000 is less interesting than his relationship with the sporting public, which, by all accounts, never gave up its infatuation with this deceptive and defiant athlete. "Yes," *Der Spiegel* commented, "Richard has been lying to the public for a year, but people could not care less, since he is the only hero France has right now." According to the Danish cycling journalist Henrik Jul Hansen, Virenque was supported at the time by 65 percent of the French population. At his public confession, Virenque would say that his fans and doping drugs were what enabled him to endure the pain of cycling. But Jul Hansen saw a more tangled relationship between the star and his fan base:

> It is not the support from the public that fuels him, even if that is, of course, what he says. The French people offer him an unrequited love. He looks the other way when they cheer him, and he writes autographs mechanically. What fuels him is the rage of the pariah, and this year it is evident that it is being poured on a talent that for years has been obscured by the man's moods and arrogance.

Here is the ultimate logic of sheer celebrity, which encourages the crowd to invest its emotions in a triumphant figure who is under no obligation to reciprocate their affections. But the crowd looks to their cycling hero with more than affection and admiration. The hunger for an exciting spectacle is the harder and potentially cold-blooded aspect of this relationship. "The truth," another British journalist commented in June 1999, "is that many fans are as hooked on drugs as the riders: they don't want the sport to have to ease the severity of its competitions or move down a gear in performance levels." The need to produce great performances makes riders suffer, and riders will therefore often dope themselves so that they can keep their jobs while suffering less in the process.

This causal relationship between public demand for high-performance cycling and doping existed long before the age of blood-boosting drugs such as erythropoietin (EPO). In 1969, for example, a five-time Tour de

France champion, Jacques Anquetil, offered the following analysis: "I dope myself. Everyone dopes himself. Those who claim they don't are liars. For 50 years bike racers have been taking stimulants. Obviously, we can do without them in a race, but then we will pedal 15 miles an hour [instead of 25]. Since we are constantly asked to go faster and to make even greater efforts, we have no choice but to take stimulants." Many years later the Italian rider Dario Frigo repeated Anquetil's claim about systemic drug use: "Everyone is doping. All of cycling is contaminated. As an amateur I never took anything. But among us professionals it's a system."

Such candid self-portraits do not, however, address some important questions about the physiological and psychological demands that are imposed on the riders. Who creates this alleged requirement for faster races, and how can we confirm that such a demand exists independent of media claims that it is, in fact, what the public wants? A related question concerns the riders' attitudes toward producing peak performances. Do they resent the need to produce faster races? Do they resent these "inhuman" norms only if they are denied the analgesic benefits of doping? Do they embrace the challenge, with or without doping, to transcend their own limits? Because survey research has never been done, the evidence on which we can draw to answer such questions is limited. In fact, as we shall see, it is possible that the sporting public's acquiescence to doping by athletes expresses a widespread and thoroughly utilitarian attitude toward drugs—an attitude held by large numbers of ordinary people.

The public has also displayed indifference when athletes were revealed to be traffickers in doping products or consumers of recreational drugs. Unlike the athletes in the preceding examples, these have not been sanctioned for taking performance-enhancing substances. Nevertheless, both situations invite the expression of judgments about athletes' behavior when faced with the temptation of using drugs. Such episodes are one more challenge to the apparently indestructible hope that model behavior by athletes can be a positive influence on their pill-popping fellow citizens. These cases also allow us to define and compare public attitudes toward the use of different categories of banned drugs inside and outside the sports world—for example, employing doping drugs versus enjoying recreational intoxicants. One might argue that since doping products have "public" effects on athletic competitions, while intoxicants belong to the sphere of "private" life, athletes have a social obligation to abstain from doping but not necessarily from the recreational use of drugs. How the public feels about such distinctions should have some bearing on how policy makers regulate different kinds of drugs.

Public indifference to the drug-trafficking athlete can originate in nationalist feeling and a public's fascination with an extroverted celebrity. Now it is March 15, 1985, and Karl-Heinz Radschinsky, a West German weightlifter who won a gold medal at the 1984 Los Angeles Olympic Games, has just confessed to police that he is a steroid dealer. He had begun by selling protein supplements to bodybuilders and then moved on to selling the anabolic steroids he obtained from East Bloc lifters and his hometown pharmacist. The indictment would charge him with selling $50,000 worth of steroids—pills, bottles, and capsules—on the black market. Following his interrogation by police, he appears at a Strength Sports Center and is greeted with thunderous applause by fans who regard his drug dealing as a trivial offense. The West German weightlifting federation (Bundesverband Deutscher Gewichtheber, or BVDG) refuses to disqualify him from competition pending a conviction in court. At a commercial appearance in Frankfurt he persuades an admiring crowd that his drug trafficking does not really matter. He is still the most popular West German athlete who came back from Los Angeles with gold. In 1986 he was convicted and sentenced to eighteen months of probation and fined $20,000—a drug-dealing weightlifter who had tested negative for steroids. In May 1987, having served his two-year ban, Radschinsky became the West German champion in his weight division and was nominated by the BVDG for the 1988 Olympic Games in Seoul. "For us the Radschinsky case presents no problems at all," a BVDG vice president said in 1988, since the offense "did not occur within the realm of sport itself." It was eventually the Athletes Commission and the Medical Commission of the International Olympic Committee (IOC) that made sure Radschinsky was not allowed to compete at the Seoul Games. Given their mandate to produce medal winners for the nation, West German sports officials could not be counted on to clean their own house. This nationalist fervor accounted for their willingness to endorse the almost surreal idea that steroid trafficking had nothing whatsoever to do with an athlete's Olympic eligibility.

Radschinsky's popularity was another factor that made the sports bureaucrats reluctant to sanction even a confessed drug dealer. For "Radi," as his fans called him, was one of the more attractive types of scoundrel, the sort of person who is born to be the life of the party. This father of four children was also a local nightclub personality whose favorite trick was to explode rubber hot-water bottles by blowing into them until they burst. His slangy, slightly mangled German was always fresh and quotable. "I am not a criminal," he insisted, and many people accepted this self-assessment from a provocative and charming rogue who had brought home Olympic gold.

Publicity surrounding the recreational drug use of a popular athletic champion creates another kind of event that appears to offer the public an opportunity to give its hero a thumbs-up or thumbs-down. Yet once again, we must be careful to distinguish between autonomous public opinion and the views of those who invoke it to lend authority to their own words and actions. The following story reveals how public opinion can be manipulated when the fate of a national hero is at stake.

In April 1997 the Austrian ski jumper Andreas Goldberger, a three-time World Cup champion, admitted that he had recently used cocaine, but only once. (A drug dealer had told Viennese police that he supplied Goldberger with cocaine on three separate occasions.) According to the German Press Agency, this confession provoked public declarations of sympathy in the general population. The press noted that it had been a generation since the Austrian nation had rallied behind an athlete in this manner. This curious scenario raises two questions. First, why did the theme of exculpation dominate the reporting of this scandal? And second, how much do we really know about how the public really felt about this case?

One factor that worked in Goldberger's favor was the absence of a classic doping offense. Because no standard protocol was automatically and immediately applied to the athlete, influential people—who saw him as a symbol of national pride—had valuable time to intervene. At the same time, the athlete's celebrity status may have influenced popular opinion. That casual use of cocaine counts as a kind of normal behavior in this glamorous demimonde may well have deflected the charge of social deviance that is the real stigma borne by drug users. The uncertain nature of the offense left the Austrian Skiing Federation (Österreichischer Skiverband, or ÖSV) in a difficult position as it attempted to adjudicate Goldberger's fate. "We have treated this offense as a kind of doping case in the wider sense," said the ÖSV chairman as he announced a six-month suspension that had been carefully calibrated to expire just in time for the star jumper to rejoin his teammates for the winter season. Yet even this kid-glove treatment could not appease the more virulent sportive nationalists to be found among Austrian fans. The adjudication committee had required police protection during its meetings, and there were threats that the ÖSV would be bombed if Goldberger were suspended.

This vigilantism notwithstanding, the real mob that railroaded Goldberger's exoneration through the court of public opinion was composed not of street hooligans but of tabloid journalists and politicians. Austria's largest paper, the tabloid *Kronenzeitung,* ran a headline that read "Our Andy Cannot Lie"—an odd concession to a cocaine abuser on the part of a newspaper that had always taken a tough and uncompromising position on drugs. The *Salzburger Nachrichten* invited its readers to participate in an opinion survey, and an overwhelming majority opposed Goldberger's suspension. A columnist at the tabloid went so far as to appoint himself the ski jumper's "guardian angel." Politicians criticized the ÖSV president for issuing the suspension, calling his response "exaggerated." The sheer ingenuity of the publicity campaign became evident when some of Goldberger's advocates advised him to make donations to agencies that treat drug abusers and to give anti-drug lectures to young audiences—a tactic also adopted by the repentant Ben Johnson. Goldberger went so far as to announce that he wanted to remain a role model for young people and participate in the "Athletes against Drugs" campaign.

This cynical farce illustrates the crucial role the tabloid press can play in promoting an indifference to drugs when it has the means and motive to do so. Austrian newspapers had used the same rhetorical tactics four years earlier when Andreas Berger, the fastest white man in the world, tested positive for a banned substance. Here, too, the Austrian press went into action, complaining bitterly of a (Nazi-style) "Night-and-fog raid," "The Lobby of the Rats," and "Mafia methods." Even the German nationality of the doping control officer, a tough former policeman and 800-meter runner named Klaus Wengoborski, was treated as suspicious. "One thing is clear," said the other Vienna tabloid, the *Kurier.* "The successes of Berger (the fastest German-speaking sprinter in years) have brought a lot of envious people out of the closet," and the result was "a campaign of revenge."

There is a tradition in Europe of tabloid resistance to anti-doping campaigns. As early as 1963, following the disqualification of many Austrian riders who were caught carrying large quantities of amphetamines and other stimulants at the Around Austria race, the Austrian press waged a nasty campaign against the race doctor who exposed them, the Viennese sports physician Ludwig Prokop. Other opponents of anti-doping measures were small cliques of thugs behind some of the top riders. Prokop reported that tabloid attacks on "conscientious sports physicians" occurred regularly during the 1960s. We may assume that the instigators of these attacks believed they were meeting the emotional needs of a sporting public that cared little about doping.

After reunification, as the West German sports establishment went about absorbing the best and the brightest among the former East German athletes and coaches who had been involved with doping, popular media showed they were indifferent to the practice. In 1990, for example, the tabloid *Bild* claimed that the incriminating testimony of one coach who opposed doping had been prompted by his unsatisfied sexual appetites. On the ZDF television network, the moderator of a sports talk show, who also handled television rights to sporting events, called anti-doping witnesses greedy and dismissed the investigation of doping as a pointless enterprise. A year later, after the former East German sprinter Katrin Krabbe had evaded drug testers for a second time, "there was more public criticism of the testers who had to chase her all the way to the Bahamas to get a urine sample than there was of the suspected doper." But "public criticism" from whom? The public had no more input into Krabbe's interminable doping drama than it does when the authorities are chasing any other sort of fugitive. The public is, in effect, an enormous and amorphous spectator at an event that unfolds on television screens and sports pages controlled by media professionals.

Tabloid hostility to doping controls can also scapegoat dissenters from the sportive nationalist line and then enlist the public to vilify these unpatriotic critics of doped athletes. Following the spectacular success of the Irish swimmer Michelle Smith at the 1996 Atlanta Olympic Games, a famously polemical columnist named Eamonn Dunphy earned widespread antipathy in Ireland by suggesting that Smith's Olympic victories were the result of her using drugs. As the *Weekly Telegraph* reported, "For three days, he appeared on the front page of the *Daily Mirror*'s Irish edition with the picture of his head on the body of a rat and when the newspaper conducted a readers' phone-in, 92 per cent agreed that he was a rat." Eventually, the Irish public was forced to conclude that Smith was, in fact, a doper. Today her reputation remains suspended in that peculiar purgatory that awaits the athletic champion who has fallen under permanent suspicion of doping in the absence of definitive proof that he or she actually used banned drugs.

Another example of tabloid vigilantism appeared in the *Gazzetta dello Sport* in 2000, as Italian authorities pursued the long-standing doping investigation of Marco Pantani, the enormously popular champion of the scandal-plagued 1998 Tour de France. "Five state prosecutors are working on Pantani, while the Mafia bosses are running around wherever they like," complained the *Gazzetta*. The same year, even an accusation by the state prosecutor that Richard Virenque was involved in drug smuggling did not damage his standing with the fans, in part because the media preferred to suppress coverage of doping and encourage talk about great cycling instead. "His Sweetest Revenge," headlined *Le Dauphiné Liberé*. In the meantime, Virenque magnanimously dedicated a stage victory to a twelve-year-old boy who had been killed by a car during an earlier stage of the race.

A year later, the same kind of public relations savvy sent the Olympic champion sprinter Linford Christie, following his doping conviction, into a primary school in Leicester, England, to present prizes to children. As in the cases of Ben Johnson and Andreas Goldberger, Christie's use of a banned doping substance did not disqualify him from serving as a role model for young people in the global war on drugs. Such episodes offer additional evidence that doping offenses do not automatically create the sort of social stigma that removes offenders from respectable society. Indeed, on July 9, 1992, Queen Elizabeth II hosted a garden party on the grounds of Buckingham Palace that welcomed, among many hundreds of celebrated athletes, four men—a weightlifter and three powerlifters—who had been banned for life from their sports because they had used illicit drugs.

Informal survey data about public attitudes toward doping reveal a modern sports audience that is divided about whether athletes dope and what should happen to them if they do. A 1998 Gallup poll sponsored by two Danish publications surveyed opinion in six countries—Denmark, Germany, England, France, Italy, and Spain—and found that about half of the respondents believed that a majority of professional athletes were using doping drugs. These Europeans even believed that drug use among track-and-field athletes and cyclists was comparable to that found among bodybuilders. In Italy 72 percent of those surveyed had become aware of the doping problem in professional soccer. Spaniards had the most permissive view of doping. While just over half said that the blood-boosting hormone erythropoietin should be banned, fully a third of those questioned said that the use of EPO should be permitted if it were medically supervised—a permissive view of EPO endorsed by every sixth respondent in the six countries as a whole. This survey also found that doping scandals caused a significant number of people to lose at least some of their interest in elite sport. Whether this disaffection has actually caused defections from stadium or television audiences remains unclear. Endorsing the ideal of drug-free sport in a survey is one thing; actually refusing to consume drug-assisted sports entertainment is another. As we shall see below, the outcomes of doping scandals can be both surprising and difficult to confirm.

The results of the 1998 poll correspond reasonably well with later surveys of varying quality. The German television show *Sports in the West*, for example, reported in June 1999 that 52.9 percent of its viewers believed that the professional riders for the German-sponsored Telekom team were doping. Six months before the Sydney Olympic Games opened in September 2000, almost half of the Australians polled said they believed that athletes were using banned substances. A full 65 percent of this group supported lifetime bans for athletes caught doping. (A British survey carried out in 1994 found that "over half of those questioned felt that athletes who used steroids should be given lifetime bans.") The Crédit Suisse bank gave up sponsoring professional cycling in 1999 when its own survey found that the Swiss public regarded cycling as by far the most doping-compromised sport. A nonrepresentative survey carried out by German Television in May 1996 found that 48 percent of the 20,000 viewers who were asked said they would rather see "doped medal winners than clean losers" at the 1996 Atlanta Olympic Games. This disquieting response shows how sportive nationalism can subvert the anti-doping campaign. Five months later, the German anti-doping official Hans Evers stated: "If you were to do an opinion survey—Do you want clean sport or medals?—I am sure that most would want the medals. And I believe that is how the federations think, as well."

Various observers have registered similar impressions. A month after the Italian police raided professional cyclists' hotel rooms during the 2001 Giro d'Italia, the German journalist Holger Gertz was reporting a general mood of hostility toward anti-doping efforts: "Anyone who goes looking for doping, be it a policeman or a state prosecutor or a journalist, is regarded as making trouble for the Big Game. The willingness to forgive is striking. On the Internet cycling fans devote pages to the mistakes not of the presumed dopers but rather of those who hunt dopers with new methods, such as the Italians with their new anti-doping law." In a similar vein, the Italian anti-doping activist Sandro Donati appears resigned to a sporting public that is willing to overlook doping as the price of athletic entertainment: "The fans only get excited about the great athletes and the great performances, instead of loving normal, human sport. It's as if the public needed stronger and stronger doses of emotion, like a drug."

Growing acceptance of athletic doping in the United States is evident in two public opinion surveys that appeared in November and December 2003. The *Denver Post* reported that 28 percent of its sample of 500 Denver-area sports fans said an athlete's use of banned or illegal performance-enhancing drugs would bother them only "a little" or "not at all." Twenty-four percent of these people endorsed athletes' use of legalized performance-enhancing drugs under medical supervision, while 10 percent were "not sure" about approving of such a procedure. Two-thirds of this group thus continued to resist the legalization of medically regulated doping as a solution to the doping crisis in sport. A *New York Times* poll of 1,057 adults nationwide came to very similar conclusions. A striking finding in both surveys shows a significant generational difference in attitudes toward drug use by athletes. The *Times* found that while 31 percent of those older than thirty were very disturbed by doping by professional athletes, only 15 percent of those between the ages of eighteen and twenty-nine expressed this view. A full 34 percent of the *Times* sample of those over thirty said they were unconcerned by doping professionals, while an even greater proportion (41 percent) of the younger age group expressed this opinion. The *Post* survey found that more than half of their respondents between the ages of eighteen and thirty-four had little or no objection to athletic doping and that a full 39 percent favored the legalization of performance-enhancing drugs under medical supervision.

These data are entirely consistent with the growing acceptance of pharmacological solutions for an expanding catalogue of human problems. Any society that permits the pharmaceutical industry to engage in direct-to-consumer advertising of its products inevitably subverts its own efforts to promote "drug-free" lifestyles. A modern society cannot ask athletes to be drug-free while ordinary people are routinely encouraged to use a variety of prescription and over-the-counter drugs for performance-enhancing purposes. The growing respectability of this kind of libertarian pharmacology can also affect how politicians manage the war on drugs. When in February 2004 Attorney General John Ashcroft announced that the government was indicting four individuals in the "designer steroid" scandal, a *New York Times* columnist speculated that he was "moving slowly as he gauges public support for unmasking steroid use by popular athletes during an election year." No American politician, after all, had dared to criticize the wildly popular Mark McGwire for serving as the role model who encouraged thousands of American adolescents to consume an unregulated anabolic steroid.

Such hypocrisy in the prosecution of the war on drugs shows that the definition of "doping" can be based on political calculations as well as more legitimate public health criteria.

The modern public's addiction to an upward spiral of escalating performances is a natural corollary of the internal logic of high-performance sport. Twentieth-century imaginations were conditioned to believe that the limits to human athletic performance could be pushed back indefinitely in measurable increments. This dream of expanding athletic horizons was eventually disrupted by the doping crisis that first attracted widespread attention during the 1980s. From then on, a global public would have to confront fundamental questions about the physiological and ethical costs of athletic achievements that tested human limits.

This appetite for spectacular performances may also have its limits. One observer has argued that audiences actually prefer the dramatic success of the underdog to the chilly perfection of the flawless performer: "Perfection produces suspicion or even revulsion when it appears in an unnatural manner, as it does in sport: No one in that world is so thoroughly spurned as the doper." Despite the naïveté of this overly categorical assertion, which is contradicted by the entire history of professional cycling, the fact remains that at least one segment of a sporting public may reject superlative performances if it intuits unnatural powers in the performers. A rare event of this kind occurred at the World Track and Field Championships at Stuttgart in 1993, when Chinese female distance runners ran so far ahead of the other women in the field that some in the stadium crowd whistled in derision as the accelerating Chinese circled the track. Two weeks later, three of the Chinese runners set world records at 1,500 meters (3:50.46), 3,000 meters (8:06.11), and 10,000 meters (29:31.78) that have never since been approached. They remain, in fact, the most mysterious performances in the history of the sport. It is still impossible for the outsider to know whether they were drug-assisted or the result of brutal training regimens inflicted on young peasant women by the tyrannical coach from whom they eventually fled. What we do know is that some spectators at the Stuttgart meet rejected the performances they were watching, presumably on the grounds that they were of unnatural origin. A similar protest erupted at the same championship when it was held in Edmonton, Alberta, in 2001. As the Russian runner Olga Yegorova ran to victory in the 5,000-meter race, she was jeered by spectators aware that she had tested positive for EPO and that only a technical error in administering the test had kept her from being barred from the competition. Upon her return home, she was hailed by *Sovyetsky Sport* as "the Golden Girl of Russia."

The humble origins and quiet suffering of the Chinese superathletes mentioned above point to the much-ignored relationship between poverty and doping that many sports fans understand. "Early in life I realized I did not have intellectual potential," Richard Virenque said at his trial, "so I dedicated myself to cycling." The Swiss rider Alex Zülle, having confessed to doping during the 1998 Tour de France scandal, described his predicament as a choice between dramatically different economic fates: "I had two alternatives: either fit in and go along with the others or go back to being a house painter. And who in my situation would have done that?" The price of upward social mobility for these men was a life of physical and mental suffering. The British rider Robert Millar, who finished fourth in the 1984 Tour de France, described this ordeal as follows: "The riders reckon that a good Tour takes one year off your life, and when you finish in a bad state, they reckon three years. . . . You can't describe to a normal person how tired you feel. . . . You can't divide the mental and the physical suffering; you tend to let go mentally before you crack physically." Given the degree of suffering, added Millar, "I can understand guys being tempted to use drugs in the Tour." Or, as the German journalist and physician Hans Halter put it: "No one can seriously expect that these extreme athletes, tortured by tropical heat and freezing cold, by rain and storm, should renounce all of the palliatives that are available to them."

Establishing medically defensible procedures to provide pain relief for these extreme athletes would appear to be an appropriate topic for public discussion. Yet neither sports officials nor media commentators have shown much interest in teaching the public the medical facts of life about professional cycling. Negotiating appropriate pain therapies in an open forum would take some of the sting out of the doping issue by removing the aura of secrecy from media coverage. At the same time, a transparent medical policy that presented the athletes as patients who require constant medicating just to stay on the course might pose other risks, as such an image would threaten the heroic tradition that has cast tough and sinewy Tour riders as "giants of the road." Whatever their motives, cycling officials have chosen to minimize public awareness of the medical support that riders get. Only police raids have allowed the public to learn about self-medicating riders discarding syringes and fleeing hotel rooms with bloody tubes hanging out of their arms. Few observers seem to realize that ordinary citizens might see these athletes as victims rather than as villains.

Some public indifference to doping may reflect the conviction that doping offers endurance athletes like professional cyclists the pain relief they deserve—a compassionate drug policy that is comparable to the medical marijuana initiatives American voters have favored over and over again in referenda, despite the constant stream of propaganda trumpeting a government war on drugs. Ordinary French citizens displayed this attitude during the drug scandal that rocked the 1988 Tour de France. The Tour's eventual winner, the Spanish rider Pedro Delgado, tested positive for a steroid-masking agent during the race. The whole world understood the implications of what he had done, yet he was not disqualified because this substance (probenecid) was still a month away from appearing on the International Cycling Federation's official list of banned drugs. Did this obvious doping violation turn the offender into a pariah? Quite the contrary. Delgado returned home a "Hero of Spain" and was awarded the gold medal of his native city of Segovia. Meanwhile, back in France, the Irish rider Paul Kimmage was observing the compassionate reactions of ordinary fans: "Few of them held any grudge against Delgado: 'Poor Pedro,' that's what they all said, 'Poor Pedro.' The consensus among the *pastis* drinkers of the Café de la Gare was that it was humanly impossible to ride a race like the Tour without taking stuff. Most ordinary people in France were of the same opinion. Delgado was encouraged like never before from the roadside: 'Poor Pedro.' " Small wonder that a *France Soir* opinion survey found 57 percent of the French public favoring the continuation of the 1998 Tour even at the height of the doping scandal, while hundreds of thousands of fans continued to line the roads.

> The opponents of doping simply could not grasp that the revelations and the scandalizing media coverage during the summer of 1998 did not cause the cycling public to turn its back on the event. Given that the whole thing was presented as cheating and fraud, the Tour route should have been wholly depopulated when the riders passed by. But it was not. On the contrary, the public was eager to demonstrate its sympathy and offer its support to the embattled field. It was obvious that these people did not feel cheated.

One reason they did not feel cheated was their appreciation of the physical ordeal the riders had to endure. Many ordinary people who depended on cigarettes, caffeine, or alcohol to make it through their days had no trouble sympathizing with men whose suffering could be read on their drawn and haggard faces.

Public compassion for doping athletes is based on the idea that sport is a form of labor that causes suffering. And the idea that athletic laborers require some kind of doping follows inevitably from the professionalizing of Olympic sport initiated by IOC president Juan Antonio Samaranch in 1981. The view that athletes are workers has been embraced by some of the most powerful sports officials in the world, with fateful consequences for doping policy. The political incorrectness of this position has produced some cryptic statements from officials who dare only hint at the necessary compromises demanded by the economic interests that rule professional sport. "Society and sport are becoming increasingly adjusted to high-tech medical methods," the president of the International Cycling Union (Union Cycliste Internationale, or UCI), Hein Verbruggen, warned in 1999. "It's an irreversible reality. The fight against doping has to adjust to that reality." Three years earlier, the head of the IOC Medical Commission, the late Prince Alexandre de Merode, was recommending a softening of doping sanctions on the grounds that Olympic athletes were professionals. "Strict sanctions were appropriate when we were dealing with top amateurs," he said, "but since sport has become a profession, we are faced with a major social problem. These sanctions have deep repercussions on people and their standard of living." In January 1999, just prior to the IOC-sponsored World Anti-Doping Conference in Lausanne, Merode once again expressed his conviction that harsh sanctions to deter doping were outmoded in an age of Olympic professionalism. Opposing minimum two-year suspensions for serious doping offenses, he proposed that athletes be allowed to compete in some events even as they were serving out their sentences for doping violations. Nor was Merode entirely off the mark when he argued, only half facetiously, that the real dopers were "people in show business and the arts, truck drivers, and government ministers [who take drugs] after long parliamentary sessions." Why should athletes be singled out for special opprobrium? In September 1998, at the height of the Tour de France furor, Merode declared that the high-performance athlete had become a worker pure and simple: "We need labour laws for high-level athletes," he said, "something like putting limits on their working time. We are going toward something of that sort." Asked about doping scandals, Merode replied that elite athletes had not been granted the protections enjoyed by industrial workers: "Labour is protected in all trades, why not in sport? High-level sport has become a trade like any other. One can imagine that we will not authorize whatever event in whatever conditions." It was this view of professionalism that in February 1999 prompted the IOC leadership to reject a mandatory two-year doping penalty that was being adamantly opposed by the international soccer, cycling, and tennis federations, all of which administer competitions featuring professional athletes.

But Olympic officials are not eager to publicize the medical predicaments of professional Olympians—the worker-athletes who are expected to train and perform at or beyond the limits of human ability without depending on drugs. The distasteful medical realities of the athletic labor-market harmonize poorly with the familiar Olympic celebrations of idealistic young people who long to fulfill their dreams. Better, then, to promise drug testing and the "clean" sport it makes possible. At the same time, one might ask whether the worried strategists at the IOC really understand their audience's complex attitudes toward doping. "What we are dealing with here is a certain kind of public relations issue," the Prince de Merode said in 1991. "The public must be persuaded that something is being done." Apparently, he could not imagine that a considerable segment of the public actually shared his sympathy for overstressed athletes who might be tempted to take drugs. How the IOC attempted to persuade the public that it was leading a crusade on behalf of drug-free sport is described in the next chapter of this book. Now it is time to summarize the results of the preceding analysis of public responses to doping.

The common presumption that the public flatly condemns all doping, though inaccurate, plays a significant role in the drug politics of modern societies. A successful illusion is always interesting from a sociological or political standpoint because it helps us to understand how interest groups can promote and benefit from its effects. Illusions, or distortions of reality, may be seen by interest groups as genuine representations of the real world; or they may be viewed as socially necessary falsehoods that serve a greater good, such as discouraging the use of drugs. The idealized image of "drug-free" athletes, which is promoted to a population that heavily consumes drugs while it looks for pharmacological abstinence in the sports sector, misrepresents the status of both therapeutic and recreational drugs in the lives of millions of people. This illusion also strengthens the mutually reinforcing relationship between the anti-doping campaign in sport and the more controversial war on drugs that has formed the basis of American drug policy since the late 1960s. A comparison of these anti-drug crusades, and an examination of how they may interact, appears toward the end of the next chapter.

The preceding analysis of public responses to doping should inspire in us the intellectual humility the subject requires. Indeed, the very concept of public opinion tends to flatten out differences, encouraging us to attribute to people's attitudes a homogeneity that is entirely speculative. What few data we do have suggest that public opinion on this subject must be subdivided in a number of ways. To begin with, there are those who care about doping and those who don't. There are distinct (and frequently overlapping) "sporting publics" for various sports that further split into those who attend events and those who watch them on television. The stadium audience that has an opportunity to register its feelings about a doping accusation will include individuals with both active and passive temperaments as well as those holding a variety of opinions that are difficult or impossible to articulate from the midst of a crowd. Those who do pay attention to doping may regard it as a private matter or as a public scandal. And as we see again and again, public reactions to doping cases are often affected by nationalistic feelings. After the blood doping scandal involving American cyclists at the 1984 Los Angeles Olympic Games, "reaction from the general public ranged from heated defense of the athletes to disappointment, resentment, and indignation." In North America as in Europe, the assumption that there is uniformity of public opinion about doping is an illusion.

The duration of a doping scandal can also affect an athlete's public image. The accused doper who vigorously disputes a positive test may at first do well in the media and enjoy what appears to be public support. But a doping controversy that drags on for months or even years can work to the athlete's disadvantage as a result of "compassion fatigue," new and unfavorable revelations, or even a declining performance level that disappoints the fans. Michelle Smith eventually lost favor with the Irish public because of several years of damaging revelations. The Danish rider Bjarne Riis, who returned home a hero after his victory in the 1996 Tour de France, fell into disfavor after it became known that his red blood cell level in 1995 had been measured at 56.3 percent of total blood volume—clearly above the normal level of 44 percent. This information did not prevent him from going on to manage corporate-sponsored cycling teams in Denmark, but his reputation has never fully recovered from this revelation and the aftershocks of the 1998 Tour scandal.

We should also recognize that public responses to doping often ex-

press intense feelings that are not centered on the ethics of using or refusing certain drugs but on patriotism or celebrity. We have already seen
how sportive nationalism can neutralize ethical concerns about doping
while creating what appears to be a public demand for top performances.
How politicians and sports officials react to such demands for nationalistic gratification is the single most important factor in determining the
success or failure of doping control. A German physician and world-class
distance runner named Thomas Wessinghage described the basic conflict
in 1985: "The spectators, too, will have to learn to accept the fact that
a girl who throws the shot is satisfied with 17 meters rather than 22. Our
national pride should not be threatened by this." In fact, this common-
sensical position has been rejected by a long series of German politicians
and sports functionaries. Like their counterparts in many other countries, these officials have made athletic performances a national security
issue, thereby creating political demands for performance that drug-free
athletes cannot always meet.

Sportive nationalist interference in the doping control process was exemplified by the histrionic behavior of the Greek sports minister, Gior-
gio Lianos, in February 2004. Facing an allegation that tied a prominent
Greek coach to the "designer steroid" scandal that had broken in the
United States in October 2003, Lianos denounced "anti-Greek propaganda that defames and insults Greek sport." Only six months before the
opening of the 2004 Athens Olympics, Lianos found himself under pressure to defend what he called "the credibility of the Greek athletes, their
coaches and the credibility of the Olympic Games." His problem was
that the credibility of Greece's male and female sprinting champions,
Kostas Kenteris and Ekaterina Thanou, had been under suspicion for
years, as they evaded drug testing at every opportunity. In 1997 their
coach, Christos Tsekos, was suspended for two years by the governing
body for international track and field (the International Association of
Athletics Federations) for physically assaulting a doping control officer
who intended to collect urine samples from two of his sprinters. In April
2003 an Athens newspaper had demanded an end to these evasive tactics. But the sports minister continued to play to a Greek public that
could be counted on to prefer Olympic medals to drug-free competition.
"I consider the accusations baseless," he declared, "because our distinguished athletes have passed and continue to go through checks and they
have never tested positive." The Greek government had paid Kenteris
300,000 euros for winning the European championship in the 200-meter
sprint in 2002, and he was selected as Greece's athlete of the year three

times in a row. His 2002 time of 19.85 seconds remains the fastest ever recorded by a white sprinter under standard conditions. Given that no sprinter the modern world would categorize as "white" has ever run 100 meters in under 10 seconds, one may speculate that Kenteris's presumed use of steroids overcame a genetic disadvantage vis-à-vis athletes of West African origin. His unique and conspicuous role as the only white man in the world capable of defeating the familiar legion of black champions can only have intensified Greeks' emotional investment in his performances and thus their indignation in the face of the doping accusations directed at their national hero.

The turbulent careers of Kenteris and Thanou came back to haunt the 2004 Athens Olympic Games as well as the Greek sports officials and politicians who for years had let them and their coach get away with anything. One day before the opening ceremony that was to have featured Kenteris lighting the Olympic torch, both stars missed an IOC drug test, thereby precipitating a public relations nightmare that changed the mood of the Games. Both athletes eventually withdrew from Olympic competition. "How," *Der Spiegel* asked, "could Kenteris and Thanou retain the support of a nation given the many reasons to distrust them, such as Kenteris's enormous thighs and [the athletes'] constant evasion of doping controls?" In fact, a great deal of pro-Kenteris feeling survived the public relations problems intact. On the night of the 200-meter final, the Greek stadium crowd that had expected to watch Kenteris defend his Olympic title became loud and unruly enough to delay the race.

Evidence of the Italian public's attitude toward doping was on display in February 2004 following the sudden death of the popular cycling champion Marco Pantani. In 1999 his elevated red blood cell count prompted cycling authorities to remove him from the Giro d'Italia, a race he had won the year before. From that point on Pantani was widely regarded as a suspected doper. In 2000 he was convicted of "athletic fraud," and in 2001 a syringe containing trace amounts of insulin was discovered in his hotel room. The reaction of Italian society to Pantani's death made it clear that his stature as a national folk hero outweighed the doping stigma. Television networks interrupted their scheduled programming to announce the discovery of his lifeless body in the beachside hotel room in which he was found with various drugs. The nation's press united in a chorus of mourning. The organizers of the Giro announced that henceforth the race would celebrate a "Pantani Day" each year. Tens of thousands attended the funeral as a regional television station projected the ceremony onto a giant screen set up in the town square.

Few observers noted at the time that Pantani had been one of three "patients" of the notorious sports physician Francesco Conconi to die within just over a year. All three were professional cyclists, and all three died of cardiac arrest.

Perhaps the most mysterious aspect of the popular response to doping is how celebrity can affect the status of the accused doper. The athlete who delivers tabloid-style diversion in the midst of his notoriety, even if only in the form of intrepid defiance, may be forgiven a multitude of sins, at least during the first phase of publicity. Whether it involves a charismatic rascal (Karl-Heinz Radschinsky) or a surly rogue who threatens to unleash his lawyers (Andreas Berger), a doping scandal can offer real entertainment to a public for which doping is simply not a life-and-death issue. It is likely, in fact, that the increasing tendency to present athletes as entertainers will further trivialize athletic doping as an ethical issue, since the public expects entertainers to use drugs. The pretty blonde sprinter whose pierced navel and tattooed back attract the television cameras is an unconvincing representative of the drug-free life. What is more, a significant number of people already accept drug-induced intoxication as a component of artistic creativity. This widespread acceptance may account for the results of an opinion poll taken in 1986 in the United States, which showed significantly more support for drug-testing athletes than entertainers. Why? Because athletes were still expected to exercise a degree of self-control that other performers are not.

Finally, public response to doping is one dimension of a larger sociopolitical process that is analyzed in the next chapter of this book. For while doping scandals invariably focus on individuals, doping is in fact a social practice that involves political institutions, international federations, professional networks, and powerful commercial interests—including corporate sponsors, media companies, pharmaceutical and supplement manufacturers, and the sports journalism business itself. "Doping is an economic problem, and that is how it should be seen," says Professor Helmut Digel, a German sociologist and reform-minded sports administrator. The athlete, he says, is a de facto "drug expert" who is constantly maneuvering between his sponsors and managers for the purpose of "selling his performance as a commodity." Here, once again, is the athlete-as-worker, for whom doping is a matter more practical than ethical, bearing on the athlete's certification and employment by large organizations. Doping, adds the French sociologist Georges Vigarello, should be less an object of anathema than a matter of public responsibility. Alas, as we shall see, social and political institutions have evaded their responsibilities to deal with doping honestly and realistically.

"You murderers! You damned murderers!" the exhausted French rider Octave Lapine shouted at the organizers of the Tour de France in 1910 as he finally completed a long mountain climb. "Damn the swine who do this to us!" cursed the Swiss rider Ferdi Kübler during the 1955 Tour. As doctors struggled to save the life of another doped rider, Kübler, full of amphetamines, locked himself in his hotel room and screamed: "Ferdi is going to explode!" whenever someone knocked on the door. Confronted by a doctor who threatened to take them to court, the organizers ordered the first drug raid in the history of the Tour. On this occasion, the raiders were not the police but the "swinish" organizers themselves.

For most of the next fifty years the riders and organizers of the Tour abided by a tacit arrangement that covered up systematic doping with a tissue of lies and evasions. Until the watershed year of 1998, similar arrangements allowed the International Olympic Committee and many international sports federations to conduct doping control as a form of public relations. Now let us examine how an informal global arrangement worked out by sports officials, politicians, and commercial interests has ensured the failure of doping control over many years.

CHAPTER 7

A War against Drugs?

The Politics of Hormone Doping in Sport

INTERNATIONAL DOPING CONTROL BEFORE REFORM

Over the past four decades illicit drug use in Olympic sport has reached epidemic proportions. The widespread and often undetected use of potentially dangerous synthetic hormones such as anabolic steroids, human growth hormone, and erythropoietin has provoked a crisis of confidence in the integrity of such Olympic sports as track and field, swimming, cycling, and weightlifting. Hormone doping has made possible, or rendered suspect, numerous world records. Signs of demoralization among athletes and sports officials have been evident for many years. In 1991, for example, the spokesman for Germany's track-and-field athletes claimed that highly placed officials had simply given up on the anti-doping campaign in the face of apparently insurmountable obstacles. A month later, the former president of the German Swimming Federation, Harm Beyer, called for the "controlled" use of steroids on the grounds that German sports officials had shown themselves to be both unwilling and unable to eradicate doping. Beyer, a Hamburg judge who has served as secretary general of the European Swimming Association and is now the head of doping control for the International Swimming Federation (Fédération Internationale de Natation Amateur, or FINA), proposed the formation of a "circus troupe" of elite athletes "subject to different rules and laws," who would be eligible to take steroids and other performance-enhancing drugs. Like others before him, this prominent official had simply resigned himself to doping as a fact of life.

The failure of national and international sports federations to control doping is primarily a political phenomenon, though it is conventionally misrepresented as being caused by the moral degeneracy of individual athletes. Media reports of doping scandals invariably stress the ethical failures of athletes and portray sports federations as beleaguered but honest regulators whose methods for detecting drugs cannot match the scientific ingenuity of the cheaters and those who aid and abet them. But the reality of doping is far more complicated. As noted in the previous chapter, one prominent anti-doping reformer has pointed out that "doping is an economic problem, and that is how it should be seen." The historical record shows that the minority of sports officials who have been openly dedicated to the eradication of doping have been unable to prevail against less-dedicated colleagues bent on tolerating or covering up the doping practices of their athletes, coaches, and doctors.

We have already seen that medical professionals are essential to the doping system. At the same time, we need to understand why modern societies and so many of their politicians demand elite athletic performances in the first place. For the failure of doping control originates in these demands and in the resulting accommodations that have been made over many years at both the national and international levels of sports administration. Many sports officials have assumed that effective doping control threatened their operations or was simply unachievable to begin with, and they have often responded with strategies designed to subvert or delay the advent of effective drug testing. This tacit holding action against reform has been less a conspiracy than a loose arrangement entered into by international sports bodies and the national federations that operate under their authority. The Olympic Games are, after all, an arrangement for promoting competitions between nations under the rubric of "the Olympic idea" and its internationalist doctrine of reconciliation between nations. The doping arrangement described above has been one aspect of this mutually beneficial collaboration between nationalists and internationalists.

The doping predicament of the International Olympic Committee (IOC) developed during the presidency of Juan Antonio Samaranch (1980–2001) and first became a public relations crisis for the IOC during the difficult year of 1988. It was then that the anti-doping campaign became a global ideology, with the elite athlete pressed into service as a drug-free role model. Samaranch took the lead in this crusade, to which he contributed an anti-doping rhetoric that sometimes took on a liturgical flavor. "Above all," he proclaimed at the Calgary Winter Games, "such behavior makes a mockery of the very essence of sport, the soul of what we, like our predecessors, consider sacrosanct ideals." "Doping," he added, "is alien to our philosophy, to our rules of conduct. We shall never tolerate it." In September of that year, only two weeks before the Ben Johnson steroid scandal at Seoul, Samaranch intensified the rhetorical assault against the doping evil. "Doping equals death," he declared, calling drugged athletes "the thieves of performance" and denouncing the medical personnel who assisted them as unprincipled people who "attach little importance to their oath or the code of ethics they are supposed to respect." He continued, "Yes, doping equals death. Death psychologically, with the profound, sometimes irreversible alteration of the body's normal processes through inexcusable manipulation. Physical death, as certain tragic cases in recent years have shown. And then also the death of the spirit and intellect, by the acceptance of cheating. And finally moral death, by placing oneself de facto outside the rules of conduct demanded by any human society."

Almost a decade later, the IOC president revived this idiom on the eve of the 1996 Atlanta Games. Athletes who dope, he said, "commit a series of acts that transgress and violate certain immutable principles." While these pronouncements do convey the sermonizing tone that was sometimes affected by this IOC president, such sentiments also represent what much of the world has expected of athletes since the Victorian age. Far from being only one man's eccentricity, this idealization of the athletic hero is a cultural preoccupation that feeds the doping crisis by producing an endless parade of "sinners" who have failed to live up to the moral standards expected of celebrated role models. This oratorical campaign eventually persuaded Samaranch that the IOC had, indeed, "spearheaded the anti-doping campaign on a worldwide scale."

The historical record suggests, however, that the rhetorical campaign against doping was not matched during this period by concerted actions, or even by public statements with more content than bombast. The IOC rationalized its political passivity as the necessary consequence of its own policy of decentralization, which left the difficult implementation of policy to national and international federations whose commitment to effective doping control has seldom been evident. Nowhere have the effects of this policy been clearer than in the case of Germany.

Reacting in late 1990 to revelations about the East German doping program, the IOC press director commented that the IOC saw no need to act and would await a report from the German National Olympic Committee. Samaranch himself called the growing scandal "a German problem." Unknown to the IOC, or perhaps viewed as irrelevant, was the unreliability of the (West) German National Olympic Committee on the subject of East German doping: West German officials were unlikely to reveal its full scope when they were hiring for their own purposes the most highly regarded coaches who had been involved in doping athletes under State Plan 14.25. In fact, Samaranch's basic policy on doping was to trust the untrustworthy and thereby avoid the confrontations that would have complicated his presidency. He had long appreciated the spectacular success of East Germany's Olympic athletes, and this admiration made his behavior vis-à-vis the East Germans conspicuously obtuse. In 1985 he conferred Olympic Orders on Communist Party boss Erich Honecker and on Manfred Ewald, the sports chief who would eventually be convicted of doping crimes against children. In 1988 he bestowed another Olympic Order on the East German swimmer Kristin Otto after she had won six gold medals at the Seoul Games with the help of steroids. By November 1991 revelations about East German doping had made headlines around the world, but this did not deter Samaranch from meeting with Ewald at a party hosted by the German National Olympic Committee. Paragraph 7 of the Olympic Charter empowers the IOC to remove an Olympic Order if a recipient has damaged the honor and dignity of the Olympic movement, but Samaranch chose not to exercise this option, despite the many Olympic medals awarded to doped East German athletes. As we shall see, the IOC categorically refused to condemn doped performances at Olympic Games until the 2002 Salt Lake City Olympic Games.

Samaranch was similarly generous toward the Chinese sports establishment. When several Chinese athletes tested positive for steroids at the swimming world championships in 1994, an IOC spokesman adroitly deflected the problem onto the individual sport's federation, FINA. The fact that Chinese swimmers, runners, and weightlifters had been producing an improbable number of mind-boggling performances prompted neither an investigation nor anything resembling critical commentary from the IOC. "The Chinese have problems," the IOC's director general said, "but they are not the only ones." The head of the IOC Medical Commission, Prince Alexandre de Merode, called the Chinese positives "accidents that could happen anywhere." In April 1995 this view was seconded by the IOC president himself: "We are carrying out a decisive struggle against the doping evil," he declared, "but there can be no sweeping condemnations of individual nations."

The IOC's primary anti-doping strategy has been the drug-testing program it initiated in 1968; tests for anabolic steroids were first carried out at the 1976 Montreal Olympic Games. But an effective anti-doping campaign did not become a real priority of the IOC until the 1998 Tour de France scandal fundamentally changed the politics of doping. The French government's decision to unleash the power of state prosecutors—who brought criminal charges against athletes, managers, and physicians—produced an upheaval that forced the IOC into an anti-doping partnership with governmental agencies. The result of this initiative was the World Anti-Doping Agency (WADA), which began operating on January 13, 2000. Before 1998, Olympic drug testing was little more than a cosmetic procedure designed to reassure the sporting public that something was being done about drugs. Between 1968 and 1996, approximately one in every thousand Olympic athletes tested positive for a banned substance at the Games. As late as the 1996 Atlanta Games, the chief medical officer stated even before drug testing began that he expected the 10,700 athletes to yield a minuscule total of twelve to fifteen positive tests, or just over the traditional 0.1 percent. In fact, the 1,923 drug tests carried out in Atlanta yielded only two steroid positives. Only four steroid positives were recorded at the 2000 Sydney Games, although this total was certainly reduced by the abrupt departure of twenty-seven Chinese athletes just before the competitions began and the disqualification of twenty others in the period leading up to the Games. A new test for synthetic erythropoietin (EPO), a hormone that increases the concentration of red blood cells, yielded no positives. Despite these low numbers, the Sydney Games are widely regarded as the first Olympic competition at which drug testing deterred doping to a significant degree.

The Olympic testing program was widely regarded as a sham, and with good reason. In the meantime, the IOC had delegated the task of additional drug testing to national and international federations. For IOC president Juan Antonio Samaranch and his closest associates, doping was primarily a public relations problem that threatened the lucrative television and corporate contracts that are now worth billions of dollars.

The IOC has frequently been ignorant of or indifferent to developments that any organization with a serious anti-doping program would have investigated, criticized, and taken action against. The booming export trade in former East German coaches with steroid doping expertise is a case in point. West German sports federations began to hire such people shortly after the Berlin Wall came down in November 1989 and continued on a scale that astonished many West German athletes and coaches. In 1991, for example, twenty-four compromised coaches who had been exposed in Brigitte Berendonk's authoritative *Doping-Dokumente* (1991) were cleared and had their contracts extended by the German Track and Field Federation (Deutscher Leichtathletik-Verband, or DLV). In the same year the West German swimming coach Georg Weinzierl initiated a campaign to oppose the hiring of former East German coaches who had admitted to doping their athletes. This action did not deter the German Swimming Federation from hiring people such as Volker Frischke and Uwe Neumann, both of whom were eventually convicted of having engaged in child doping in East Germany. East German coaches accused of doping were still being employed by the DLV as late as May 2000. Nor was the demand for this East German talent pool limited to Germany. The former head swimming coach, Wolfgang Richter, found work in Catalonia. Another swimming coach, Rolf Gläser, was hired by the Austrians and eventually convicted of administering steroids to girls. "I see no other coach in Austria who is as professionally competent to coach me," said an Austrian protegée who was surprised by Gläser's confession. Another East German who found a position in Austria was the biathlon coach Kurt Hinze, who eventually lost a court case to an Olympic champion (Jens Steinigen) who had accused him of promoting doping. Former East German coaches also found employment in Denmark, Holland, France, Switzerland, Great Britain, Spain, Italy, Greece, Norway, Sweden, Egypt, South Africa, South Korea, Brunei, New Zealand, and Australia. The spread of East German doping expertise around the world has never been addressed by the IOC.

Perhaps the most interesting emigrant of the 1990s was Ekkart Arbeit, who had served the East German sports establishment as head throwing coach (1982–83) and as head track-and-field coach (1989–90). In late 1997 Athletics Australia hired Arbeit as chief administrator for Australian track and field with an eye to producing medals at the 2000 Sydney Olympic Games. Before the end of 1990 Arbeit had been hired by Colonel Gianni Gola, president of the Italian track-and-field federation, to coach discus throwers. As the German anti-doping activist Dr. Werner Franke told an Australian journalist in October 1997: "He can't find a job in Germany so he has been to Italy and Greece. Wherever he goes there is a smell, and now the smell is in your country." He added, "You can quote me that Arbeit was responsibly involved with giving steroids to minors." The Arbeit hiring created a firestorm of publicity in Australia, but his appointment was not canceled until it was learned that he had served the East German secret police for twenty years as a spy. The ideological solidarity of the international coaching fraternity became evident when Frank Dick, the British president of the European Athletic Coaches Association, declared his support of the hiring: "Ekkart Arbeit enjoys the confidence and respect of all coaches and athletes with whom he has worked around the world." In October 2001 Arbeit was flown to South Africa in the hope that he would apply for a position as Athletics South Africa's first national coach. His disappointed hosts were told that he preferred to be a consultant. In April 2002 Athletics South Africa confirmed his position as chief consultant, offering a series of rationalizations to justify this appointment. It is clear that Arbeit's documented participation in the East German doping program has barely affected demand for his services. Such careers are sustained by the ambitions of sportive nationalists in many countries. The IOC's reluctance to regulate this job market underscores that the Olympic Games themselves are an arrangement that satisfies the ambitions of sportive nationalists around the globe. Samaranch's stern insistence that there can be "no sweeping condemnations of individual nations" was essentially a political maneuver to provide cover for national and international federation officials, who were allowed to deal (or not deal) with the doping problem as they saw fit.

The infiltration of international sports medical commissions by physicians who tolerate or encourage doping presents another aspect of IOC silence and passivity. Subversion of the drug-testing process from within was already under way at a 1974 meeting of the medical commission of the governing body for international track and field (the International Amateur Athletic Federation, or IAAF). The subject of this heated session was the introduction of doping controls to detect the use of anabolic steroids at the upcoming European championships. Dr. Ludwig Prokop of Vienna, a former president of the World Federation of Sports Physicians, expressed his concern about the future of high-performance athletics. The exploitation of sport as an instrument of national prestige had already led to the use of medically dangerous androgens, and he appealed for an unambiguous resolution to ban these drugs from sport. He was opposed by the West German sports physician Dr. Joseph Keul, who argued that anabolic steroids were indispensable regenerative drugs that could be safely administered in small doses. Eventually, Prokop's anti-doping resolution was seriously watered down by a committee consisting of himself, Keul, and Manfred Höppner, director of the East German Sports Medical Service (Sportmedizinischer Dienst der DDR, or SMD). According to an East German secret police report on this meeting, Keul upbraided Prokop for sounding like a spokesman for the Catholic Church. Twenty years later Prokop recalled his interaction with these high-performance sports physicians: "In fact, these people just wanted to know how to minimize side effects. The whispering campaign among the physicians—so many milligrams of this and of that—was revolting. What I find just as immoral is their knowing complicity."

Three decades later we are in a position to assess the careers of these men and the course of the doping epidemic to which they are connected in different ways. The late Joseph Keul was decorated by the federal government in Bonn and served as West Germany's official Olympic sports physician for two decades. During much of this time he was described repeatedly in the press as a compromised figure whose insincere criticisms of doping concealed his membership in the medical pro-steroid lobby. Following the drug-related death of the West German heptathlete Birgit Dressel in 1987, Keul told the German parliament that the doping problem was being exaggerated, that doping did not occur in most sports, that steroids were safe and effective. At the height of the 1998 Tour de France scandal, Keul recommended EPO as a safe alternative to altitude training. Manfred Höppner is today the disgraced former director of the SMD, convicted along with Manfred Ewald for doping crimes in the former East Germany. Both men received suspended prison sentences. Ludwig Prokop has maintained his independence from elite sports medical circles. In 1994 he described the high-performance sports world as "a big mafia."

Investigating and disqualifying doping-tainted medals and performances was never acceptable to the IOC during the Samaranch era. Documented proof of the systematic doping of former East German Olympic champions and world-record holders has opened up the possibility of reassigning the medals won by doped athletes to those who finished immediately behind them in Olympic competitions. Proposals to reassign medals came from the United States, Britain, and Australia. "With this information we can rewrite records and send a loud message to our youngsters that you can break records without drugs," a British coach and former athlete said in September 1997. This proposal was endorsed by Dr. Werner Franke, a prominent German molecular biologist and doping expert. "It has been said that records could not be reset because there wasn't any proof," he stated at a seminar in London in September 1997. "Well, there is now."

But German sports officials of varying credibility on the doping issue strenuously resisted these initiatives as discriminatory and unfair—yet another example of how sportive nationalism subverts the building of a global anti-doping coalition by mobilizing feelings of national pride. The conservative (Christlich-Demokratische Union, or CDU) German interior minister Manfred Kanther angrily rejected the whole idea as "absurd," claiming that Germany had dealt with its doping past in a "meticulous" manner and (even more implausibly) that German sport was now "manipulation-free." Even the reformist president of the German track-and-field federation, Professor Helmut Digel, described these demands as hypocritical, because doping had been a global problem for many years. These protests demonstrated how much German reunification had changed sports' political landscape, as West Germans who had once resented the doping-tainted victories of their East German adversaries now embraced these performances as part of a common national heritage of achievement.

But such protests were not necessary, because the IOC was not interested in new information and never had been. As early as the doping-rhetoric offensive launched at Calgary, the head of the IOC Medical Commission had pointedly rejected the idea of using information about doping to revise the results of tainted competitions. Athletes who confessed to doping, said the Prince de Merode, would not be penalized. "Some things belong to history. We are not going to apply sanctions from [sic] an event that happened four years ago. We'll never have retroactive sanctions." When Samaranch was asked in 1990 whether an Olympic champion who later confessed to doping would be retroactively disqualified, the IOC president deflected the question by saying, "Those are hypotheses. We proceed only on the basis of facts." Seven years later, as those facts were pouring out of newly accessible East German documents, Samaranch declared them irrelevant. When asked whether doped East German athletes would have to surrender their Olympic medals, Samaranch stated: "There are time limits, one cannot go back that far." IOC director-general François Carrard claimed that the organization was already in the process of working out a procedure for handling such matters between Olympiads and that the IOC Executive Board would be discussing the British demands a month later in Nagano, Japan, the site of the 1998 Winter Olympic Games. Both of the German IOC members, Thomas Bach and Walther Tröger, asserted that sports history simply could not be rewritten.

These pronouncements about the immutability of Olympic history were also embraced by the IAAF. When asked in September 1997 about the possibility of changing doping-tainted world records, an IAAF spokesman replied: "We can only deal with athletes individually. The documents would mean nothing to us." Another IAAF official declared: "The rule is quite clear. After six years it is not possible to cancel any results. It is too late." An IAAF press officer referred to a six-year statute of limitations in the IAAF rules that would govern allegations of doping violations.

This legalistic defense of doping-compromised performances was opposed by Frank Shorter, the 1972 Olympic marathon champion, who is also a lawyer. Shorter believes, and not without reason, that the East German runner who outran him for the gold medal at the 1976 Montreal Games benefited from steroid doping. "Six years," he has argued, "is an arbitrary statute of limitations. Also, since I maintain participation in international athletics is a privilege and not a right, it is always revocable and the federations should have total discretion in this regard. Laws have been changed in the past because of social need. 'The greatest good for the greatest number' is part of common law. The whole point is that the users should know there is no statute of limitations." Why, indeed, should there be such fastidiousness about preserving the reputations of compromised people whose doping-tainted performances were now a matter of public record?

Arbitrary statutes of this kind are formulated and enforced by supranational entities such as the IOC and the IAAF that are supposed to function as courts of last resort, transcending national claims and rivalries. As the IAAF general secretary put it in 1988 when a Swiss runner challenged her doping sanction in a Swiss court: "We can't have the national courts of 181 member nations telling us what to do." The problem is that the international federations have never developed a caste of reliable international civil servants who might have administered a viable system of doping controls. Too many of these federations become autocratic fiefdoms where the president's word is law, the IOC of Juan Antonio Samaranch being a prime case in point. Autocratic bodies of this kind are not receptive to internal reform, as became evident in 1999 when external forces compelled the IOC to adopt reforms over the objections of most of its members. It is hardly surprising, then, that such a group would be unwilling to revise the results of past competitions to which it has lent its prestige. Once the medals are awarded, discussion is forbidden. In a similar fashion, the canonization of a saint by a pope is irreversible: "New information coming into the scholars' hands after the pope has spoken does not matter." Indeed, the Vatican and the IOC share a grandiosity that declares the glorious past to be a monument that is, in effect, beyond examination or negotiation.

The IOC's unwillingness to remove its doped champions from the historical record may also derive from a profound sense of insecurity about the integrity of its competitions. For revising medal and record lists would require more than simply undertaking protracted investigations and holding contentious committee meetings. Such a reckoning with the past would probe the network of relationships between various IOC and federation officials that makes the whole Olympic enterprise possible, a network that had always operated on the premise that doping is a public relations issue to be "controlled" primarily in the media. Helmut Digel's proposal to deal with suspect world records by starting a new list as of January 1, 2000, went nowhere. The most powerful IOC and federation officials will continue to resist such reforms unless unanticipated developments compel them to do otherwise. Restoring hope to young athletes who are demoralized by competing against steroid-assisted records has been less important than preserving intact the egos and reputations of sports officials who were accountable to no one but themselves.

SPORTIVE NATIONALISM AND DOPING

That international sports officials had the latitude for many years to run doping control as a public relations operation points to a larger societal ambivalence toward performance-enhancing drugs. Their partners in this enterprise were the national Olympic committees (NOCs) and national sports federations in countries around the world, which have encouraged or covered up doping practices to promote success in international sports competitions. These practices belong under the heading of *sportive nationalism,* which may be defined as the use of elite athletes by governments or other national bodies to demonstrate national fitness and vitality for the purpose of enhancing national prestige. Sportive nationalism takes different forms, depending in part on the nature of the government that seeks prestige in the athletic arena. The East German dictatorship was able to operate in an uninhibited manner that maximized the efficient use of its relatively small population while secretly mobilizing more than a thousand scientists, doctors, and other personnel to operate a comprehensive doping program for elite athletes. Many of these people, particularly the young women, were medically harmed by these procedures. The sheer efficiency and brutality of such a project are both unusual and incompatible with the ethos of a democratic society.

Sportive nationalism in open societies is more interesting than its authoritarian counterpart because elected officials can debate in an open forum the national vitality hypothesis and its consequences. We shall examine the German argument over doping in greatest depth because no other society has debated the issue so intensely over so long a period of time, with so many high government officials taking part. The office responsible for national sports strategy in Germany has been the Interior Ministry, which funds elite athlete training and sports research. Federal funding means that the German parliament (Bundestag) bears a legal and moral responsibility for the development of elite athletes and for any attendant doping problems. Public hearings in the Bundestag thus force politicians to declare their allegiances on the subject of performance-enhancing drugs. Are they more committed to winning medals or to fielding drug-free athletes? In other words, when it comes to doping, are they nationalists bent on athletic glory or regulatory internationalists bent on effective regulation of doping in sport?

Government sponsorship of elite athletes therefore requires a delicate balancing act: it must promote national competitiveness while supporting, or appearing to support, the campaign against performance-enhancing drugs. In West Germany, for example, as preparations were under way for the 1988 Seoul Olympic Games, the interior minister asserted that medical support for elite athletes would not include doping and that the Olympic mobilization would place the best interests of the athlete ahead of nationalistic pressures: "The athlete must not be turned into a plaything of political interests," he declared. Several weeks later, the president of the Federal Republic, Richard von Weizsäcker, addressed the issue of national vitality at a ceremony honoring some of West Germany's top athletes: "Recently," he said, "there have been a number of comments made concerning the weak performance of German sport at its highest level. It is my view that premature condemnations in this area should be avoided, *since it would be wrong to measure the quality of a country by the number of its Olympic medals*" (emphasis added). The West German Olympic and world champion swimmer Michael Groß seconded this position: "I do not share the view that an inability to win medals says anything about our society's ability to compete."

German sportive nationalism has always prevailed over this kind of sober-minded rationality, and this imbalance of power has promoted the doping of (West) German athletes as well as their East German counterparts. The most candid display of pro-doping sentiment occurred back in 1977, when the conservative (CDU) parliamentary representative Wolfgang Schäuble told the Bundestag that West German athletes should have access to anabolic steroids to advance the national interest: "We advocate only the most limited use of these drugs," he stated, "and only under the complete control of the sports physicians . . . because it is clear that there are [sports] disciplines in which the use of these drugs is necessary to remain competitive at the international level." Fifteen years later, during Schäuble's term as interior minister, the federal government once again refused to ratify a European Anti-Doping Charter that called for banning all pharmacological, chemical, and mechanical forms of performance enhancement. Given the prominent government support of highly publicized anti-doping initiatives such as the *Keine Macht den Drogen* (No Power to Drugs) and *Fair-Play geht vor* (Fair Play Comes First) campaigns, one might ask why the interior ministry would oppose the ratification of a comprehensive anti-doping treaty. One explanation was proposed by the sports journalist Thomas Kistner:

> The striking degree of restraint in Bonn may well have to do with the fact that the charter also prescribes procedures for dealing with those who provide doping substances. Signing the treaty would thus create a legal foundation for proceeding against physicians, coaches, and officials who practice doping. And with that, by a stroke of the pen, unified Germany—which is to say, the East German State Doping Plan—would acquire a host of problems.

In 1989 Schäuble warned against a "doping hysteria" that unfairly tainted elite sport and the use of doping, calling it "manipulation." "The limits of human performance must be respected," the interior minister declared, even as he called for a "new definition of the doping concept" that would not deny the athlete appropriate regenerative treatments. In 1991 Schäuble demanded an end to the doping problem even as he was refusing to give up sportive nationalism as a national priority. "I reject," he said, "the demands that the federal government should put an end to its promotion of elite sport on the grounds that the end of the East-West conflict means that sport has lost one of its basic functions—to express the competition between political systems." At the same time, he also rejected more investment in sport for the masses, dismissing this egalitarian proposal behind the slogan "Mass sport and elite sport are a unity." Five years later, the president of the German Sports Federation

(Deutscher Sportbund, or DSB), Manfred von Richthofen, denounced the government's refusal to promote sport as a public health measure. It appeared that for the government of Chancellor Helmut Kohl, the medals won by elite athletes served the national interest more effectively than did the fitness of the body politic.

Schäuble's successor at the Ministry of the Interior, Manfred Kanther, shared his predecessor's view that elite sport was an indispensable expression of national vitality. The policies of both men demonstrated once again that sportive nationalism imposes limits on anti-doping initiatives. In May 1994 Kanther released a federal anti-doping report, surveying the period from 1989 to April 1994; it concluded that new laws against doping were not necessary. Meanwhile, the indifference of conservative deputies killed a Social Democratic (Sozialdemokratische Partei Deutschlands, or SPD) proposal for a law punishing those who doped children. In April 1997 Kanther was still opposing a change in the drug law that would have exposed doping coaches to legal penalties. He justified this position by arguing that such a law would represent an unwarranted intrusion into the autonomous world of sport organizations, which already had the doping problem under control. To more skeptical observers, Kanther's refusal to support a sharpening of the drug law appeared consistent with Schäuble's argument in 1977 that Germany had no obligation to practice unilateral disarmament in the area of performance-enhancing pharmacology. By the 1980s it was clear that the sheer political incorrectness of this position required a countervailing rhetoric of "clean" sport. In conformity with this political requirement, and like his predecessor, Kanther obscured the sportive-nationalist position by combining a series of anti-doping pledges with a robust discourse of nationalist self-assertion. "The successes of our athletes," he declared in September 1996, "demonstrate that the government's investment in elite sport is fully justified." "Sports medals," he said in January 1997, "are a national priority. They are proof of a people's ability to compete." In June 1997 Kanther and his political allies in the Bundestag opposed yet another SPD-sponsored anti-doping law, and for the Social Democratic sports spokesman Eckhard Fischer the reason was clear: "The CDU," he said, "is scared to death that elite sport is going to come in for criticism."

The sportive nationalism of important German politicians is a matter of record: the real challenge is to understand why they say what they say. It is possible, for example, that some politicians offer the public a feigned concern about German sporting prowess because they believe many voters to be receptive to this sort of chauvinism. Yet it is also possible that at least some of these statements are sincere, in that they express a genuine anxiety about the "fitness" of the body politic in an expansive sense that includes the military and economic viability of the nation. This elastic sense of national fitness encourages the idea that athletic success in international competitions is a kind of national security issue that warrants the toleration of performance-enhancing drugs. "[German] sport must remain internationally competitive," Chancellor Helmut Kohl declared in October 1995. In May 1997 the German president, Roman Herzog, endorsed elite sport as a healthy influence against what he described as a sort of national malaise. "Pessimism," he lamented, "has become the prevailing mood among us," and he pointed to "a paralysis in our society." The antidote was the "dynamism" of sport. The idea that German society had succumbed to a kind of mood disorder had appeared a year earlier in the remarks of Chancellor Kohl, as he received the team that had just won the European soccer championship. German athletes who had rebounded from adversity, he said, set a good example at a time when "many of us at home call in sick on account of a little head cold." Endorsements of elite athletic success at the highest political level can only encourage the tacit bureaucratic acceptance of doping that has long been evident in the most ambitious sports establishments around the world.

The overt sportive nationalism that marked the tenure of Chancellor Helmut Kohl (1982–98) is more often associated with conservative politicians than with their Social Democratic counterparts, and this ideological divide has also shaped the German debate about doping. Disagreements about anti-doping policy in the Bundestag during the 1980s and 1990s typically featured a minority of Greens and Social Democrats arguing for stronger laws and sanctions against doping and its practitioners, while a conservative (Christian Democrat) majority resisted these initiatives. At the same time, the harder anti-doping line forced its left-wing sponsors into the difficult position of opposing sportive nationalism itself. "Even if the 1992 Olympics turn out to be a debacle for us," the SPD sports spokesman said a year before the Games, "we can engage in elite sport only if it is clean." We have already seen that German politicians of the past generation have not seen fit to enforce this standard of conduct.

The same contest between nationalist ambition and anti-doping norms occurs in various societies around the world. Heads of state and other officials have often intervened when athletes representing the nation were suspected of doping. When the Australian Institute of Sport's swim coach faced charges of anabolic steroid possession in 2001, Prime Minister John Howard issued a statement declaring the innocence of Australia's leading swimmers. When the prominent sprinter Merlene Ottey tested positive for a steroid in 1999, the president of Jamaica declared that the country supported her, while his minister for sport and labor demanded a new test. When a Russian cross-country skier was disqualified for doping at the 2002 Salt Lake City Olympic Games, the head of the Russian Olympic Committee's anti-doping team insisted that "we have no intention of going back on our decision to defend the honor of our skier Larisa Lazutina." These are just a few examples of the reflexive sportive nationalism that has subverted doping controls for decades.

Nationalist resistance in Italy to anti-doping measures has been fueled in recent years by the struggle for power between politicians of the left and right. Years before he took political office in 2001, the right-wing media patriarch Silvio Berlusconi had demonstrated his penchant for a sportive nationalism that was sure to appeal to many Italian voters. In 1993 Berlusconi named his new political party (Forza Italia) after a soccer chant. He announced that his professional soccer team (AC Milano) would be playing for "the colors of Italy." "Sports will come first again," he promised at a Forza Italia Sports Day rally just before he was elected prime minister.

In October 1998 the Rome doping laboratory operated by the Italian National Olympic Committee (Comitato Olimpico Nazionale Italiano, or CONI), the world's most powerful NOC, was shut down following a major scandal implicating CONI laboratory personnel and its physicians. The CONI president, Mario Pescante, was forced to resign. Berlusconi declared that this scandal, which exposed the official Italian anti-doping program as a sham, was the result of a left-wing plot. (Pescante retained his seat on the International Olympic Committee, which almost never investigates domestic corruption charges against its members.) As the government's sports minister, Giovanna Melandri, used the spreading doping scandal to attempt to reform the politics of CONI and promote an anti-doping policy, powerful sports officials denounced her as "a left-wing dictator" and as "Stalin's niece." Following his election as prime minister, Berlusconi replaced Giovanna Melandri with his own sports minister—Mario Pescante.

This political power play did not put an end to Italian anti-doping reforms, however. In November 2000, before Berlusconi took power, the Italian Senate had passed an innovative anti-doping law that made it a crime to distribute or use illicit doping drugs. In January 2002, a new anti-doping commission operating under the authority of the Italian Health Ministry passed a rule requiring Italian pharmaceutical companies to declare if any product contained performance-enhancing substances. State prosecutors have continued to pursue doping investigations of Italian soccer and cycling. Berlusconi's open hostility toward Italy's independent judiciary did not shut down these investigations or directly sabotage the trials of the accused doping doctors Francesco Conconi and Michele Ferrari. In November 2003 Conconi was acquitted by a judge who ruled that the statute of limitations had expired. In March 2004 another judge announced that despite his formal acquittal, Conconi was guilty as charged. As of that time, the doping charges against Ferrari had not yet been resolved.

On another front, the anti-doping campaign led by Sandro Donati, a former CONI research official and track-and-field coach, has enraged powerful Italian sports officials for whom anti-doping reform is a provocation rather than a policy objective. It is not yet clear whether they will finally prevail over anti-doping activists like Donati, who are at a clear political disadvantage while Berlusconi is in office. Berlusconi's attitude toward doping control has even given encouragement to athletes who run afoul of Italy's strict anti-doping laws. When the cycling star Marco Pantani was accused in May 2002 of injecting himself with insulin during the 2001 Giro d'Italia, he appealed to Berlusconi to defend cycling against the "persisting and unjustified suspicions and slanders" that had sullied the reputation of the sport.

Such struggles between ambitious sports officials and anti-doping reformers are not limited to politically volatile Italy. A thousand miles to the north, in politically stable, social democratic Norway, a similar conflict became a major public controversy shortly after the 2000 Sydney Olympic Games. A senior sports expert at the Ministry of Culture, Hans B. Skaset, threatened to withdraw government support for elite sport if Norwegian sports officials continued to employ techniques, such as "dietary supplements" and altitude chambers, that Skaset identified with the ethically dubious "gray zones" in which doping practices occur. Norway's sports leaders, he said, were "indirectly sanctioning experimentation that borders on doping." Skaset argued that such exploitation of "gray zone" techniques to win medals was beneath the dignity of the Norwegian state. This statement of principle put the minister of culture, whose lack of expertise in this area was well known, in a difficult position. But when the president of the Norwegian Sports Federation

(Norges Idrettsforbund, or NIF), a prominent business executive, demanded that she clarify the state's position regarding performance-enhancing technologies, she promptly aligned herself with the NIF and its sportive nationalist ambitions. Skaset was left out in the cold, and after ten years of service to the Ministry of Culture he had no choice but to resign.

The Skaset affair illuminated several aspects of the relationship between doping and state power in Norway. Unlike in Germany and Italy, the politics of doping in this small society, which is renowned for the depth of its nationalist feeling, is not a matter of left versus right. In Norway the sportive nationalism that can lower resistance to doping is a bipartisan affair; for example, both of the NIF vice presidents who supported their president from the world of big business were social democratic rather than conservative politicians. It was, in fact, right-of-center politicians who raised questions at a parliamentary hearing about the relationship between the state and the NIF, or precisely the reverse of what one would expect to find in Germany or Italy. The Norwegian public also learned that parliamentary scrutiny of the national elite sport budget had been quietly dropped in 1999 for reasons no one could explain. We may presume that Norwegian sports officials persuaded key politicians to look the other way while the sports establishment went about enhancing Norway's prestige in the international arena. This concession to the competitive ethos is one aspect of the Americanization of Norwegian society that has been under way since the 1980s, and it would appear that there is no going back to the quieter world Norwegians once knew. A principled refusal to push the envelope, one commentator argued, would surely mean the end of Norway's ability to compete in the sports at which it has traditionally excelled.

Such conflicts between dissenting insiders and sports officials who are on a nationalist mission to win international medals is inherent in any ambitious sports establishment, including that of the United States. In July 2000 Dr. Wade Exum, a former director of Drug Control Administration for the United States Olympic Committee (USOC), filed a lawsuit that claimed the USOC had subverted the anti-doping program he had been hired to carry out. In his complaint to the United States District Court for Colorado, he described the USOC as a "national ministry of sport" that had imposed "absolutely no sanction . . . on roughly half of all the American athletes who have tested positive for prohibited substances" during the late 1990s. Synthetic testosterone, he said, "continues to be routinely abused by athletes," not one of whom had ever been sanctioned for using that substance. Like his Norwegian counterpart, Exum found his own elite sports establishment violating the norms of drug-free sport, in that "the USOC actually encourages fringe performance enhancing and/or potential doping practices by such means as the use of so called nitrogen [altitude] tents on USOC premises." Neither of these dissenters trusted the sports officials who employed them to exercise appropriate self-restraint when tempted by performance-enhancing technologies.

A similar drama had marked the departure from the USOC of Dr. Exum's predecessor. Dr. Robert O. Voy was appointed as chief medical officer of the USOC in 1985. On October 15, 1987, he gave a candid speech on the realities of doping to the General Assembly of International Sports Federations in Colorado Springs. Almost a year before the Ben Johnson scandal shook the world of Olympic sport, Voy saw the looming crisis of high-performance sports medicine and tried to alert his colleagues. For taking this position Voy was vilified and marginalized, and he eventually left the USOC in early 1989. For anyone interested in the mentality of the USOC during the 1980s regarding the doping issue, Voy's memoir is essential reading. It offers the perspective of an insider who was forced into a position of independence vis-à-vis the USOC bureaucracy he had attempted to serve in a principled manner. That his successor, Dr. Exum, found himself in the same predicament raises obvious questions about the USOC leadership's commitment to pursue a serious anti-doping program and the "educational" project such a program would require.

The reluctance of the USOC to take decisive action against doping is rooted in sportive nationalism, the idea that athletes who are successful in international competition bring glory to the nation and the sports bureaucrats who produce them. The USOC's corporate ethos thus has failed to accommodate forceful disciplinary responses to even the most flagrant doping violations. For example, following the unethical and medically dangerous blood doping of seven American cyclists at the 1984 Los Angeles Olympic Games, the USOC imposed no sanctions on any of the doctors, officials, or athletes involved, leaving it to the U.S. Cycling Federation to hand out perfunctory thirty-day suspensions. Shortly after the head of the USOC's Sports Medicine Council denounced this blood doping as "unethical, unacceptable and illegal," he was dismissed.

USOC indifference to the ethical implications of doping reached its nadir during the 1980s. The Exum lawsuit and the $20 million sponsorship fee accepted by the USOC in 2000 from a supplements manufacturer suggest that its leadership had learned little about the doping problem in recent years. A similar intransigence was evident in the doping-related behavior of USA Track & Field (USATF), which, according to an official report, failed to "administer an effective and out-of-competition drug testing program" and had yet to inculcate in its member athletes "a no-nonsense attitude toward doping."

Another incident comparable to the 1984 cycling fiasco was the Kerry Lynch blood-doping scandal, which erupted at the end of 1987. This incident involved Jim Page, the chief U.S. Nordic coach, and Doug Petersen, head coach of the U.S. Nordic combined team. Both men knew about and covered up Lynch's cheating. (Page had arranged for a New Hampshire doctor to fly to Germany to perform Kerry Lynch's blood transfusion.) The response of the International Ski Federation (Fédération Internationale de Ski, or FIS) was to impose lifetime suspensions on the two Americans. The USOC's response was to retain Page in his position, put him on probation, and issue a reprimand. He remained at the USOC until 2002 as managing director of sports performance, and he was given anti-doping responsibilities during the 1990s. Lynch stated that he had engaged in blood doping in response to "direct and indirect pressures from the administration, media and the American society on athletes to succeed in top international competitions."

The USOC's handling of the Page scandal demonstrated once again its reluctance to take disciplinary action against blatant doping offenses. USOC president Robert Helmick offered stern words of moral caution. "It is morally wrong," he said, "for an athlete to be involved and particularly reprehensible for a physician and coaches to supervise." But Helmick's ultimate purpose was to exonerate his subordinate: "Jim Page should have said no, he didn't, and he recognizes that mistake. He has a long history of fighting against the procedure, and there is no need to make him a scapegoat. We think the athletes of the future will be better served by having him [with the USOC] than not having him." Helmick did not substantiate his claim that this compromised coach had actually opposed the illicit procedure he first expedited and then covered up, and more impartial observers saw what Page had done in a different light. Dr. Bud Little, an American member of the FIS council, commented: "I felt the recommended position of the U.S. Ski Association was inadequate. The punishment should have been more severe. This was obviously a very premeditated act." Three years later, USOC president Helmick was forced to resign in disgrace from the International Olympic

Committee on account of his self-serving financial deals. It turned out that the USOC's enforcer of ethical standards had some ethical problems of his own. Indeed, the rise of Robert Helmick to the presidency of the USOC and then to membership in the IOC raises important questions about the frequency with which dubious individuals climb into the upper echelons of sports federations around the world. The presence of these self-recruited opportunists in key positions has been a principal obstacle in many sports federations to formulating and enforcing effective anti-doping measures.

The USOC's lack of interest in a transparent drug-testing operation was clearly explained as far back as the late 1980s by its drug-testing expert Dr. Don Catlin, chairman of its Committee on Substance Abuse, Research, and Education. In 1986 Catlin advised caution in introducing drug testing into some sports governing bodies where performance-enhancing drugs had been used. As he bluntly put it: "If you go in with a sickle and scythe, you could put all their athletes out of business. In some sports, you could wipe out the whole team." (In other words, the USOC was aware of systematic doping and was doing almost nothing about it.) His suggestion was "to announce testing well in advance of the implementation of a program and to encourage the sport's governing body to educate its athletes." Such a plan both would be likely to allow athletes more than sufficient time to evade positive test results and would put unwarranted faith in an "educational" process at cross-purposes to the ambitions and the ethical standards of many elite athletes as well as of the USOC itself. In 1989 Catlin stated: "I think that, when the sports organization identifies a drug user through a test and imposes a sanction, that's the penalty. I don't see the necessity of making a public announcement. The public has a right to know, but not necessarily to know instantaneously." Thus the athlete's right to privacy outweighed the public's right to know about doping—an attitude we encountered earlier in the context of "client-centered" sports medicine. Dr. Voy's view of the same situation provides a stark contrast. We may assume that key USOC executives shared the position that effective doping control could have put some of their sports federations out of business.

To the best of my knowledge, no government has ever renounced sportive nationalism as its fundamental approach to international athletic competition. This transnational loyalty to performance has undermined the international campaign against doping by giving national sports officials tacit permission and even encouragement to withhold support from effective anti-doping measures that might limit the performances of their athletes.

The conflict between sportive nationalists and anti-doping policy makers will be with us for some time to come. Nationalist ambition continues to influence the formulation of national sports policy, and the officials responsible for producing impressive medal totals at Olympic Games and world championships will continue to seek every technological and pharmacological advantage they can get away with. At the same time, anti-doping activists and officials enjoy a new prestige and political momentum following the 1998 Tour de France scandal. But the outcome of this struggle, which models in some ways the much larger conflict over regulating drugs in the wider world, remains uncertain.

INTERNATIONAL DOPING CONTROL AFTER REFORM

The IOC's relationship to doping control was dramatically altered by three events that occurred during the second half of 1998. First, the Tour de France scandal that erupted in July transformed the politics of doping by revealing that an entire athletic community—athletes, trainers, physicians, and officials—had been practicing and concealing comprehensive doping as a way of life. By demonstrating that a major professional sport could not reform itself, it opened the door to unprecedented state involvement in anti-doping activism. In addition, the Tour debacle finally made it acceptable to say in public what some journalists had long known—namely, that long-distance cycling was the most consistently drug-soaked sport of the twentieth century.

The Tour thus became a proving ground for state prosecution of doping offenses in accordance with existing law, in this case the French anti-doping law of 1989. The long-delayed crackdown that decimated the 1998 Tour was a political as much as it was a legal event. "For as long as the Tour has existed, since 1903, its participants have been doping themselves," one journalist noted. "No dope, no hope. The Tour, in fact, is only possible because—not despite the fact—there is doping. For 60 years this was allowed. For the past 30 years it has been officially prohibited. Yet the fact remains: great cyclists have doped themselves, then as now." Indeed, the riders and their handlers were dumbfounded precisely because everyone involved, including the press, had for so long been turning a blind eye in the interest of doing business as usual. What no one had expected was prosecutorial activism backed by politicians who meant business. It is not by chance that the Tour prosecutions had to wait for a Socialist prime minister (Lionel Jospin) who was willing to appoint a Communist minister of Youth and Sport (Marie-Georges Buffet). Similarly, it was a Social Democratic German interior minister, Otto Schily, who on February 2, 1999, told the IOC-sponsored World Conference on Doping that it was "not good for sport when we are dealing with a kind of constitutional monarchy." For the past two decades, left-of-center politicians in western European parliaments have been more willing to prosecute doping offenses than conservative colleagues, who are more motivated by sportive nationalism.

IOC president Samaranch opposed this threat to the IOC's authority by insisting that the sports world was still able to regulate itself. In his usual fashion, Samaranch expressed confidence in the beleaguered federation in question by calling on the International Cycling Union (Union Cycliste Internationale, or UCI) to take a "very hard and serious" approach to the anti-doping struggle. The possibility that UCI inaction had directly contributed to the scandal seemed not to occur to an IOC president who had always refused to interfere in the federations' management of doping. In contrast, Klaus Müller, chief of the anti-doping laboratory at Kreischa, pointed to UCI management of doping control not as a solution but as a root cause of the problems that had ruined the 1998 Tour. Some sports officials were also rethinking the role of the state in the fight against doping. "Sport cannot possibly solve this problem by itself," said Walther Tröger, president of the German National Olympic Committee and a member of the IOC. "State agencies must also help." The old order was dissolving, but it remained unclear what sort of new arrangement might replace it.

The second event that changed the political landscape was Samaranch's proposal to "drastically reduce" the number of substances banned from elite sport. Alarmed by the spectacle of Tour riders being hauled off to jail cells and police interrogations, Samaranch imagined a comparable Olympic fiasco and resolved to prevent it by redefining many doping offenses out of existence. In the July 26 edition of the Spanish newspaper *El Mundo* Samaranch thus declared: "For me everything that does not injure the health of the athlete is not doping." This apparent reversal of long-standing IOC anti-doping policy was harshly criticized by a wide range of sports officials, scientists, and physicians. Even Samaranch's ally Thomas Bach distanced himself from this sort of "reform," insisting that the distinction between harmful and performance-enhancing substances was artificial and that the IOC was obligated to pursue doping aggressively. In retrospect, we can see that Samaranch's candid and heretical comments were a public relations faux pas that called into question his commitment to the campaign against doping. To repair his damaged reputation, he called for a World Anti-Doping Conference under his leadership that would convene in early 1999, and by November the IOC had published an agenda for this event. But this strategy did not restore Samaranch's political stature just before the worst Olympic crisis of them all arrived to shatter his prestige and that of the entire IOC.

The Olympic bribery scandal that erupted in December 1998—the third cataclysmic event of the year—weakened the authority of the IOC to the point where Samaranch eventually found it necessary to create both an IOC Reform Commission and an IOC Ethics Commission featuring celebrities such as Henry Kissinger and former United Nations secretary-general Javier Perez de Cuellar. A secondary effect of the bribery scandal was to push the doping issue out of the public eye before the Anti-Doping Conference convened in Lausanne. This conference led to the founding of the World Anti-Doping Agency (WADA), which went into operation on January 13, 2000. The removal of anti-doping authority from the IOC resulted in more aggressive drug testing at both the 2000 Sydney Olympic Games and the 2002 Salt Lake City Olympic Games, where three cross-country skiers tested positive for a blood-boosting drug and were immediately stripped of their medals. Now, for the first time in history, there was reason to believe that the IOC was prepared to support a serious campaign against hormone doping in sport. In March 2003 WADA convened a conference in Copenhagen to announce a World Anti-Doping Code that would eventually be administered uniformly around the globe.

A WAR ON DRUGS?
ATHLETES AND THE DOPING OF EVERYDAY LIFE

The rhetorical similarities between the war on drugs in American society and the anti-doping campaign in sport encourage the idea that these crusades benefit from a synergistic and mutually reinforcing relationship. Both campaigns are presented as exercises in public hygiene that can improve physical and moral health (of ordinary people and athletes, respectively), and there is good reason to believe that these parallel initiatives will succeed or fail together. In the eyes of many public officials around the world, "the lifting of the ban on drugs in sport would almost certainly be seen . . . as socially irresponsible." Conversely, sports officials who are serious about driving performance-enhancing drugs out of sport must fear the relaxation of anti-drug laws, since that would undercut the ethical basis of their anti-doping message.

One problem with the synergy model is that apart from their shared condemnation of drugs these two crusades pursue different goals. While the war on drugs aims to maximize human productivity, the anti-doping campaign must seek to limit athletic productivity in favor of drug-free competition. Some of the problems that result from this awkward attempt at self-regulation have been presented in earlier chapters of this book. While the anti-doping campaign is supposed to discourage the use of performance-enhancing drugs, we have seen how its impact around the world has been subverted by escalating demands for performance that encourage doping. The passive enforcement strategies of international officials became particularly evident during the 1998 Tour de France scandal, the greatest doping scandal of the twentieth century, when official drug testing did not unmask a single doping cyclist. Only the power of the French state could break through the wall of silence and separate riders from their drugs. We have also seen how doping is driven by the unrelenting pressures generated by sportive nationalism, which have become the most deeply rooted threat to drug-free sport. The anti-doping campaign is thus undermined from within, as sports officials simultaneously demand escalating performances and pharmacological self-discipline. A fateful consequence of the pressure to boost performance has been the emergence of a legal market for doping products that serve both athletes and others who find it necessary to produce at ever-escalating levels in their private and professional lives.

The War on Drugs proclaimed in 1968 derives much of its emotional power from the idea that national survival depends on a national efficiency that is fatally impaired by drug abuse. Richard Nixon exploited this latent anxiety as he campaigned to be president of the United States when he declared drugs "a modern curse" that was "decimating a generation of Americans." A month after his election, research sponsored by the Michigan Health Department concluded that "drug use by young people, particularly use of marijuana, represents a social form of recreation far removed in nature from the traditional problem of narcotics addiction or alcoholism." In a word, drug use of this kind posed no credible threat to social stability or national productivity.

The war on drugs can be thought of as a fateful contest between the catastrophic view of drug abuse and a more realistic view that does not employ the hysterical rhetoric of the most vehement prohibitionists. The theme of productivity has played a crucial role in alarmist anti-drug rhetoric since 1968—especially during the 1980s, when the Reagan presidency produced the famous slogan "Just Say No." Ironically, it was Nixon's own National Commission on Marijuana and Drug Abuse that in 1972 debunked the notion that marijuana conflicted with "the operating functions of our society" and recommended legalization (to no avail).

Warnings about falling productivity became a standard feature of the war on drugs. In 1981, for example, a Menninger Foundation psychiatrist described a marijuana-induced "Organic Brain Syndrome" that included "diminished will power" among its symptoms. The cover story of the May 16, 1983, issue of the *U.S. News and World Report* was "How Drugs Sap the Nation's Strength." "No one has measured how all this pill popping, injecting, and inhaling has affected the national output," the magazine noted, but this lack of knowledge did not deter the writer from tying "US productivity" to the country's "drug problem." The August 22, 1983, issue of *Newsweek* reported that "the use of illegal drugs on the job has become a crisis for American business." In 1986 the prestigious Research Triangle Institute announced it had found "reduced productivity due to daily marijuana use." Shortly thereafter, Congressman Jim Wright, Democrat of Texas, spoke of drugs as "a menace draining away our economy." In 1989 Reagan's commissioner of customs called drugs the "most serious threat to our national health and security." This was also the year that Reagan's drug czar (i.e., director of the White House Office of National Drug Control Policy), William Bennett, told an audience at Harvard's Kennedy School of Government that drug use "subverts productivity." The fact that the United States has survived its massive consumption of marijuana, cocaine, and other recreational drugs to become the world's only military, economic, and cultural superpower does not appear to have prompted any revision of the theory that drug use presages national decline.

Only a deeply irrational view of drug abuse explains this selective approach to productivity-subverting behaviors that regards economically and medically disastrous drugs such as alcohol and nicotine as socially acceptable, while demonizing recreational drugs that do far less damage to health and to workplace productivity. Given this mind-set, it made strategic sense for alcohol and tobacco companies to contribute money to the Partnership for a Drug-Free America, thereby fortifying the social convention that exempts alcohol and tobacco from the stigma of drugs that do significant harm.

The productivity issue has also haunted the anti-doping campaign in sport, but in a very different form. Because hormone doping promotes too much productivity rather than too little, it erases the alleged contradiction between drug use and performance that has animated the campaign against recreational drugs such as intoxicants and soporifics that subvert efficiency. "The use of anabolic steroids is too consistent with societal values—bigger, stronger, taller, faster—to be eradicated," as one steroid expert put it in 1989. A year later a congressional committee heard a Department of Justice representative testify that "many steroid users were very goal oriented and did not take steroids 'to get high or to escape from reality.' " The functional (as opposed to recreational) use of these drugs thoroughly confounds the logic of a war on drugs that emphasizes the importance of productivity. Indeed, the drugs' effectiveness is why medical arguments against steroid use occur along with the traditional arguments about preserving fair competition, since it is becoming increasingly difficult to construe performance-enhancing techniques as unfair.

An important result of the selective blindness about drugs has been the development of parallel markets for intoxicants and stimulants that are either lightly or heavily regulated, depending on the drug's social status. While alcohol, nicotine, caffeine, ephedrine, Ritalin, and Prozac are regarded as compatible with the goals of social stability and efficiency, marijuana in particular still symbolizes a threat to the morale of a society that must produce and consume to survive. I would emphasize that my analysis is not intended as an endorsement of recreational drug use; on the contrary, the abuse of one substance does not legitimate the abuse of another on the grounds of consistency. My point is rather that hysterical claims rooted in "the belief that drugs radiate a supernatural evil" will inevitably stigmatize certain drugs in a way that shields other harmful drugs that are protected by politicians and corporate interests. Drug use, as F. Allan Hanson observes, "currently plays a role in American thinking similar to witchcraft a few centuries ago: it is insidious, pervasive, but not easily recognizable, an evil that infuses social life and is responsible for many of the ills that beset us." An obsession of this kind readily produces a deeply gratifying and even violent sense of indignation that can be directed at any emotionally convenient target. William Bennett, the U.S. drug czar whose nicotine addiction forced him to check into a treatment facility, had no compunctions about rejecting the medical model of drug abuse, identifying drugs with absolute evil and even endorsing the beheading of drug dealers.

Today the sports world promotes the doping of everyday life by providing a public showcase for performance-enhancing products that associate athletic performance and productive human functioning. Sports medicine credentials can give endorsers an air of authority they may or may not deserve. For example, the career of Karlis Ullis, M.D., the medical director of the Sports Medicine and Anti-Aging Medical Group in Santa Monica, California, has benefited from the merging of athleticism and health into a single vague category. Athleticism conveys here a special biological dynamism that can supposedly maintain the vigor of all aging individuals. "Under new federal regulations," reads an Internet advertisement for Ullis's book, "consumers have access to a whole new group of supplements that boost the body's natural testosterone levels. Available without a prescription, these 'T boosters,' including androstenedione, promise to revolutionize health, fitness, and weight management regimens for men and women." Countless promotional messages of this sort have made hormone-related procedures a form of alternative medicine that remains exempt from legal and professional regulation.

More prominent are the athletic role models who advertise various drugs or other enhancements inadvertently or as paid spokesmen. The publicity generated by Mark McGwire's initially private use of the anabolic steroid androstenedione (Andro) is the most prominent example of unintended advertising of a doping product. That this substance continued to be sold freely for more than five years, regardless of the wishes of prosecutors, politicians, federal agencies, or public moralists, speaks to a profound indifference shown toward legal doping by our social institutions and by the general public. Endorsements of herbal stimulants like ephedrine promote what one observer has called "a new teenage drug subculture: the world of legal steroid substitutes and speed." The St. Louis Rams running back Marshall Faulk thus calls the ephedrine product Xenadrine—a stimulant that mimics the doping drug amphetamine—"the most effective performance-enhancement supplement I've ever taken." In May 2002 the National Football League banned the ephedrine-based stimulants that have been used by hundreds of NFL players.

Athletes have also endorsed drugs that are taken to enhance nonathletic capacities. The strong and healthy baseball star Rafael Palmeiro has been recruited to remove the stigma of erectile dysfunction by serving as a spokesman for Viagra. The pitcher Pete Harnisch has endorsed the antidepressant Paxil. The Pharmacia/Pfizer company exhorts customers taking its arthritis pain reliever Celebrex to "Celebrate the Olympic

Spirit!" and take their rightful place alongside the elite athletes who inspire them: "Unsung, in a similar spirit, thousands of arthritis patients rise to meet the challenges of everyday life." Stars and fans alike thus share in a ritual of performance enhancement and medical redemption in which anyone can participate. In a similar vein, the golfing superstar Tiger Woods has endorsed a surgical procedure whose benefits can be enjoyed by ordinary people: "Thanks to TLC [Laser Eye Centers], the hole and everything now looks bigger," he says. "Following surgery," this advertisement continues, "Tiger went on to win 5-straight official PGA tournaments. A feat that hasn't been duplicated in over 50 years." Such advertising weaves the ethos of performance enhancement into the fabric of everyday life and points to the social respectability of performance-enhancing techniques, such as dietary supplements, that are by any reasonable definition forms of doping.

Media resistance to advertising claims made by supplement manufacturers is minimal or nonexistent, and there are few powerful interests that see any benefit in taking on the supplement companies. "Major national newspapers, magazines, television, cable and radio stations seem ready to accept the substantial advertising dollars of this industry without question, often airing patently fraudulent ads," a federal trade commissioner stated in May 2002. The MET-Rx sports nutrition company, which once distributed androstenedione and now manufactures products containing creatine, sponsored the *Superstars* competition on CBS-TV in May 2002 that featured two high-profile 2002 Winter Olympic athletes, Jim Shea and Apolo Anton Ohno. Given the United States Olympic Committee's endorsement deal with its own supplements manufacturer (Pharmancx), it is not surprising that a USOC spokesman argued that the Olympians' participation did not imply endorsement. Only the health insurer Blue Cross and Blue Shield opposed USOC sponsorship of potentially hazardous products and "asked CBS to air public-service announcements to tell viewers of the supplements' risks." Needless to say, CBS refused to broadcast a public health message that would have stigmatized its sponsor's product.

But the sports world's promotion of the doping mentality transcends the testimonials offered by famous athletes. The public is becoming increasingly aware that healthy high-performance athletes require comprehensive medical support that can border on or fall into the category of a doping regimen. Medical support for the professional athlete is also legitimized by his or her status as a performer—as someone being productive and socially responsible by doing a job. Acknowledging the physiological predicament of the athlete-worker removes the stigma from doping procedures and thus facilitates the emergence of a legal market for performance-enhancing products.

The idea that doping and athletic achievement are mutually compatible aspects of a modern fixation on performance may surprise readers who associate athletes with the anti-doping campaign that aims to remove drugs from sport. My argument, however, is that modern society both embraces the productive effects of doping drugs and disapproves of them with a prohibitionist passion that is rooted in the traditional idea that socially disreputable drugs are consumed by dysfunctional addicts. The sports world thus at the same time promotes doping and the campaign to abolish it. The drug-testing industry that has undergone a vast expansion over the past two decades owes much of its authority to the anti-doping campaign in sport. Large-scale drug testing was pioneered in the United States by the Department of Defense in the early 1980s—particularly the U.S. Navy, which was administering almost 2 million tests a year by 1986. The declared purpose of this testing was workplace safety, which is one aspect of productivity. Yet athletes have been far more visible than military personnel as the subjects of drug tests.

The drug testing of high school and college student-athletes in the United States has been justified in several ways that bear indirectly on the issue of productivity. This testing campaign has adopted the central argument of the war on drugs: that drug use amounts to nothing less than a social emergency requiring a full-scale assault, even if the individual's right to privacy is diminished in the process. It is worth noting that this mind-set commanded less authority in the 1980s than it has acquired in the intervening years. In 1987, for example, a California superior court judge, Conrad L. Rushing, rejected the "clear and present danger" argument when he refused to endorse the testing program of the National Collegiate Athletics Association (NCAA): "Mandatory drug testing has usually required proof that the social consequences of drug use are likely to be so immediate that the public health and safety are threatened, as with railroad operators or air-traffic controllers."

This approach to drug testing was reversed in a landmark 1995 ruling by the United States Supreme Court, which allowed public schools to test student athletes for drugs. In June 2002 the Supreme Court reaffirmed the widespread practice of random drug testing of public school students in a decision that went well beyond the previous ruling that allowed drug testing of students engaged in athletics. The rationales for testing young athletes include their medical safety, their responsibility to serve as role models for other young people, and their obligation not to harm the reputation of the schools they represent in interscholastic competition. Conspicuously absent from this list is any concern about the unethical enhancement of athletic performance.

Whether such testing constitutes good social policy is a complex question that deserves far more analysis than this chapter can provide. It is clear, however, that the student-athlete population in the United States has been forced by schools and courts into playing a cutting-edge role in the war on drugs. When the Supreme Court "opened the door to drug testing in schools by permitting the testing of athletes," it unleashed a potential juggernaut that has been expanding its powers ever since. Like their counterparts in the sports world, the public officials who manage testing programs can make policy in two important areas. First, they have the power to determine whether a drug will or will not be deemed compatible with social stability and productivity. But they are also authorized to turn athletes into supercompliant role models who are expected to accept drug testing on behalf of serving a larger community. For this reason F. Allan Hanson has called drug testing "a disciplinary drill" that "develops automatic docility." He has also found student-athletes to accept such treatment more docilely than, for example, the railroad workers who are also subject to testing. Second, the drug testing of athletes who are minors enhances the social prestige of the war on drugs by associating testing with the formation of character and with training for citizenship. In this sense, the war on drugs represents an enormous state initiative that employs athletes as role models. The anti-doping campaign thus takes on a social mission quite distinct from promoting an ideal of drug-free athletic competition. But there is little evidence that the anti-doping campaign can really change how athletes and other people think about drugs.

The fundamental question posed by this chapter is whether the anti-doping campaign—the sports world's own war on drugs—can prevail over the many obstacles that confront it. Success would be marked by the creation of a relatively drug-free sports culture that might even diminish the demand for doping products in the larger society; indeed, certain European officials have made it clear that they expect a tangible public health benefit from their investment in anti-doping work. Assessing the prospects of this campaign requires us to examine the most powerful institutions and interest groups that have declared an interest in the war against drugs in sport. We have already seen how sportive nationalism, public attitudes, international sports organizations, and sports physicians often encourage, or fail to discourage, the doping practices that officials everywhere routinely deplore. Other major actors in the global doping drama include governments, professional sports leagues, and the pharmaceutical industry, which produces drugs that are diverted onto the athletic black market. (How much pharmaceutical companies have known about these diversions remains an open question.) What kind of support can the World Anti-Doping Agency expect from these institutions?

National governments created WADA in partnership with the IOC in November 1999. Its role is to carry out the international anti-doping work the IOC proved unwilling or unable to do, and its first few years in operation gave WADA a credibility that the IOC never earned. But two problems undermine the effectiveness of this international arrangement. First, WADA is dependent on funding from dozens of countries that do not always meet their payment deadlines; only time will tell what WADA can accomplish around the world with an annual budget of about $17 million. Second, few governmental authorities have shown a willingness to pursue doping control aggressively—that is, to use police raids and arrests as in France and Italy. Effective enforcement is thus left in the hands of those few dedicated civil servants who are willing to enforce state-sponsored anti-doping initiatives. The 1998 Tour de France prosecutions, for example, occurred only because the French minister of youth and sport, the Communist Marie-Georges Buffet, demonstrated the political will to send in the police to confiscate drugs, to jail riders, and to establish independent oversight of sports physicians. Her politically conservative predecessor, the Olympic champion hurdler Guy Drut, had eliminated funding for the national doping laboratory and had investigated few athletes who tested positive for drug use.

In France, as in Italy and Germany, left-of-center officials confront right-of-center counterparts who tend to show more interest in winning Olympic medals than in restricting the use of doping drugs. The left-wing approach, apart from prosecuting athletes and their handlers, emphasizes the threat posed by doping to public health and the need to protect the health of athletes who are seen as exploited workers. The Italian state prosecutor Raffaele Guariniello, who specializes in occupational diseases, has investigated the high death rates of professional athletes and whether they have been doped against their will. He is also convinced that the prevalence of doping among athletes influences the drug-consuming habits of children. These priorities are not shared by Prime Minister Berlusconi, however, or by the professional cycling federations that represent the riders. The state prosecutor who goes in for anti-doping activism is likely to be a political dissident who is at odds with powerful interests who do not share his goals.

The professional sports leagues that showcase the most popular athletes have been among the most recalcitrant opponents of doping control. While professional cycling has endured an endless series of doping scandals, European soccer has shown little interest in dealing with its own serious doping problems. Italian police found hundreds of drugs at the Juventus Turin training center—"enough to cater to the needs of a small hospital," according to the investigating judge.

Professional leagues and players' unions in the United States have also resisted drug testing. Those testing programs that do operate catch few drug-using athletes, in part because high-profile players in the National Football League (NFL) have been spared exposure while lower-level players were punished for the same violations. Between 1984 and 2000 the National Basketball Association (NBA) announced a total of seven positive drug tests. The National Hockey League (NHL) did not test for drugs until it decided in 2001 to allow the World Anti-Doping Agency to test its potential Olympians; as of 2002 it was still not testing its players for anabolic steroids.

But the most blatant example of entrenched resistance to drug testing in professional sports is Major League Baseball (MLB), which tests minor league players for steroids while doing no random or regular drug testing of major leaguers. MLB executives claim that while they favor testing, the Players Association adamantly opposes steroid tests as a violation of individual privacy. As the *New York Times* commented in 2002: "Major League Baseball has asked for steroid testing, but has never regarded it as a make-or-break issue in collective bargaining." In a word, baseball executives have declined to participate in the sports world's war on drugs.

Baseball's public drug problem dates from the Mark McGwire controversy of August 1998. In the years that have passed since Andro became a household word, MLB has done everything it could to prevent or defer the banning or labeling of this anabolic steroid as a drug. In February 1999 MLB's chief labor executive stated: "Our policy will not be driven by public relations but by what the scientific information shows." When a clinical study partially funded by MLB and the Players Association showed that androstenedione raises estrogen and testosterone levels in young men, Commissioner Bud Selig announced that MLB was "pleased to have played a part in the advancement of science" and took no further action. When an author of this study called the growing use of this drug a "serious public health issue, beyond being a sports issue," baseball executives simply ignored him. "Every ballplayer I've ever seen has a locker filled with 19 bottles of secret stuff," MLB's own medical chief, Dr. Robert Millman, commented in 2000, but this observation changed nothing. At the same time, baseball executives showed no qualms about invoking a "player's position as a role model to children." As many commentators have pointed out, the men who run baseball fear that revelations about past and present steroid use will tarnish the image of their game. But even as they pursue this policy of silence and hypocrisy, speculation about steroid use in baseball has been mounting in the mainstream media. A steroid testing program implemented by MLB and the players' union in 2002 was widely (and correctly) dismissed as ineffectual.

The remarkable aspect of this story is that MLB executives have carried off this strategy of stonewalling and deception with such impunity. Every prediction that they could be pressured into regulating their athletes' hormone consumption has proven to be wrong. In June 2000 the White House drug policy director, General Barry R. McCaffrey, predicted that the U.S. government would reclassify androstenedione as a steroid "within a few months." He was mistaken. Two months later a sportswriter predicted that MLB would ban the drug "in the near future" following the publication of clinical research. He, too, got it wrong. In October 2000 an MLB vice president, Sandy Alderson, told an interviewer that steroid testing was "very likely" as early as the next season. It never happened. The same month he told another journalist that "Major League Baseball and the players association are reviewing this situation"—a consultation that, judging from past performance, would only confirm once again their shared reluctance to test for steroids. And there was no sign whatsoever that the public had any objection to this arrangement. In March 2004 the FDA warned twenty-three companies to stop including androstenedione in their products or they would face substantial penalties. At this time a bill to prohibit the sale of androstenedione had been introduced in the U.S. Senate and was expected to become law.

Labor-management collusion on this scale for the purpose of preserving a doping subculture has long been a familiar arrangement in European professional cycling. Indeed, the great irony of anti-doping activism by public health–minded officials such as Marie-Georges Buffet and Raffaele Guariniello is that many of the competitors they want to protect do not want to be protected; the same is true of many professional athletes in the United States. But outsiders who are unversed in the politics of doping may well assume otherwise. Commenting on the NFL's drug-testing scandal in March 2000, the chairman of the Senate Caucus on International Narcotics Control, Senator Charles E. Grassley, concluded: "The league, the players, and the players union all recognize the value of a drug-free workplace." The problem with this statement, as we saw earlier, is that many sports executives and professional athletes have shown little interest in creating a drug-free workplace. The willingness of a U.S. senator to resort to this sort of wishful thinking about the motives of labor and management helps to explain the absence of political pressure on professional sports leagues to carry out effective drug testing. It would appear that constant exposure to the vocabulary of the war on drugs has created an impression that everyone recognizes the "drug-free workplace" as an urgent priority. In fact, the strategy of the professional sports industry has been to publicly embrace the rhetoric of the anti-doping campaign while establishing ineffectual drug-testing programs or simply refusing to challenge the pro-doping policies of the players' unions.

Our final protagonist in this doping drama is the pharmaceutical industry. At the height of the Tour de France scandal in August 1998, a prominent member of the IOC announced that drug companies would be expected to participate in the IOC-sponsored anti-doping conference scheduled for February 1999. "It's time we made it clear to major drug manufacturers of steroids, EPO's, human growth hormones," he boldly declared, "that if they're not careful and don't apply more stringent controls, and the public perceives that drugs are bringing down the character of sport, their reputation is at stake." The response from the pharmaceutical industry was to ignore this invitation and the warning that went along with it.

Pharmaceutical companies have in fact demonstrated some concern about the misuse of their products by athletes. When the four-minute milers were accused of using amphetamines in 1957, the industry issued a statement claiming that "amphetamine sulphate is one of the safest drugs available to medical practice." In 1982 reports of serious side effects prompted Ciba-Geigy to stop production of the anabolic steroid it was marketing under the name Dianabol, thereby ensuring that it not appear to be promoting doping. In 1988 Searle took the anabolic steroid Anavar off the market on account of "its misuse in sport." As of 1992 the German drug firm Schering AG was concerned about the image of testosterone as a doping drug because it was investigating the possibility of a testosterone-based male contraceptive. In 2001 a spokesman for the German pharmaceutical industry promised to help fund anti-doping work and emphasized that no drug company wanted "its medications used for the purpose of doping." It was, in fact, Amgen, the largest biotechnology company in the world, that made it possible for the IOC to detect the use of its blood-boosting product darbepoietin by the three cross-country skiers at the Salt Lake City Winter Games. But Amgen has refused to attach a chemical marker to Epogen (the brand name of erythropoietin), on the grounds that the procedure would be expensive and might require the FDA to put the drug through another round of clinical trials.

The pharmaceutical industry is in an awkward position vis-à-vis athletic doping. Testosterone products are important for treating hypogonadism and wasting disease. Genentech makes Protropin, a recombinant growth hormone for hormone-deficient children; Amgen makes Epogen for kidney patients with chronic anemia; Biopure makes the blood substitute Hemopure. All these products have wound up on the black market for doping drugs. Exactly how athletes obtain these drugs remains unexplained. How, for example, did the Italian cyclist Dario Frigo obtain the blood product Hemassist in 2001, even before it was to go onto the market and after it had been withdrawn from clinical trials? Sandro Donati, then head of scientific research at the Italian Olympic Committee, stated in 1998 that only 20 percent of the EPO being used in Italy, a $600 million market, was serving legitimate medical purposes. He also said that the EPO market was now an attractive target for organized crime. We do not know how much pharmaceutical companies know about the diversion of their products into the doping underground, but they clearly still regard doping scandals as a recurrent nuisance rather than as a real threat to their marketing of hormones.

ATHLETIC DOPING AND THE HUMAN FUTURE

We embarked on this extended tour of hormone doping in the sports world because it models in important ways the biomedical future that both fascinates and frightens us. The central drama of the doping story is the ongoing contest between illicit drugs and regulation. Its principal lesson is that up to this point, regulation has failed to eliminate hormone doping from sport. Another important lesson is that the persistence of doping is due not simply to the pharmacological ingenuity of athletes and doctors but also to political and economic demands that athletes are expected to meet. Our purpose, therefore, has been to identify the actors and the social forces that have promoted doping as a way of life within elite athletic communities. The sportive nationalism that drives doping grows out of the self-interested decisions of politicians and out of ideas about national vitality that are manipulated by a variety of social actors. Corporate sponsors of teams and individual athletes exert additional pressures on competitors to produce top performances. In short, systematic doping must be understood as resulting from a social system and its values.

Our examination of hormone doping has also revealed modern society's profound ambivalence toward performance-enhancing drugs. Doping control languished during the last two decades of the twentieth century because modern societies elected to tolerate ineffectual testing programs at the Olympic Games and in professional sports.

Finally, we have learned that the apparently straightforward choice between "doping" and "drug-free" sport is an illusion. This is especially true at elite levels, where athletes are subjected to constant physical and psychological stresses that are treated with drugs. Lance Armstrong, the six-time champion of the Tour de France, sleeps in an altitude chamber to boost his red blood cell level. So does Paula Radcliffe, the British world-record holder in the marathon (as of this writing) and a prominent anti-doping crusader. The crucial advantage of this artificial manipulation of an athletically important physiological variable—in short, this doping procedure—is that it does not involve swallowing or injecting a drug. Doping has also spread to recreational sport and even sport for the handicapped, demonstrating once again how the modern fascination with performance extends far beyond the exclusive ranks of elite performers.

EPILOGUE

Testosterone as a Way of Life

Testosterone has infiltrated modern life in ways that often escape both our attention and our censure. Anabolic steroids made possible, for example, the cinematic and political careers of Arnold Schwarzenegger, who was elected governor of California in November 2003. The former bodybuilding champion has prospered as a prototype of the hypermuscular male body that entered the American mainstream through the film (*Pumping Iron*, 1977) in which he first starred. As the father of small boys, I often encountered copycat versions of his swollen male torso in toy stores in the form of "action figures." These grotesquely muscle-bound plastic creatures also star in the sadistic video games that are now a part of popular culture for children around the world. Here, and in the violent and vulgar world of professional wrestling, testosterone manifests itself not as a prohibited drug but as the entertaining consequences of the drug's offstage use. Wrestling as well as sports fans "want to see bigger-than-life people do bigger-than-life things. At its extreme, it's a freak show. They want to see people who don't look like them do things they can only dream of doing," as the steroid expert Charles Yesalis once put it. These drug-dependent spectacles are legal, and very few prosecutors will find that it is in society's interest to trace such performances back to their pharmacological origins for the purpose of ensuring drug-free mayhem onstage. The same sort of discretion has long concealed the use of steroids by professional athletes, who have grown conspicuously larger and stronger in the absence of any serious effort to uncover the drug habits that have boosted their appeal to spectators who crave violent action on the field.

This lack of interest in stigmatizing the effects of testosterone drugs has also shielded many steroid-using police officers from public scrutiny. In recent years there have been numerous reports from around the world concerning the use of steroids by policemen. Dr. Robert Kerr, the steroid evangelist whose career is described in chapter 5, testified in the Superior Court of California in Los Angeles County in June 1985 that he had prescribed steroids to about 500 policemen in the Los Angeles area. In 1985 and 1986 the Texas Department of Public Safety suspended seven of its officers for using steroids. In 1989 a white police officer in Houston, Texas, who was known to be a steroid user was finally dismissed from the force after he killed three black motorists. In Britain the use of steroids by police was discussed in the House of Commons in 1996. In 1998 police in Liverpool were ordered to undergo random drug testing after two officers were suspended for using steroids. In Denmark, Copenhagen's Police Station No. 1 experienced a major doping scandal, along with charges of racism and brutality, in 2000 and 2001. Police involvement with steroids was reported from Australia in 1998, 2000, and 2003. The use of steroids by police officers is publicly censured by officials around the world for two principal reasons. First, the drugs can produce overly aggressive behavior in some people; and second, because police officers who use steroids are breaking the law, the drug traffickers with whom they often deal might be able to blackmail them or otherwise influence police operations.

Official censure of steroid use by police officers is frequently undermined by official reluctance to discipline or condemn the compromised individuals. For example, a county sheriff in Texas who was investigated for steroid use in 1988 "was not disciplined when the investigation revealed he wasn't buying or selling the drug, only using steroids that had been given to him." When Georg Andersen was banned from sport for life in 1993 as a steroid-using shot-putter, the very idea that he might be expelled from police service in his rural district in Norway did not even come up for discussion. On the contrary, Andersen became a folk hero who earned widespread popular sympathy as the victim of meddling officials in metropolitan Oslo. When a Denver police sergeant was under investigation in 2003 for receiving a package of anabolic steroids from England, the county sheriff in charge of the case commented: "We have no indication that these [drugs] were for anything other than personal use." In July 2003 a highly regarded police officer in Ohio was sentenced to ninety days of house arrest for illegal possession of steroids. At his arraignment in June a special prosecutor had announced his intention to recommend probation on the grounds that the officer had ordered the drugs only for his own use. Possession of illegally acquired steroids by a policeman, the prosecutor implied, was a private matter—a striking endorsement of libertarian pharmacology by a representative of the state. The officer himself, a 1999 Deputy of the Year who had served in the U.S. Marine Corps during the Persian Gulf War, said that steroids helped him to deal with the chronic fatigue syndrome that might have been a result of his military service. So here, too, we encounter the classic conundrum of performance-enhancing drugs: are they to be allowed because they are therapeutic drugs to which the suffering patient has a right, or are they to be vilified because they confer an unfair or potentially hazardous advantage? Another Ohio police officer convicted of using testosterone in 2003 blamed his positive drug test on contamination caused by his legal dietary supplements. "The supplements I'm taking are banned from so many sporting events because they are performance-enhancing," he explained. The idea that he might have a more legitimate claim to performance-enhancing drugs than do athlete-entertainers does not seem to have occurred to him.

The special treatment accorded to police officers who use steroids is largely a reaction to the physical demands of police work, which serves public safety. As representatives of law and order, the police benefit from a halo effect that gives their motives for using drugs the benefit of the doubt: the drug use that fortifies them is assumed (tacitly rather than publicly) to serve the vital interests of society. As in the case of soldiers and aviators, it is difficult to argue against drug use that promotes the operational viability and survival of those who must put themselves in harm's way. From this standpoint, a steroid-soaked activity like body-building appears to be compatible with police work because it promotes physical strength. It is thus not surprising that both the former Chicago police officer Sergio Oliva and the former Dallas policeman Ronny Coleman became champion bodybuilders after leaving public service.

But it is the practical rather than the narcissistic aspect of steroid use that informed observers invariably emphasize. "Bodybuilding," says one British expert, "is most often the entrée to taking steroids, but people who take the drugs often do it because they see their body as important to their job. Some people have the stereotypical image of a bodybuilder as unemployed. But in a sample of steroid-users that we looked at, there were a range of occupations, particularly among professions where your body can be instrumental to your job." In a similar vein, an employee of the Drugs and Sport Advisory Service in Liverpool noted in 1996 that many men in physically active professions use steroids and that steroid users can be active in more than one role requiring physical prowess: "Steroids cross all barriers. One rugby player to test positive for steroids recently was a member of a police force in South Wales. But I am aware of instances of steroid use in the police, armed forces, and fire service, as well as in private security firms." An Australian expert confirmed in 2003 that steroid users include police, security guards, members of the armed services, and nightclub bouncers who take the drugs to achieve the "frilled neck lizard response" that conveys physical dominance. This veneer of male dominance is coveted by millions of male adolescents around the world, who form a major black market for anabolic steroids.

Testosterone's covert presence in the ranks of the world's policemen contrasts with its more overt, and even flamboyant, manifestations in the body-conscious world of male homosexuals. According to Michelangelo Signorile, the spread of steroid use among gay men in the United States occurred along with the growing devastation of the AIDS epidemic during the 1980s. "Don't you see," one of his sources, an HIV-negative Californian, asked in 1997, "that there is suddenly an explosion of *natural, genetically superior* gay men all over the place, popping up like pod people? It's all steroids—they're all doing them, almost everyone who has that particular perfect and cut body is doing them, just like I'm doing them. But nobody's telling." Steroids have brought this "gay male body aesthetic" within reach of large numbers of men, who embrace "the hypermasculine paradigm" as a way of coping with the stigma of effeminacy. Their reticence about admitting to steroid use stems from a wish to appear naturally, rather than artificially, endowed with a superior musculature and thus more sexually attractive.

The AIDS catastrophe has made steroid use among homosexuals a medical strategy as well as a way to boost sexual appeal, since the drugs are used to stave off AIDS-related wasting disease. In fact, these rationales for steroid use are related in that the same drugs given to patients as a form of therapy can enhance muscular development in the much larger population that buys steroids on the black market, gets them from HIV-positive friends, or obtains them by means of "off-label" prescriptions. A male nurse who was treating gay men with AIDS at one urban clinic explained: "We were much more circumspect and cautious in the beginning, but now we're giving out steroids quite liberally. There's no question too that steroid use in the HIV community has normalized steroid use in the gay community [among HIV-negative men]." What is unique about steroid use among gay men is that a legitimate medical purpose is driving the spread of the drugs. In the athletic and police subcultures, in contrast, demands for more functional bodies come first; an appeal on medical grounds tends to be an ex post facto justification that is invoked when athletes or policemen are caught doping.

That most steroid use in the gay and athletic subcultures is illicit ensures that the "lesser harm" rationale for its covert supervision appears in both groups. The sports physician tells himself that his supervised doping regimen protects the athlete from potentially dangerous self-medication. Similarly, the gay fitness trainer who shows his clients how to take steroids explains that "they're going to use them anyway, so they should know what they're taking and know how to take it. I'd rather help them out than see them do damage to themselves." These decisions, by physicians and laymen alike, to give medical advice outside legal and professional guidelines are among the various strategies that are used to circumvent the Anabolic Steroids Control Act of 1990. "We struggle with [this issue] all the time," says one San Francisco doctor who treats many HIV-positive patients. "It is common to prescribe steroids as a way to counteract wasting. But I draw the line at giving them for purely cosmetic reasons." The refusal of many doctors to observe this distinction promotes the rise of client-centered medicine described in chapter 5 of this book.

A related challenge to the medical and legal orthodoxy that has regulated the use of steroids originates within the ranks of those AIDS physicians who have revived the idea that testosterone drugs can have a "tonic" or prophylactic effect on healthy people:

> To rebuild muscle tissue in those patients infected with HIV who are experiencing wasting, some doctors prescribe anabolic steroids in addition to testosterone therapy or as a replacement for it. More controversial, however, is the practice by some doctors with large AIDS practices in the urban centers of prescribing testosterone and anabolic steroids for patients who are not wasting or have no other symptoms associated with low testosterone. These doctors believe that the steroids can be used as a preventive or prophylaxis for people with AIDS, including those who may be quite healthy and whose BIA [bioelectric impedance analysis] tests and other indicators of wasting are normal; they believe that building up the body acts in this case as a sort of insurance against wasting, should it ever occur.

The idea that testosterone therapy should be available to men who have normal hormone levels has been controversial since the 1950s—for two distinct reasons (a crucial point). One reason is technical: the long-term effects of prolonged testosterone therapy in normal individuals are unknown, and it is widely assumed that testosterone promotes the growth of cancer in the prostate gland. At the same time, these concerns of medical safety have always been entangled with deeper cultural anxieties about promoting sexual activity by enhancing and thereby transforming normal people into hypersexual beings.

Physicians who treated men during the early phase of androgen therapy frequently observed no effect at all on men who showed no hormone deficiency. One report from 1939 found no "significant aphrodisical effect in the normal man" and sounded a cautionary note that is still heard from many physicians today: "It must be emphasized that the use of glandular substances for the purpose of stimulating sex urge is at present highly speculative and the wise practitioner will refrain from prescribing them in these conditions until a great deal more is learned about them and their undesirable side effects." In 1944 two authors found that "normal men experience little, if any, increase in sexual potency or in well being by taking the male sex hormone." Even the testosterone advocate Paul de Kruif reported in 1945 that "normal" young men experienced no "sexual effect" at all from the administration of synthetic testosterone. An article from 1949 made the same point about female patients: "Testosterone supplementation produced no increase in libido in post-menopausal women with normal testosterone levels."

Estrogenic drugs were seen as equally ineffective in stimulating sexual desire in women. "The prevailing experience," JAMA noted in 1941, "is that endocrine preparations [estrone and its derivatives] almost invariably fail when they are given to otherwise normal individuals for this purpose." Estrogen would reestablish sexual desire only in women whose ovaries had been removed. Nor would estrogen increase the size of women's breasts if the patient lacked a "congenital gonadal deficiency." Women with "normally developed but nevertheless small breasts" would have to be satisfied with the bodies they already had. A British report reiterated the futility of topical estrogenic stimulation of normal women: "In women who menstruate regularly, but whose breasts are small, the addition of ointments or creams containing estrogen will be ineffectual, since they have already received adequate stimulation."

We have already seen that different eras employ different criteria to define what constitutes "adequate stimulation" for adults who are interested in being sexually active. But what about those who desire additional stimulation beyond the norm? During the 1940s and 1950s, cultural predisposition and medical custom discouraged such ambitions and promoted acceptance of the physiology and the anatomy with which one had been born. During the sexual revolution of the 1960s, an interest in "stimulating sex urge" gained a new kind of social acceptability that challenged the traditional inhibitions about hormone therapy, including the dogma that discouraged the administration of hormone drugs to physiologically normal people.

The incompatibility of traditional medical thinking about hormone therapy and the idea of enhancing people with extra testosterone was described with admirable clarity by the British gerontologist and sexologist Alex Comfort, whose book *The Joy of Sex* (1972) became a worldwide best seller. In 1967 Comfort noted that "the therapy of age changes is still a dangerous subject" and that physicians generally continued to deny the therapeutic efficacy of certain substances: "The geriatrician who uses hormones or high-protein diets still feels under the obligation to indicate that he really does not expect any results from them." Testosterone remained "a gerontologically notorious substance" that Comfort suspected of being a "euphoriant" whose physiological effects remained poorly understood. Unlike the prudish physicians of the 1940s who were embarrassed by discussions of sex, Comfort downplayed the effects of testosterone because he did not want to make a scientific fool of himself.

There are important differences between Comfort's perspective on testosterone therapy and that of the physicians who administer the drug to men today. For one thing, therapeutic approaches to aging have ceased to be "a dangerous subject," because gerontology enjoys a respectability it did not have in the 1960s. For another, the physiological as well as psychological effects of testosterone are now better understood. What remains the same is a widespread feeling that responsible physicians have an obligation to doubt the efficacy of testosterone therapy and to discourage its use among "normal" people.

There are two major reasons why physicians and medical researchers feel pressured to prevent testosterone therapy from spreading among physiologically normal people. First, the history of glandular and later hormone therapies is littered with quackery and medical experiments of ill repute. Testosterone, as Comfort observes with a wince, has generated "the largest and most depressing anecdotal literature" of any substance associated with "sexual hopes and fears." Today's market in male menopause products, promoted on the Internet and in other media by entrepreneurs with and without medical degrees, continues this tradition and inspires instinctive disapproval in those physicians who are concerned about the lack of long-term studies of testosterone therapy. The sudden discrediting in 2003 of hormone replacement therapy for women only reinforced the skeptics' position vis-à-vis testosterone for aging men. Second, some physicians may be reluctant to defy what they sense to be lingering societal disapproval of pharmacologically enhanced sexual activity. Many physicians will refuse to prescribe drugs for what they regard as "lifestyle" enhancements as opposed to genuine medical needs.

This conservatism has persisted even as more doctors than ever before are rejecting the cautionary approach and prescribing testosterone to men with normal hormone levels. The divide in medical opinion came into sharp focus after the publication in November 2003 of a report on testosterone therapy by the congressionally chartered Institute of Medicine (IOM), a division of the National Academy of Sciences. The conservative position was articulated by Dan Blazer, chair of the committee and a professor of psychiatry and behavioral sciences at Duke University: "People are really looking for an anti-aging drug, and this is a very popular candidate." But "it is inappropriate for wide-scale use to prevent possible future disease or to enhance strength or mood in otherwise healthy men." "For men whose testosterone is already in the normal range," added Deborah Grady, a panel member, "there is no proof that it makes them better in any way. If there is no proven benefit for them, they shouldn't be taking testosterone no matter what the risk." Dr. John B. McKinlay of the New England Research Institutes in Watertown, Massachusetts, an epidemiologist and a historian of the male menopause concept, claimed that so-called normal testosterone levels in older men and techniques for measuring them remain unknown. "What we are about to do for men is repeat what we've done for women," he said. "Testosterone is a drug in search of a disease."

Unvoiced but unmistakable in this conservative consensus was a conspicuous lack of interest in promoting the subjective "well-being" of middle-aged men. While most users of testosterone are between forty-six and sixty-five years old, with only 13 percent older than sixty-five, the IOM committee recommended a small clinical trial that would exclude all men under that cutoff and anyone who did not have a low testosterone level. More than a half century after Paul de Kruif had campaigned for testosterone therapy for male rejuvenation, the Institute of Medicine was refusing to recognize this type of enhancement as legitimate medicine. Similarly, the requirement that testosterone be administered only to the hormone deficient, a standard dating from 1939, was reaffirmed as official policy sixty-five years later.

Yet the reality in 2003 was that many physicians were defying this policy. Prescription sales of testosterone drugs increased by more than 500 percent between 1993 and 2003. The IOM committee reported that most of the 1.75 million testosterone prescriptions written in 2002 went to men who did not suffer from hypogonadism, the principal indication for which the drug is supposed to be prescribed. In other words, testosterone had already become a predominantly off-label drug that was, by IOM standards, out of control—and some physicians were prepared to defend their discretionary use of the drug in the court of public opinion.

Abraham Morgentaler, a urologist affiliated with Harvard Medical School and a paid speaker for two drug companies that make testosterone, argues that the conservative consensus ignores the medical realities encountered when treating the emotional and sexual problems of middle-aged men. "There is a disconnect between some of the conclusions and recommendations that come out of this, and what I and other doctors see in clinical practice," he charges. In his experience, the drug works: "Among those of us who do any work with sexual medicine, there's no question this is beneficial. Men come to me because they're noticing a loss of vitality, increased fatigue, and sexual symptoms, such as diminished libido and sexual dysfunction. Many of these men see very beneficial response with treatment." Morgentaler's debunking of the standard medical warnings against testosterone therapy, which appeared in the prestigious *New England Journal of Medicine* in January 2004, marked a turning point in how testosterone is presented in the American medical literature.

The activist approach to testosterone therapy has been standard practice for years in the offices of two Harley Street physicians in London. Malcolm Carruthers, a specialist in men's health, estimates that the male menopause (or andropause) affects half of all men in their fifties. "Female hormone replacement therapy (HRT) is well established and women get lots of care and attention," he declared in 2000. "Men get told that it's just their age, or that they are depressed." Malcolm Whitehead, a gynecologist, notes that he has "prescribed testosterone implants for female politicians in Westminster who want to compete better with their male colleagues in committee meetings and parliamentary debates. They claim the hormone boosts their assertiveness and makes them feel more powerful."

The unresolved conflict over testosterone therapy, like the unending doping crisis in sport, is a de facto referendum on the cultural status of enhancements for the general population. In the meantime, divided medical opinion presents another threat to physicians' credibility on the potential value of hormone therapy. The conservatives' dogmatic reluctance to acknowledge the reported benefits of testosterone therapy for aging men reflects both scientific caution and a discomfort about enhancement procedures for "normal" people. Dr. Shalender Bhasin, an endocrinologist who has published clinical studies of anabolic steroids, has pointed to the societal context of the uneasiness about testosterone drugs: "There is some degree of denial and hypocrisy with the use of these compounds. We discourage it by punishing a few people now and then to show our displeasure, but we tolerate their use. We haven't taken a stand as a society, and the widespread use of these agents is reflective of our ambivalence." There is a historical precedent that illustrates the medical consequences of such denial and hypocrisy. Until 1984 the American Academy of Sports Medicine held to the view that anabolic-androgenic steroids did not enhance athletic performance. (A sports physician had already published this mistaken view in *JAMA* in 1972.) The athletes, of course, knew this assertion to be false, and the physicians' naïveté undermined their authority for years afterward. It is likely that the Institute of Medicine's obstructive approach to testosterone research will, in a similar fashion, enlarge rather than narrow the gap between orthodox clinical medicine and the wide-open hormone markets that are now thriving around the world.

NOTES

INTRODUCTION. Testosterone Dreams

2   This scientific achievement was driven by a competition   See John M. Hoberman and Charles E. Yesalis, "The History of Synthetic Testosterone," *Scientific American* 272 (February 1995): 76–81.

2   An association between testosterone treatment and muscular enlargement George N. Papanicolaou and Emil A. Falk, "General Muscular Hypertrophy Induced by Androgenic Hormone," *Science* 87 (March 11, 1938): 238–39.

2   "Androgens exert a tonic and stimulating action"   "Climacteric in Aging Men," *Journal of the American Medical Association* (hereafter *JAMA*) 118 (February 7, 1942): 460.

2   Scientists were already distinguishing   W. O. Thompson and N. J. Heckel, "Male Sex Hormone," *JAMA* 113 (1939): 2128; August A. Werner, "The Male Climacteric: Report of Fifty-four Cases," *JAMA* 127 (March 24, 1945): 710.

2   Excerpted in *Reader's Digest*   Paul de Kruif, "Can Man's Prime Be Prolonged?" *Reader's Digest* 45 (July 1944): 21–24; "Hormones for He Men," *Newsweek*, May 28, 1945, 90.

2   "The male hormone"   Paul de Kruif, *The Male Hormone* (New York: Harcourt, Brace, 1945), 208.

2   Commending his "courageous honesty"   H. M. Parshley, "A Rhetorical Rhapsody," *Herald Tribune Weekly Book Review*, May 27, 1945, 10.

3   Two companies   "Sex Hormones in Legal Battle," *Business Week*, December 22, 1945, 48.

3   By 1937 testosterone propionate   Samuel A. Vest, Jr., and John Eager Howard, "Clinical Experiments with the Use of Male Sex Hormones," *Journal of Urology* 40 (July 1938): 158.

3   By 1938 the production of testosterone   "Sex Hormones in Legal Battle," 48.

3   de Kruif predicted in 1945   De Kruif, *The Male Hormone,* 187.

3   De Kruif declared   Ibid., 222, 199, 66, 162.

3   Physicians described the optimal effect of testosterone   Ibid., 200, 108–9, 218, 201.

3   "The present results"   "Hormones in Geriatrics," *JAMA* 154 (April 17, 1954): 1336.

4   "these substances"   "Of Fires and Frying Pans," *JAMA* 155 (May 15, 1954): 302.

4   "social and economic responsibilities"   "Androgen for Male Climacteric and Gonadal Insufficiency," *JAMA* 113 (July 29, 1939): 452.

4   "We know how"   De Kruif, *The Male Hormone,* 223.

4   In March 1944   Maj. Gen. David N. W. Grant, " 'Pep' Pills for Bomber Pilots," *Science Digest,* June 1944, 85.

5   After two U.S. Air Force pilots   Thom Shanker with Mary Duenwald, "Bombing Error Puts a Spotlight on Pilots' Pills," *New York Times,* January 19, 2003.

5   the consent form   "Informed Consent for Operational Use of Dexedrine" includes the following passage: "Should I choose not to take it [Dexedrine] under circumstances where its use appears indicated . . . my commander, upon advice of the flight surgeon, may determine whether or not I should be considered unfit to fly a given mission" (William Walker, "U.S. Pilots Stay Up Taking 'Uppers,' " *Toronto Star,* August 1, 2002). For a detailed description of stimulant use by U.S. Air Force pilots, see "The Memory Hole—Navy Publication on Giving Speed to Military Pilots" (2002), www.thememoryhole.org/mil/pilot-speed.htm (accessed February 2004).

5   "The aviation community"   John Pike, director of Globalsecurity.org, quoted in Walker, "U.S. Pilots Stay Up Taking 'Uppers.' "

5   the tacit drug policy   See John Hoberman, " 'A Pharmacy on Wheels': Doping and Community Cohesion among Professional Cyclists following the Tour de France Scandal of 1998," in *The Essence of Sport,* ed. Verner Møller and John Nauright (Odense: University Press of Southern Denmark, 2003), 107–27.

5   They responded   "Kamikaze-Pillen," *Süddeutsche Zeitung* (Munich), August 19/20, 1998.

5   "apparent increase in illegal drug use"   "Elite Soldiers Face Charges as 'Police Uncover Drug Use,' " *Sydney Morning Herald,* July 24, 2002.

6   "How might a substance"   Peter D. Kramer, *Listening to Prozac* (New York: Viking, 1993), 16.

6   "People think they've got to keep up"   Dr. Joseph Glenmullen, of Harvard University Health Services, quoted in Craig Lambert, "The Downsides of Prozac," *Harvard Magazine,* May–June 2000, 21.

6   "We work against"   Jeffrey R. Young, "Prozac Campus," *Chronicle of Higher Education,* February 14, 2003, A37.

6   "showing signs of becoming"   Andrew Pollack, "A Biotech Outcast Awakens," *New York Times,* October 20, 2002. Pollack continues, "By year-end, Cephalon hopes to have results of a clinical trial in which Provigil is being tested to reduce sleepiness in people who work the graveyard shift. If the trial is successful, the com-

pany will ask the Food and Drug Administration to expand the approved uses of Provigil from just narcolepsy to excessive sleepiness associated with any medical condition."

6 **"Even as sleep disorders increase"** Jerome Groopman, "Eyes Wide Open," *New Yorker*, December 3, 2001, 54.

7 **"The employee may"** "Specific Problems of Women in Industry," *JAMA* 124 (March 11, 1944): 696.

7 **"With more and more women"** Robert A. Wilson, *Feminine Forever* (New York: M. Evans, 1966), 100; McKinlay, quoted in Margaret Morganroth Gullette, "Menopause as Magic Marker," in *Reinterpreting Menopause: Cultural and Philosophical Issues,* ed. Paul A. Komesaroff, Philipa Rothfield, and Jeanne Daly (New York: Routledge, 1997), 188.

7 **"Hormonal replacement therapy"** Bettina Leysen, "Medicalization of Menopause: From 'Feminine Forever' to 'Healthy Forever,' " in *Between Monsters, Goddesses and Cyborgs: Feminist Confrontations with Science, Medicine and Cyberspace,* ed. Nina Lykke and Rosi Braidotti (London: Zed Books, 1996), 174, 186.

8 **"Patients come in"** Polan, quoted in Stephen Rae, "Rx: Desire," *Modern Maturity,* March–April 2001, 88.

8 **"many people will feel"** Graham Hart and Kaye Wellings, "Sexual Behaviour and Its Medicalisation: In Sickness and in Health," *British Medical Journal,* April 15, 2002, 898.

8 Thus **"lifestyle" medicine** Gullette, "Menopause as Magic Marker," 189.

8 **Sensational coverage** De Kruif, *The Male Hormone,* 85.

9 *Science Digest* **reported** Dr. Albert Hemming, "The Truth about Testosterone," *Science Digest,* April 1946, 75.

9 **In addition, the idea** See, for example, "Ovaries, Estrogens and Libido," *JAMA* 113 (July 8, 1939): 168; Carl G. Heller and Gordon B. Myers, "The Male Climacteric, Its Symptomatology, Diagnosis and Treatment," *JAMA* 126 (October 21, 1944): 475; Ernst Simonsen, Walter M. Kearns, and Norbert Enzer, "Effect of Methyl Testosterone Treatment on Muscular Performance and the Central Nervous System of Older Men," *Journal of Clinical Endocrinology* 4 (1944): 533.

9 **"The prevailing experience"** "Frigidity in Women," *JAMA* 117 (November 15, 1941): 1750–51.

9 **The same principle applied** "Testosterone as a Treatment for Prematurity," *British Medical Journal,* January 29, 1949, 190; P. M. F. Bishop, "The Use of Sex Hormones in Therapeutics," *British Medical Journal,* January 29, 1949, 168.

9 **The marketing of testosterone** This idea preceded the availability of synthetic testosterone. "There must be a definite insufficiency on the part of one of the endocrine glands, so that the exhibition of a single glandular product fills a specific need and is true replacement therapy" ("Endocrine Products in Sterility," *JAMA* 92 [April 20, 1929]: 1372). See also "Sterilization without Unsexing," *JAMA* 92 (February 2, 1929): 374.

10 **Today it is the aging process** See, for example, Gina Kolata, "Growth Hormone Changed Older Bodies, for Better and Worse," *New York Times,* November 13, 2002.

10   The dramatic increase   Shalender Bhasin and William J. Bremner write:

> On the other hand, several recent trends in androgen use are alarming. Be-
> cause a substantial portion of the androgen market is underground, exact
> estimates of androgen use in the United States are not available. However,
> audits of direct and indirect sales indicate that the androgen sales in this
> country are growing 20–30% each year. There is reason to believe that a
> substantial portion of the overall androgen market involves the illicit use of
> testosterone for unapproved indications, particularly for muscle building by
> athletes and recreational body builders. The use of testosterone in human
> immunodeficiency virus (HIV)-infected men is growing, although clinical
> trials to examine the effectiveness of testosterone in reversing HIV-wasting
> syndrome are still in progress. It is distressing that a significant proportion
> of hypogonadal men continue to be undiagnosed, diagnosed late, or inap-
> propriately treated. Thus a paradoxical situation has developed in which
> testosterone replacement therapy continues to be underutilized or inappro-
> priately used for legitimate indications, while its use for unapproved indi-
> cations continues to expand. (Bhasin and Bremner, "Emerging Issues in An-
> drogen Replacement Therapy," *Journal of Clinical Endocrinology and
> Metabolism* 82 [1997]: 3)

According to other researchers, "Since 1995, the use of AAS [anabolic-androgenic
steroids] is estimated to have increased 400%, mostly attributable to treatment of
AIDS-associated wasting" (Shehzad Basaria, Justin T. Wahlstrom, and Adrian S.
Dobs, "Anabolic-Androgenic Steroid Therapy in the Treatment of Chronic Diseases," *Journal of Clinical Endocrinology and Metabolism* 86 [2001]: 5108).

10   **"Improvement of clinical symptoms"**   Pekka Kunelius et al., "The Effects of
Transdermal Dihydrotestosterone in the Aging Male: A Prospective, Randomized,
Double Blind Study," *Journal of Clinical Endocrinology and Metabolism* 87
(2002): 1467. Other researchers observe:

> It is now generally agreed that male aging is associated with a slow and pro-
> gressive decrease in serum T[estosterone] concentrations. The decreases in
> serum T may be accompanied by a constellation of symptoms including sex-
> ual dysfunction, lack of energy, loss of muscle and bone mass, increased
> frailty, loss of balance, cognitive impairment, and decreased general well
> being—a condition termed "andropause" or "androgen deficiency of aging
> men." Some of these clinical symptoms are relieved by replacement therapy
> with intramuscular T injections or transdermal T applications. ("Editorial:
> Should the Nonaromatizable Androgen Dihydrotestosterone Be Considered
> as an Alternative to Testosterone in the Treatment of the Andropause?"
> *Journal of Clinical Endocrinology and Metabolism* 87 [2002]: 1462)

10   **"symptoms that are often denied"**   "ACCE Clinical Practice Guidelines for the
Evaluation and Treatment of Hypogonadism in Adult Male Patients," *Endocrine
Practice* 2 (November–December 1996): 440, 441.

10   **"designer androgens"**   "Editorial: Should the Nonaromatizable Androgen Dihydrotestosterone Be Considered as an Alternative to Testosterone?" 1462.

10   **the long-standing medical concern**   Basaria, Wahlstrom, and Dobs, "Anabolic-
Androgenic Steroid Therapy," 5115.

10   **the standard warning**   The disclaimer given in the report is typical:

> Our results in no way justify the use of anabolic-androgenic steroids in
> sports, because, with extended use, such drugs have potentially serious ad-

verse effects on the cardiovascular system, prostate, lipid metabolism, and insulin sensitivity. Moreover, the use of any performance-enhancing agent in sports raises serious ethical issues. Our findings do, however, raise the possibility that the short-term administration of androgens may have beneficial effects in immobilized patients, during space travel, and in patients with cancer-related cachexia, disease caused by the human immunodeficiency virus, or other chronic wasting disorders. (Shalender Bhasin et al., "The Effects of Supraphysiologic Doses of Testosterone on Muscle Size and Strength in Normal Men," *New England Journal of Medicine* 335 [July 4, 1996]: 6)

11 **"They linked up"**   Quoted in Gina Kolata with Melody Petersen, "Hormone Replacement Study a Shock to the Medical System," *New York Times,* July 10, 2002.

11 **According to the same study**   Gina Kolata, "Hormone Therapy, Already Found to Have Risks, Is Now Said to Lack Benefits," *New York Times,* March 18, 2003.

11 **Finally, access to testosterone**   "The prescription must be for a legitimate medical reason and written in the course of the practitioner's professional practice" ("Memorandum of the Basic Elements for the Effective Control of Steroids" [n.d.]). I thank Charles E. Yesalis for providing me with a copy of this document.

11 *Testosterone* **magazine**   Cy Willson, "Your Doctor, Your Dealer," *Testosterone,* April 2001, 86–91.

11 **A far more significant work-around**   Julie Magno Zito et al., "Trends in the Prescribing of Psychotropic Medications to Preschoolers," *JAMA* 283 (February 23, 2000): 1025.

11 **Even though this federal agency's approval**   Pollack, "A Biotech Outcast Awakens."

11 **"the vast majority"**   Zito et al., "Trends in the Prescribing of Psychotropic Medications to Preschoolers," 1028.

11 **"estimates suggest"**   Mary Lee Vance, "Can Growth Hormone Prevent Aging?" *New England Journal of Medicine* 348 (February 27, 2003): 780.

CHAPTER 1.   Hormone Therapy and the New Medical Paradigm

13 **"No one," he says, "can age with dignity"**   Quoted in "Eine Art von Doping," *Der Spiegel,* September 20, 1999, 178–79. All translations are mine, unless otherwise noted.

14 **The American Academy of Anti-Aging Medicine**   "Shot of Youth," *Modern Maturity,* March–April 2000, 70. The medical establishment's response to the anti-aging movement within its own ranks has been generally subdued rather than openly hostile. For example:

Although many physicians advertise that they're "board-certified" in this area, anti-aging medicine isn't a recognized medical specialty. This designation simply means that the physician has attended conferences and passed an examination sponsored by the American Academy of Anti-Aging Medicine (AAAAM)—an organization that promotes anti-aging products and services. It doesn't represent a course of study at any certified medical school, and it isn't sanctioned by the American Medical Association. ("Who Are the Anti-Aging Specialists?" *Harvard Women's Health Watch,* December 2001, 4; this publication is sponsored by the Harvard Medical School)

14   *Newsweek*'s "Testosterone" cover story   Geoffrey Cowley, "Attention: Aging Men," *Newsweek,* September 16, 1996, 70.

14   "In the next few years"   Gail Sheehy, "Endless Youth," *Vanity Fair,* June 1996, 68.

14   "The menopausal man"   Carruthers, quoted in "When the Competitive Spirit Starts to Flag," *Times* (London), January 27, 1997.

14   "was like being turbo-boosted"   "Gym and Tonic," *Sunday Times* (London), November 10, 1996.

14   Finally, we want to know   "How common is the use of a medicine, hormone, or treatment to enhance sexual performance? Only 10 percent of men said they used any of these. Nearly half of them cited Viagra, and most men and their partners said the drug had increased their sexual enjoyment" ("The Chemical Factor," *Modern Maturity,* September–October 1999, 44). Just over 20 percent of men ages sixty-five to sixty-nine and just under 20 percent of men ages seventy to seventy-four reported using any of these procedures.

14   "I strongly suspect"   Charles E. Yesalis, "Replacement or Doping?" *Muscular Development,* January 1999, 165.

15   "We are being steamrollered"   Allolio, quoted in "Power ohne Ende," *Der Spiegel,* September 3, 2001, 65.

15   "medically reinforced normality"   The researcher referred to is the Danish scientist Claus Møldrup. See "Doping i dagligdagen," *Berlingske Tidende* (Copenhagen), May 27, 2001.

15   Plastic surgeries   Advertisements for cosmetic surgeries have proliferated in recent years in the United States. For an American physician's sardonic reaction to this development, see Selma Harrison Calmes, "Aesthetic Surgery," *JAMA* 282 (August 11, 1999): 591. See also the articles on this subject published in *Medical Student JAMA* 286 (November 7, 2001). The popularity of cosmetic surgery is also advancing in Germany. See, for example, "Verschrumpelte Mickeymäuse," *Der Spiegel,* March 20, 2000, 84–85, 88–89.

15   The booming trade   See, for example, Paul Solotaroff, "Killer Bods," *Rolling Stone,* February 14, 2002, 55–56ff.

16   "The use of dietary supplements"   Quoted in "Is Kava Safe? European Nations Say No, but U.S. Is Still Studying It," *Austin American-Statesman,* January 19, 2002.

17   "We are rapidly becoming"   Professor Arvid Carlsson of the Pharmacological Institute at the University of Gothenburg, Sweden, won a Nobel Prize for Medicine and Physiology in 1999; he is quoted in "Nobelprisvinner:—Lykkepillen blir like vanlig som kaffe," *Aftenposten* (Oslo), January 5, 2002.

18   "Why worry"   Erik Parens, "Is Better Always Good? The Enhancement Project," in *Enhancing Human Traits: Ethical and Social Implications,* ed. Erik Parens (Washington, D.C.: Georgetown University Press, 1993), 1, 23.

18   The "normal function model"   Ibid., 4–5, 7.

18   "medicine really has no proper boundaries"   Eric T. Juengst, "What Does Enhancement Mean?" in Parens, ed., *Enhancing Human Traits,* 34.

18   "One takes one's cues"   Ibid.

19   "I'm talking about the performance-enhancing drugs"   Okun, quoted in Barbara Crossette, "U.N. Board Says Legal Drug Use Increases in Rich Countries," *New York Times,* February 21, 2001.

19   "Some colleagues and competitors"   "Beyond Prozac," *Newsweek*, February 7, 1994, 40.
19   "Imagine," Parens wrote   Parens, "Is Better Always Good?" 15.
20   "The capability to resist"   Jerome Groopman, "Eyes Wide Open," *New Yorker*, December 3, 2001, 55, 54.
20   The East German doctors   For English-language accounts of the East German doping program, see John Hoberman, *Mortal Engines: The Science of Performance and the Dehumanization of Sport* (New York: Free Press, 1992): 222–24; Werner W. Franke and Brigitte Berendonk, "Hormonal Doping and Androgenization of Athletes: A Secret Program of the German Democratic Republic Government," *Clinical Chemistry* 43 (1997): 1262–79. See also Steven Ungerleider, *Faust's Gold: Inside the East German Doping Machine* (New York: St. Martin's Press, 2001).
20   the United States Air Force   Groopman, "Eyes Wide Open," 53.
20   In 1997 the Drug Enforcement Administration   Lawrence Diller, *Running on Ritalin: A Physician Reflects on Children, Society, and Performance in a Pill* (New York: Bantam Books, 1998), 34–35, 314–15.
20   "conspired to create a market for Ritalin"   Quoted in Barry Meier, "Suits Charge Conspiracy to Expand Ritalin Use," *New York Times*, September 14, 2000.
20   Peter Kramer wonders   Peter D. Kramer, "Female Troubles," *New York Times Magazine*, October 1, 2000, 18.
21   "the most tempting drug"   Dinges, quoted in Groopman, "Eyes Wide Open," 57.
21   "The ideas surge forth"   Honoré de Balzac, "Traité des excitants modernes" (1838), in *Études analytiques* (Paris: Les Bibliophiles de l'Originale, 1968), 263; see also Maurice Bardèche, *Balzac* (Paris: Juillard, 1980), 266–67. On Balzac's theory of coffee as a stimulant *(excitant)*, see Hoberman, *Mortal Engines*, 111–14.
21   It is a curious fact   On the use of beta blockers by musicians, see Mary L. Wolfe, "Correlates of Adaptive and Maladaptive Musical Performance Anxiety," *Medical Problems of Performing Artists*, March 1989, 49–56; see also Hoberman, *Mortal Engines*, 110.
21   "There is something indeed odd"   Parens, "Is Better Always Good?" 12.
22   A gradual shift   Jennifer Steinhauer, "Doctors Eliminate Wrinkles, and Insurers," *New York Times*, January 18, 2000.
23   Indeed, the influence of the supplements industry   See, for example, Stephanie Mencimer, "Scorin' with Orrin," *Washington Monthly*, September 2001, 27–35. On the relationship between Senators Orrin Hatch and Tom Harkin and the supplements industry, see also Chuck Neubauer, Judy Pasternak, and Richard T. Cooper, "Senator, His Son Get Boosts from Makers of Ephedra," *Los Angeles Times*, March 5, 2003.
24   As two fertility experts once described it   Quoted in Gina Kolata, "On Cloning Humans, 'Never' Turns Swiftly into 'Why Not,' " *New York Times*, December 2, 1997.
25   "The quest for sex hormones"   Nelly Oudshoorn, *Beyond the Natural Body: An Archeology of Sex Hormones* (London: Routledge, 1994), 150.
25   "Scientists have only recently recognized"   Sue DeCotiis, M.D., quoted in Susan Crain Bakos, "From Lib to Libido: How Women Are Reinventing Sex for Grown-Ups," *Modern Maturity*, September–October 1999, 56.

25 **"Anabolic steroids"** Adrian Sandra Dobs, "Is There a Role for Androgenic Anabolic Steroids in Medical Practice?" *JAMA* 281 (April 14, 1999): 1326. The earliest citation by this author is from 1975; almost all the rest date from the 1990s.

26 **papers asking the same question** See W. O. Thompson, "Uses and Abuses of the Male Sex Hormone," *JAMA* 132 (September 28, 1946): 185–88; Jean D. Wilson and James E. Griffin, "The Use and Misuse of Androgens," *Metabolism* 29 (1980): 1278–95; Carrie J. Bagatell and William J. Bremner, "Androgens in Men—Uses and Abuses," *New England Journal of Medicine* 334 (March 14, 1996): 707–14.

26 **Finally, testosterone is now undergoing** David France, "Testosterone, the Rogue Hormone, Is Getting a Makeover," *New York Times,* February 17, 1999.

26 **"the uninformed continue to believe"** Dr. Albert Hemming, "The Truth about Testosterone," *Science Digest,* April 1946, 75.

26 **"It is well known"** "Torpedomiljø hardner," *Aftenposten,* November 7, 2000.

26 **"Many officers around the country"** "Police Taking Steroids to Counter Thugs," *Sunday Times* (London), December 6, 1998.

26 **Steroid use by police officers** See "Steroid Use by Law Officers Raises Fears," *Austin American-Statesman,* November 5, 1989; "Researchers Say Police Steroid Use a Dangerous Trend," *Houston Post,* November 18, 1989.

27 **In the United States, increasing numbers** Avery D. Feigenbaum et al., "Anabolic Steroid Use by Male and Female Middle School Students" (abstract), *Pediatrics* 101 (May 5, 1998): 914.

27 **Steroid use among female adolescents** Holcomb B. Noble, "Steroid Use by Teen-Age Girls Is Rising," *New York Times,* June 1, 1999.

27 **Of an estimated 83,000 teenage steroid users** "Youth Popping Pills at Alarming Rate, RCMP Says," *Globe and Mail* (Toronto), November 18, 1998.

27 **its long career as a sexual stimulant** "Doctors sometimes prescribe testosterone to increase energy and sexual activity" (James McBride Dabbs, *Heroes, Rogues, and Lovers: Testosterone and Behavior* [New York: McGraw-Hill, 2000], 100).

27 **rampant drug use among Tour de France riders** See John Hoberman, " 'A Pharmacy on Wheels': Doping and Community Cohesion among Professional Cyclists following the Tour de France Scandal of 1998," in *The Essence of Sport,* ed. Verner Møller and John Nauright (Odense: University Press of Southern Denmark, 2003), 107–27.

28 **"Attempts have been made"** H. Climenko, "Corpus Luteum in Neurological Practice," *Endocrinology* 3 (1919): 1.

28 **Reports that testicle transplants** See, for example, R. G. Hoskins, "Studies on Vigor. IV: The Effect of Testicle Grafts on Spontaneous Activity," *Endocrinology* 9 (July–August 1925): 281–82, 290.

28 **"Now for the first time"** Edward Huntington Williams, *How We Become Personalities: The Glands of Health, Virility, and Success* (1926); quoted in Bernice L. Hausman, *Changing Sex: Transsexualism, Technology, and the Idea of Gender* (Durham, N.C.: Duke University Press, 1995), 23.

28 **Commenting in 1952** Herman Rubin, quoted in Hausman, *Changing Sex,* 35.

28 **"a high-testosterone approach to life"** Dabbs, *Heroes, Rogues, and Lovers,* 3, 50, 29.

29 "the new anabolic Tarzan" Stephen S. Hall, "The Bully in the Mirror," *New York Times Magazine*, August 22, 1999, 100.

29 "gargantuan mummies come to life" Jack McCallum, "Titans of Testosterone," *Sports Illustrated*, October 18, 1999, 100.

29 "the men-behaving-badly genre" Andrew Ross Sorkin, "On Newsstands in Britain, Beer and Babes Are in Decline," *New York Times*, August 6, 1999.

29 "a testosterone-addled, myopic car nut" Bruce McCall, "King of the Road," *New York Times Book Review*, July 18, 1999, 6.

29 "a testosterone drought" John Tierney, "Monkey Business: Strippers, Testosterone and the Dow," *New York Times*, November 9, 1998.

29 a "testosterone backlash" Gail Collins, "Pumped-Up Politics," *New York Times*, October 5, 1999.

29 "The testosterone flowed freely" George Rush and Joanna Molloy with Marcus Baram and K. C. Baker, "This Is Rich: Fund Set Up for Wildenstein," *Daily News* (New York), November 12, 1998.

29 The Hyundai Corporation Jane L. Lee, "Korea's Hyundai Kicks Off 'Apron War,' " *Wall Street Journal*, May 6, 1999.

29 "a Tonka toy on steroids" Marco R. della Cava, "Marine Convoy Steadily Makes Its Way to Mission," *USA Today*, June 11, 1999.

29 "humorless, unnecessarily sadistic" Rita Kempley, " 'Soldier' Misfortune," *Washington Post*, October 23, 1998.

29 "Corporations on Steroids" Thomas Friedman, "Corporations on Steroids," *New York Times*, February 4, 2000.

29 "Anabolic steroids build muscle mass" Advertisement in *New York Times Magazine*, February 21 and 28, 2000.

30 "Many of baseball's most talented players" Skip Bayless, "Survival of the Fittest Drives Homer Totals," *Austin American-Statesman*, October 3, 2001.

31 "Prozac's enormous appeal" David J. Rothman, "Shiny Happy People," *New Republic*, February 14, 1994, 34.

31 "an all-purpose personality enhancer" Christine Gorman, "Prozac's Worst Enemy," *Newsweek*, October 10, 1994, 64.

31 Kramer believes Peter D. Kramer, *Listening to Prozac* (New York: Viking, 1993), 17, 297.

31 "a quintessentially American drug" Rothman, "Shiny Happy People," 36.

31 "the ultimately capitalist pill" Lauren Slater, *Prozac Diary* (1998; reprint, New York: Penguin Books, 1999), 162.

32 Kramer himself uses the steroid analogy Kramer, *Listening to Prozac*, 246, 15, 248.

32 "It is one thing" Slater, *Prozac Diary*, 188, 195.

33 Benzedrine might produce "Benzedrine: Mental Scores Improve after a Dose of Pills," *News-Week*, January 2, 1937, 18.

33 The United States Olympic Committee's Selena Roberts, "Athletes Must Guess on Supplements," *New York Times*, January 30, 2002.

33 the Coca-Cola Company Ludy T. Benjamin, Jr., Anne M. Rogers, and Angela Rosenbaum, "Coca-Cola, Caffeine, and Mental Deficiency: Harry Hollingworth and the Chattanooga Trial of 1911," *Journal of the History of Behavioral Sciences* 27 (1991): 45.

34 "a general cell stimulant"   R. G. Hoskins, "Some Current Trends in Endocrinology," *JAMA* 77 (November 5, 1921): 1460.

34 "testicular substance"   L. L. Stanley, "An Analysis of One Thousand Testicular Substance Implantations," *Endocrinology* 6 (November 1922): 794.

34 "Androgens," a *JAMA* editorial   "Climacteric in Aging Men," *JAMA* 118 (February 7, 1942): 460.

34 "natural stimulants"   V. Korenchevsky, "The War and the Problem of Aging," *JAMA* 119 (June 20, 1942): 629, 630.

34 "is usually adequate"   "Dosage of Testosterone Propionate," *JAMA* 128 (July 14, 1945): 838.

34 "a general body stimulant"   Lespinasse, quoted in August A. Werner, "The Male Climacteric," *JAMA* 132 (September 28, 1946): 194.

34 "general stimulative effects"   Joseph L. Decourcy and Cornelius B. Decourcy, "Steroid Hormones in Geriatric Practice," *Geriatrics* 6 (1951): 28.

34 "tonic and dynamogenic" effects   "Androgen Therapy in Gynecology," *JAMA* 153 (December 19, 1953): 1468.

34 "anabolic tonic"   Robert N. Rutherford, "The Male and Female Climacteric," *Postgraduate Medicine* 50 (October–December 1971): 127, 128.

34 "tonic and stimulating influence"   "Testicle and Ovary Endocrine Therapy," *JAMA* 75 (December 4, 1920): 1598.

34 Reports appearing in 1949 and 1961   "Testosterone as a Treatment for Prematurity," *British Medical Journal,* January 29, 1949, 189–90; "Use of Anabolic Hormones as Growth Stimulants," *Nutrition Reviews* 19 (1961): 2–4.

34 "perfectly safe"   "Methyl Testosterone in Premature Infants," *JAMA* 142 (January 28, 1950): 287. The safety of testosterone for premature infants is reiterated in A. M. Earle, "Methyl Testosterone and Plasma for Premature Infants," *Journal of Pediatrics* 36.87 (January 1950); abstract in *Archives of Pediatrics* 67 (1950): 243–44. See also "Testosterone Therapy in Stunted Children," *Lancet,* June 29, 1957, 1341.

34 "a general growth stimulant"   Joseph Schwartzman, "Testoserone: A Study of Its Effect upon Anorexia and Underweight in Children—Review of 19 Cases," *Archives of Pediatrics* 71 (April 1954): 105. Another researcher noted, "These unwanted side-effects of testosterone therapy—virilism and advanced skeletal maturation—have caused clinicians to be cautious in using it to stimulate growth in children" ("Testosterone Therapy in Dwarfism," *British Medical Journal,* October 12, 1957, 870).

35 It is rather the notoriety   France, "Testosterone, the Rogue Hormone, Is Getting a Makeover."

35 "The promiscuous use"   "Minutes of House of Delegates," *JAMA* 74 (June 19, 1920): 1322.

35 "An extravagant use"   Lewellys F. Barker, "The Principles Underlying Organotherapy and Hormonotherapy," *Endocrinology* 6 (September 1922): 592.

35 "The laity are becoming versed"   R. G. Hoskins, "Some Recent Work on Internal Secretions," *Endocrinology* 6 (September 1922): 622–23.

35 "the bad impression"   Stanley, "An Analysis of One Thousand Testicular Substance Implantations," 787.

36 "the over-conservative group"   Hoskins, "Some Recent Work on Internal Secretions," 632.

36   "There prevails a widespread feeling"   Barker, "The Principles Underlying Organotherapy and Hormonotherapy," 591-92.

36   "pseudoscientific rubbish"   "Disappointments of Endocrinology," *JAMA* 76 (June 11, 1921): 1686.

36   comparable editorials and warnings   For example:

> Studies, to date, in short, offer tantalizing evidence that androgens may play an important role in women, but they are not fully convincing because most have been performed in women who are only partly deficient in androgens, and most have been performed with doses of androgens that are probably at least somewhat excessive. (Peter J. Snyder, "Editorial: The Role of Androgens in Women," *Journal of Clinical Endocrinology and Metabolism* 86 [2001]: 1007)

Also:

> The concept of developing androgenic compounds with variable biological actions in different organs (anti-androgenic in the prostate) is currently being pursued, but the selection of aging men with clinically important and well-defined hypogonadism remains difficult, a situation that contrasts sharply with abrupt menopause in women. (Steven W. J. Lamberts, Annewieke W. van den Beld, and Aart-Jan van der Lely, "The Endocrinology of Aging," *Science* 278 [October 17, 1997]: 422)

Just as the first article speaks of "tantalizing evidence" that might favor androgen therapy, so too does the second article conclude that "a number of aspects of the aging process of the endocrine system invite the development of 'routine' medical intervention programs offering long-term replacement therapy with one or more hormones, in order to delay the aging process and to allow us to live for a longer period in a relatively intact state" (423). This ambivalent presentation of views and evidence is characteristic of the current state of the debate about androgen therapy.

37   the intravenous injection of adrenal extract   See Merriley Borell, "Organotherapy and the Emergence of Reproductive Endocrinology," *Journal of the History of Biology* 18 (Spring 1985): 3, 5, 9.

37   "the use of animal glandular extracts"   Theodore A. McGraw, Jr., "Clinical Experiences in Organotherapy with Special Reference to the Stimulation of Body Growth," *Endocrinology* 8 (1924): 196.

37   the French physiologist Charles-Édouard Brown-Séquard   On Brown-Séquard, see Hoberman, *Mortal Engines,* 72-76. See also Merriley Borell, "Organotherapy, British Physiology, and Discovery of the Internal Secretions," *Journal of the History of Biology* 9 (Fall 1976): 235-68; Borell, "Brown-Séquard's Organotherapy and Its Appearance in America at the End of the Nineteenth Century," *Bulletin of the History of Medicine* 50 (Fall 1976): 309-20.

38   Brown-Séquard complained in 1889   Brown-Séquard, quoted in Borell, "Brown-Séquard's Organotherapy," 313.

39   "There is always a class of medical men"   Quoted in Borell, "Organotherapy, British Physiology, and Discovery of the Internal Secretions," 241.

39   "manufacturing chemists"   Quoted in ibid., 253.

40   Brown-Séquard was reporting   Borell, "Organotherapy and the Emergence of Reproductive Endocrinology," 4n.

40   "The attempt to estimate the significance"   Hoskins, "Some Current Trends in Endocrinology," 1459.

40   "The literature of the day"   McGraw, "Clinical Experiences in Organotherapy," 196.

41   "The antagonism of certain pharmaceutical houses"   "Council on Pharmacy and Chemistry," *JAMA* 106 (April 4, 1936): 1171.

41   "the tremendous abuse"   Morris Fishbein, "Glandular Physiology and Therapy," *JAMA* 104 (February 9, 1935): 463.

41   "commercial interests have seized"   "Abuses of Organotherapy," *JAMA* 79 (November 11, 1922): 1723.

41   "our best pharmaceutical houses"   Leonard G. Rowntree, "An Evaluation of Therapy, with Special Reference to Organotherapy," *Endocrinology* 9 (1925): 185–86.

41   Even five years later   E. M. K. Geiling, "The Need for Conservatism in Endocrine Therapy and Research," *JAMA* 101 (September 2, 1933): 743.

41   "the principle that the physician or laboratory investigator"   "Endocrinology and Pseudo-Endocrinology," *JAMA* 77 (November 5, 1921): 1499.

42   "To what extent is the scientific staff"   "Introducing a New Drug," *JAMA* 79 (September 30, 1922): 1149.

42   "the outer appearance of these subjects"   "The Rejuvenation Method of Professor Steinach," *JAMA* 76 (April 9, 1921): 1026–27.

42   The Paris-based surgeon Serge Voronoff   See David Hamilton, *The Monkey Gland Affair* (London: Chatto and Windus, 1986).

42   "Sometimes boldly"   "Fraudulent Exploitation of 'Organo Tablets,' " *JAMA* 76 (March 26, 1921): 887.

43   "an ever expanding public conversation about sex"   Julia A. Ericksen, *Kiss and Tell: Surveying Sex in the Twentieth Century* (Cambridge, Mass.: Harvard University Press, 1999), 21, 37.

44   "I appreciate that this is not a life"   "Treatment of Impotence," *JAMA* 107 (October 17, 1936): 1325.

44   "a blessing in disguise"   Oswald S. Lowsley and James L. Bray, "The Surgical Relief of Impotence," *JAMA* 107 (December 19, 1936): 2035.

44   "Are we to uphold the idea"   "Period of Potency in Man," *JAMA* 109 (September 11, 1937): 891.

45   The commissioner of baseball   Murray Chass, "Baseball Tries to Calm Down Debate on Pills," *New York Times,* August 27, 1998.

45   The Boston Red Sox slugger Mo Vaughn   Gordon Edes, "Vaughn Says Legal Supplements Are Fair," *Boston Globe,* August 26, 1998.

46   But the absence of research in this area   See, for example, Luke Cyphers, "Chemistry Clash," *Daily News* (New York), November 1, 1998.

46   "This is a snake-oil exemption"   Wolfe, quoted in Sheryl Gay Stolberg, "Rule on Ads for Diet Supplements Is Revised," *New York Times,* January 6, 2000.

46   "What the agency is doing"   Quoted in ibid.

47   "special artificial foods"   Ove Bøje, "Doping: A Study of the Means Employed to Raise the Level of Performance in Sport," *Bulletin of the Health Organization of the League of Nations* 8 (1939): 449. For a more extended discussion of this issue, see Hoberman, *Mortal Engines,* 107–8.

47   The head of the Office of National Drug Control Policy   Bill Pennington, "From the Highest Level, a Call for Action," *New York Times,* July 11, 1998.

47   The General Nutrition Companies   The *Wall Street Journal* described these studies as follows:

> But here are the five [research studies] GNC was talking about: an article written by a sometime spokesman for an andro supplier; favorable comments by a professor who was doing andro research at Eastern Michigan University, research financed by the same andro supplier; and three papers that didn't address the substance's long-term safety. One of the researchers, Conrad Earnest, says that there is "certainly no data that (a) andro is safe and (b) it has any effect." (Dan Morse, "GNC Resisted Offering a Hot Pill, Losing Sales and Irking Franchisees," *Wall Street Journal,* August 16, 1999)

47   By 1997 the supplement market   Kirk Johnson, "As Drugs in Sports Proliferate, So Do Ethical Questions," *New York Times,* August 31, 1998.

47   "Anyone who takes these products"   McLellan, quoted in Murray Chass, "Senate Posse Is Passing Steroids Buck to Baseball," *New York Times,* March 16, 2004.

48   "Several manufacturers said"   Amy Shipley, "Andro's Ban Effect May Be Small: Manufacturers Say More Potent Products Have Replaced Supplement," *Washington Post,* March 18, 2004.

48   "infantile" to equate hormone precursors   Connolly, quoted in Bill Pennington and Jack Curry, "Andro Hangs in a Quiet Limbo," *New York Times,* July 11, 1999.

48   "Androstenedione is a steroid"   Catlin, quoted in ibid.

48   a "sex steroid"   Yesalis and Leiken, quoted in William C. Rhoden, "Baseball's Pandora's Box Cracks Open," *New York Times,* August 25, 1998. See also Timothy Gower, "Safety and the Search for Muscle in a Bottle," *New York Times,* February 17, 1999.

48   "Chemically and pharmacologically, these substances"   Victor P. Uralets and Paul A. Gillette, "Over-the-Counter Anabolic Steroids 4-Androsten-3,17-dione; 4-Androsten-3beta,17beta-diol; and 19-nor-4-Androsten-3,17-dione: Excretion Studies in Men," *Journal of Analytical Toxicology* 23 (September 1999): 357–66.

49   "There is this belief"   Connolly, quoted in Pennington and Curry, "Andro Hangs in a Quiet Limbo."

49   "You will not reach"   Arnold, quoted in Johnson, "As Drugs in Sports Proliferate, So Do Ethical Questions."

49   "natural Viagra alternative"   Cyphers, "Chemistry Clash."

49   "Let's target the old guys"   Quoted in Morse, "GNC Resisted Offering a Hot Pill."

49   "It's good for your sex life"   McGwire, quoted in Pennington and Curry, "Andro Hangs in a Quiet Limbo."

49   Casual aphrodisia of this kind   Morse, "GNC Resisted Offering a Hot Pill."

49   East German scientists devised a use for this hormone   Thomas Kistner, "Das letzte Geheimnis des Staatsplans 14.25," *Süddeutsche Zeitung* (Munich), November 9, 1998. See also "Viagra für den ganzen Körper," *Der Spiegel,* November 9, 1998, 242–44.

50   "reprehensible advertising policy"   "Progynon-B and the Ovarian Follicular Hormone," *JAMA* 105 (August 31, 1935): 676.

50   In 1940 and 1941 this scenario was repeated   *JAMA*'s reactions were just as severe:

> The evidence in the literature, which forms the basis of this report, except for several lesser references, is definitely inadequate as a basis for the recommendation of therapy with mare gonadotropin. Our knowledge of the physiologic and pathologic action in primates, especially man, is still most uncertain. Certainly there is little justification for claims of consistent therapeutic success in gonadal disorders on the basis of the physiologic reactions obtained in laboratory animals and the meager clinical data reported up to the present time. ("The Present Status of the Gonadotropic Hormone from the Serum of Pregnant Mares: Gonadogen [The Upjohn Company], Anteron [Schering Corporation] and Gonadin [Cutter Laboratories] Not Acceptable for N.N.R.," *JAMA* 115 [December 7, 1940]: 1999)

> It must be pointed out that this substance [pregneninolone] was placed on the market over a year ago and that physicians were induced to use this substance on the advertising claims of the firm, as there was a distinct lack of evidence in the scientific literature. ("Regneninolone and Pranone [Schering Corporation]," *JAMA* 116 [March 15, 1941]: 1054)

50   "An adequate level of male sex-hormone"   Ernst Simonsen, Walter M. Kearns, and Norbert Enzer, "Effect of Methyl Testosterone Treatment on Muscular Performance and the Central Nervous System of Older Men," *Journal of Clinical Endocrinology* 4 (1944): 528.

51   Male hormone replacement therapy   See, for example, "Clinical Use of Synthetic Male Sex Hormone," *JAMA* 113 (July 29, 1939): 452.

51   Schering tried to promote the idea of male menopause   "Medical Motion Pictures," *JAMA* 146 (June 9, 1951): 580.

51   As of 1992 the company was concerned   "Jeden Dreck, jeden Blödsinn reingehauen," *Der Spiegel*, September 14, 1992, 286. By 1997 Schering had concluded that production of a testosterone-based male contraceptive was not commercially viable, given development costs of about $250 million. See "Falschmeldung ans Hirn," *Der Spiegel*, March 31, 1997, 176.

51   In 1997 Schering executives   "Wie ein Hund an der Kette," *Der Spiegel*, June 16, 1997, 122. Also in 1997, an endocrinologist at the Free University of Berlin, Horst Lübbert, who was collaborating with Schering on anabolic steroid research, found himself involved in one of the Berlin trials of former East German doping personnel. A former East German athlete who alleged she had been harmed by state-administered steroids refused to be examined by Lübbert. See "Bärte nach hinten," *Der Spiegel*, August 10, 1998, 106–7.

51   Schering had acquired a top expert   Oettel's activities in the East German doping program are described in Brigitte Berendonk, *Doping-Dokumente: Von der Forschung zum Betrug* (Berlin: Springer-Verlag, 1991), 122–24.

52   In October 2002 Schering announced   "Schering hilft," *Süddeutsche Zeitung*, October 21, 2002; "Schering macht Witze," *Süddeutsche Zeitung*, October 21, 2002.

52   Today Schering is trying to promote testosterone   "Die geheimen Sorgen des Mannes," *Süddeutsche Zeitung*, January 18, 2000.

52   Testosterone therapy now appears   A product that is alleged to boost testosterone levels (Testosterol) has been advertised on the *Rush Limbaugh Show* to the largest

radio audience in the United States. I heard this advertisement on KLBJ-AM radio in Austin, Texas, on November 19, 2001.

52 **"Studies indicate that roughly one in three men"** Russell Wild, "10 Hidden Energy Drains," *Modern Maturity*, November–December 2001, 38. See also Jim Thornton, "Man Power," *Modern Maturity*, January–February 2001, 47–48, 50, 70; Stephen Rae, "Rx: Desire," *Modern Maturity*, March–April 2001, 88–90, 94.

53 **"Whatever the mechanism of hypogonadism"** Ramzi R. Hajjar, Fran E. Kaiser, and John E. Morley, "Outcomes of Long-Term Testosterone Replacement in Older Hypogonadal Males: A Retrospective Analysis," *Journal of Clinical Endocrinology and Metabolism* 82 (1997): 3793. The caveat that the administration of testosterone "cannot be considered harmless therapy" for older hypogonadal men gets less attention than what testosterone therapy might do for these patients (Rahmawati Sih et al., "Testosterone Replacement in Older Hypogonadal Men: A 12-Month Randomized Controlled Trial," *Journal of Clinical Endocrinology and Metabolism* 82 [1997]: 1666).

53 **"leads to the possibility"** Paul G. Cohen, "Sexual Dysfunction in the United States" (letter), *JAMA* 282 (October 6, 1999): 1229.

53 **An analogous diagnosis** Sexual dysfunction has been reported to affect 43 percent of women in the United States. See Edward O. Laumann, Anthony Paik, and Raymond C. Rosen, "Sexual Dysfunction in the United States: Prevalence and Predictors," *JAMA* 281 (February 10, 1999): 537–44.

53 **"Enormous numbers of women"** Quoted in Rae, "Rx: Desire," 94.

53 **"If the administration of testosterone"** Susan Rako, M.D., *The Hormone of Desire: The Truth about Sexuality, Menopause, and Testosterone* (New York: Harmony Books, 1996), 33.

54 **"The development of transdermal testosterone preparations"** Snyder, "Editorial: The Role of Androgens in Women," 1006.

54 **Organized medicine's response** For example:

> These days, it's hard to ignore the ads, infomercials, and mailings that promise wrinkle-free skin, flexible joints, clear arteries, and a youthful sex drive. Americans spend billions of dollars each year trying to fight aging. Some of us visit physicians specializing in "anti-aging medicine" who offer therapy with hormone injections, patches, and pills. Many are intrigued by anti-aging supplements found in health food stores. ("Can Supplements Rewind Our Body Clocks?" *Harvard Women's Health Watch*, November 2001, 2)

54 **"flamboyant exploitation"** "Sex Hormones Hold the Stage," *JAMA* 112 (May 13, 1939): 1970.

CHAPTER 2. The Aphrodisiac That Failed

55 **"German and Swiss chemical laboratories"** "Testosterone," *Time*, September 23, 1935, 42–43. Four years later *Time* had become disillusioned with the male hormone: "Some medical discoveries are over-ballyhooed. Among them is testosterone, now sometimes puffed as a great rejuvenator. Actually there is no such thing as a

rejuvenator" ("Testosterone Tested," *Time,* July 24, 1939, 25). This gloomy prognosis was based on the work of the British gerontologist V. G. Korenchevsky.

55 **"the secretion that one day"** "Chemistry: Fertility Vitamins, Sex Hormones, Radioactive Salt," *News-Week,* August 31, 1935, 28.

56 **"Rub sex chemicals"** "Rub Sex Chemicals on Gums to Prevent Loss of Teeth," *Science News Letter* 37 (January 27, 1940): 53.

56 **"the medical grapevine"** Paul de Kruif, *The Male Hormone* (New York: Harcourt, Brace, 1945), 211, 212.

56 *Newsweek* **devoted a full page** Paul de Kruif, "Can Man's Prime Be Prolonged?" *Reader's Digest* 45 (July 1944): 21–24; "Hormones for He Men," *Newsweek,* May 28, 1945, 90–91.

57 **"I will candidly say"** Quoted in Marc H. Hollender, "The 51st Landmark Article," *JAMA* 250 (July 8, 1983): 228.

57 **"With all due respect"** Kelley, quoted in ibid.

58 **"any physician"** Darrow, quoted in ibid.

58 **"the instinct that dictates"** Denslow Lewis, "The Gynecologic Consideration of the Sexual Act" (1899), *JAMA* 250 (July 8, 1983): 222, 223.

59 **"Did women enjoy sex"** Edward Shorter, *A History of Women's Bodies* (New York: Basic Books, 1982), 9, 13, 16.

59 **"She should be informed"** Lewis, "The Gynecologic Consideration of the Sexual Act," 223.

59 **"bring disaster to many"** Ibid.

60 **The threat here** For example, Julia A. Ericksen writes:

> Although communities of male "fairies" had existed in most large American cities since the turn of the century, lesbians continued to be invisible. Lesbians represented a distinct threat; their existence meant that women could live without men. For experts who were just beginning to imagine that women might have sex drives, it was hard to understand the existence of women who not only experienced desire but initiated sex with other women. (Ericksen, *Kiss and Tell: Surveying Sex in the Twentieth Century* [Cambridge, Mass.: Harvard University Press, 1999], 33)

60 **Under the unsuspecting** Ornella Moscucci writes:

> Throughout the sixteenth and seventeenth centuries, it was accepted that the clitoris was the seat of woman's sexual pleasure; medical writers were not worried about the potential of the clitoris for lesbianism or masturbation, nor about its size, which was seen positively, as a healthy mark of female lustfulness. By the end of the eighteenth century, however, the clitoris had become much more problematic. As the emerging notion of two opposite sexes made heterosexual coupling "natural," the capacity of the clitoris for homo- and autoeroticism was increasingly perceived as a threat to the social order. Clitoral eroticism became synonymous with masturbation in the male, attracting widespread condemnation as the "solitary vice." (Moscucci, "Clitoridectomy, Circumcision, and the Politics of Sexual Pleasure in Mid-Victorian Britain," in *Sexualities in Victorian Britain,* ed. Andrew H. Miller and James Eli Adams [Bloomington: Indiana University Press, 1996], 69)

60 **"In one case, the clitoris"** Lewis, "The Gynecologic Consideration of the Sexual Act," 225.

61 **"absolutely devoid"** Ibid., 224.

61 "a judicious circumcision" Ibid., 225.

61 "sufficient passion" Ibid.

61 the female strategy of faking orgasm Michael Mason, *The Making of Victorian Sexuality* (Oxford: Oxford University Press, 1994), 176.

61 "I have known husbands" Lewis, "The Gynecologic Consideration of the Sexual Act," 225.

61 "I shall never forget" Kelly, quoted in ibid., 226.

62 "I do not believe" Kelly, quoted in ibid.

62 "singularly deficient in excitability" Ibid., 225.

62 "I believe any deviation" Ibid., 223.

62 Clitoridectomy Moscucci writes:

> During the 1850s, however, both the removal of the hood of the clitoris and the more radical form of clitoridectomy, involving the excision of the clitoris and labia, were occasionally suggested by medical practitioners as a cure for masturbation. . . . Much favored by American practitioners, who appear to have performed it well into the twentieth century, clitoridectomy never became established in Britain as an acceptable treatment for female masturbation. The majority of practitioners had grave misgivings about the operation, which they regarded as sexual mutilation[.] ("Clitoridectomy, Circumcision, and the Politics of Sexual Pleasure," 61)

On the history of the clitoridectomy, see Ornella Moscucci, *The Science of Woman: Gynaecology and Gender in England, 1800–1929* (Cambridge: Cambridge University Press, 1990), 159ff.; Ann Dally, *Women under the Knife: A History of Surgery* (London: Hutchinson Radius, 1991), 159ff.

62 "As we view the matter" "Clitoridectomy" (editorial), *Southern Journal of Medical Science* (1866–67): 794; quoted in John Duffy, "Masturbation and Clitoridectomy: A Nineteenth-Century View," *JAMA* 186 (October 19, 1963): 247.

63 "The spate of gynecologic activity" G. J. Barker-Benfield, "Sexual Surgery in Late Nineteenth-Century America," in *Seizing Our Bodies: The Politics of Women's Health*, ed. Claudia Dreifus (New York: Vintage Books, 1977), 22.

63 "grown stouter" Bloch, quoted in Duffy, "Masturbation and Clitoridectomy," 248.

63 Clitoridectomy may have been performed Barker-Benfield, "Sexual Surgery in Late Nineteenth-Century America," 23, 24.

63 "What is the general opinion" "Frigidity and the Clitoris," *JAMA* 130 (February 23, 1946): 546. See also "Operations on Clitoris for Frigidity," *JAMA* 130 (March 30, 1946): 908.

63 A more drastic and dangerous procedure On the history of the ovariotomy, see Moscucci, *The Science of Woman*, 135ff.; Dally, *Women under the Knife*, 135ff.

64 "the castration of women" Blackwell, quoted in Ann Douglas Wood, " 'The Fashionable Diseases': Women's Complaints and Their Treatment in Nineteenth-Century America," *Journal of Interdisciplinary History* 4 (1973): 48.

64 Female castration was officially known See, for example, "The Surgical Menopause," *JAMA* 78 (February 11, 1922): 470–71; "After-Effects of Intra-Uterine Radium for Production of Artificial Menopause," *JAMA* 96 (January 3, 1931): 74; William P. Boger, "Methyl Testosterone and Surgical Castration in the Treatment of Carcinoma of the Breast," *JAMA* 6 (1946): 88–98.

64   "but surgeons soon extended"   Dally, *Women under the Knife,* 147–48, 157–58.

64   "She becomes tractable"   Quoted in Barker-Benfield, "Sexual Surgery in Late Nineteenth-Century America," 27.

64   "My condition is all I could desire"   Quoted in ibid., 32–33, 40.

64   Surgical or X-ray-induced "castration"   Howard Schwander and Horace N. Marvin, "Treatment of Carcinoma of the Human Breast with Testosterone Propionate: A Report of Five Cases," *Journal of Clinical Endocrinology* 7 (1947): 423.

64   "castration entails atrophy"   "The Surgical Menopause," 470–71.

64   "What chance, if any"   "Ovaries, Estrogens and Libido," *JAMA* 113 (July 8, 1939): 168. See also "Cancer, Artificial Menopause and Libido," *JAMA* 129 (October 20, 1945): 584.

65   "patients with nymphomania"   "Oophorectomy and Libido," *JAMA* 97 (October 24, 1931): 1246.

65   "What treatment do you advise"   "Dipsomania and Nymphomania," *JAMA* 107 (July 4, 1936): 61.

65   In the 1920s these techniques   R. G. Hoskins, "Some Recent Work on Internal Secretions," *Endocrinology* 6 (September 1922): 631; "Stimulation of Endocrine Glands with Radium," *JAMA* 87 (August 28, 1926): 700.

65   As early as 1932   "Sex Desire and Menopause—High Voltage Roentgen Therapy in Cancer," *JAMA* 98 (June 4, 1932): 2009.

65   "Not only do hot flushes occur"   P. M. F. Bishop, "The Use of Sex Hormones in Therapeutics," *British Medical Journal,* January 29, 1949, 66.

65   "a safe and effective method"   Hugh C. McLaren, "Ill Effects of the Radium Menopause," *British Medical Journal,* July 8, 1950, 79.

66   Electrotherapy for male and female sexual problems   Rachel P. Maines writes:

> In the second half of the nineteenth century and the early part of the twentieth, there was considerable medical and scientific interest in electrolytes, human skin conductivity, and the effects of electrical stimulation on the health of plants and animals. Some doctors thought that electrical contraction of muscles could be useful as a substitute for exercise. Of particular interest to physicians was the perceived potential of electrotherapeutic treatment of impotence and "sexual debility" in men, both thought to be caused at least in part by masturbation. Popular medical literature and advertising encouraged men's anxiety about losing virility to the solitary vice, and thousands of electrical devices were sold directly to consumers on the strength of their alleged ability to restore masculine powers; some physicians specialized in providing electrotherapeutic services. (Maines, *The Technology of Orgasm: "Hysteria," the Vibrator, and Women's Sexual Satisfaction* [Baltimore: Johns Hopkins University Press, 1999], 82)

66   In the late nineteenth century   Ibid., 82, 66.

66   "For this purpose"   "Treatment of Impotence," *JAMA* 107 (October 17, 1936): 1326.

66   Electric current was also prescribed   In 1931 a German physician had employed a vaginal electrode as "diathermic treatment" for gynecological problems unrelated to sexual response ("Diathermic Treatment of Gynecologic Conditions," *JAMA* 95 [July 26, 1930]: 311).

66   At the turn of the century   Maines, *The Technology of Orgasm,* 82, 83.

66   "sensitization of the vaginal mucous membrane"   "Sexual Frigidity," *JAMA* 102

(February 3, 1934): 394; "Frigidity in Women," *JAMA* 114 (March 23, 1940): 1100.

66 **"The most remarkable"** Quoted in "Electric Shock Treatment for Menopausal Symptoms," *JAMA* 128 (June 30, 1945): 697.

67 **"The beauty of sex research"** James H. Jones, *Alfred C. Kinsey: A Public/Private Life* (New York: W. W. Norton, 1997), 503.

67 **"mild faradic current"** Maines, *The Technology of Orgasm,* 57.

67 **"clitoridectomists and castrators"** Barker-Benfield, "Sexual Surgery in Late Nineteenth-Century America," 41.

67 **a standard treatment for "hysteria"** Maines, *The Technology of Orgasm,* 3.

67 **"absolutely anesthetic in those regions"** A. L. Wolbarst (letter), "Frigidity in Women," *JAMA* 114 (May 11, 1940): 1952.

67 **In the late nineteenth century** Ann Dally writes:

> In America the influential Charles Meigs, a professor in Philadelphia . . . believed that modesty was a good reason for not trying to further knowledge in the field. It is, he says: ". . . perhaps best, on the whole, that this great degree of modesty should exist even to the extent of putting a bar to researches, without which no very clear and understandable notions can be obtained of the sexual disorders. I confess I am proud to say, that in this country generally, certainly in many parts of it, there are women who prefer to suffer the extremity of danger and pain rather than waive those scruples of delicacy which prevent their maladies from being fully explored." (*Women under the Knife,* 51)

68 **"had been informed of the examiner's intentions"** "Examination of a Virgin," *British Medical Journal,* June 8, 1946, 899.

68 **"Although some women"** "Vaginal Examination and the Patient," *British Medical Journal,* December 24, 1955, 1576.

68 **"ample evidence that gynecologists"** Barker-Benfield, "Sexual Surgery in Late Nineteenth-Century America," 24.

68 **"The conspiratorial theory"** Gail Pat Parsons, "Equal Treatment for All: American Medical Remedies for Male Sexual Problems: 1800–1900," *Journal of the History of Medicine* 32 (1977): 70.

68 **"There are many historical examples"** Maines, *The Technology of Orgasm,* 51.

68 **"Castration," Barker-Benfield writes** Barker-Benfield, "Sexual Surgery in Late Nineteenth-Century America," 33.

69 **a British physician who found himself "appalled"** "Marriage Neurosis," *British Medical Journal,* April 9, 1949, 635.

69 **the popular diagnosis of "ovariomania"** Dally, *Women under the Knife,* 151.

69 **"disintegrate into crones"** "Can a Woman Be Feminine Forever?" *New Republic,* March 19, 1966, 15.

70 **"I'm just not interested in sex"** Ira Levin, *The Stepford Wives* (New York: Random House, 1972), 59, 82, 56, 65–66.

70 **popular women's magazines were filled with articles** "My Husband Was Afraid of Sex," *Good Housekeeping,* January 1972, 34; "Fighting Words: American Women Are Lousy Lovers," *Vogue,* July 1971, 91; "Must Marriage Cheat Today's Young Women?" *Redbook,* February 1971, 66–67; "All about the New Sex Ther-

apy," *Newsweek,* November 27, 1972, 65–67; "Why Some Women Respond Sexually and Others Don't," *McCalls,* October 1972, 86–87.

70   "Disorderly women were handed over"   Barker-Benfield, "Sexual Surgery in Late Nineteenth-Century America," 38.

71   "indifferent to the conjugal embrace"   Lewis, "The Gynecologic Consideration of the Sexual Act," 225.

71   "and even if the sexual passion"   "Sex Instinct in Woman after Menopause," *JAMA* 99 (November 5, 1932): 1624.

71   "In hormone therapy"   "The Bases for Hormone Therapy," *JAMA* 76 (January 15, 1921): 210.

72   The carnival atmosphere   "Gold Medal Brand Sexual Pills," *JAMA* 80 (March 3, 1923): 645; "New Life Corporation Fraud," *JAMA* 98 (June 18, 1932): 2230; "Sex and Gland Rejuvenators," *JAMA* 108 (June 5, 1937): 1987; "Kelpep, Prostax and Glanmend," *JAMA* 111 (December 10, 1938): 2229; "The Nathan Peikes Quackery," *JAMA* 112 (February 11, 1939): 569; "Another Fraudulent 'Electric Belt,' " *JAMA* 114 (January 6, 1940): 74.

72   "lost all sense of proportion"   Robert T. Frank et al., "Present Endocrine Diagnosis and Therapy," *JAMA* 103 (August 11, 1934): 393.

72   Physicians' naïveté   As the pioneering American sexologist Robert Latou Dickinson put it in 1925: "We have trained students and interns with an outlook on laparotomy and pathology rather than on physiology, life-adjustments, and pelvic social problems" (Robert L. Dickinson and Henry H. Pierson, "The Average Sex Life of American Women," *JAMA* 85 [October 10, 1925]: 1113).

72   still being lamented in *JAMA*   "Sex Experts and Medical Scientists Join Forces against a Common Foe: AIDS," *JAMA* 259 (February 5, 1988): 641.

72   "By and large"   William F. Sheeley, "Sex and the Practicing Physician," *JAMA* 195 (January 17, 1966): 196.

72   One technique was to refer women   Robert Latou Dickinson, "Medical Analysis of a Thousand Marriages," *JAMA* 97 (August 22, 1931): 535.

73   "does not sense"   Robert Latou Dickinson, "Premarital Consultation," *JAMA* 117 (November 15, 1941): 1688.

73   "should hardly be of any great concern"   "Impotence," *JAMA* 163 (February 23, 1957): 704.

73   "Are we to uphold the idea"   "Period of Potency in Man," *JAMA* 109 (September 11, 1937): 891.

73   "Fortunately," *JAMA* comments   "Increased Libido after Menopause," *JAMA* 131 (July 6, 1946): 873.

74   "to the extent that she is afraid"   "Increased Sexual Desire at Climacteric," *JAMA* 98 (April 2, 1932): 1207; "Sexual Libido after Menopause," *JAMA* 99 (December 24, 1932): 2204.

74   "Occasionally androgens will decrease"   "Increased Libido of Menopause," *JAMA* 139 (January 22, 1949): 273.

74   For the standard menopausal symptoms   See Robert Jay Lifton, *The Nazi Doctors: Medical Killing and the Psychology of Genocide* (New York: Basic Books, 1986), 273.

74   "avoidance of coffee"   "Sexual Libido after Menopause," *JAMA* 99 (December 24, 1932): 2204.

74   "Are the talk of other women"   "Increased Libido of Menopause," 273.

74   the treatment of sexual feeling as a problem   By this time, doctors knew that these surgeries did not usually present a threat to the sex drives of their patients: "In most women the change of life does not seem to influence their sex desires and gratification. In some there is a diminution in these reactions, whereas in others there is an intensification of the libido" ("Sexual Libido after Menopause," 2204).

74   the renunciation of sexual activity by older people   See, for example, Richard A. Knox, "Boomers Take '60s Sexual Mores to Later Life," *Boston Globe,* August 4, 1999.

75   "If a woman broods"   "Relief of Symptoms at Menopause," *JAMA* 106 (March 21, 1936): 1030.

75   "For the severer types"   "Excessive Libido in a Woman," *JAMA* 110 (March 5, 1938): 761.

75   "morbidly oversexed females"   H. S. Rubenstein, H. D. Shapiro, and Walter Freeman, "The Treatment of Morbid Sex Craving with the Aid of Testosterone Propionate," *American Journal of Psychiatry* 97 (1940): 703–10.

76   Would a virgin go through menopause   "Pregnancy at Various Ages," *JAMA* 95 (October 18, 1930): 1197.

76   Would the sex instinct survive   "Sex Instinct in Woman after Menopause," 1624.

76   Would castrating a male   "Castration," *JAMA* 158 (August 20, 1955): 1483.

76   Could sex crimes be caused   "Hormones in Food," *JAMA* 163 (February 9, 1957): 515.

76   Could lack of sexual excitement   "Sexual Excitement and Nervous System of Women," *JAMA* 111 (October 8, 1938): 1400.

76   Could circumcising a woman   "Circumcision in the Female," *JAMA* 158 (August 27, 1955): 1576.

76   Was there a drug to suppress   "Sublimation of Sexual Urge," *JAMA* 165 (September 14, 1957): 203.

76   Why did prostitutes   "Infertility of Prostitutes," *JAMA* 166 (March 8, 1958): 1262.

76   Was a post-childbirth distaste   "Frigidity after Childbirth," *British Medical Journal,* July 22, 1944, 135.

76   Was there a safe aphrodisiac   "Sexual Frigidity," *British Medical Journal,* June 21, 1947, 911.

76   Was there a "sex-gland treatment"   "Size of Penis," *British Medical Journal,* April 22, 1944, 579.

76   Was there a hormone therapy   "Hormones and the Bust," *British Medical Journal,* February 2, 1955, 368. At least one physician treated women with "infantile breasts" by means of a topical application of the estrogenic substances estradiol or estradiol benzoate ("Local Application of Sex Hormones," *JAMA* 117 [September 9, 1941]: 473).

76   Could sex hormone injections   "Sex Hormones and Infertility," *British Medical Journal,* January 12, 1946, 76.

76   Women have feared and believed   "Oophorectomy and Libido," 1246.

76   "They have been told"   John D. Weaver, "Estrogenic Hormones, Often Only a Psychotherapeutic Agent," *Southern Medical Journal* 39 (1946): 582.

76   A British woman   "Marriage after Oophorectomy," *British Medical Journal,* May 13, 1944, 676.

77   Fear and hope combined   " 'Holding back'—a deliberate suppression of orgasm—is practised by women who mistakenly believe that pregnancy can be avoided if an orgasm is not permitted" (Joan Malleson, "Sexual Disorders in Women: Their Medical Significance," *British Medical Journal,* December 22, 1951, 1483).

77   "All know"   "Increased Libido after the Menopause," *JAMA* 100 (January 14, 1933): 136.

77   "The sad reality"   Mason, *The Making of Victorian Sexuality,* 203.

77   "this pathetic hope"   "The Climacteric," *British Medical Journal,* February 21, 1953, 454.

77   Fears that youthful masturbation   Wilfred C. Hulse, "The Management of Sexual Conflicts in General Practice," *JAMA* 150 (November 1, 1952): 848.

78   "still equate virility and potency"   E. B. Strauss, "Impotence from the Psychiatric Standpoint," *British Medical Journal,* March 25, 1950, 697.

78   A related stereotype holds   "Sexual Potency in Aging Males," *JAMA* 170 (July 18, 1959): 1393.

78   Some assumed that sex hormone injections   "Artificial Insemination," *British Medical Journal,* January 15, 1944, 95.

78   an analogous idea that testosterone injections   See, for example, G. I. M. Swyer, "Effects of Testosterone Implants in Men with Defective Spermatogenesis," *British Medical Journal,* November 14, 1953, 1080–81; Charles W. Charny, "Treatment of Male Infertility with Large Doses of Testosterone," *JAMA* 160 (January 14, 1956): 98–101; "Hormones and Human Fertility," *JAMA* (August 11, 1956): 1500–1501; "Male Sterility," *JAMA* 178 (December 16, 1961): 1122; "Testosterone Therapy and 'Rebound,' " *JAMA* 197 (August 15, 1966): 600.

78   "impressed by the idea"   T. N. A. Jeffcoate, "Male Infertility," *British Medical Journal,* August 10, 1946, 187.

78   "the type of placebo"   Hulse, "The Management of Sexual Conflicts in General Practice," 847.

78   "a fancied magical pill"   Sheeley, "Sex and the Practicing Physician," 196.

79   Sponsorship of this initiative by the NRC   See Vern L. Bullough, *Science in the Bedroom: A History of Sex Research* (New York: Basic Books, 1994), 116–17; Bullough, "The Development of Sexology in the USA in the Early Twentieth Century," in *Sexual Knowledge, Sexual Science: The History of Attitudes to Sexuality,* ed. Roy Porter and Mikuláš Teich (Cambridge: Cambridge University Press, 1994), 313–16; Ericksen, *Kiss and Tell,* 48; Jonathan Gathorne-Hardy, *Sex the Measure of All Things: A Life of Alfred C. Kinsey* (London: Chatto and Windus, 1998), 93; "National Research Council Committee for Research on Sex Problems," *JAMA* 81 (November 24, 1923): 1811–12.

79   "underground fact-finding research"   Bullough, "The Development of Sexology in the USA," 306; Gathorne-Hardy, *Sex the Measure of All Things,* 88.

80   "was a Christian gentleman"   Jones, *Alfred C. Kinsey,* 504.

80   The courage of these convictions   Dickinson and Pierson, "The Average Sex Life of American Women," 1113–17; "Medical Analysis of a Thousand Marriages," *JAMA* 97 (August 22, 1931): 529–34 (quotation, 534).

80   "If we can utilize scientific research"   "Sex and Medicine," *JAMA* 197 (July 18, 1966): 214.

80   the reader-response sex surveys published by Shere Hite   Shere Hite, *The Hite Report: A Nationwide Study on Female Sexuality* (New York: Macmillan, 1976); Hite, *The Hite Report on Male Sexuality* (New York: Knopf, 1981).

80   "Our present beliefs"   Dickinson and Pierson, "The Average Sex Life of American Women," 1113.

80   Dickinson himself translated principle   Bullough, "The Development of Sexology in the USA," 313.

81   a patriarchal ideology   I was pleased to find Julia Ericksen using the term *patriarchal* to characterize the mind-set of the men who carried out some of the early sex surveys: "Male surveyors whose agenda was to save marriage and maintain a patriarchal social order turned their attention away from unmarried men as subjects and toward the spousal couple" (*Kiss and Tell*, 35). Ericksen's portrait of the male medical attitudes of the interwar period is fully supported by my research on the medical context for sex hormone therapies at this time.

81   "the marriage act"   "Tests of Impotence," *JAMA* 94 (June 14, 1930): 1940; Hulse, "The Management of Sexual Conflicts in General Practice," 849.

81   "Techniques had to be learned"   Cate Haste, *Rules of Desire: Sex in Britain: World War I to the Present* (London: Chatto and Windus, 1992), 145.

82   "Now that the country"   "Marriage and Parenthood," *British Medical Journal*, April 15, 1944, 540; see also "What Is Marriage Guidance?" *British Medical Journal*, March 17, 1945, 377.

82   "the appalling breakdown rate"   "Marriage Guidance by Doctors," *British Medical Journal*, July 9, 1949, 101; see also "Pain in Childbirth," *British Medical Society*, July 17, 1948, 172.

82   "the acme of her sex life"   "Sexual Disorders in Women," *British Medical Journal*, January 12, 1952, 106; the same point had already been made in "Pain in Childbirth," 172-73.

82   "I have been consulted lately"   "Psychological Impotence after Long Separation," *British Medical Journal*, August 10, 1946, 216.

82   "Soldiers abroad idealize"   "Frigidity after Separation," *British Medical Journal*, February 16, 1946, 263.

83   "Soldier's impotence"   Strauss, "Impotence from a Psychiatric Standpoint," 698; see also "The Returned Prisoner of War," *British Medical Journal*, October 10, 1953, 820-21.

83   various drugs   See, for example, *Lancet* General Advertiser, November 14, 1942, 8; *Lancet* General Advertiser, October 24, 1942, 8.

83   The testosterone drugs advertised   See, for example, *Lancet* General Advertiser, March 27, 1943, 4.

83   "Is there any safe aphrodisiac"   "Sexual Frigidity," *British Medical Journal*, 911.

83   the sexually stimulating effect   "A Local Use for Testosterone," *Lancet*, September 23, 1939, 722.

83   Reports about the libido-boosting effects   See, for example, Udall J. Salon, "Rationale for Androgen Therapy in Gynecology," *Journal of Clinical Endocrinology* 1 (1941): 167-68; Robert B. Greenblatt, Frank Mortara, and Richard Torpin, "Sexual Libido in the Female," *American Journal of Obstetrics and Gynecology*

44 (1942): 659; Robert B. Greenblatt, "Androgenic Therapy in Women," *Journal of Clinical Endocrinology* 2 (1942): 666; Udall J. Salmon and Samuel H. Geist, "Effect of Androgens upon Libido in Women," *Journal of Clinical Endocrinology* 3 (1943): 235–38.

84   **"At the center of that religion of marriage"**   Quoted in Haste, *Rules of Desire,* 158.

84   **In 1660 in England**   *The Oxford English Dictionary,* s.v. "frigid." It is interesting to note that *JAMA* uses two different terms within the space of two years during the 1920s ("Impotence in Women," *JAMA* 78 [May 27, 1922]: 1673–74; "Sexual Frigidity in Women," *JAMA* 82 [January 19, 1924]: 251).

85   **While female "frigidity" and male "impotence"**   On the history of the terms *frigidity* and *impotence,* see Mark L. Elliott, "The Use of 'Impotence' and 'Frigidity': Why Has 'Impotence' Survived," *Journal of Sex and Marital Therapy* 11 (Spring 1985): 51–56.

85   **"There is no greater personal tragedy"**   Amram Scheinfeld, " 'Cold' Women— And Why," *Reader's Digest* 53 (August 1948): 124.

85   **"Scientists," he reports**   "Why a Wife Says 'No,' " *Popular Science,* August 1956, 112, 114.

86   **The medical term *frigidity***   See, for example, Malcolm Faulk, " 'Frigidity': A Critical Review," *Archives of Sexual Behavior* 2 (1973): 258.

86   **Freudian doctrine held**   For a long series of citations from Freud and other psychoanalytic commentators on clitoral and vaginal sensations and orgasm, see Alfred C. Kinsey, Wardell B. Pomeroy, Clyde E. Martin, and Paul H. Gebhard, *Sexual Behavior in the Human Female* (Philadelphia: W. B. Saunders, 1953), 582–83.

86   **Kinsey infuriated many psychoanalysts**   Ibid., 579–84.

87   **"This question is one of considerable importance"**   Ibid., 584.

87   **"an irascible New York analyst"**   Gathorne-Hardy, *Sex the Measure of All Things,* 319.

87   **the "beautiful, coquettish woman"**   Edmund Bergler, "The Problem of Frigidity," *Psychiatric Quarterly* 18 (1944): 382, 383, 386, 389.

87   **"homosexuals, aggressive old maids"**   William S. Kroger and S. Charles Freed, "Psychosomatic Aspects of Frigidity," *JAMA* 143 (June 10, 1950): 527.

87   **"the passive rôle"**   Bergler, "The Problem of Frigidity," 383; Kroger and Freed, "Psychosomatic Aspects of Frigidity," 528.

88   **The vaginal doctrine decreed**   See, for example, Dickinson, "The Average Sex Life of American Women," 1115; "Treatment of Frigidity," *JAMA* 96 (January 3, 1931): 62; "Frigidity in Women," *JAMA* 101 (November 4, 1933): 1501; "Frigidity in Women," *JAMA* 114 (March 23, 1940): 1100; "Frigidity and the Clitoris," *JAMA* 131 (May 11, 1946): 188; "Frigidity," *JAMA* 173 (June 25, 1960): 971.

88   **"is so widespread in our culture"**   Edmund Bergler and William S. Kroger, "Sexual Behavior" (letter), *JAMA* 154 (January 9, 1954): 168.

88   **"As a mass problem"**   Bergler, "The Problem of Frigidity," 375, 388.

88   **"I have repeatedly seen"**   "Frigidity and the Clitoris," *JAMA* 131 (May 11, 1946): 188.

88   ***Ramparts* magazine took up**   Susan Lydon, "Understanding Orgasm," *Ramparts* 7 (December 14–28, 1968): 61.

89 **"But now there are groups"** Elizabeth Fishel, "Sex 101: Continuing Education," *Ms.*, September 1975, 22.

89 **some participants in group therapy** Barbara Schneidman and Linda McGuire, "Group Therapy for Nonorgasmic Women: Two Age Levels," *Archives of Sexual Behavior* 5 (1976): 245.

89 **The first recorded case** Salmon and Geist, "Effect of Androgens upon Libido in Women," 235.

89 **"several elderly women"** Salmon, "Rationale for Androgen Therapy in Gynecology," 167–68.

89 **"Her physicians were amazed"** Herbert S. Kupperman, "Hormonal Aspects of Frigidity," *Quarterly Review of Surgery, Obstetrics and Gynecology* 16 (October–December 1959): 255.

90 **"since if administered in excess"** Udall J. Salmon, a physician quoted in Robert B. Greenblatt, "Testosterone Propionate Pellet Implantation in Gynecic Disorders," *JAMA* 121 (January 2, 1943): 24.

90 **In fact, the early androgen episodes** One researcher noted, "These observations must be considered as reliable and objective, since the steroid is being given for menstrual pain alone and not for any sexual inadequacies. When these patients offer the information that, in addition to relief of dysmenorrhea, libido is increased, we have unbiased evidence on the effect of androgens in increasing libido in the female" (Kupperman, "Hormonal Aspects of Frigidity," 255).

90 **"Theoretically," *JAMA*'s editors commented** "Increased Libido after Menopause," 873.

90 **In 1922 a German physician** "Impotence in Women," 1673; see also Allen Wright, "Materia Aphrodisia," *American Mercury*, July 1939, 350.

90 **Alcohol and wheat germ oil** "Treatment of Sexual Impotence," *JAMA* 87 (September 25, 1926): 1066.

91 **"inserting a large vaginal electrode"** Max Huhner, *The Diagnosis and Treatment of Sexual Disorders in the Male and Female* (Philadelphia: F. A. Davis, 1942), 407.

91 **It is worth noting** See, for example, "Psychologic Treatment of Frigidity," *JAMA* 97 (August 22, 1931): 560; William H. Barrow, "The Patient and the Art of Living," *JAMA* 114 (February 24, 1940): 708. On the use of hypnotherapy, see Kroger and Freed, "Psychosomatic Aspects of Frigidity," 531.

91 **Some physicians, in conformity** "The rapid return of normal libido in certain menopausal women who are treated with potent estrogens is occasionally striking" (William H. Perloff, "Role of the Hormones in Human Sexuality," *Psychosomatic Medicine* 11 [May–June 1949]: 135).

91 **A report in 1941** "Local Application of Sex Hormones," 473.

91 **"psychosexual panic"** "Theelin," *JAMA* 100 (June 3, 1933): 1793. A contemporary textbook identifies theelin as a monoatomic keto alcohol having the formula $C_{18}H_{21}O(OH)$ (Philip B. Hawk and Olaf Bergeim, *Practical Physiological Chemistry* [Philadelphia: P. Blakiston's Son, 1931], 571).

91 **Testosterone propionate ointment** Robert B. Greenblatt et al., "Sexual Libido in the Female," *American Journal of Obstetrics and Gynecology* 44 (1942): 660.

91 **"Many married women volunteered"** Robert B. Greenblatt, "Hormone Factors in Libido," *Journal of Clinical Endocrinology* 3 (1943): 306.

91 **By 1943 testosterone propionate** Harold D. Palmer and Margaret De Ronde,

"Reversible Testosterone-Induced Virilism," *Journal of Clinical Endocrinology* 3 (1943): 428.

91 **"the effect of androgens"** Anne C. Carter, Eugene J. Cohen, and Ephraim Shorr, "The Use of Androgens in Women," *Vitamins and Hormones* 5 (1947): 363.

91 **"causing, a) a heightened susceptibility"** Salmon and Geist, "Effect of Androgens upon Libido in Women," 237.

92 **One physician, for example** Kupperman, "Hormonal Aspects of Frigidity," 256.

93 **This reform turned tradition upside down** Stanley E. Harris, "Aversion Therapy for Homosexuality," *JAMA* 259 (June 10, 1988): 3271.

93 **"the enormity of the retributive sentences"** "Homosexuality," *British Medical Journal*, February 2, 1946, 179.

94 **"a dirty, unaesthetic, and abnormal practice"** "Homosexuality and the Law," *British Medical Journal*, April 6, 1946, 550.

94 **Less punitive proposals** "Homosexuality," *British Medical Journal*, April 6, 1946, 550.

94 **"repulsively feminized boys"** "Endocrine Therapy of Hypertrichosis and Acne," *British Medical Journal*, January 10, 1942, 54.

94 **"It would be rash to assume"** "Homosexuality," *British Medical Journal*, April 6, 1946, 550.

94 **In 1730 the Court of Holland** Theo van der Meer, "Sodomy and Moral Panic in the Low Countries," in *Sexuality*, ed. Robert A. Nye (New York: Oxford University Press, 1999), 66.

94 **At the end of the nineteenth century** Chandak Sengoopta, "Glandular Politics: Experimental Biology, Clinical Medicine, and Homosexual Emancipation in Fin-de-Siècle Central Europe," *Isis* 89 (1998): 449.

95 **"the purpose of nature"** Richard von Krafft-Ebing, "Perversity and Perversion," in Nye, ed., *Sexuality*, 149.

95 **the German physician Albert Moll claimed** Albert Moll, "Hegemony of the Two-Sex Model: Males," in Nye, ed., *Sexuality*, 154.

95 **Brown-Séquard noted that** Charles-Édouard Brown-Séquard, "Remarques sur les effets produits sur la femme par des injections sous-cutanées d'un liquide retiré d'ovaires d'animaux," *Archives de physiologie normale et pathologique*, 5th ser., 2 (1890): 456.

95 **He assumed that injecting** M. Tausk, "The Emergence of Endocrinology," in *Discoveries in Pharmacology*, ed. M. J. Parnham and J. Bruinvels, vol. 2, *Haemodynamics, Hormones and Inflammation* (Amsterdam: Elsevier, 1984), 222.

95 **Brown-Séquard noted that an American** C. E. Brown-Séquard, "On a New Therapeutic Method Consisting in the Use of Organic Liquids Extracted from Glands and Other Organs," *British Medical Journal*, June 10, 1893, 1213.

96 **By 1907 the British scientist Edward Schäfer** Merriley Borrell, "Organotherapy and the Emergence of Reproductive Endocrinology," *Journal of the History of Biology* 18 (Spring 1985): 13n29, 13, 17.

96 **The 1912 edition of** *Psychopathia sexualis* Richard von Krafft-Ebing, *Psychopathia sexualis*, 14th ed. (1912; reprint, Munich: Matthes und Seitz, 1984), 43.

96 **"energetic and manly aspect"** Robert Lichtenstern, "Über 'Innere Sekretion und Sexualität,'" *Zeitschrift für Urologie* 15 (1921): 20–202; see also "The Puberty Glands," *JAMA* 75 (September 11, 1920): 755; "Testicle Implants," *JAMA* 78

(January 21, 1922): 256; "Transplantation of Testes in Relation to Homosexuality," *JAMA* 79 (August 12, 1922): 598; Sengoopta, "Glandular Politics," 465–67.

97   The surgeon Richard Mühsam   Sengoopta, "Glandular Politics," 468.

97   Perhaps the most scientifically interesting case   R. G. Hoskins, "Studies on Vigor. IV: The Effect of Testicle Grafts on Spontaneous Activity," *Endocrinology* 9 (July–August 1925): 282, 289.

97   "If homosexuality is merely"   Julius Baur, "Homosexuality as an Endocrinological, Psychological, and Genetic Problem," *Journal of Criminal Psychopathology* 2 (October 1940): 188.

97   "Perhaps when we understand"   Norman E. Himes, *Your Marriage: A Guide to Happiness* (New York: Farrar and Rinehart, 1940), 23–24.

98   The idea that the bodies of homosexuals   C. A. Wright in the *Medical Record* 142 (November 6, 1935): 407.

98   "such highly suggestive hormonal differences"   S. J. Glass, H. J. Deuel, and C. A. Wright, "Sex Hormone Studies in Male Homosexuality," *Endocrinology* 26 (1940): 593. See also Rudolph Neustadt and Abraham Myerson, "Quantitative Sex Hormone Studies in Homosexuality, Childhood, and Various Neuropsychiatric Disturbances," *American Journal of Psychiatry* 97 (November 1940): 533–35.

98   This theory was also endorsed   "Endocrine Treatment in Homosexual Men," *Medical Record* 155 (1942): 65. For this reference I am indebted to Tracy D. Morgan, "Written on the Body: Rethinking the Medical History of Homosexuality," paper presented at the Annual Meeting of the American Historical Association, Atlanta, Georgia, January 1996.

98   In fact, the Dutch drug company Organon   Nelly Oudshoorn, *Beyond the Natural Body: An Archeology of Sex Hormones* (London: Routledge, 1994), 59.

98   "an abnormality of the chromosomal structure"   Baur, "Homosexuality as an Endocrinological, Psychological, and Genetic Problem," 194.

98   This report described   Saul Rosenzweig and R. G. Hoskins, "A Note on the Ineffectualness of Sex-Hormone Medication in a Case of Pronounced Homosexuality," *Psychosomatic Medicine* 3 (January 1941): 88, 89.

99   "More basic than any error"   Alfred C. Kinsey, "Criteria for a Hormonal Explanation of the Homosexual," *Journal of Clinical Endocrinology* 1 (1941): 425, 426.

99   "It is impossible at the present stage"   John Money, "Sex Hormones and Other Variables in Human Eroticism," in *Sex and Internal Secretions*, ed. William C. Young (Baltimore: Williams and Wilkins, 1961), 1385.

99   "Organotherapy by compulsion"   S. J. Glass and Roswell H. Johnson, "Limitations and Complications of Organotherapy in Male Homosexuality," *Journal of Clinical Endocrinology* 4 (1944): 540, 542, 543.

100   "The 'fairy' is easily recognized"   Louis A. Lurie, "The Endocrine Factor of Homosexuality: Report of Treatment of 4 Cases with Androgen Hormone," *American Journal of Medical Science* 208 (1944): 177.

100   "There are popular and even clinical concepts"   Kinsey, "Criteria for a Hormonal Explanation of the Homosexual," 427.

100   "The homosexual trends and drives"   Lurie, "The Endocrine Factor of Homosexuality," 185.

101   "The results were startling"   Ibid., 180, 185, 186.

101   "hypogonadal subjects are more vulnerable"   Glass and Johnson, "Limitations and Complications of Organotherapy in Male Homosexuality," 543.

101   Indeed, with the benefit of hindsight   The endocrine-imbalance theory has been discredited for half a century: "In our experience, no patient, either male or female, has shown any consistent reversal of the endocrine pattern to explain homosexual tendencies. We have never observed any correlation between the choice of the sex object and the levels of hormonal excretion" (Perloff, "Role of the Hormones in Human Sexuality," 136). A contemporary researcher noted, "It may be stated categorically that no convincing demonstrations of endocrine imbalance in 'homosexuals' have been forthcoming" (G. I. M. Swyer, "Homosexuality: The Endocrinological Aspects," *Practitioner* 172 [1954]: 375). More recently, a scholar declared: "It is the author's thesis that, on the basis of the available evidence, it cannot be concluded that there is any hormonal cause of homosexuality in either women or men and that the often unquestioned assumptions of the medical model are leading researchers to ask questions which are at least irrelevant and at times result in measures designed to 'control' homosexuality" (Lynda I. A. Birke, "Is Homosexuality Hormonally Determined?" *Journal of Homosexuality* 6 [Summer 1981]: 37). The verdict at the end of the century is the same: "Workers [researchers] once thought an adult's androgen and estrogen levels determined orientation, but this hypothesis withered for lack of support" (William Byne, "The Biological Evidence Challenged," in Nye, ed., *Sexuality*, 295).

101   The demise of the endocrine theory   The endocrine-imbalance theory of homosexuality made a short-lived comeback during the 1970s. See Heino F. L. Meyer-Bahlburg, "Sex Hormones and Male Homosexuality in Comparative Perspective," *Archives of Sexual Behavior* 4 (1977): 301–2.

101   "A patient was made to stand"   "Aversion Therapy," *JAMA* 258 (November 13, 1987): 2564.

102   A variation on this treatment   N. McConaghy and R. F. Barr, "Classical, Avoidance and Backward Conditioning Treatments of Homosexuality," *British Journal of Psychiatry* 122 (1973): 151.

102   "This began with an explanation"   Basil James, "Case of Homosexuality Treated by Aversion Therapy," *British Medical Journal*, March 17, 1962, 769. On the use of testosterone propionate injections for this purpose, see also M. P. Feldman and M. J. MacCulloch, "A Systematic Approach to the Treatment of Homosexuality by Conditioned Aversion: Preliminary Report," *American Journal of Psychiatry* 121 (1964): 167.

102   A 1987 review   "Aversion Therapy," 2565.

102   West German surgeons reported   "Stereotaxic Surgery Results in 'Cures' of German Sex Offenders," *JAMA* 229 (September 23, 1974): 1716. See also I. Rieber and V. Sigusch, "Psychosurgery on Sex Offenders and Sexual 'Deviants' in West Germany," *Archives of Sexual Behavior* 8 (1979): 523–27; G. Schmidt and E. Schorsch, "Psychosurgery of Sexually Deviant Patients: Review and Analysis of New Empirical Findings," *Archives of Sexual Behavior* 10 (1981): 301–23.

102   The sexually deadening effects   See, for example, M. A. F. Murray et al., "Endocrine Changes in Male Sexual Deviants after Treatment with Anti-Androgens, Oestrogens or Tranquillizers," *Journal of Endocrinology* 67 (1975): 179–88.

102   Almost entirely absent from the biomedical campaign   One researcher has noted, "I was unable to find any concrete clinical reports on actual attempts at 'curing' lesbianism by compensatory administration of estrogens or by antiandrogen treatment. . . . To my knowledge, there have been no investigations concerning the sexual orientation of female hypogonadal patients and the effects of hormone therapy on it" (Heino F. L. Meyer-Bahlburg, "Sex Hormones and Female Homosexuality: A Critical Examination," *Archives of Sexual Behavior* 8 [1979]: 103). See also Birke, "Is Homosexuality Hormonally Determined?" 47; Sengoopta, "Glandular Politics," 446; Simon LeVay, "The Sexual Brain," in Nye, ed., *Sexuality*, 290.

103   a speculative proposal to prevent female homosexuality   G. Dörner, "Hormonal Induction and Prevention of Female Homosexuality," *Journal of Endocrinology* 42 (1968): 163–64.

103   Dörner's proposal   Günter Dörner et al., "A Neuroendocrine Predisposition for Homosexuality in Men," *Archives of Sexual Behavior* 4 (1975): 2.

103   This hypothetical treatment   Dörner declares, "These results suggest that androgen-induced male homosexuality may be prevented by androgen administration during the critical period of the hypothalamic mating centre(s)" (G. Dörner and G. Hinz, "Induction and Prevention of Male Homosexuality by Androgen," *Journal of Endocrinology* 40 [1968]: 387–88).

103   "When does the male homosexual"   Meyer-Bahlburg, "Sex Hormones and Male Homosexuality in Comparative Perspective," 319. He continues:

Our view is as follows: First, the analogy of sexual motor patterns of rats (lordosis, mounting) with the sexual life of human beings is not only rash and arbitrary, but also anthropological nonsense. Second, comparisons between various species show that prenatal or perinatal hormone influences vary considerably even on the physiological level (e.g., as regards the cyclic secretion of sex hormones). Third, clinical observations of prenatal hormone disturbances in humans (adrenogenital syndrome) do not offer any evidence for the validation of Dörner's hypothesis; even serious hormonal malfunctions of this kind do not favor homosexual development.

See also Volkmar Sigusch et al., "Official Statement by the German Society for Sex Research [Deutsche Gesellschaft für Sexualforschung e.V.] on the Research of Prof. Dr. Günter Dörner on the Subject of Homosexuality," *Archives of Sexual Behavior* 11 [1982]: 445–49; Birke, "Is Homosexuality Hormonally Determined?" 46; Luis J. G. Gooren et al., "Biomedical Theories of Sexual Orientation," in *Homosexuality/Heterosexuality: Concepts of Sexual Orientation*, ed. David P. McWhirter, Stephanie A. Sanders, and June Machover Reinisch (New York: Oxford University Press, 1990), 80–84.

103   "a preventive therapy"   Dörner et al., "A Neuroendocrine Predisposition for Homosexuality in Men," 7.

103   "endocrinological euthanasia of homosexuality"   Sigusch et al., "Official Statement," 448.

104   medical malpractice   Harris warns, "Clinicians who persist in misdiagnosing and mistreating their homosexual and bisexual patients with aversion therapy may soon find themselves confronted with malpractice litigation" ("Aversion Therapy for Homosexuality," 3271).

104   Dörner lashed back at his critics   Günter Dörner, "Letter to the Editor," *Archives of Sexual Behavior* 12 (1983): 577–82.

104   **"As long as society"**   Gunter Schmidt, "Allies and Prosecutors: Science and Medicine in the Homosexuality Issue," *Journal of Homosexuality* 10 (Winter 1984): 137.

104   **Simon LeVay, like Dörner**   LeVay, "The Sexual Brain," 292.

104   **"The male hormone"**   De Kruif, *The Male Hormone*, 208.

105   **In 1931 Organon**   Oudshoorn, *Beyond the Natural Body*, 99–100.

106   **"It occurred to me"**   Elmer Bobst, *Bobst: The Autobiography of a Pharmaceutical Pioneer* (New York: McKay, 1973), 161–63.

106   **"almost incredible"**   Ibid., 163.

107   **Fishbein scolded Bobst**   "Sex Hormones Hold the Stage," *JAMA* 112 (May 13, 1939): 1970.

107   **"Within the past few months"**   "The Present Status of Testosterone Propionate: Three Brands, Perandren, Oreton and Neo-Hombreol (Roche-Organon) Not Acceptable for N.N.R.," *JAMA* 112 (May 13, 1939): 1949. In this report the council declares Perandren (Ciba), Oreton (Schering), and Neo-Hombreol (Roche-Organon, Hoffmann-LaRoche) to be "unacceptable for inclusion in New and Nonofficial Remedies" (1951).

107   **"A substance which may be"**   "The Public Be Warned," *JAMA* 114 (May 11, 1940): 1886.

108   **gynecomastia**   *Gynecomastia* refers to "an abnormal swelling of one or both breasts in men. The condition is usually temporary and harmless. It may be caused by hormonal imbalance, tumor of the testis or pituitary, drugs containing estrogen or steroids, or failure of the liver to dissolve estrogen in the bloodstream" (*The Signet Mosby Medical Encyclopedia*, ed. Walter D. Glanze, Kenneth N. Anderson, and Lois E. Anderson, rev. ed. [New York: Signet Books, 1996], 361). On the relationship between gynecomastia and anabolic-androgenic steroids, see Karl E. Friedl, "Effects of Anabolic Steroids on Physical Health," in *Anabolic Steroids in Sport and Exercise*, ed. Charles E. Yesalis (Champaign, Ill.: Human Kinetics, 1993), 110, 113, 116.

108   **"Recently many reports"**   "Climacteric in Aging Men," *JAMA* 118 (February 7, 1942): 458.

108   **the male climacteric syndrome**   On the history of the male climacteric, see John B. McKinlay, "Is There an Epidemiologic Basis for a Male Climacteric Syndrome? The Massachusetts Male Aging Study," in *Menopause: Evaluation, Treatment, and Health Concerns*, ed. Charles B. Hammond, Florence P. Haseltine, and Isaac Schiff (New York: Alan R. Liss, 1989), 163–92.

108   **"What treatment would you suggest"**   "Decrease of Potency in a Man of Sixty," 682.

108   **"A 64-year-old patient"**   "Impotence," 704.

109   **"The effect of impotency"**   "Impotence in Diabetics," *JAMA* 153 (November 14, 1953): 1067.

109   **"It is probably not worth while"**   "Impotence and Administration of Endocrines," *JAMA* 124 (April 29, 1944): 1320.

109   **"She wants to know"**   "Frigidity in Women," *JAMA* 117 (November 15, 1941): 1750.

109 "I have had requests" "Testosterone Therapy," *JAMA* 140 (May 28, 1949): 438.

110 "a vigorous man in his middle seventies" "Dosage of Testosterone Propionate," *JAMA* 128 (July 14, 1945): 838.

110 As early as 1939 "Androgen for Male Climacteric and Gonadal Insufficiency," *JAMA* 113 (July 29, 1939): 451–52.

110 "is an important syndrome" Dunn, quoted in August A. Werner, "The Male Climacteric," *JAMA* 127 (March 24, 1945): 710.

111 "Androgens," a *JAMA* editorial declared "Climacteric in Aging Men," 460.

111 "when they complain" Stanley F. Goldman and Mark J. Markham, "Clinical Use of Testosterone in the Male Climacteric," *Journal of Clinical Endocrinology* 2 (1942): 242.

111 "An adequate level of male-sex hormone" Ernst Simonsen, Walter M. Kearns, and Norbert Enzer, "Effect of Methyl Testosterone Treatment on Muscular Performance and the Central Nervous System of Older Men," *Journal of Clinical Endocrinology* 4 (1944): 528.

111 popular magazines had addressed marital problems "Why Marriages Fail," *Atlantic,* September 1907, 289–98; "Why So Many Married People Are Discontented," *Good Housekeeping,* August 1912, 231–34; "Things Women Keep Quiet About," *Ladies Home Journal,* November 16 and December 22, 1913.

111 By the 1940s the popular magazine "The Psychology of Sex," *Hygeia* 18 (February 1940): 124ff; "Sex Education for the Woman at Menopause," *Hygeia* 19 (September 1941): 699ff; "Marital Frustration in Women," *Hygeia* 21 (April 1943): 271–72ff; "Marriage as a Doctor Sees It," *Woman's Home Companion* 69 (June 1942): 20–21; Scheinfeld, " 'Cold' Women—And Why," 124–26.

112 "Gynecologists and psychiatrists" Kroger and Freed, "Psychosomatic Aspects of Frigidity," 526, 530.

112 "readily amenable to substitution therapy" Carl G. Hartman, "Sex Education for the Woman at Menopause," *Hygeia* 19 (September 1941): 747.

112 "One of the greatest sins" Richard W. Te Linde, "The Menopause," *American Journal of Nursing* 54 (August 1954): 952.

113 "It has been demonstrated" "Cancer, Artificial Menopause and Libido," 584.

113 "certain chemicals in responsible medical use" Maxine Davis, *The Sexual Responsibility of Woman* (New York: Dial Press, 1956), 208.

113 all that *The Complete Medical Guide* was telling Benjamin F. Miller, M.D., *The Complete Medical Guide,* rev. ed. (New York: Simon and Schuster, 1967), 77.

114 "contrasexual mutilation of the woman" E. C. Hamblen, "Androgen Therapy in Women," *Journal of Clinical Endocrinology* 2 (September 1942): 575.

114 "Testosterone propionate will restore libido" Greenblatt, "Androgenic Therapy in Women," 666.

114 "One out of every five men" "Of Fires and Frying Pans," *JAMA* 155 (May 15, 1954): 302.

114 "aggravate and accelerate some processes" V. Korenchevsky, "Research Schemes on Endocrinologic Aspects of Aging in Males," *Journal of Gerontology* 7 (1952): 299.

114 *The Complete Medical Guide* (1956), for example Miller, *The Complete Medical Guide,* 77. The disreputable nature of "rejuvenation" research is emphasized by de Kruif in *The Male Hormone* (55, 59).

115 "The drug itself produced obvious" Edward S. Tauber and George E. Daniels, "Further Observations on Androgenic Hormones and Psychic Conflict," *Psychosomatic Medicine* 11 (1949): 141–42.

115 "may only help prolong" "Impotence," *JAMA* 154 (January 16, 1954): 288.

115 "pathologically increased sex desire" "Oophorectomy and Libido," 1246; Charles Mazer, David R. Meranze, and S. Leon Israel, "Evaluation of the Constitutional Effects of Large Doses of Estrogenic Principle," *JAMA* (July 27, 1935): 262; Greenblatt, "Testosterone Propionate Pellet Implantation in Gynecic Disorders," 24.

115 "In the case of the sex hormones" V. Korenchevsky, "The War and the Problem of Aging," *JAMA* 119 (June 20, 1942): 629.

115 "marital complications" Greenblatt, "Testosterone Propionate Pellet Implantation in Gynecic Disorders," 24.

115 "Fortunately," *JAMA* declared "Increased Libido after Menopause," 873.

116 "without normal channels for satisfaction" Carter, Cohen, and Shorr, "The Use of Androgens in Women," 364.

116 "not to stimulate tissues" August A. Werner, "The Male Climacteric," *JAMA* 132 (September 28, 1946): 194.

116 "A general knowledge of the hormones" Kinsey et al., *Sexual Behavior in the Human Female*, 721.

116 The evidence presented in his book For example:

> When testosterone, for instance, is given the normal human male, there may be an increase in the frequency of his morning erections, the frequency of his erotic response to various stimuli, the frequency of his masturbation, and the frequency of his socio-sexual contacts. This is ordinarily true of adult males of ages ranging at least from the twenties into the fifties or sixties.

And:

> There is some clinical experience in administering testosterone to normal human females, and the results obtained are quite similar to those obtained in males. Once again, the levels of physical activity may be increased, and the general level of aggressiveness may be increased. (Ibid., 747, 748)

116 Kinsey hints broadly Ibid., 747n51.

116 "the hormone plays a prime part" Ibid., 748, 761.

117 "One of the most controversial subjects" William H. Masters, "Endocrine Therapy in the Aging Individual," *Obstetrics and Gynecology* 8 (1956): 67.

117 "Steroid replacement technics" Ibid., 67.

117 "There is no reason why" William H. Masters and Virginia E. Johnson, *Human Sexual Response* (Boston: Little, Brown, 1966), 246–47, 263.

118 Masters and Johnson damn testosterone therapy William H. Masters, Virginia E. Johnson, and Robert C. Kolodny, *Heterosexuality* (New York: HarperCollins, 1994), 143–47.

118 "What are the contraindications" "Testosterone for Older Men," *JAMA* 153 (December 26, 1953): 1598.

CHAPTER 3.   The Mainstreaming of Testosterone

119   "If there is such a thing"   "Are You Man Enough?" *Time*, April 24, 2000, 59.
120   "a syringe full of manhood"   Andrew Sullivan, "The He Hormone," *New York Times Magazine*, April 2, 2000, 48, 48.
120   "received permission to begin clinical trials"   "FDA Reviewed Clinical Protocol: Growth Hormone Replacement" (advertisement), *Austin American-Statesman*, May 2, 2000.
121   Sullivan declared vaguely   Sullivan, "The He Hormone," 46, 73.
121   "Testosterone can make a difference"   "Are You Man Enough?" 59.
121   "Fatigued? Depressed mood?"   Advertisement, *Business Week*, December 2, 2002, 15.
121   "we're verging on a moment"   "Are You Man Enough?" 64.
122   Sexual dysfunction has been inflated   On the process of medicalization in this context, see Graham Hart and Kaye Wellings, "Sexual Behaviour and Its Medicalisation: In Sickness and in Health," *British Medical Journal* 324, April 15, 2002, 896–900. For a general description of medicalization, see Susan E. Bell, "Changing Ideas: The Medicalization of Menopause," *Social Science and Medicine* 24 (1987): 535. According to Bell, "The values and organizational structure of American society make the experiences of women especially compatible with medicalization" (535).
122   "a new phylum of illness"   Jack Hitt, "The Second Sexual Revolution," *New York Times Magazine*, February 20, 2000, 36.
122   While *Health* magazine had published   Daniel Goleman, "Death of a Sex Life," *Health*, June 1990, 54–57.
122   "turned the armamentarium of clinical medicine"   Janice M. Irvine, *Disorders of Desire: Sex and Gender in Modern American Sexology* (Philadelphia: Temple University Press, 1990), 210.
122   "The so-called aphrodisiacs"   "Treatment of Sexual Impotence," *JAMA* 87 (September 25, 1926): 1066.
123   "Despite lack of supporting evidence"   Irvine, *Disorders of Desire*, 213–14.
123   "is engaging in sexual activity"   Goleman, "Death of a Sex Life," 56, 56, 56, 57.
124   "A postmodern revision of aging"   David B. Morris, *Illness and Culture in the Postmodern Age* (Berkeley: University of California Press, 1998), 236.
124   "has become a quasi-public performance"   Ibid., 65.
125   "a culturewide hypochondria"   Ibid., 65, 64, 236.
126   "Unless you have a treatment"   Goldstein, quoted in Hitt, "The Second Sexual Revolution," 36.
127   extrapolates it into a mass diagnosis   Bell has pointed out that the diagnosis of female menopause followed this course in the 1930s and 1940s:

> For most women (85% was the figure most often cited) menopause was "physiologic," not "pathologic." However clinical studies of menopause were comprised almost exclusively of patients: women seeking medical help for their menopausal symptoms. Thus, specialists' conclusions about menopause were drawn from a biased sample. Even though specialists argued that most women negotiated menopause successfully these women were not included in their studies. ("Changing Ideas," 538)

127 "The syndrome of ISD" Irvine, *Disorders of Desire*, 215–16.

127 "a trend toward pathologizing daily life" McMullen, quoted in Craig Lambert, "The Downsides of Prozac," *Harvard Magazine*, May–June 2000, 21–22.

128 "I worry absolutely" Quoted in Lynda Gorov, "The Latest Fad from La-La Land: A 'Designer Vagina,' " *Boston Globe*, August 23, 1999. See also Hart and Wellings, "Sexual Behaviour and Its Medicalisation," 898.

128 "If you don't get" Ron Kennedy, M.D., "It's Not Just Your Bat; It's the Amount of Testosterone behind It That Makes a Difference!" *Journal of Longevity* 5.3 (1999): 23.

128 "implies a shift" Morris, *Illness and Culture in the Postmodern Age*, 39.

129 The empowered patient enjoys Jennifer Steinhauer, "Doctors Eliminate Wrinkles, and Insurers," *New York Times*, January 18, 2000.

129 "the confusing welter of self-help programs" Morris, *Illness and Culture in the Postmodern Age*, 17.

129 "has captured the fancy" Robert Marcus and Gerald M. Reaven, "Editorial: Growth Hormone—Ready for Prime Time?" *Journal of Clinical Endocrinology and Metabolism* 82 (1997): 725.

130 a treatment for the female menopause On the early medical and social construction of the female menopause, see Bell, "Changing Ideas," 535–42.

130 "there is a perception" Bush, quoted in Malcolm Gladwell, "The Estrogen Question," *New Yorker*, June 9, 1997, 59.

130 In 1977, for example Frances B. McCrea, "The Politics of Menopause: The 'Discovery' of a Deficiency Disease," *Social Problems* 31 (October 1983): 119.

131 "the public anxiety created" Paul Meier and Richard L. Landau, "Estrogen Replacement Therapy," *JAMA* 243 (April 25, 1980): 1658.

131 "According to feminists" McCrea, "The Politics of Menopause," 117.

131 "male-dominated, profit-oriented" Marilyn Grossman and Pauline Bart, quoted in ibid., 118.

131 "unnecessary treatment with hormones" Richard W. Te Linde, "The Menopause," *American Journal of Nursing* 54 (August 1954): 952.

132 "probably has a paunchy husband" "Estrogen Therapy: What Is Its Role in Treatment of Menopausal Women?" *JAMA* 194 (November 8, 1965): 31.

132 the influence of their colleague Robert Wilson Wilson's role in the promotion of estrogen therapy is by no means forgotten. In its 1995 cover story on estrogen, *Time*'s writer begins her essay by introducing him as the early prophet of hormonal rejuvenation for women (Claudia Wallis, "The Estrogen Dilemma," *Time*, June 26, 1995, 46).

132 "Estrogen therapy is a treatment" Rossi, quoted in Anita Diamant, "Hype on Ills of Menopause Is Reported to Be Unfounded," *Boston Globe*, August 16, 1992.

132 "Sex hormones may best be portrayed" Nelly Oudshoorn, *Beyond the Natural Body: An Archeology of Sex Hormones* (London: Routledge, 1994), 108, 93–96.

133 women—even feminists—may use As one feminist notes, "One should not too readily adopt a moralizing stance toward restoring or normalizing efforts because such moralizing ends up essentializing the body as a biological entity that must 'naturally' age. The refusal of age as decline, as Friedan has argued, is in general admirable and essential" (E. Ann Kaplan, "Resisting Pathologies of Age and Race," in *Reinterpreting Menopause: Cultural and Philosophical Issues*, ed. Paul

A. Komesaroff, Philipa Rothfield, and Jeanne Daly [New York: Routledge, 1997], 107).

133 "most medical opinion was hardened" Robert A. Wilson, *Feminine Forever* (New York: M. Evans, 1966), 17, 112.

133 "Menopause is not the onset of disease" " 'Planning' for Menopause," *Harvard Women's Health Watch,* July 1996, 1.

134 "It is no accident" Roy Porter, *The Greatest Benefit to Mankind: A Medical History of Humanity* (New York: W. W. Norton, 1999), 706.

134 "Throughout her entire life" Quoted in Oudshoorn, *Beyond the Natural Body,* 108, 60.

135 "This wide range of applications" Ibid., 92–95, 95.

135 a 1963 news item "Submissive Women Arise—And Marriages Fall," *JAMA* 184 (April 13, 1963): 47.

135 "no woman can be sure" Wilson, *Feminine Forever,* 43, 44.

135 "There is hardly anything lovelier" Ibid., 78, 16, 85.

136 "lack of basic sympathy for women" Ibid., 17–18, 142, 145, 142, 27, 19.

136 "lifelong penchant for the more magic attributes" Ibid., 196.

137 "a constant undertone of hissing" "Do Aging Processes Differ in Men and Women?" *JAMA* 223 (February 19, 1973): 846.

137 "There is no convincing proof" Robert A. Wilson, "The Roles of Estrogen and Progesterone in Breast and Genital Cancer," *JAMA* 182 (October 27, 1962): 327, 331.

137 "officially expressed his distrust" Richard L. Landau, "What You Should Know about Estrogens: Or the Perils of Pauline," *JAMA* 241 (January 5, 1979): 47, 51. A year later the same physician was complaining about "the public anxiety created by the Food and Drug Administration" concerning the dangers of ERT (Meier and Landau, "Estrogen Replacement Therapy," 1658).

138 "estrogen makes women adaptable" Wilson, *Feminine Forever,* 64.

138 "is that intercourse becomes painful" Kistner, quoted in "Durable, Unendurable Women," *Time,* October 16, 1964, 72.

138 "The menopausal syndrome" Wilson, *Feminine Forever,* 100.

138 "one of the greatest biological revolutions" Wilson, quoted in "Pills to Keep Women Young," *Time,* April 1, 1966, 50.

138 Research scientists began to realize See, for example, McCrea, "The Politics of Menopause," 116.

138 "There is no persuasive evidence" This statement appears in the *Medical Letter on Drugs and Therapeutics,* January 19, 1973. See "Long-Term Estrogen Therapy Rarely Helps Much," *JAMA* 223 (February 19, 1973): 847.

139 "some of the normal things" Dr. Anthony Scialli, a professor of obstetrics and gynecology at the Georgetown University School of Medicine in Washington, D.C.; quoted in Alex Kuczynski, "Menopause Forever," *New York Times,* June 23, 2002.

139 "A number of husbands have asked" Robert N. Rutherford, "The Male and the Female Climacteric," *Postgraduate Medicine* 50 (October–December 1971): 126.

139 "intense subjective nervousness" August A. Werner, "The Male Climacteric," *JAMA* 112 (April 15, 1939): 1442.

140 "A man remains male" Wilson, *Feminine Forever,* 51, 154.

140   **"Males in western culture"**   Kaplan, "Resisting Pathologies of Age and Race," 102.

140   **"The fact is"**   Margaret Morganroth Gullette, "Menopause as Magic Marker," in Komesaroff, Rothfield, and Daly, eds., *Reinterpreting Menopause,* 183.

140   **"Midlife men"**   Ibid., 193.

141   **"In the late 1930s"**   Oudshoorn, *Beyond the Natural Body,* 94, 95.

141   **"It seems reasonable to believe"**   Werner, "The Male Climacteric," 1441.

141   **"The male climacteric"**   Stanley F. Goldman and Mark J. Markham, "Clinical Use of Testosterone in the Male Climacteric," *Journal of Clinical Endocrinology* 2 (1942): 237.

142   **"a crucial element of ambiguity"**   Morris, *Illness and Culture in the Postmodern Age,* 58.

142   **"The climacteric symptoms in men"**   Werner, "The Male Climacteric," 1442.

142   **"reasonable to believe"**   Carl G. Heller and Gordon B. Myers, "The Male Climacteric, Its Symptomatology, Diagnosis and Treatment," *JAMA* 126 (October 21, 1944): 477.

143   **"the so-called male climacteric"**   "Is There a True Male Climacteric?" *JAMA* 155 (August 14, 1954): 1427.

143   **"most elderly men exhibit"**   Heller and Myers, "The Male Climacteric," 472.

143   **"testicular insufficiency"**   Julius Bauer, "The Male Climacteric—A Misnomer," *JAMA* 126 (December 2, 1944): 914.

143   **"In our experience"**   William H. Masters, Virginia E. Johnson, and Robert C. Kolodny, *Heterosexuality* (New York: HarperCollins, 1994), 469. They also note:

> Since these are relatively nonspecific symptoms that could be seen with a variety of illnesses, including depression, cancer or severe anemia, to establish the diagnosis accurately it is necessary to find a markedly subnormal testosterone level *and* to see significant improvements in the symptoms within two months of implementing adequate testosterone replacement therapy. (468)

143   **"an aging population"**   John B. McKinlay, "Is There an Epidemiologic Basis for a Male Climacteric Syndrome? The Massachusetts Male Aging Study," in *Menopause: Evaluation, Treatment, and Health Concerns,* ed. Charles B. Hammond, Florence P. Haseltine, and Isaac Schiff (New York: Alan R. Liss, 1989), 163.

143   **"I don't believe in the male mid-life crisis"**   McKinlay, quoted in "Midlife Myths: What about Men?" *International Herald Tribune,* May 21, 1992.

144   **"Is Her Majesty's government"**   Quoted in Gail Sheehy, "The Unspeakable Passage: Is There a Male Menopause?" *Vanity Fair,* April 1993, 226.

144   **"It's becoming popular to blame"**   Andrew A. Skolnick, "Is 'Male Menopause' Real or Just an Excuse?" *JAMA* 268 (November 11, 1992): 2486.

144   **"The emphasis on performance"**   Sheehy, "The Unspeakable Passage," 164–67, 219–27; quotation, 220.

144   **Inevitably, however, one effect of creating a public climacteric**   Hart and Wellings write:

> Mass [sexual] surveillance inadvertently establishes norms and standards for sexual behaviour against which people can measure themselves and be measured. This can bring benefits—when Kinsey reported on the heterogeneity of sexual conduct in America, Americans who had previously felt

deviant gave a collective sigh of relief. There are also risks attached to such transparency—many people will feel "inadequate" when faced with evidence about extremes of sexual performance. ("Sexual Behaviour and Its Medicalisation," 898)

144 **"older couples fearful"** "Sex Manuals: How Not to . . . ," *Newsweek,* October 18, 1965, 100–101; quoted in Irvine, *Disorders of Desire,* 72.

144 **"Nowhere in the course of history"** Schnarch, quoted in Barbara Mathias-Riegel, "Intimacy 101," *Modern Maturity,* September–October 1999, 47.

144 **"One commonly recognized belief"** Gustave Newman and Claude R. Nichols, "Sexual Activities and Attitudes in Older Persons," *JAMA* 173 (May 7, 1960): 33.

145 **"many patients and doctors have"** McKinlay, quoted in Susan Jacoby, "Great Sex: What's Age Got to Do with It?" *Modern Maturity,* September–October 1999, 44.

145 **"We used to treat older people"** Stephen B. Levine, M.D., quoted in ibid., 42.

145 **"Somehow,"** Janice Irvine wrote Irvine, *Disorders of Desire,* 222.

146 **"Like a man of thirty-five"** "Ölwechsel für den Körper," *Der Spiegel,* April 24, 2000, 166, 172.

147 **Marital status is highly significant** See, for example, "Sex—genauso bunt und vielfältig wie in anderen Lebensaltern," *Süddeutsche Zeitung,* April 10/11, 1999; Jacoby, "Great Sex," 41.

147 **Many older women, for example** Jacoby notes, "About 5 percent of men 75 and older—but more than 35 percent of women in that age group—say they would be quite happy if they never had sex again. Among women in their 40s and 50s, only 9 percent are sanguine about such a prospect" ("Great Sex," 43).

147 **"putting themselves at risk"** Alex Kuczynski, "Psst: Want to Buy Some Wrinkle Remover?" *New York Times,* February 16, 2003. He reports, "Dr. Arthur Kaplan, the director of the Center for Bioethics at the University of Pennsylvania, said that he was disturbed that any doctor in this country would use Restylane without government approval."

CHAPTER 4. "Outlaw" Biomedical Innovations

150 **"Sometimes I wonder"** Sauer, quoted in Frank Bruni, "The Gods of Fertility," *New York Times,* July 8, 1997.

150 **"The result is a tiering effect"** Quoted in Jennifer Steinhauer, "Doctors Eliminate Wrinkles, and Insurers," *New York Times,* January 18, 2000.

151 **"It creates a financial conflict of interest"** Saunders, quoted in Abigail Zuger, "Doctors' Offices Turn into Salesrooms," *New York Times,* March 30, 1999.

151 **"The United States"** Rebecca Mead, "Eggs for Sale," *New Yorker,* August 9, 1999, 59.

152 **There are egg auctions** Gina Kolata, "Clinics Selling Embryos Made for 'Adoption,' " *New York Times,* November 23, 1997.

152 **"examining scenarios"** John Maddox, "Exploring Life as We Don't Yet Know It," *Nature* 380 (March 14, 1996): 89.

152 **"it's eerie how many"** Robin Marantz Henig, "Adapting to Our Own Engineering," *New York Times,* December 17, 2002.

152   doctors in London refused in 1993   William E. Schmidt, "Birth to a 59-Year-Old Generates an Ethical Controversy in Britain," *New York Times,* December 29, 1993.

152   "There was so much negative pressure"   Bilotta, quoted in Alessandra Stanley, "Couple Leave Italy after Being Rebuffed on Surrogate Motherhood," *New York Times,* May 11, 2000.

153   When the Italian infertility specialist Severino Antinori   "Maverick Fertility Expert Plans First Human Clone," *Sunday Times* (London), October 25, 1998.

153   the maverick American physicist Richard Seed   Richard Saltus, "Would-Be Cloner Says He'll Start with Himself," *Boston Sunday Globe,* September 6, 1998.

153   "Outlaw the exploration of human cloning"   Daniel Kevles, "Study Cloning, Don't Ban It," *New York Times,* February 26, 1997.

153   "Such a move tries to defy"   Quoted in "Abortions aboard Ship Planned to Skirt Law," *Boston Globe,* June 16, 2000.

153   As late as 1995   Celestine Bohlen, "Almost Anything Goes in Birth Science in Italy," *New York Times,* April 4, 1995.

154   As of June 2002   "Italian Fertility Bill 'Danger to Women,' " *BBC News* (June 30, 2002), www.bbc.co.uk. The absence of regulation as of May 2000 is cited in Stanley, "Couple Leave Italy after Being Rebuffed on Surrogate Motherhood." See also "Why Italy Is the Wild West of Infertility Treatment," *Guardian Unlimited* (August 8, 2001), www.blackstar.co.uk.

154   "much of our political world"   Francis Fukuyama, *Our Posthuman Future: Consequences of the Biotechnology Revolution* (New York: Farrar, Straus and Giroux, 2002), 217, 218, 128.

155   "Americans say they are appalled"   Mary Leonard, "Beyond the Breakthrough," *Boston Sunday Globe,* June 29, 1997.

155   "most people" objected   "Fear of Cloning," *Economist,* January 17, 1998, 18.

155   "The mere thought of cloning"   "Cloning for Good or Evil" (editorial), *New York Times,* February 25, 1997.

155   "How drastically"   Bruni, "The Gods of Fertility."

155   "I certainly understand"   Gaylin, quoted in Gina Kolata, "A 63-Year-Old Has Given Birth; What Does That Say about Life?" *New York Times,* April 27, 1997.

155   "Human cloning means"   Quoted in "Maverick Fertility Expert Plans First Human Clone."

155   "To pollution and perversion"   Leon R. Kass, "The Wisdom of Repugnance," *New Republic,* June 2, 1997, 21, 18, 19.

156   "whose moral boundaries"   Ibid., 18.

156   "Each human life"   Clinton, quoted in Rick Weiss, "Clinton: No Money for Human Cloning," *Austin American-Statesman,* March 5, 1997.

156   "For now," wrote the historian   Kevles, "Study Cloning, Don't Ban It."

157   "the very decision to use the law"   Laurence H. Tribe, "Second Thoughts on Cloning," *New York Times,* December 5, 1997. The legal philosopher Ronald Dworkin has also argued in favor of scientific freedom in this vein: "If playing God means struggling to improve what God deliberately or nature blindly has evolved over eons, then the first principle of ethical individualism commands that struggle, and its second principle forbids, in the absence of positive evidence of danger, hobbling scientists and doctors who volunteer to lead it" (quoted in Fukuyama, *Our Posthuman Future,* 107).

157   "I absolutely think"   Andrews, quoted in Gina Kolata, "On Cloning Humans, 'Never' Turns Swiftly into 'Why Not,' " *New York Times*, December 2, 1997.

157   "The biotech revolution raises"   Fukuyama, quoted in Thomas L. Friedman, "The Parallel Universe," *New York Times*, May 12, 2000.

158   In Britain, human cloning   Steve Farrar, "Rebel Baby Maker Plans the First Human Clone," *Sunday Times* (London), October 25, 1998.

158   "processes that would change"   Sabra Chartrand, "Patents," *New York Times*, June 26, 2000.

158   Two months later, the European Parliament   "Londons Haltung zum Embryo-Klonen gerügt," *Süddeutsche Zeitung*, September 8, 2000.

158   "When issues of international scientific"   Maddox, "Exploring Life as We Don't Yet Know It," 89. See also "Vom Klonen und der Illusion eines Verbots," *Süddeutsche Zeitung*, April 30/May 1, 1997.

158   the Chinese government had made stem cell research   "Chinas revolutionäre Zellen," *Der Spiegel*, June 10, 2002, 162–64.

158   "By turning itself into a 'regulatory haven' "   "Send in the Clones," *Economist*, August 24, 2002, 58–59.

158   "a class of genetically well-endowed"   David Papineau, "Hello, Dolly, Dolly, Dolly . . . ," *New York Times Book Review*, September 6, 1998, 2. As one *New York Times* editorial put it:

> The most troubling issues involve the potential for cloning adult humans. Nightmares envisioned in literature and popular entertainment have ranged from cloning dozens of Hitlers to cloning hordes of drones to perform menial work. Would some entrepreneur seek to clone enough Michael Jordans to make an unbeatable basketball dynasty? Would societies try to engineer a more "perfect" population by replicating geniuses or athletes or the most beautiful by current norms? Would a wealthy egomaniac want his legacy to be not a foundation or a university building, but a copy—or multiple copies—of his very own self? ("Cloning for Good or Evil")

158   "Human cloning isn't inevitable"   Emanuel, quoted in Leonard, "Beyond the Breakthrough."

159   "The big drug companies"   Bond, quoted in Lizette Alvarez, "Senate, 54–42, Rejects Republican Bill to Ban Human Cloning," *New York Times*, February 12, 1998.

159   By the end of 1997   Kolata, "On Cloning Humans, 'Never' Turns Swiftly into 'Why Not.' "

159   At that time, human cloning research   Leonard, "Beyond the Breakthrough."

159   "We are much closer to cloning humans"   "Genes out of the Bottle," *New Republic*, February 28, 2000, 9.

159   "If a global ban on the cloning"   Heidrun Graupner, "Der Baby-Dealer," *Süddeutsche Zeitung*, November 28, 2002.

159   "It's been a public and media assumption"   Quoted in "F.D.A. Is Prepared to Block Unapproved Cloning Efforts," *New York Times*, January 20, 1998.

159   "whether a regulatory body charged"   Arthur L. Caplan, "Why the Rush to Ban Cloning?" *New York Times*, January 28, 1998.

160   "These researchers are not crazed"   Holt, quoted in Sheryl Gay Stolberg, "House Votes to Ban All Human Cloning," *New York Times*, February 28, 2003.

160   At the end of 2003   Kirk Semple, "U.N. to Consider Whether to Ban Some, or All, Forms of Cloning of Human Embryos," *New York Times,* November 3, 2003.

160   "Where is Washington"   Rebecca L. Skloot, "The Other Baby Experiment," *New York Times,* February 22, 2002.

160   "The Federal Government"   Brent Staples, "Turning People into Product," *New York Times,* February 28, 1997.

160   "Just a few years ago"   "From Monsters to Mainstream" (editorial), *New York Times,* March 1, 1992.

160   "Like most technologies"   "Cloning for Good or Evil."

161   "listen to the radio call-in shows"   Jean Bethke Elshtain, "Ewegenics," *New Republic,* March 31, 1997, 25.

161   "opinion polls showing overwhelming opposition"   Kass, "The Wisdom of Repugnance," 17.

161   "We have no law"   D'Agostino and Antinori, quoted in Bohlen, "Almost Anything Goes in Birth Science in Italy."

162   "I went to church"   Quoted in Tom Hundley, "Fertility Clinic Sparks Debate in Poland," *Chicago Tribune,* April 9, 1995.

163   In November 1996   Christopher S. Wren, "Votes on Marijuana Are Stirring Debate," *New York Times,* November 17, 1996.

163   "a public health dilemma"   Varmus, quoted in Christopher S. Wren, "U.S. Plans Meeting to Study Issue of Medical Marijuana," *New York Times,* January 31, 1997.

163   "Marijuana for medicinal purposes"   Kleber, quoted in Sam Howe Verhovek, "What Is the Matter with Mary Jane?" *New York Times,* October 15, 2000.

163   AIDS activists of the late 1980s   See, for example, Harlan Dalton, "AIDS in Blackface," *Daedalus* 118 (Summer 1989): 205–27.

164   A survey of two thousand oncologists   Michael Pollan, "Living with Medical Marijuana," *New York Times Magazine,* July 20, 1997, 29.

164   "Marijuana's active components"   Quoted in Katharine Q. Seelye, "Gore Retreats from Earlier Signal of Support for Medical Use of Marijuana," *New York Times,* May 17, 2000.

164   "Doctors have long recognized"   "Misguided Marijuana War" (editorial), *New York Times,* February 4, 2003.

164   "The noxious sensations that patients experience"   Jerome P. Kassirer, "Federal Foolishness and Marijuana," *New England Journal of Medicine* 336 (January 30, 1997): 366.

165   McCaffrey threatened the doctors of California   Pollan, "Living with Medical Marijuana," 28.

165   In response, a group of doctors   Tim Golden, "Marijuana Advocates File Suit to Stop U.S. Sanctions," *New York Times,* January 15, 1997.

165   On July 17, 2000   "Ruling in California Favors the Medicinal Use of Marijuana," *New York Times,* July 18, 2000.

165   In September 2000   "Medical Marijuana and Free Speech" (editorial), *New York Times,* September 20, 2000.

165   "not a medical proposition"   McCaffrey, quoted in Pollan, "Living with Medical Marijuana," 28, 26.

165   "they personally knew someone"   Pollan, "Living with Medical Marijuana," 26.

165   prior to the California referendum   Carey Goldberg, "Medical Marijuana Use Winning Support," *New York Times,* October 30, 1996.

166   In January 2003 a federal jury   Dean E. Murphy, "Clash on Medical Marijuana Puts a Grower in U.S. Court," *New York Times,* January 21, 2003. A medical marijuana activist argues: "There is no doubt among knowledgeable physicians and researchers that marijuana is a medicine. It has proven anti-spasmodic, analgesic and anti-nausea properties, and has an incredible safety record. There are no recorded deaths from its use and overindulgence results in drowsiness and a sound sleep" (quoted in Ed Rosenthal, "A Marijuana Crusader Defends His Healing Mission," *Forward,* February 21, 2003, 9).

166   Once they realized that the defendant   Dean E. Murphy, "Jurors Who Convicted Marijuana Grower Seek New Trial," *New York Times,* February 5, 2003.

166   "shows that the misguided federal war"   "Misguided Marijuana War."

166   the public delivered its unwelcome verdict   Murphy notes, "Eight other states [in addition to California] allow the sick and dying to smoke or grow marijuana with a doctor's recommendation" ("Jurors Who Convicted Marijuana Grower Seek New Trial").

167   "Whatever their reasons"   Kassirer, "Federal Foolishness and Marijuana," 366. Almost four years later, the *New York Times* endorsed Kassirer's view in an editorial: "The Clinton administration should stop threatening doctors and make marijuana available to sick individuals who need relief" ("Medical Marijuana and Free Speech").

167   "California's experiment with medical marijuana"   Pollan, "Living with Medical Marijuana," 25, 24, 24–25.

167   "inflamed public opinion"   Nurith C. Aizenman, "Smoked Out," *New Republic,* November 30, 1998, 19.

168   Government attempts to restrict   On June 21, 1991, Dr. James O. Mason, chief of the Public Health Service, announced the abrupt ending of the Compassionate Investigative New Drug (IND) program, which had made marijuana available to mitigate the nausea caused by chemotherapy. His explanation was that continuing the program would improve the reputation of marijuana in a socially dangerous way. Dan Baum describes what happened next: "The public, which until now had generally cheered each escalation of the War on Drugs, finally balked. Massachusetts quickly became the thirty-sixth state to pass a resolution recognizing marijuana's medical value; governors and legislators from every corner of the country went on the air to denounce Mason's decision, and most major medical associations weighed in against the decision" (Baum, *Smoke and Mirrors: The War on Drugs and the Politics of Failure* [Boston: Little, Brown, 1996], 110–11).

168   "a complex conversation"   Aizenman, "Smoked Out," 19. Proposition 215, General McCaffrey argued, "isn't part of the medical process—there's no physical exam, no prescription. An aromatherapist, a 'care giver,' even a patient can grow their own in the backyard. We don't tell people to grow their own heart medicine! We don't decide flight rules for L.A. airport by plebiscite!" (quoted in Pollan, "Living with Medical Marijuana," 29).

168   "What is a symptom?"   Peter D. Kramer, "Female Troubles," *New York Times Magazine,* October 1, 2000, 18.

169   "a gray area of uncertainty"   Jeffrey Hedges, "The Anabolic Steroids Act: Bad Medicine for the Elderly," *Elder Law Journal* 5 (Fall 1997): 316.

169   "Certain steroid hormones"   Joseph L. DeCourcy and Cornelius B. DeCourcy, "Steroid Hormones in Geriatric Practice," *Geriatrics* 6 (1951): 28.

169   "is whether to prosecute physicians"   Hedges, "The Anabolic Steroids Act," 314.

169   the legitimate purpose of combating wasting disease   On the effectiveness of anabolic steroids for this purpose, see Joseph Cofrancesco, Jr., John J. Whalen III, and Adrian S. Dobs, "Testosterone Replacement Treatment Options for HIV-Infected Men," *Journal of Acquired Immune Deficiency Syndrome* 16 (December 1, 1997): 254–65; Colleen Corcoran and Steven Grinspoon, "Treatments for Wasting in Patients with the Acquired Immunodeficiency Syndrome," *New England Journal of Medicine* 340 (June 3, 1999): 1740–50; Shalender Bhasin et al., "Testosterone Replacement and Resistance Exercise in HIV-Infected Men with Weight Loss and Low Testosterone Levels," *JAMA* 283 (February 9, 2000): 763–70.

169   "With the failure of AZT"   Dave Purdy, quoted in "Unfounded Fear of Anabolic Steroids Prevents Major Health Benefits for HIV/AIDS Patients" (typescript, Hollywood, Calif., n.d.). See also Tony Kahane, "Steroids Used to Combat Aids," *London Observer*, June 13, 1993.

169   "This threat of prosecution"   Hedges, "The Anabolic Steroids Act," 316–17.

170   "It has been stated"   Donald L. Cooper, "Drugs and the Athlete," *JAMA* 221 (August 28, 1972): 1010.

170   "Use of anabolic steroids"   Jaime Prat et al., "Wilms Tumor in an Adult Associated with Androgen Abuse," *JAMA* 237 (May 23, 1977): 2323.

170   "extending down to the junior high school level"   P. Gunby, "Olympics Drug Testing: Basis for Future Study," *JAMA* 252 (July 27, 1984): 454.

170   "It is apparent"   M. A. Frankle, G. J. Cicero, and J. Payne, "Use of Androgenic Anabolic Steroids by Athletes" (letter), *JAMA* 252 (July 27, 1984): 482.

170   "Every professional football player"   Virginia Cowart, "Some Predict Increased Steroid Use in Sports Despite Drug Testing, Crackdown on Suppliers," *JAMA* 252 (June 12, 1987): 3025.

170   By 1988 the Council on Scientific Affairs   "Drug Abuse in Athletes: Anabolic Steroids and Human Growth Hormone," *JAMA* 259 (March 18, 1988): 1703–5.

170   the Ben Johnson doping scandal   The official Canadian response to this scandal was the formation of a Commission of Inquiry into the Use of Drugs and Banned Practices Intended to Increase Athletic Performance, under the leadership of Charles L. Dubin. The report of the Dubin Commission was published as *Commission of Inquiry into the Use of Drugs and Banned Practices Intended to Increase Athletic Performance* (Ottawa: Canadian Government Publishing Centre, 1990).

171   one study showed that 7 percent   Virginia S. Cowart, "Issues of Drugs and Sports Gain Attention as Olympic Games Open in South Korea," *JAMA* 260 (September 16, 1988): 1513.

171   The American Medical Association protested   Hedges, "The Anabolic Steroids Act: Bad Medicine for the Elderly," 310–11. A position paper issued by the AMA's Council on Scientific Affairs declares: "The AMA reaffirm [sic] its opposition to scheduling of AAS [anabolic-androgenic steroids] under the federal Controlled Substances Act" ("Medical and Nonmedical Uses of Anabolic-Androgenic Steroids," *JAMA* 260 [December 12, 1990]: 2927).

171 The American Academy of Anti-Aging Medicine   Alex Kuczynski, "Pursuing Potions: Fountain of Youth or Poisonous Fad?" *New York Times,* April 14, 1998. For current membership figures, see the Academy's home page, "The World Health Network," www.worldhealth.net (accessed February 2004).

172 "has intervened in several cases"   John A. Fromson, "Growth Hormone Therapy in Adults and Children," *New England Journal of Medicine* 342 (February 3, 1997): 359.

172 "Usually the referral comes from peers"   John A. Fromson, M.D., personal communication, October 6, 2000.

173 "A series of injections of human growth hormone"   Kuczynski, "Pursuing Potions."

173 "Our goal," he says   Mintz and Nadler, quoted in ibid. Physicians who lead by example also include dermatologists who inject Botox and use it themselves. BotoxCosmetic.com advertised its services in *Newsweek* (January 19, 2004), a year and a half after the magazine's cover story on Botox (David Noonan and Jerry Adler, "The Botox Boom," *Newsweek,* May 13, 2002, 50ff).

175 "a dramatic improvement in their sense"   Ludwig, quoted in "Wind in der Glut," *Der Spiegel,* October 2, 2000, 271–72.

175 some offshore physicians on the Internet   Donald E. deKieffer, "Direct Sale of Sildenafil (Viagra) to Consumers over the Internet," *New England Journal of Medicine* 342 (March 9, 2000): 742.

176 "the practice by some doctors"   Michelangelo Signorile, "The Incredible Bulk," *Out,* May 1997, 73.

CHAPTER 5.   Hormone Therapy for Athletes

179 In fact, a long series of attempts   See John Hoberman, *Mortal Engines: The Science of Performance and the Dehumanization of Sport* (New York: Free Press, 1992).

179 Such a perspective would acknowledge   The red blood cell limits instituted by the International Skiing Federation in 1997 marked a preliminary step in this direction. It also acknowledged the commonness of doping among the athletes being tested. Yet the fact that doping was routine for many years before the advent of the blood-boosting drug erythropoietin (EPO) is either unknown or ignored by the sports officials, journalists, and politicians who make public pronouncements about it.

180 "Sports is simply one segment"   Dr. Richard Strauss, quoted in Virginia Cowart, "State-of-Art Drug Identification Laboratories Play Increasing Role in Major Athletic Events," *JAMA* 256 (December 12, 1986): 3074.

180 "Should you penalize an aging athlete"   Dr. Charles E. Yesalis of Pennsylvania State University, in his "Replacement or Doping?" *Muscular Development,* January 1999, 165.

180 "Either the public hasn't figured out"   Quoted in Harvey Araton, "One Issue Is Settled; Others Await," *New York Times,* February 29, 2000.

182 "A drug addict"   Review of E. W. Adams, *Drug Addiction* (1937), in *Lancet,* September 11, 1937, 634.

183   "They definitely do stimulate"   "Amphetamines, Athletes, and Performance,"
       JAMA 168 (October 11, 1958): 775.
183   The doping practices of the professional cyclists   In a letter to the *Times*, C. R.
       Woodard wrote:

> So specialized have officials in sport become that they are inclined to fail to
> appreciate what goes on in other sports than their own particular one.
> However, I think such people have quite a lot to learn, at least in the form
> of being forewarned, from a practice that has occurred for many years in
> the sport of cycling. Three years ago I did a thorough investigation of this
> subject of doping among cyclists on the Continent, and I found the habit
> quite common. The three principal drugs that were used were strychnine,
> caffeine, and benzedrine. (Woodard, " 'Doping' of Athletes" (letter), *Times*
> [London], July 23, 1953)

183   Before the 100-kilometer team road race   "Olympic Trainer Admits Giving Drug
       to Danish Cyclist Who Died," *New York Times*, August 29, 1960.
183   "Deaths are rare"   Robert Daley, "Survival of the Fastest," *New York Times*, Au-
       gust 30, 1960.
184   "a persistent belief among athletes"   This is a paraphrase of Abrahams's actual
       remarks. See "Athletic Training," *JAMA* 157 (April 16, 1955): 1430.
184   "those drugs which by inhibiting"   Adolphe Abrahams, " 'Doping' of Athletes"
       (letter), *Times* (London), July 10, 1953.
184   Abrahams reverses field   Ibid.
185   "drugs that could stimulate the body"   Sir Adolphe Abrahams, "Should Athletes
       Take 'Pep' Drugs?" *Sunday Times* (London), June 16, 1957.
185   must have disturbed many of his readers   Abrahams's position certainly disturbed
       an editorialist at *JAMA*, who commented: "His statement is open to attack on the
       ground of sportsmanship—particularly in amateur athletics. The statement also
       emphasizes the use, rather than the abuse, of amphetamine. Yet is even judicious
       use safe? And if it is, what are the perils of misuse?" ("Amphetamines, Athletes,
       and Performance," 775).
185   "If it were practicable"   Abrahams, quoted in ibid., 775. Abrahams was not the
       first British physician to wonder about the possible effects of these drugs on ath-
       letic performance. See "Cortisone and Athletic Performance" (letter), *British Med-
       ical Journal*, December 13, 1952, 1320.
185   "Either sporting competitions would be"   H. Crichton-Miller, " 'Doping' of
       Athletes," *Times* (London), July 14, 1953.
186   "largely a matter of opinion"   Abrahams, "Should Athletes Take 'Pep' Drugs?"
186   At the time, no one knew   Responding to the 1957 controversy, Professor
       Thomas K. Cureton of the University of Illinois commented: "The major point is
       the release of potential energy. Obviously a quick release makes for a better effort.
       At this time, no scientist knows whether drugs can create this release or whether
       an athlete who takes them is merely wasting his time" (quoted in "The Milers
       Speak Up," *Newsweek*, June 17, 1957, 100). Research on the performance-
       enhancing effects of amphetamine on athletes was first published in 1959 (Gene M.
       Smith and Henry K. Beecher, "Amphetamine Sulfate and Athletic Performance,"
       JAMA 170 [May 30, 1959]: 542-57).

186 "In the 1950s," he told me   Forbes Carlile, personal communication, December 3, 2000.

186 "Some of our champion swimmers"   Davies, quoted in "Athletes Report Use of 'Pep Pills,' " *New York Times,* June 8, 1957.

187 "What I most remember"   Bruce Kidd, personal communication, February 18, 2001.

187 "Sudden staggering performances"   Gordon Pirie, *Running Wild* (London: W. H. Allen, 1961), 28. Pirie continues: "Athletes of many nations are probably addicted to stimulants, too, though of course concrete evidence is difficult to get. In Rome [at the 1960 Olympic Games] a doctor asked me what stimulants I used. When I indignantly replied that I used none, I was told, 'well, you must be one of the few mugs who don't.' I have frequently seen athletes sniffing inhalants, presumably benzedrine" (28–29). I am indebted to John Bale for bringing Pirie's book to my attention.

187 In 1954 a Soviet team doctor   Terry Todd, "Anabolic Steroids: The Gremlins of Sport," *Journal of Sport History* 14 (1987): 93–94. According to the German sport scientist Wildor Hollmann, "Anabolic steroids were first used in the United States after the 1956 Melbourne Olympic Games and were brought to Europe by American athletes in conjunction with the 1960 Rome Olympic Games" (Hollmann, "Risikofaktoren in der Entwicklung des Hochleistungssports," in *Sportmedizin—Kursbestimmung,* ed. H. Rieckert, Deutscher Sportärztekongreß, Kiel, 16.–19. Oktober 1986 [Berlin: Springer-Verlag, 1987], 19).

187 "there were reports of used hypodermic needles"   Cowart, "State-of-Art Drug Identification Laboratories Play Increasing Role in Major Athletic Events," 3073.

187 "If I could not win a race"   Russell Mockridge, *My World on Wheels: The Posthumous Autobiography of Russell Mockridge,* completed by John Burrowes (London: Stanley Paul, 1960), 132, 130–31, 131. I am indebted to Graem Sims for providing me with material from Mockridge's book and offering valuable comments on Mockridge's personality.

188 "Recent reports of university students"   Ibid., 131.

188 "the more or less paradoxical attitude"   Albert Salisbury Hyman, M.D., "Use of Drugs in Sport" (letter), *New York Times,* September 12, 1960.

188 "Certainly, if approached scientifically"   Mockridge, *My World on Wheels,* 132.

188 The Danish doctor accused   "Inquiry to Last Several Weeks," *New York Times,* August 30, 1960.

189 "a low blow. I am myself an opponent"   Mathiesen and others, quoted in "Danske roere fik hormonpiller af læge," *Politiken,* November 27, 2000. This article is a reprint; the original account of the DIF meeting appeared in *Politiken* on November 27, 1950.

190 This ethically ambiguous medical style   See John Hoberman, "Sports Physicians and the Doping Crisis in Elite Sport," *Clinical Journal of Sport Medicine* 12 (2002): 203–8.

190 The purveyors of glandular remedies   "Gold Medal Brand Sexual Pills," *JAMA* 80 (March 3, 1923): 645; "Sex-Co Restorative Tablets," *JAMA* 80 (March 3, 1923): 645; "Enter the 'Master Hormones' as Therapeutic Agents," *JAMA* 99 (October 29, 1932): 1529–30.

190   "many physicians collaborate in steroid abuse"   Jonathan P. Jarow and Larry I. Lipschultz, "Anabolic Steroid-Induced Hypogonadotropic Hypogonadism," *American Journal of Sports Medicine* 18 (1990): 429.

190   "I am well aware"   Evers, quoted in "Zu viele reden mit," *Süddeutsche Zeitung,* January 17, 1995.

191   "The physician must oppose all methods"   Quoted in Michael Sehling, Reinhold Pollert, and Dieter Hackfort, *Doping im Sport: Medizinische, sozialwissenschaftliche und juristische Aspekte* (Munich: BLV Verlagsgesellschaft, 1989), 100.

191   "Every type of prohibited performance enhancement"   Quoted in "Hemmungslos," *Süddeutsche Zeitung,* November 17/18, 1984.

192   In 1986, for example   "Rekord oder Medaille," *Süddeutsche Zeitung,* August 7, 1986.

192   "We have reached the maximum"   Hollmann, quoted in "Typen wie aus dem Panoptikum," *Der Spiegel,* July 23, 1984, 71.

192   "Sports medicine must seriously consider"   Hollmann, quoted in "Sportärzte kritisieren Samaranch," *Süddeutsche Zeitung,* October 29, 1985.

192   the physician "adapts to pressures"   "Gefahren durch Flickschusterei," *Der Spiegel,* November 5, 1985, 242.

192   "I said eleven years ago"   Hollmann, quoted in "Eine fünfte Kategorie für den Sport," *Süddeutsche Zeitung,* January 10, 1989.

192   some sports were not as severely affected   Ibid.

192   "Sports medicine takes the pulse"   Hollmann, quoted in "Gefahren durch Flickschusterei," 242, 245.

193   "do not change the fact"   Hollmann, quoted in "Der Sport ist wie ein ungepflügtes Land," *Süddeutsche Zeitung,* February 4, 1985.

193   "Elite sport," he said in 1988   Liesen, quoted in "Sportmediziner uneins," *Süddeutsche Zeitung,* February 2, 1988.

193   "Anabolic steroids can be used"   Liesen, quoted in "Zuviel Theater um Anabolika," *Süddeutsche Zeitung,* January 23, 1985.

193   "I regard it as better"   Liesen, quoted in "Liesen: Rufmord," *Süddeutsche Zeitung,* June 11, 1999.

194   "It is well known"   Quoted in "Funktionäre mitschuldig," *Süddeutsche Zeitung,* October 2, 1986.

194   "Anyone who, like Mr. Liesen"   Reindell, quoted in "Doping mit erlaubten Mitteln," *Süddeutsche Zeitung,* January 22, 1987.

194   A year later Manfred Steinbach   "Wider die Doping-Mentalität der Scharlatane," *Süddeutsche Zeitung,* May 24, 1988.

194   Steinbach participated in the recruitment   "Schocktherapie am Runden Tisch," *Süddeutsche Zeitung,* January 25, 1993.

194   "I want to drink deeply"   Steinbach, quoted in "Nach der Demonstration Signale der Gemeinsamkeit," *Süddeutsche Zeitung,* September 3, 1990.

195   Major League Baseball still rejects   Buster Olney, "The Bigger They Are, the More They're Falling," *New York Times,* March 31, 2002.

195   "the private domain of the individual athlete"   Klümper, quoted in "Die ärztliche Kunst der Selbstverteidigung," *Frankfurter Allgemeine Zeitung,* February 16, 1990.

195 "Everything that helps is permitted" Klümper, quoted in "Siegen um jeden Preis," *Der Spiegel*, November 26, 1984, 197.

196 "As a physician" Liesen, quoted in "Liesen: Rufmord."

196 "The limits of human performance" Schäuble, quoted in "Minister Schäuble warnt vor einer 'Doping-Hysterie,' " *Süddeutsche Zeitung*, October 21, 1989.

197 many athletes refused to cooperate Virginia Cowart, "State-of-Art Drug Identification Laboratories Play Increasing Role in Major Athletic Events," *JAMA* 256 (December 12, 1986): 3073.

197 "they really did not consider themselves" D. A. Johnson, "Use of Anabolic Steroids by Athletes" (letter), *JAMA* 251 (March 16, 1984): 1430.

197 "it was within their individual rights" Richard H. Strauss, Mariah T. Liggett, and Richard R. Lanese, "Anabolic Steroid Use and Perceived Effects in Ten Weight-Trained Women Athletes," *JAMA* 253 (May 17, 1985): 2872.

198 "It is my duty to help athletes" Liesen, quoted in "Trinken, um Leistung zu bringen," *Süddeutsche Zeitung*, June 7/8, 1986.

198 "If what is being done is allowed" Quoted in "Da müssen Sie schon Herrn Conconi fragen," *Süddeutsche Zeitung*, February 22, 1988.

198 "The doped East German athletes" Evers, quoted in "Zufällige Versorgung," *Süddeutsche Zeitung*, July 5, 1989.

198 Another West German track-and-field athlete "Blödsinn?" *Süddeutsche Zeitung*, October 31/November 1, 1990.

198 Kerr left behind a frequently cited manifesto Robert Kerr, *The Practical Use of Anabolic Steroids with Athletes* (San Gabriel, Calif.: Research Center for Sports, 1982). "Believe me, I'm the most ethical doctor you ever saw anywhere," Robert Kerr said in 1983. "I really do not condone anything that I consider unethical practice. If the state medical board here told me not to do it, I'd stop it right away" (quoted in ". . . There's a Doctor to Help," *Los Angeles Times*, December 4, 1983).

199 "I think you will agree" Kerr, *The Practical Use of Anabolic Steroids with Athletes*, 2.

199 "To my way of thinking 'doping' " Ibid., 3.

199 "Body building," he declares Ibid.

199 The obstacle to mainstreaming steroids For discussions of the potential medical and psychological hazards of anabolic steroid use, see Charles E. Yesalis, ed., *Anabolic Steroids in Sport and Exercise* (Champaign, Ill.: Human Kinetics, 1993).

200 "Anabolic steroids will never be viewed" Kerr, *The Practical Use of Anabolic Steroids with Athletes*, 90.

200 "They have been used, and sometimes abused" Quoted in "Styrkeexpert vill legalisera anabola steroider," *Svenska Dagbladet* (Stockholm), September 12, 1984.

200 "I think it [the anabolic steroid] is" Dr. Peter Jokl, quoted in "Steroid Drug Use: Concern Is Rising," *New York Times*, August 19, 1987.

200 "Athletes are going to take anabolic steroids" Kerr, quoted in ". . . There's a Doctor to Help."

200 to protect the athlete "Den Hammer weggelegt," *Frankfurter Rundschau*, September 27, 1984.

200 "anabolic steroids must be removed" Kindermann, quoted in "Kontrollen in den Trainingsphasen," *Süddeutsche Zeitung*, August 11, 1988.

334 / NOTES TO PAGES 201-206

201 "It is true that pharmacologic administration"   Jean D. Wilson and James E. Griffin, "The Use and Misuse of Androgens," *Metabolism* 29 (1980): 1289.

201 "safe, stable, effective, and reversible contraception"   "Contraceptive Efficacy of Testosterone-Induced Azoospermia in Normal Men," *Lancet*, October 20, 1990, 958.

201 "The safety of androgens"   Frederick C. W. Wu et al., "Effects of Testosterone Enanthate in Normal Men: Experience from a Multicenter Contraceptive Efficacy Center," *Fertility and Sterility* 65 (1996): 627.

201 "balanced assessment of the risks and benefits"   "Contraceptive Efficacy of Testosterone-Induced Azoospermia and Oligozoospermia in Normal Men," *Fertility and Sterility* 65 (1996): 828.

202 "The doping problem will not be eliminated"   Keller, quoted in "Erhard Keller befürwortet maßvolle Anabolika-Freigabe," *Süddeutsche Zeitung*, November 18, 1989.

202 Reichenbach called steroids "medically defensible"   Reichenbach, quoted in "Heuchelei um Anabolika," *Süddeutsche Zeitung*, January 5/6, 1989.

202 The concept of substitution therapy   The term *hormone substitution therapy* first appears in Samuel H. Geist et al., "The Biologic Effects of Androgen (Testosterone Propionate) in Women," *JAMA* 114 (April 20, 1940): 1539.

202 "These are drugs that help"   Wright, quoted in Virginia S. Cowart, "Study Proposes to Examine Football Players, Power Lifters for Possible Long-Term Sequelae from Anabolic Steroid Use in 1970s Competition," *JAMA* 257 (June 12, 1987): 3025.

202 "The world-famous hormone researcher"   Liesen, quoted in "Zuviel Theater um Anabolika."

203 The former East German shot-putter Grit Hammer   "Eine Athletin, die auf Abstand bedacht ist," *Süddeutsche Zeitung*, February 24, 1995.

204 "We are not the ones"   Buhl, quoted in "Doping aus Fürsorge," *Süddeutsche Zeitung*, February 15, 1990.

204 "whether the administration of small doses"   Quoted in "Und es war doch Doping," *Süddeutsche Zeitung*, July 5, 2001.

205 "out of concern for the athlete"   Buhl, quoted in "Doping aus Fürsorge."

205 The real purpose of the research   "DDR-Forscher geben systematisches Doping zu," *Frankfurter Allgemeine Zeitung*, February 16, 1990.

205 "In our country there was no Dressel case"   Höppner, quoted in "Doping nach Plan im DDR-Spitzensport enthüllt," *Süddeutsche Zeitung*, November 29, 1990. On the death of Birgit Dressel, see John Hoberman, *Mortal Engines: The Science of Performance and the Dehumanization of Sport* (New York: Free Press, 1992), 1-2.

205 "Anabolic steroids," two of them wrote   R. Häcker and A. Lehnert, "Sportliche Höchstleistung aus medizinisch-biowissenschaftlicher Sicht," in *Hormonelle Regulation und psychophysische Belastung im Leistungssport*, ed. R. Häcker and H. de Marées (Cologne: Deutscher Ärzteverlag, 1991), 17-18.

206 they courted the approval   The two distinguished West German guests at this conference were Dr. Manfred Donike, the world's foremost authority on the detection of performance-enhancing drugs in sport, and Dr. Horst de Marées, the new director of the Federal Institute for Sports Sciences (BISP).

206   many scientists, doctors, and athletes   See, e.g., Brigitte Berendonk, *Doping-Dokumente: Von der Forschung zum Betrug* (Reinbek bei Hamburg: Rowohlt, 1992).

206   "A sports physician is the only physician"   Quoted in "Staatsanwaltschaft untersucht Dopingvorwürfe," *Frankfurter Allgemeine Zeitung*, August 29, 1991.

206   "it was made quite clear to me"   Quoted in "Sportarzt klagt Leverkusener Dopingnest an," *Süddeutsche Zeitung*, March 3, 1995.

206   "We haven't given the athletes"   Hacker, quoted in "Menschenversuche mit neuen Dopingmitteln: Funktionäre haben Athleten gezwungen," *Frankfurter Allgemeine Zeitung*, December 5, 1990.

206   "It would be much more honest"   Höppner, quoted in "Bonn fordert schnelle Untersuchung," *Süddeutsche Zeitung*, November 30, 1990.

207   In July 2000 Höppner was convicted   "Ex-East German Sports Chief Is Convicted in Doping Trial," *New York Times*, July 19, 2000.

207   East German trainers who gave steroids   Berendonk, *Doping-Dokumente: Von der Forschung zum Betrug*, 71, 276.

207   "The effect on the sexual drive"   Höppner, quoted in Werner W. Franke and Brigitte Berendonk, "Hormonal Doping and Androgenization of Athletes: A Secret Program of the German Democratic Republic Government," *Clinical Chemistry* 43 (1997): 1274.

208   "Among some [male] athletes"   Gehrmann, quoted in "Bundestag gegen Generalamnestie," *Süddeutsche Zeitung*, September 4, 1991. On Christian Gehrmann's doping practices, see Berendonk, *Doping-Dokumente: Von der Forschung zum Betrug*, 270–76.

208   the German distance runner Martin Bremer   "Die Sünder mit der Unschuldsmiene," *Süddeutsche Zeitung*, December 30, 1994.

208   the professional cyclist Christian Henn   "Probleme in der Familie," *Der Spiegel*, August 16, 1999, 114–16.

209   Steroids were administered to some members   Giselher Spitzer, *Doping in der DDR: Ein historischer Überblick zu einer konspirativen Praxis* (Cologne: Sport und Buch Strauß, 2000), 116.

209   In 1992, for example   "Im Nest der Staatsförderung," *Der Spiegel*, April 27, 1992, 294.

209   "neither the DEA"   Michael Colgan, "New Testosterones," *Muscular Development*, January 1999, 94.

209   "Historically, the Federal motivation"   Quoted in Michael T. Risher, "Controlling Viagra-Mania," *New York Times*, July 20, 1998.

210   "The biggest problem with the women"   Lawrence Diller, quoted in Amanda Ripley, "Ritalin: Mom's Little Helper," *Time*, February 12, 2001, 73. Diller is the author of *Running on Ritalin: A Physician Reflects on Children, Society, and Performance in a Pill* (New York: Bantam Books, 1998).

210   "nearly everyone else—all the citizens"   Diller, *Running on Ritalin*, 16.

211   "see labor as a kind of performance"   Margaret Talbot, "Pay on Delivery," *New York Times Magazine*, October 31, 1999, 20.

212   "encounter groups, sensory awareness enhancement"   Janice M. Irvine, *Disorders of Desire: Sex and Gender in Modern American Sexology* (Philadelphia: Temple University Press, 1990), 109.

212   "opposed to thinking about human beings"   Quoted in ibid., 108.

212   In Ireland, Viagra has been fed   "Viagra—nichts für Windhunde," *Süddeutsche Zeitung,* June 23/24, 2001.

212   Even a so-called mind-expanding drug   See, for example, Matthew Klam, "Experiencing Ecstasy," *New York Times Magazine,* January 21, 2001, 43.

213   During the 2001 Tour de France   "Tour-medicinmænd," *Information* (Copenhagen), June 21, 2001.

CHAPTER 6.   "Let Them Take Drugs"

215   "If the American public ever thought"   Quoted in Athelia Knight, "USOC: Drugs Are Top Concern," *Washington Post,* June 29, 1999.

215   "the credibility of sport"   Donike, quoted in "Die Grenzen der Doping-Analyse sind erreicht," *Frankfurter Allgemeine Zeitung,* April 4, 1990.

215   "going to be accepted in this society"   Quoted in "Schicksalsstunde des Sports," *Der Spiegel,* December 10, 1990, 267.

215   "the scourge of drugs"   "Track at the Crossroads," *Track & Field News,* May 1991, 5.

215   "The public is disappointed again"   "Die Maske fällt," *Frankfurter Allgemeine Zeitung,* November 29, 1990.

215   "generally felt to be the worst"   Richard Williams, *Guardian,* August 1, 1998; quoted in Ivan Waddington, *Sport, Health and Drugs: A Critical Sociological Perspective* (London: E and FN Spon, 2000), 96.

215   "the public response to the use of drugs"   Waddington, *Sport, Health and Drugs,* 111.

215   "I am just as disturbed about this"   Ulrich, quoted in "Ullrich fordert lebenslange Sperre für Dopingsünder," *Frankfurter Allgemeine Zeitung,* June 11, 2001.

216   "the record-breaking craze"   Ove Bøje, "Doping: A Study of the Means Employed to Raise the Level of Performance in Sport," *Bulletin of the Health Organization of the League of Nations* 8 (1939): 439–40.

216   "The public demands it"   Meyer, quoted in "Aufforderung zum Doping," *Der Spiegel,* November 13, 1989, 259.

217   "I was really moved by the public"   Couto, quoted in "Klagen über geschäftsschädigende Kontrollen," *Süddeutsche Zeitung,* April 24, 2001.

217   Eventually, Couto was suspended   "Zufälliges Doping," *Süddeutsche Zeitung,* September 8/9, 2001.

218   Upon returning to competition   "Proteste gegen Leipolds Rückkehr," *Süddeutsche Zeitung,* January 29, 2001.

218   "Because nobody really cares"   Krause, quoted in "Verkauft mich nicht für blöd," *Süddeutsche Zeitung,* August 11, 1999.

218   "a startlingly affectionate reception"   Richard O'Brien, "A New Start," *Sports Illustrated,* January 21, 1991, 26.

218   meet promoters had been pursuing him   "Sponsoren liegen Johnson zu Füßen," *Süddeutsche Zeitung,* November 23, 1990.

218   "totally shocked"   Quoted in "Die meisten Zuschauer sprechen Johnson frei," *Frankfurter Allgemeine Zeitung,* January 16, 1989.

219   "In ten days there will be"   Leblanc, quoted in "Voet belastet Festina," *Süddeutsche Zeitung,* July 15, 1998.

219   "The Tour must remain clean"   Leblanc, quoted in "Ein Sprengsatz bedroht die ganze Tour," *Süddeutsche Zeitung,* July 13, 1998.

219   "On one side are the journalists"   Peter Burghardt, "Ein Verdacht in 22 Etappen," *Süddeutsche Zeitung,* July 28, 1998.

219   "that the scandal had a positive effect"   Samuel Abt, "Riders Are Still Critical of the French Police and Courts for Their Role in Drug Affair," *New York Times,* October 11, 1998.

219   Three years later, it was still being reported   Holger Gertz, "Dope und Spiele," *Süddeutsche Zeitung,* July 7/8, 2001.

220   "Despite negative publicity"   Jeremy Whittle, "Tour's Uneasy Riders Get Tour Back on the Road," *Times* (London), June 29, 1999.

220   "Yes," *Der Spiegel* commented   "Die Friedensfahrt der Nr. 69," *Der Spiegel,* July 12, 1999, 111.

220   "It is not the support"   Henrik Jul Hansen, *Man brænder da hekse: Tour de France 1999* (Copenhagen: Informations Forlag, 2000), 111.

220   "The truth"   Andrew Longmore, "Cycling—Time to Stop Cheating, Pleads Millar," *Independent,* June 27, 1999.

221   "I dope myself"   Anquetil, quoted in Bil Gilbert, "Something Extra on the Ball," *Sports Illustrated,* June 30, 1969, 32.

221   "Everyone is doping"   Frigo, quoted in "Auch Ullrich auf der Schwarzen Liste," *Süddeutsche Zeitung,* June 15, 2001.

222   Now it is March 15, 1985   "Werberummel um Radschinsky," *Süddeutsche Zeitung,* May 7, 1985; "Schurke oder tragischer Held?" *Süddeutsche Zeitung,* March 23/24, 1985.

222   "For us the Radschinsky case"   Quoted in "Mit Daume reden," *Süddeutsche Zeitung,* April 11, 1988.

222   Radschinsky's popularity was another factor   Ibid.

223   In April 1997 the Austrian ski jumper   "Durch Dealer beschuldigt," *Süddeutsche Zeitung,* April 24, 1997.

223   The press noted   "Urteil unter Krämpfen," *Süddeutsche Zeitung,* May 16, 1997.

223   "We have treated this offense"   Quoted in ibid.

224   Austria's largest paper   Ibid.

224   Politicians criticized the ÖSV president   "Die Sucht nach benebelten Sinnen," *Süddeutsche Zeitung,* April 22, 1997

224   a tactic also adopted by the repentant Ben Johnson   "Sponsoren liegen Johnson zu Füßen."

224   Goldberger went so far as to announce   "Goldberger gibt Kokainkonsum zu und wird sofort gesperrt," *Süddeutsche Zeitung,* April 27, 1997.

224   Here, too, the Austrian press went into action   "Dopingskandal brodelt in der Gerüchteküche," *Süddeutsche Zeitung,* July 21, 1993.

224   the Austrian press waged a nasty campaign   L. Prokop, "Praktische Erfahrungen mit dem Doping in Österreich," *Der Sportarzt* (1966): 58.

224   Prokop reported that tabloid attacks   Ludwig Prokop, "Zur Geschichte des Dopings," in *Rekorde aus der Retorte: Leistungssteigerung im modernen Hochleistungssport,* ed. Helmut Acker (Stuttgart: Deutsche Verlags-Anstalt, 1972), 27.

225 In 1990, for example "Aus einer anderen Welt," *Der Spiegel,* December 24, 1990, 141.

225 "there was more public criticism" "Goldschatz für alle," *Der Spiegel,* March 4, 1991, 236.

225 "For three days, he appeared" "Smith's Olympic Heroics Shrouded in Scepticism," *Weekly Telegraph,* November 13–19, 1996.

225 "Five state prosecutors are working" Quoted in "Pantani wird zum Präzedenzfall," *Süddeutsche Zeitung,* June 8, 2000.

226 The same year, even an accusation "Das schlechte Gewissen der Tour de France," *Süddeutsche Zeitung,* July 20, 2000.

226 the Olympic champion sprinter Linford Christie Personal communication from Ivan Waddington, June 15, 2001. I wish to express my appreciation to Professor Waddington for this information.

226 Queen Elizabeth II hosted a garden party "Banned Champions Join Elite for Garden Party at Palace," *Times* (London), July 9, 1992. See also "Star Gazing at the Royal Sports Party," *Times* (London), July 10, 1992.

226 A 1998 Gallup poll sponsored by two Danish publications "Dyb europæisk mistillid til sporten," *Idrætsliv,* November 20, 1998, 4–5.

227 The German television show "Das übliche Komplott?" *Süddeutsche Zeitung,* June 15, 1999, "Schon ein bißchen merkwürdig," *Der Spiegel,* June 21, 1999, 145.

227 almost half of the Australians polled "Skepsis in Sydney," *Süddeutsche Zeitung,* March 15, 2000.

227 "over half of those questioned felt" Waddington, *Sport, Drugs and Health,* 96.

227 The Crédit Suisse bank gave up Gertz, "Dope und Spiele."

227 A nonrepresentative survey carried out "Der Doping-Betrug prosperiert," *Süddeutche Zeitung,* May 10, 1996.

227 "If you were to do an opinion survey" Evers, quoted in "Angewidert von der Doppelbödigkeit der Antidoping Politik," *Süddeutsche Zeitung,* October 2, 1996.

227 "Anyone who goes looking for doping" Gertz, "Dope und Spiele."

227 "The fans only get excited" Donati, quoted in "Die Lawine rollt," *Der Spiegel,* January 24, 2000, 146.

228 The *Denver Post* reported Bill Briggs, "Swifter, Higher, Stronger, Dirtier?" *Denver Post,* November 16, 2003.

228 A *New York Times* poll Jere Longman and Marjorie Connelly, "Americans Suspect Steroid Use in Sports Is Common, Poll Finds," *New York Times,* December 16, 2003. For additional commentary on the American public's indifference to doped professional baseball players, see Tom Verducci, "Totally Juiced," *Sports Illustrated,* June 3, 2002, 48.

228 a *New York Times* columnist speculated Harvey Araton, "Do You Recall Balco? Baseball Hopes Not," *New York Times,* February 16, 2004.

229 "Perfection produces suspicion" "Menschlichkeit siegt," *Frankfurter Allgemeine Zeitung,* June 11, 2001.

229 Chinese female distance runners ran so far ahead "Dong Chaoxia kommt zu einer schönen Reise nach Göteborg," *Süddeutsche Zeitung,* August 2, 1995; "Als die Leichtathleten abhoben," *Süddeutsche Zeitung,* August 1, 2001.

230   Upon her return home   "Russia's 'Golden Girl,' " *BBC Sport* (August 21, 2001), http://news.bbc.co.uk/sport1/hi/in_depth/2001/world_athletics/1490321.stm.

230   "Early in life I realized"   Virenque and Zülle, quoted in "Hier sitzen nur Schwerverbrecher," *Süddeutsche Zeitung*, July 27, 1998.

230   "The riders reckon that a good Tour"   Millar, quoted in Waddington, *Sport, Health and Drugs*, 161.

230   "No one can seriously expect"   Hans Halter, "Alles verstehen, alles verzeihen," *Der Spiegel*, August 3, 1998, 97.

231   Delgado returned home a "Hero of Spain"   "Wie weh das tut," *Der Spiegel*, July 17, 1989, 171.

231   "Few of them held any grudge"   Paul Kimmage, *Rough Ride: Behind the Wheel with a Pro Cyclist* (London: Yellow Jersey Press, 1990), 177–78.

231   a *France Soir* opinion survey   "Das Schweigen der Renner," *Süddeutsche Zeitung*, July 27, 1998.

231   "The opponents of doping"   Verner Møller, *Dopingdjævlen—analyse af en hed debat* (Copenhagen: Gyldendal, 1999), 137–38.

232   "Society and sport are becoming"   Verbruggen, quoted in Whittle, "Tour's Uneasy Riders Get Tour Back on the Road." Hein Verbruggen is also a member of the World Anti-Doping Agency (WADA) and the IOC.

232   "Strict sanctions were appropriate"   The Prince de Merode, quoted in "We're Too Hard on Drug Cheats: Olympic Boss," *Weekend Australian*, December 21–22, 1996.

232   "people in show business"   Merode, quoted in "Europas Sportminister setzen IOC unter Druck," *Süddeutsche Zeitung*, February 3, 1999.

232   "We need labour laws"   Merode, quoted by Reuters, September 3, 1998.

233   "What we are dealing with here"   Merode, quoted in "Die Mühen mit der Manipulation," *Süddeutsche Zeitung*, September 20, 1991.

233   the status of both therapeutic and recreational drugs   Ivan Waddington has pointed out "how public attitudes and anxieties towards the use of controlled drugs in society generally have 'spilled over' into the sports arena and have influenced anti-doping policies in sport" (*Sport, Health and Drugs*, 112).

234   "reaction from the general public"   Harvey G. Klein, "Blood Transfusion and Athletics," *New England Journal of Medicine* 312 (March 28, 1985): 854.

234   But a doping controversy that drags on   Marco Pantani's popularity was reported to be in decline after his disappointing performance in the Dolomites during the 2001 Giro d'Italia ("Der Kreuzzug des Piraten," *Süddeutsche Zeitung*, June 5, 2001). His conviction on a doping charge dating from 1999 did not appear to threaten his reputation in Italy.

234   The Danish rider Bjarne Riis   Hansen, *Man brænder da hekse*, 32.

235   "The spectators, too"   Wessinghage, quoted in "Würden Sie Ihrer Tochter dazu raten?" *Der Spiegel*, August 26, 1985, 133.

235   Lianos denounced "anti-Greek propaganda"   "Greek Coach Says He Will Sue British Newspaper," Associated Press, February 18, 2004.

235   In 1997 their coach   "Pfiffe des Zweifels," *Süddeutsche Zeitung*, August 12, 2002.

235   In April 2003 an Athens newspaper   "Auf der Flucht," *Süddeutsche Zeitung*, April 3, 2003.

235 "I consider the accusations baseless" Duncan Mackay and Helena Smith, "Greek Fury over Dope Claim," *Guardian*, February 17, 2004.

236 His 2002 time See "Der undurchsichtige Adonis," *Der Spiegel*, August 11, 2003, 87. The only faster time ever recorded by a white runner was run by the Italian Pietro Mennea in 1972 in Mexico City, which is situated 7,500 feet above sea level. Significantly faster times are possible at high altitude because of the thinness of the air. Apart from Mennea and Kenteris, the only other white sprinter to have run 200 meters in under 20 seconds is a Pole, Marcin Urbas, who ran 19.98 seconds in Seville in 1999.

236 no sprinter the modern world would categorize The Australian sprinter Patrick Johnson, who ran a time of 9.93 in Mito, Japan, on May 5, 2003, is the son of an Irish-born Australian father and an Aboriginal mother. On the history of ideas about racial athletic aptitude, see John Hoberman, *Darwin's Athletes: How Sport Has Damaged Black America and Preserved the Myth of Race* (New York: Houghton Mifflin, 1997), 187–207.

236 their indignation in the face of the doping accusations One Greek told a British journalist that the British and the Americans were conspiring to spread doping rumors about Greek athletes "because they did not want their 'Negro sprinters' to be beaten by a white Greek." See Duncan Mackay, "Hate Figure in Greece—But I'm Unrepentant," *Observer* (London), February 22, 2004.

236 In 1999 his elevated red blood cell count Nicole Winfield, "Italy Mourns 'Lost Hero,' " *Austin American-Statesman*, February 16, 2004.

236 The reaction of Italian society Eric Jozsef, "L'Italie pleure son 'roi des montagnes,' " *Libération*, February 16, 2004.

236 The organizers of the Giro Eric Jozsef, "L'Italie enterre son héros sans se remettre en question," *Libération*, February 19, 2004.

236 Tens of thousands attended "Pantani in Cesenatico beigesetzt," *Neue Zürcher Zeitung*, February 18, 2004.

237 Pantani had been one of three "patients" The Italian rider Denis Zanette died in January 2003 (see Thomas Kistner, "Plötzlicher Herzfehler," *Süddeutsche Zeitung*, January 16, 2003; Torben Rask Larsen, "Tunge beviser mod død rytter," *Ekstra Bladet* [Copenhagen], January 17, 2003). The Spanish rider Jose-Maria Jimenez died in November 2003 in a psychiatric hospital in Madrid (see Jean-Louis le Touzet, "Le 'pirate' a sombré," *Libération*, February 16, 2004). On Conconi's role, and his friendship with the president of the European Commission, Romano Prodi, see Jozsef, "L'Italie pleure son 'roi des montagnes.' "

237 The pretty blonde sprinter "Love Parade in Spikes," *Der Spiegel*, June 25, 2001, 176.

237 an opinion poll taken in 1986 F. Allan Hanson, *Testing, Testing: Social Consequences of the Examined Life* (Berkeley: University of California Press, 1993), 128.

237 "Doping is an economic problem" Digel, quoted in "Das Kalkül der Athleten," *Süddeutsche Zeitung*, July 28/29, 2001. Digel, a sport sociologist, was president of the German Track and Field Federation (Deutscher Leichtathletik-Verband, or DLV) from 1993 to 2001.

237 Doping, adds the French sociologist Georges Vigarello, "Le sport dopé," *Esprit*, January 1999, 76.

238 "You murderers! You damned murderers!" Lapine, quoted in "Atemzug für zwei," *Der Spiegel*, July 20, 1992, 191.

238 "Damn the swine who do this" Kübler, quoted in "Fahren mit Dynamit," *Der Spiegel*, August 3, 1955, 34.

238 For most of the next fifty years Consider, for example, how the Tour de France riders responded to the scandal of 1998. One step they took was to elect a former rider named Francesco Moser as the president of a new association to represent the interests of professional cyclists. In other words, less than a year after the doping scandal, the riders chose as their spokesman a man who admitted to blood doping his way to a world-record time trial in 1984 and who proclaimed in 1999: "We will have to live with doping. Clean cycling is just an illusion" ("Zabel soll es richten," *Süddeutsche Zeitung*, April 10/11, 1999). Moser's election only weeks before the Tour of Redemption exemplifies the schizophrenic relationship between the athletes and society at large.

CHAPTER 7. A War against Drugs?

239 Over the past four decades Significant passages from this section have been taken or adapted from my essay "How Drug Testing Fails: The Politics of Doping Control," in *Doping in Elite Sport: The Politics of Drugs in the Olympic Movement*, ed. Wayne Wilson and Edward Derse (Champaign, Ill.: Human Kinetics, 2000), 241–74. On the international politics of doping control, see also John Hoberman, *Mortal Engines: The Science of Performance and the Dehumanization of Sport* (New York: Free Press, 1992), 229–68.

239 Hormone doping has made possible It is known as fact that the holder of the world record in the women's 400-meter run, Marita Koch of East Germany, consumed 3,680 milligrams of the East German anabolic steroid Oral-Turinabol during the period 1981–84. She set the (still unbroken, at this writing) record of 47.60 seconds in 1985 (Brigitte Berendonk, *Doping-Dokumente: Von der Forschung zum Betrug* [Reinbek bei Hamburg: Rowohlt, 1992], 151). A longitudinal survey of performances in the men's and women's shot put makes it clear that steroid consumption has fallen sharply in this event since the record performances of the 1970s and 1980s. The astonishing world records set by Chinese female runners in 1993 remain unexplained.

239 In 1991, for example, the spokesman "Zwischen Schönfarberei und Schwarzmalerei," *Süddeutsche Zeitung*, July 26, 1991; "Beyer fordert Doping-Freigabe," *Süddeutsche Zeitung*, August 28, 1991.

239 Like others before him Dr. Wildor Hollmann, a longtime president of the International Federation of Sports Physicians (Fédération Internationale de Médecine Sportive, or FIMS), made a similar proposal in 1989. "The chemically prepared athlete has been a reality for a long time. We must introduce a fifth category into sport, the sports show *[Sportshow]* that is no longer associated with our traditional definitions of sport. I said eleven years ago that the time would come when we would have to say good-bye to sport and its traditional values. In some sports that time has come" (quoted in "Eine fünfte Kategorie für den Sport," *Süddeutsche Zeitung*, January 10, 1989).

240 **"doping is an economic problem"** Professor Helmut Digel, former president of the German Track and Field Federation (1993–2001), currently vice president of the German National Olympic Committee and vice president of the International Association of Athletics Federations (IAAF); quoted in "Das Kalkül der Athleten," *Süddeutsche Zeitung*, July 28/29, 2001.

240 **The historical record shows** Among the anti-doping activists who have been forced out of official positions by their national Olympic committees or other national bodies over the past twenty years are Dr. Hans Howald (Switzerland), Hans B. Skaset (Norway), Sandro Donati (Italy), and Drs. Robert Voy (1989) and Wade Exum (2000) of the United States.

240 **Samaranch took the lead in this crusade** See Hoberman, "How Drug Testing Fails," 242–43, 268.

241 **"Above all," he proclaimed** Samaranch, quoted in Michael Janofsky, "Samaranch Blasts Drugs and Boycotts," *New York Times*, February 9, 1988.

241 **"Doping," he added** Samaranch, quoted in "Samaranch Tough on Drug Abusers," *Houston Chronicle*, February 9, 1988.

241 **"Doping equals death"** Samaranch, quoted in Michael Janofsky, "President of I.O.C. Condemns Drug Use," *New York Times*, September 13, 1988.

241 **"commit a series of acts"** Samaranch, quoted by Associated Press, July 23, 1996.

241 **"spearheaded the anti-doping campaign"** Samaranch, quoted by United Press International, July 14, 1996.

241 **The historical record suggests** When, for example, Olympic drug testing failed to produce a single positive test at the 1980 Moscow Games, the IOC did nothing to investigate or improve upon this improbable finding. Working off the record, the IOC drug-testing expert Manfred Donike found that "20 percent of all athletes tested—males and females—would have failed his new testosterone screen if it were officially administered" (Jan Todd and Terry Todd, "Significant Events in the History of Drug Testing and the Olympic Movement: 1960–1999," in Wilson and Derse, eds., *Doping in Elite Sport*, 77). See also Jacques Wallach, "Athletes and Steroid Drugs" (letter), *JAMA* 252 (July 27, 1984): 566.

241 **the IOC press director commented** "Probe 0708104 und andere 'Monster' der DDR: Doktor Höppner—Alchimist als Kronzeuge?" *Frankfurter Allgemeine Zeitung*, December 1, 1990. On the politics of doping in Germany, see Hoberman, *Mortal Engines*, 252–65.

242 **"a German problem"** Samaranch, quoted in "Deutsches Problem," *Süddeutsche Zeitung*, December 11, 1990.

242 **the unreliability of the (West) German National Olympic Committee** See Steven Ungerleider, *Faust's Gold: Inside the East German Doping Machine* (New York: St. Martin's Press, 2001), 171–75.

242 **In 1988 he bestowed another Olympic Order** See Berendonk, *Doping-Dokumente: Von der Forschung zum Betrug*, 291.

242 **this did not deter Samaranch** "Kopf runter und durch," *Der Spiegel*, March 9, 1992, 228; "Ewald trifft sich mit Samaranch," *Süddeutsche Zeitung*, November 12, 1991.

242 **Paragraph 7 of the Olympic Charter** "Rückgabe des IOC-Ordens," *Süddeutsche Zeitung*, March 19, 1990.

242   The fact that Chinese swimmers   See, for example, Todd and Todd, "Significant Events in the History of Drug Testing," 100.

242   "The Chinese have problems"   Quoted in "IOC stützt Chinesen," *Süddeutsche Zeitung,* April 5, 1995.

242   "accidents that could happen anywhere"   The Prince de Merode, quoted in "Zum Thema Doping sagt Samaranch nichts," *Süddeutsche Zeitung,* December 19, 1994.

242   "We are carrying out a decisive struggle"   Samaranch, quoted in "IOC stützt Chinesen."

243   The IOC's primary anti-doping strategy   Todd and Todd, "Significant Events in the History of Drug Testing," 68, 74.

243   Between 1968 and 1996   This proportion represents 52 drug positives in an athlete population of about 54,000. See Amy Shipley, "Drug Tests, Troubling Results: IOC's System Is Plagued by False Positives in Addition to Cheating," *Washington Post,* September 23, 1999; see also Amy Shipley, "With Drug Tests, Answers Are Few: The IOC Says It Is Cracking Down on Doping, but to Critics the Problem Is Only Getting Worse," *Washington Post,* September 22, 1999.

243   As late as the 1996 Atlanta Games   Jere Longman, "Drug Lab Passes Test for Atlanta Drug Tests," *New York Times,* July 6, 1996.

243   In fact, the 1,923 drug tests   Shipley, "Drug Tests, Troubling Results."

243   The booming export trade in former East German coaches   See, for example, Hoberman, *Mortal Engines,* 247-48.

244   In 1991, for example   "Vieldeutiger Rückzug," *Süddeutsche Zeitung,* November 29, 1991. See Brigitte Berendonk, *Doping-Dokumente: Von der Forschung zum Betrug* (Berlin: Springer-Verlag, 1991).

244   the West German swimming coach Georg Weinzierl   "Streit der Trainer," *Süddeutsche Zeitung,* December 9, 1991.

244   This action did not deter   See "Pioniere des Vertuschens," *Der Spiegel,* April 24, 1994, 236-38; "Das ist gut für die Zähne," *Der Spiegel,* August 18, 1997, 126-28; "Mach' Schluss, das Thema ist durch," *Süddeutsche Zeitung,* August 23/24, 1997; "Mit Handschellen gedroht," *Süddeutsche Zeitung,* December 9, 1998.

244   East German coaches accused of doping   "DLV halt an DDR-Trainern fest," *Süddeutsche Zeitung,* May 18, 2000.

244   The former head swimming coach   "Streit der Trainer."

244   "I see no other coach in Austria"   Quoted in "Zerrüttete Verhältnisse," *Süddeutsche Zeitung,* August 28, 1998.

244   the biathlon coach Kurt Hinze   "Wehmutige Gedanken an die Allerbesten," *Süddeutsche Zeitung,* March 23, 1992; "Kurt Hinze verliert," *Süddeutsche Zeitung,* May 30/31, 1992.

244   Former East German coaches also found employment   See "Traum von Medaillenregen," *Der Spiegel,* November 17, 1997: 206-8; for a summary in English, see Hoberman, "How Drug Testing Fails," 262-63.

244   Before the end of 1990 Arbeit   "Italien verpflichtet DDR-Trainer," *Süddeutsche Zeitung,* August 28, 1990.

244   "He can't find a job in Germany"   Franke, quoted in "We Have Hired a 'Major Rascal,'" *Australian,* October 4, 1997.

245 **his appointment was not canceled until** "Unmasked: Files Reveal Coach Was a Communist Spy," *Daily Telegraph* (Sydney), November 19, 1997.

245 **"Ekkart Arbeit enjoys the confidence"** Dick, quoted by Reuters Information Service, October 12, 1997. Dick had recommended Arbeit to Athletics Australia. "His experience and expertise is *[sic]* without parallel in the world, let alone Europe . . . and there has been no record or any hint of irregularity in his conduct as coach," Dick said a month before Arbeit was revealed to have been a Stasi spy (quoted in "IAAF Urged to Solve Row on Arbeit," *Sydney Morning Herald,* October 16, 1997). In early October 1997 Arbeit's candidacy was being supported by the president of the Australian Olympic Committee, John Coates, who stated that he believed Arbeit's denials of ever giving drugs to athletes ("FOR Ekkart Arbeit's Appointment," *Cool Running Australia* [October 7, 1997], www.coolrunning.com .au). Coates is now a member of the IOC.

245 **Arbeit was flown to South Africa** *Daily Mail and Guardian,* October 23, 2001. Arbeit's international search for employment continued for years. See "Athletics: New Proof of Arbeit Drug Link," *Daily Telegraph* (London), February 11, 2004.

245 **offering a series of rationalizations** For example: "ASA has no evidence whatsoever of the alleged existence of the said state-sponsored doping programme of the former East Germany. For this reason, ASA reserves the right to express an opinion as to whether such a programme did in fact exist, or not" ("ASA Boss Defends SA's New 'Doping Coach,' " *Daily News* [Johannesburg], April 23, 2002).

245 **Arbeit's documented participation** On Arbeit's involvement in the State Plan 14.25 doping program, see Giselher Spitzer, *Doping in der DDR: Ein historischer Überblick zu einer konspirativen Praxis* (Cologne: Sport und Buch Strauß, 2000), 59, 147–48.

246 **"In fact, these people just wanted to know"** Prokop, quoted in Thomas Kistner, "Die Stasi führt Olympia-Arzt Joseph Keul als Dopingbefürworter," *Süddeutsche Zeitung,* March 21, 1994.

246 **The late Joseph Keul** "Willige Sklaven," *Der Spiegel,* October 19, 1987, 226. On Keul's relationship to doping, see also Thomas Kistner, *Muskelspiele: Ein Abgesang auf Olympia* (Berlin: Rowohlt, 1996), 194–97.

246 **Keul recommended EPO** "Ausblenden und Gesundbeten," *Der Spiegel,* July 27, 1998, 105.

246 **"a big mafia"** Prokop, quoted in "Eine grosse Mafia," *Der Spiegel,* March 21, 1994, 188.

246 **"With this information we can rewrite records"** Quoted by Reuters Information Service, September 17, 1997.

246 **"It has been said that records"** Franke, quoted by Agence France-Presse, September 17, 1997.

247 **Manfred Kanther angrily rejected the whole idea** AP Sports, January 9, 1998. For a critical commentary on Kanther's position, see Thomas Kistner, "Kanther schafft das Doping ab," *Süddeutsche Zeitung,* January 13, 1998.

247 **Even the reformist president** "Zuviel Aufwand an Moral und Ethik?" *Süddeutsche Zeitung,* January 27, 1998.

247 **"Some things belong to history"** Merode, quoted in "IOC Medical Chief Criticizes Blood Doping," *Dallas Morning News,* February 11, 1988.

247 "Those are hypotheses" Merode, quoted in "Kommerzialisierung in richtige Bahnen lenken," *Süddeutsche Zeitung*, December 21, 1990.

247 "There are time limits" Merode, quoted in "IOC: Rückgabe unmöglich," *Süddeutsche Zeitung*, January 14, 1998.

248 "We can only deal" Quoted by Agence France-Presse, September 17, 1997.

248 "The rule is quite clear" Quoted by Reuters, January 5, 1998.

248 a six-year statute of limitations The IAAF Rule Book, Division III, Rule 55.8 reads: "An admission may be made either orally in a verifiable manner or in writing. For the purpose of these rules a statement is not to be regarded as an admission where it was made more than six years after the facts to which it relates." Therefore, the press officer reasoned, "any discussion about East German track and field athletes becomes redundant. The last GDR team competed at the World Championships in 1987—when [Thomas] Schönlebe set his [400-meter] mark 11 years ago" (Jim Ferstle, "East German Drug Revelations Mount; Other Athletes Begin to Ask That Sports History Be Rewritten" [January 6, 1998], www.runners world. com/dailynew/archives/1998/January/980106.html; cited in Todd and Todd, "Significant Events in the History of Drug Testing," 258).

248 "Six years," he has argued Shorter, quoted in ibid., 258–59.

248 "We can't have the national courts" Quoted in "Defiant Swiss Athlete's Case Submitted to IAAF Tribunal," *Times* (London), January 5, 1988. For an analysis of this case, see Hoberman, *Mortal Engines*, 229–37.

248 Too many of these federations become autocratic fiefdoms From 1968 to 2002 the head of the IOC Medical Commission was a Belgian nobleman, Prince Alexandre de Merode, who was neither a doctor nor a scientist and whose conduct in this position was frequently criticized. On May 22, 2001, at a conference in Oslo, I asked Dr. Arne Ljungqvist, an IOC member and IAAF doping expert, whether he had ever advised the IOC's President Samaranch to replace the Prince de Merode with a better-qualified person. Yes, he said, on several occasions he had done just that. And what, I asked, was Mr. Samaranch's response? " 'I cannot dismiss a friend,' " Dr. Ljungqvist replied. The new head of the IOC Medical Commission, Dr. Ljungqvist has adopted a harder anti-doping line than his predecessor, a position in tune with the more militant anti-doping politics of the post-Samaranch era.

249 "New information coming" Garry Wills, "The Vatican Monarchy," *New York Review of Books*, February 19, 1998, 25.

249 Helmut Digel's proposal "Das Digel-Konzept," *Süddeutsche Zeitung*, January 26, 1998.

249 the heading of *sportive nationalism* On the phenomenon of sportive nationalism, see John Hoberman, "Sport and Ideology in the Post-Communist Age," in *The Changing Politics of Sport*, ed. Lincoln Allison (Manchester: Manchester University Press, 1993), 18–29.

249 The East German dictatorship was able to operate See Werner W. Franke and Brigitte Berendonk, "Hormonal Doping and Androgenization of Athletes: A Secret Program of the German Democratic Republic Government," *Clinical Chemistry* 43 (1997): 1262–79. See also Ungerleider, *Faust's Gold*.

250 "The athlete must not be turned" Quoted in "Regierung und DSB bekennen sich zum Spitzensport: Alle Kräfte auf die Olympischen Spiele konzentrieren," *Frankfurter Allgemeine Zeitung*, December 7, 1987.

250 "Recently," he said   Weizsäcker, quoted in "Die Athleten nicht vorab unter Druck setzen," *Süddeutsche Zeitung,* January 21, 1988.

250 "I do not share the view"   Groß, quoted in "Mensch, jetzt haste Steurern verschwendet," *Der Spiegel,* October 12, 1987, 227.

250 German sportive nationalism has always prevailed   On German sportive nationalism, see John Hoberman, "Fitness and National Vitality: A Comparative Study of Germany and the United States," in *Fitness as Cultural Phenomenon,* ed. Karin A. E. Volkwein (Münster: Waxmann, 1998), 231–47.

251 "We advocate only"   Schäuble, quoted in Berendonk, *Doping-Dokumente: Von der Forschung zum Betrug,* 45. See also Hans Joachim Seppelt and Holger Schück, eds., *Anklage: Kinderdoping: Das Erbe des DDR-Sports* (Berlin: Tenea, 1999), 290.

251 "The striking degree of restraint"   Thomas Kistner, "Eine unliebsame Charta," *Süddeutsche Zeitung,* September 17, 1992.

251 "The limits of human performance"   Schäuble, quoted in "Minister Schäuble warnt vor einer 'Doping-Hysterie,' " *Süddeutsche Zeitung,* October 21, 1989.

251 "I reject," he said   Schäuble, quoted in "Schäuble mahnt Konsequenzen an," *Süddeutsche Zeitung,* October 23, 1991.

252 In May 1994 Kanther released   "Gesetz nicht nötig," *Süddeutsche Zeitung,* May 14/15, 1994; "SPD-Plan gescheitert," *Süddeutsche Zeitung,* May 20, 1994.

252 In April 1997 Kanther was still opposing   "Vertraute Vorstöße ins Vakuum," *Süddeutsche Zeitung,* April 18, 1997.

252 "The successes of our athletes"   Kantner, quoted in "217 für den Sport," *Süddeutsche Zeitung,* September 12, 1996.

252 "Sports medals," he said   Kantner, quoted in "Nationales Anliegen," *Süddeutsche Zeitung,* January 7, 1997.

252 "The CDU," he said   Fischer, quoted in "Blockade Politik in Bonn," *Süddeutsche Zeitung,* June 13, 1997.

253 "[German] sport must remain"   Kohl, quoted in "Die Sporthilfe holt sich Hilfe beim Kanzler," *Süddeutsche Zeitung,* October 27, 1995.

253 "Pessimism," he lamented   Herzog, quoted in "Langfristige Bindung gesucht," *Süddeutsche Zeitung,* May 27, 1997.

253 "many of us at home"   Kohl, quoted in "Experten für schwierige Lebenslagen," *Süddeutsche Zeitung,* July 2, 1996.

253 Disagreements about anti-doping policy   On this (West) German ideological conflict, see Hoberman, *Mortal Engines,* 244–46.

253 "Even if the 1992 Olympics"   Quoted in "Die Drohung aus Bonn wird verstanden," *Süddeutsche Zeitung,* September 28/29, 1991.

254 Prime Minister John Howard issued a statement   "PM Backs 'Clean' Swimming Stars," *Sydney Morning Herald,* April 12, 2001.

254 the president of Jamaica declared   "Denken diese Leute, wir sind Idioten?" *Süddeutsche Zeitung,* August 20, 1999.

254 "we have no intention"   Quoted in "Russia under Pressure Not to Protest Olympic Doping Cases," Reuters, February 28, 2002.

254 "Sports will come first again"   Berlusconi, quoted in *Süddeutsche Zeitung,* May 5/6, 2001.

254 In October 1998 the Rome doping laboratory   "Liebesgrüße aus dem Heizungskeller," *Süddeutsche Zeitung,* October 19, 1998.

254   Berlusconi declared that this scandal   "Klagen über geschäftsschädigende Kontrollen," *Süddeutsche Zeitung*, April 24, 2001.

254   Pescante retained his seat   As of this writing (February 2004), IOC member Mohamad (Bob) Hasan has been jailed, tried, and convicted on corruption charges in Indonesia. In 1991 Robert Helmick of the United States was forced to resign from the IOC on account of his self-serving financial dealings.

254   As the government's sports minister   "Eine Doppelspitze gegen den Werteverfall," *Süddeutsche Zeitung*, December 19/20, 1998.

254   the Italian Senate had passed   "Anti-Drug Measure Passes Italian Senate," *New York Times*, November 17, 2000.

255   a new anti-doping commission   "New Drug Labeling Rules in Italy," *Marketletter*, January 7, 2002.

255   State prosecutors have continued   See "Ermittlungen ausgeweitet," *Süddeutsche Zeitung*, November 20, 1998; "Dafür sorgen, daß Doping geächtet wird," *Süddeutsche Zeitung*, May 5, 1999; "Der Leise Herr aus der Abteilung Desaster," *Süddeutsche Zeitung*, November 14, 2001; "Auch Kappes auf der Liste," *Süddeutsche Zeitung*, December 16, 1999.

255   In March 2004 another judge   "Ein belastender Freispruch Conconis," *Neue Zürcher Zeitung*, March 13, 2004.

255   the anti-doping campaign led by Sandro Donati   "Donati proprement dérangeant," *Libération* (Paris), February 1, 2002.

255   When the cycling star Marco Pantani was accused   "Pirat am seidenen Faden," *Süddeutsche Zeitung*, May 4/5, 2002.

255   A senior sports expert at the Ministry of Culture   Skaset's commentary appeared in *Idrettsanlegg* during the fall of 2000 and appeared on the Web site of Sport Media AS. See also "Truer med å trekke offentlig støtte," *Aftenposten* (Oslo), October 27, 2000. In March 2001, the sports leader Bjørge Stensbøl staunchly defended the use of altitude chambers as a training technique comparable to lifting weights or running against the drag effect of a parachute ("Stensbøl nekter å stenge høydehuset," *Aftenposten*, March 10, 2001).

255   "indirectly sanctioning experimentation"   Skaset, quoted in "Truer med å trekke offentlig støtte."

255   But when the president of the Norwegian Sports Federation   See "Full seier til Kran," *Aftenposten*, October 28, 2000; Dag Vidar Hanstad, "Skasets selvskudd," *Aftenposten*, October 28, 2000.

256   It was, in fact, right-of-center politicians   Dag Vidar Hanstad, "Politikerne brukte sjansen," *Aftenposten*, February 3, 2001. Norway's most effective sportive nationalist politician of the 1980s and 1990s was the Social Democratic (Arbeiderparti) prime minister Gro Harlem Brundtland, who presided over the successful 1994 Lillehammer Olympic Games.

256   The Norwegian public also learned   "Vil ha strengere kontroll over idrettens penger," *Aftenposten*, November 4, 2000.

256   A principled refusal to push the envelope   Dag Vidar Hanstad, "Vil vi ha elitedrett?" *Aftenposten*, March 10, 2001.

256   "national ministry of sport"   From the Verified Complaint and Jury Demand filed by the Plaintiff, Wade F. Exum, M.D., versus United States Olympic Committee, a corporation; United States Anti-Doping Agency, a not-for-profit Colorado corpo-

ration. The press release announcing the filing of this suit was issued by Exum's attorney on July 17, 2000 (I quote from pp. 2, 5, 10, 5, 6). Like Dr. Voy, I volunteered to serve as an expert witness on Dr. Exum's behalf. All of the doping experts nominated by Exum's attorney were eventually dismissed from the case by the presiding judge. In 2001 I accepted a subpoena to testify on Dr. Exum's behalf at a trial scheduled for April 2003. It has subsequently been postponed indefinitely.

257 **On October 15, 1987, he gave a candid speech** Robert O. Voy published this speech as "Education as a Means against Doping," *Olympian*, December 1987, 43-46.

257 **Voy's memoir is essential reading** Robert O. Voy, *Drugs, Sport, and Politics* (Champaign, Ill.: Leisure Press, 1991).

257 **For example, following the unethical** See, for example, Bjarne Rostaing and Robert Sullivan, "Triumphs Tainted with Blood," *Sports Illustrated*, January 21, 1985, 12-17; Richard Ben Cramer, "Olympic Cheating: The Inside Story of Illicit Doping and the U.S. Cycling Team," *Rolling Stone*, February 14, 1985, 25, 26, 30; Harvey G. Klein, "Blood Transfusion and Athletics," *New England Journal of Medicine* 312 (March 28, 1985): 854-56; Voy, *Drugs, Sport, and Politics*, 70-72.

257 **"unethical, unacceptable and illegal"** Dardik, quoted in Rostaing and Sullivan, "Triumphs Tainted with Blood," 17. In June 1985 the USOC replaced Dr. Irving Dardik as the head of its Sports Medicine Council after eight years of service. "Dardik claimed he was replaced because he headed the investigating panel which determined 8 members of the '84 U.S. Olympic Cycling team had participated in blood boosting in Los Angeles. USOC president Robert Helmick said Dardik was replaced (by Dr. Robert Leach, head of the '84 medical staff) simply because a leadership change was due" (*Track & Field News*, June 1985, 39). This is, of course, the same Robert Helmick who would later preside over the quiet expulsion of Robert Voy and who would himself be expelled from the IOC in 1991 because of his improper financial dealings. A few years later, Dardik encountered some problems of his own. "In 1995, New York State medical licensing authorities found him guilty of fraud, exercising undue influence, guaranteeing satisfaction or a cure, and failing to maintain adequate records. Case records indicate that he had charged four MS [multiple sclerosis] patients from $30,000 to $100,000 for their treatment. His New York medical license was revoked, he was fined $40,000, and his New Jersey license was subsequently revoked" (Stephen Barrett, M.D., "Be Wary of Multiple Sclerosis 'Cures,' " *Quackwatch* [August 6, 2003], www.quackwatch.org/01QuackeryRelatedTopics/ms.html).

258 **failed to "administer an effective"** These assessments are taken from the "Report of the Independent International Review Commission on Doping Control—U.S.A. Track & Field" (July 11, 2001), 73, 96 (for other critical comments, see 32, 37n, 70, 82, 83, 90, 91, 93). This document was prepared by a four-person committee chaired by a Canadian lawyer, Richard McLaren, and is informally known as the McLaren Report.

258 **the Kerry Lynch blood-doping scandal** "U.S. Skier Suspended for 2 Years," *Chicago Tribune*, June 9, 1988; see also Voy, *Drugs, Sport, and Politics*, 72-73. The USOC and the United States Skiing Association penalized Lynch by requiring him to return $1,200 to the USOC and to serve a suspension that expired six weeks before the opening of the 1988 Calgary Olympic Games.

258   **"direct and indirect pressures"**   Lynch, quoted in "U.S. Nordic Medalist Admits to Blood Packing," *Chicago Tribune,* December 29, 1987.

258   **"It is morally wrong"**   Helmick, quoted in ibid.

258   **more impartial observers saw**   "It seemed to be an extremely modest sanction for that degree of an orchestrated, premeditated violation of Olympic ethics," said a Canadian official (quoted in "Ban Is Almost Certain for U.S. Skier Lynch," *Chicago Tribune,* January 13, 1988).

258   **"I felt the recommended position"**   Little, quoted in "Skier Lynch Voted Out of Games," *Chicago Tribune,* January 20, 1988.

259   **"If you go in with a sickle and scythe"**   Catlin, quoted in Virginia Cowart, "State-of-Art Drug Identification Laboratories Play Increasing Role in Major Athletic Events," *JAMA* 256 (December 12, 1986): 3073.

259   **"I think that"**   Catlin, quoted in Virginia S. Cowart, "Athlete Drug Testing Receiving More Attention Than Ever Before in History of Competition," *JAMA* 261 (June 23/30, 1989): 3511. Voy, on the contrary, said: "I am one who thinks that if we are going to solve the problem of drug use in sports we have to expose those who cheat. I don't go along with aggregate figures. If an athlete has cheated the process, we need to make that public" (quoted in ibid.).

259   **no government has ever renounced**   The temporary exception to this rule was the "Friendship First, Competition Second" sports policy proclaimed by Mao Zedong during the early 1970s (see John Hoberman, "Sport and Social Change: The Transformation of Maoist Sport," *Sociology of Sport Journal* 4 [1987]: 156–70). The idea that a modern country's national security requires elite athletes who can compete with the world's best may appear primitive in a technological age whose power relies on intricately designed flows of electrons rather than muscular might and agility. One might argue that cultivating athletes to enhance national stature is a more rational policy for small countries than for large nations able to project other and more tangible forms of strength into the wider world. Still, the symbolic power of athletic dynamism remains enormously appealing to governments of all kinds.

259   **giving national sports officials tacit permission**   In March 2002, the Spanish track-and-field federation was selling its coaches a book (Garcia Manso, *La Fuerza* [Madrid: Editorial Gymnos, 1999]) that includes a long chapter on the administration of anabolic steroids to elite athletes ("Betrug nach Lehrbuch," *Süddeutsche Zeitung,* March 6, 2002).

260   **the Tour de France scandal**   See John Hoberman, " 'A Pharmacy on Wheels': Doping and Community Cohesion among Professional Cyclists following the Tour de France Scandal of 1998," in *The Essence of Sport,* ed. Verner Møller and John Nauright (Odense: University Press of Southern Denmark, 2003), 107–27.

260   **the French anti-doping law of 1989**   French anti-doping legislation had been passed as early as 1964 and 1966, as contemporary *JAMA* articles noted: "A law prohibiting the use of stimulant drugs by competitors has been recently approved by the French cabinet. Fines and imprisonment for offending sportsmen, trainers, and handlers may be imposed if use of drugs can be proved. Blood, urine, and sweat tests are permissible in order to detect the illegal drug usage" ("France Bans Use of Drugs in Sports," *JAMA* 189 [September 21, 1964]: 977). And: "The use of stimulants at athletic competitions (called in French slang, doping) was recently put under repressive legislation. . . . Penalties are severe: the athlete must pay a fine

of 500 to 5000 francs, and the directors and managers must face, beside the fine, a prison penalty of a month to a year" ("French Law on Doping," *JAMA* 197 [July 25, 1966]: 306).

260 **"For as long as the Tour has existed"** Hans Halter, "Alles verstehen, alles verzeihen," *Der Spiegel,* August 3, 1998, 97.

261 **"not good for sport"** Schily, quoted in "Europas Sportminister setzen IOC unter Druck," *Süddeutsche Zeitung,* February 3, 1998.

261 **For the past two decades** On the relationship between political affiliation and doping policy in Germany, see Hoberman, *Mortal Engines,* 237–46; Hoberman, "Fitness and National Vitality."

261 **Samaranch expressed confidence** "Die Scheinheiligkeit der Sport-Funktionäre," *Süddeutsche Zeitung,* July 25/26, 1998.

261 **In contrast, Klaus Müller** "Klaus Müller: Dopingkontrolleur und Laborchef in Kreischa," *Süddeutsche Zeitung,* July 26/26, 1998.

261 **"Sport cannot possibly solve"** Tröger, quoted in "Olympischer Radsport gefährdet," *Süddeutsche Zeitung,* July 25/26, 1998.

261 **"For me everything"** Samaranch, quoted in "Kürzung der Dopingliste," *Süddeutsche Zeitung,* July 27, 1998.

261 **Thomas Bach distanced himself** "Der Vorschlag ist ein Schlag ins Gesicht," *Süddeutsche Zeitung,* July 28, 1998.

262 **the Anti-Doping Conference convened** See Jim Ferstle, "World Conference on Doping in Sport," in Wilson and Derse, eds., *Doping in Elite Sport,* 275–86.

262 **"the lifting of the ban"** Ivan Waddington, *Sport, Health and Drugs: A Critical Sociological Perspective* (London: E and FN Spon, 2000), 177.

263 **"a modern curse"** Nixon, quoted in Dan Baum, *Smoke and Mirrors: The War on Drugs and the Politics of Failure* (Boston: Little, Brown, 1996), 12.

263 **"drug use by young people"** Quoted in "Marijuana Users Are Sociable, Michigan Student Survey Finds," *New York Times,* December 17, 1968. The researchers observed: "Marijuana users, judging from our data, do not seem to be 'copping out' or withdrawing from society."

264 **it was Nixon's own National Commission** Baum, *Smoke and Mirrors,* 71.

264 **"Organic Brain Syndrome"** Quoted in Baum, *Smoke and Mirrors,* 71, 154, 187, 187, 230, 231, 278, v.

264 **Only a deeply irrational view** In this case, the emotional (and, I believe, irrational) need to condemn the sheer degeneracy associated with drug use outweighs a more objective assessment of which drugs do the most to subvert productivity. The productivity theme thus plays a powerful, but not an all-powerful, role in the war on drugs.

264 **it made strategic sense** Baum, *Smoke and Mirrors,* 297.

265 **"The use of anabolic steroids"** James E. Wright, Ph.D., quoted in "National Institute on Drug Abuse May Join in Anabolic Steroid Research," *Journal of the American Medical Society* 261 (April 7, 1989): 1855.

265 **"many steroid users"** Quoted in Jeffrey Hedges, "The Anabolic Steroids Act: Bad Medicine for the Elderly," *Elder Law Journal* 5 (Fall 1997): 309.

265 **"the belief that drugs radiate a supernatural evil"** This phrase appears in Baum, *Smoke and Mirrors,* xii. It is worth recalling that IOC president Samaranch both employed an extravagant anti-doping rhetoric and conferred Olympic decorations

(in 1985) on the architects of the East German doping system, the Communist party leader Erich Honecker and the sports bureaucrat Manfred Ewald.

265 **"currently plays a role"** F. Allan Hanson, *Testing Testing: Social Consequences of the Examined Life* (Berkeley: University of California Press, 1993), 123.

265 **William Bennett, the U.S. drug czar** Baum, *Smoke and Mirrors*, 263–65, 298. William Bennett spent eighteen months as President George H. W. Bush's drug czar.

266 **"Under new federal regulations"** This advertisement for *Super T: The Complete Guide to Creating an Effective, Safe, and Natural Testosterone Supplement Program for Men and Women* (by Karlis Ullis, with Joshua Shackman and Greg Ptacek [New York: Fireside, 1999]) appeared on the Beyond Muscle.com Web site (www.beyondmuscle.com) in April 2002.

266 **"a new teenage drug subculture"** Paul Solotaroff, "Killer Bods," *Rolling Stone*, February 14, 2002, 58, 58. "Supplements have become a huge problem for kids and for amateur sports in particular," says Dr. Gary Wadler, a professor of medicine at New York University School of Medicine and the leading expert at the World Anti-Doping Agency, which monitors drug use at the Olympics. "Take ephedrine, for instance, which these companies combine with caffeine and phenylpropanolamine. At the suggested dose—and kids take multiples of that, for maximum acceleration—it replicates the clinical effects of amphetamines, including an elevated heart rate and temperature" (quoted in ibid., 72).

266 **In May 2002 the National Football League** Mike Freeman, "N.F.L. to Begin Testing Players for the Stimulant Ephedra," *New York Times*, May 10, 2002; "Giants Trainer Says 75 Percent of Team Took Ephedra," *Daily News* (New York), May 14, 2002.

266 **The strong and healthy baseball star** Grant Wahl, "Scorecard: Off the Dole," *Sports Illustrated*, March 11, 2002, 24.

266 **The pitcher Pete Harnisch** Robert Lipsyte, "Psychiatric Medication Is Moving into the Lineup," *New York Times*, March 5, 2000.

267 **"Unsung, in a similar spirit"** From a Celebrex (celecoxib capsules) brochure titled "Celebrate the Olympic Spirit!" I found this brochure in an Eckerd's drugstore in Austin, Texas, in April 2002.

267 **Tiger Woods has endorsed a surgical procedure** "Why Did Tiger Choose TLC?" (TLC Laser Eye Centers advertisement), *New York Times Magazine*, May 5, 2002, 37.

267 **"Major national newspapers"** Quoted in "US Trade Commissioner Urges Media and Industry to Act on Deceptive Supplement Claims," *Nutraceuticals International*, May 7, 2002.

267 **"asked CBS to air"** L. Jon Wertheim and Mike Shropshire, "Scorecard: Not-So-Superstars?" *Sports Illustrated*, May 6, 2002.

268 **Large-scale drug testing** Hanson, *Testing Testing*, 124.

268 **"Mandatory drug testing has usually"** Rushing, quoted in "NCAA's Drug Tests of Athletes at Stanford U. Barred by Cal. Judge," *Chronicle of Higher Education*, September 1, 1988, A30. See also John M. Hoberman, "Drug Abuse: The Student-Athlete and High-Performance Sport," in *The Rules of the Game: Ethics in College Sport*, ed. Richard E. Lapchick and John Brooks Slaughter (London: Collier Macmillan Publishers, 1989), 83–98.

268   In June 2002 the Supreme Court   Linda Greenhouse, "Justices Allow Schools Wider Use of Random Drug Tests for Pupils," *New York Times,* June 28, 2002.

269   "opened the door to drug testing"   Jim Yardley, "Family in Texas Challenges Mandatory School Drug Test," *New York Times,* April 17, 2000.

269   For this reason F. Allan Hanson   Hanson, *Testing Testing,* 170–72.

269   certain European officials have made it clear   Viviane Reding, the European commissioner in charge of education, training, youth, audiovisual affairs, culture, sport, and civil society, has emphasized that "sport has a social dimension, an educational role" to play in modern societies, and that this social mission includes a "zero-tolerance policy" toward doping (quoted in "Schily weiß, dass die EU die Wada nicht finanzieren kann," *Süddeutsche Zeitung,* March 14, 2002).

270   How much pharmaceutical companies have known   "In the 1980s, the federal government began suspecting that drug manufacturers were producing anabolic steroids far in excess of the legitimate medical demand" (Hedges, "The Anabolic Steroids Act," 307).

270   National governments created WADA   For basic information on the formation and funding of WADA, see the World Anti-Doping Agency home page, www.wada-ama.org.

270   The 1998 Tour de France prosecutions   "Madame Buffets zwiespältige Revolution," *Süddeutsche Zeitung,* November 18, 1998. On Buffet's work after 1998 to set up a national anti-doping program, see "Ein Antennenwald gegen das Doping," *Süddeutsche Zeitung,* October 16, 2001. In November 1998 only the conservative neo-Gaullist party (Rassemblement Pour la République, or RPR) did not vote for a strengthened anti-doping law in the French National Assembly ("Verschärfte Vorlage," *Süddeutsche Zeitung,* November 20, 1998).

270   The Italian state prosecutor   See "Eine Doppelspitze gegen den Werteverfall"; "Dafür sorgen, daß Doping geächtet wird."

271   The professional sports leagues   In a direct rebuke to Marie-Georges Buffet, the president of the International Cycling Union, Hein Verbruggen, refused in March 2002 to allow an independent panel of doctors to rule on the use of medical products by professional riders—more evidence of the extraordinary political power wielded by this compromised bureaucrat ("UCI President Rejects Use of Independent Doctors on Tour de France," Agence France-Presse, March 31, 2002). As of this writing (February 2004), Verbruggen remains an influential member of the IOC.

271   European soccer has shown little interest   See, for example, "Mit dem ganz großen Schwamm," *Süddeutsche Zeitung,* October 10, 2001.

271   "enough to cater to the needs"   "No Excuses for Using Drugs: Inquiry," *Toronto Sun,* November 24, 2001.

271   in part because high-profile players   In March 2000 a U.S. Senate investigation determined that during the late 1990s, the NFL had covered up positive drug tests of prominent players but had punished lower-level players (Mike Freeman, "Panel Says Drug Policy Favored Stars," *New York Times,* March 9, 2000).

271   Between 1984 and 2000   As the *New York Times* reporter commented: "The results may have been influenced by the fact that the players knew in advance when they would be tested. In 1999 the NBA players union accepted drug testing for marijuana, steroids, amphetamines and LSD" (Mike Wise, "N.B.A. Finds Minimal Use of Marijuana in First Tests," *New York Times,* February 7, 2000).

271   The National Hockey League   Selena Roberts, "N.H.L. Unhappy with U.S.O.C. Policy," *New York Times,* March 9, 2001; "Deal Allows Olympic Testing," *New York Times,* March 20, 2001.

271   But the most blatant example of entrenched resistance   "What's More American Than Baseball? Performance-Enhancing Steroids; Baseball under Fire for Drug-Use Policies," *Salt Lake Tribune,* July 10, 2000.

271   "Major League Baseball has asked"   Buster Olney, "The Bigger They Are, the More They're Falling," *New York Times,* March 31, 2002.

271   "Our policy will not be driven"   Quoted in Murray Chass, "Science, Not Outcry, to Drive Baseball's Decision on Andro," *New York Times,* February 6, 1999.

271   "pleased to have played a part"   Selig, quoted in "Andro Boosts Testosterone," *abcNEWS.com* (July 20, 2000), http://abcnews.go.com. See Benjamin Z. Leder et al., "Oral Androstenedione Administration and Serum Testosterone Concentrations in Young Men," *JAMA* 283 (February 9, 2000): 779–82.

272   "serious public health issue"   Quoted in Harvey Araton, "One Issue Is Settled; Others Await," *New York Times,* February 29, 2000.

272   "Every ballplayer I've ever seen"   Millman, quoted in "What's More American Than Baseball?"

272   "player's position as a role model"   Quoted in Dave Anderson, "On Baseball's Soft Drug Policy," *New York Times,* March 3, 2000.

272   speculation about steroid use   In addition to the other newspaper articles and columns cited in this chapter, see Rick Reilly, "The 'Roid to Ruin," *Sports Illustrated,* August 21, 2000, 92; Ken Rosenthal, "The Hot Zone: Baseball," *Sporting News,* April 15, 2002; Terence Moore, "Canseco Might Step to Plate on Steroids," *Atlanta Journal and Constitution,* May 16, 2002; Skip Bayless, "Mr. Canseco, If You Tell All, Start with Yourself," *Austin American-Statesman,* May 20, 2002.

272   Two months later a sportswriter predicted   Steve Kettmann, "Baseball Must Come Clean on Its Darkest Secret," *New York Times,* August 20, 2000.

272   In October 2000 an MLB vice president   Howard Manly, "HBO Details Steroid Use in Baseball," *Boston Globe,* October 6, 2000.

272   "Major League Baseball"   Alderson, quoted in James C. McKinley, Jr., "Steroid Suspicions Abound in Major League Dugouts," *New York Times,* October 11, 2000.

272   And there was no sign whatsoever   As we have already seen in chapter 7, it is all too easy to assume that public support for the war on drugs translates into support for drug-free professional athletes. For example, in an otherwise thoughtful op-ed piece on steroids in baseball, Steve Kettmann asserted in August 2000 that "the players will risk widespread fan outrage if they resist the call for testing." Yet later in the column he observes, "What's striking about steroid use in baseball [is] how much public acceptance it seems to have gained" ("Baseball Must Come Clean on Its Darkest Secret"). This sort of cognitive dissonance is to be expected in a society constantly exposed to the war on drugs and its dogmatic assumptions about how "the public" feels about drug use.

272   In March 2004 the FDA   Alice Dembner, "Herbal Industry Seen Fending Off FDA," *Boston Globe,* March 26, 2004.

273   "The league, the players"   Grassley, quoted in Freeman, "Panel Says Drug Policy Favored Stars."

273   the pro-doping policies of the players' unions   The belated approach to drug testing on the part of a players' union became evident once again when the NFL announced in May 2002 that it would begin testing its players for ephedrine products. For years it was generally assumed that many players, possibly hundreds, had
been using these products to lose weight or experience a sudden charge of energy.
Following the death of one player and mounting reports of medical risks associated with these drugs, while players continued to complain of any regulation whatsoever, the executive director of the players association, Gene Upshaw, finally announced: "It's time to be proactive in this area" (quoted in Mike Freeman, "N.F.L.
to Begin Testing Players for the Stimulant Ephedra," *New York Times,* May 10,
2002; see also "NFL Blaming Ephedrine for Stringer's Untimely Death," *Austin
American-Statesman,* May 13, 2002). The crucial role of players' unions in drug
testing was pointed out by a USOC official commenting on the 2002 Salt Lake City
Olympic Games: "If professional athletes want to participate on the U.S. Olympic
team, they are going to have to voluntarily subject themselves to our no-advance-
notice drug testing program, irrespective of what their agreements with their players unions may say" (quoted in "USOC Alters Policy," *Denver Post,* February 24,
2001).

273   "It's time we made it clear"   The speaker was the Australian Kevan Gosper, a
member of the IOC executive board (quoted in "Drug Companies Invited to Meeting," *New York Times,* August 15, 1998).

273   The response from the pharmaceutical industry   This was confirmed to me by
Richard Pound, an IOC member and head of WADA, at a conference in Waterloo,
Ontario, on October 1, 2001.

273   When the four-minute milers were accused   "Athletes Deny Use of Drugs,"
Times (London), June 7, 1957.

273   In 1982 reports of serious side effects   "Plötzlich wahnsinnig aggressiv," *Der
Spiegel,* May 25, 1992, 197; "Jeden Dreck, jeden Blödsinn reingehauen," *Der
Spiegel,* September 14, 1992, 286.

273   In 1988 Searle took the anabolic steroid   Berendonk, *Doping-Dokumente: Von
der Forschung zum Betrug,* 49.

273   As of 1992 the German drug firm   "Jeden Dreck, jeden Blödsinn reingehauen,"
286.

274   "its medications used"   Quoted in "Pharma hilft Nada," *Süddeutsche Zeitung,*
December 22/23, 2001. In 1999 the prominent German sports official Helmut
Digel had demanded that the pharmaceutical industry participate in the anti-
doping effort ("Notfalls Daumenschrauben," *Süddeutsche Zeitung,* June 4, 1999).

274   It was, in fact, Amgen   "Aus der Trickkiste der Fahnder," *Neue Zürcher Zeitung,*
March 16, 2002. "EPO, short for erythropoietin, was created by Amgen in the
early 1980s and is now one of the top selling drugs in the world. It took in more
than $3 billion last year [in 1997] for its three manufacturers, Amgen, J & J and
France's Roche" ("Amgen Shares Soar on Court Victory," Associated Press, December 22, 1998).

274   But Amgen has refused to attach   Naomi Aoki, "Drug Makers Battle Bad
Sports," *Boston Globe,* September 27, 2000.

274   Testosterone products are important   See, for example, Shehzad Basaria, Justin
T. Wahlstrom, and Adrian S. Dobs, "Anabolic-Androgenic Steroid Therapy in the

Treatment of Chronic Diseases," *Journal of Clinical Endocrinology and Metabolism* 86 (2001): 5108–17.

274 **Genentech makes Protropin**   Aoki, "Drug Makers Battle Bad Sports."

274 **How, for example, did the Italian cyclist**   "Brisanter Saft," *Der Spiegel*, June 18, 2001, 168.

274 **Sandro Donati, then head**   "Italian Soccer Stricken by Doping Scandals, Corruption," *Globe and Mail* (Toronto), December 28, 1998.

275 **Lance Armstrong, the six-time champion**   Christopher Clarey, "If Doping Is Banned, Should Altitude Tents Be Allowed for Endurance Athletes?" *International Herald Tribune*, December 26, 2001.

EPILOGUE.   Testosterone as a Way of Life

277 **"want to see bigger-than-life people"**   Yesalis, quoted in Carol Slezak, "Fighting the Good Fight—and Losing Anyway," *Chicago Sun-Times*, November 30, 2003.

278 **steroid-using police officers**   "In recent years, drug abuse in law enforcement has garnered a great deal of attention. Numerous individual cases of police officers using or dealing drugs have received nationwide publicity, and police officers in various ranks and assignments have been involved. However, one area of substance abuse that has been ignored, for the most part, is police officer use of steroids" (Charles Swanson, Larry Gaines, and Barbara Gore, "Abuse of Anabolic Steroids," *FBI Law Enforcement Bulletin*, August 1991, 19–23).

278 **In 1985 and 1986 the Texas Department**   Mark Wangrin, "Steroid Use by Law Officers Raises Fears," *Austin American-Statesman*, November 5, 1989.

278 **In 1989 a white police officer in Houston**   Mary Flood and Felix Sanchez, "Researchers Say Police Steroid Use a Dangerous Trend," *Houston Post*, November 18, 1989.

278 **In Britain the use of steroids**   Doug Gillon, "Questions for House—'Explosion' in Numbers Abusing Steroids," *Glasgow Herald*, April 15, 1996.

278 **In 1998 police in Liverpool**   Julian Kossoff, "Police Must Take Random Drug Tests," *Independent on Sunday*, November 22, 1998. "Police officers are using body-building drugs to give themselves added bulk and strength to deal with violent criminals. Many officers around the country have turned to steroids as a way of minimising their chances of being hurt or humiliated" (Jon Ungoed-Thomas, "Police Taking Steroids to Counter Thugs," *Sunday Times* [London], December 6, 1998).

278 **In Denmark, Copenhagen's Police Station**   "Politianholdelse: Betjente anholdt for doping," *Jyllands-Posten*, November 23, 2000; "4 politibetjente sigtet for doping," *Ekstra Bladet*, November 23, 2000; "Politidoping: Sigtede betjente bliver i tjenesten," *Jyllands-Posten*, November 24, 2000; "Station 1: Racistisk materiale ryster politiet," *Jyllands-Posten*, November 26, 2000; "Station 1: Politielev solgte dopingmidler," *Jyllands-Posten*, November 28, 2000; "Ransaging hos politielev," *Jyllands-Posten*, November 29, 2000; "Politidoping: Dopingtest på Station 1," *Jyllands-Posten*, December 6, 2000; "Fem betjente sigtet," *Jyllands-Posten*, December 23, 2000; "Politibetjent gik selv til bekendelse," *Jyllands-Posten*, February 11, 2001; "Station 1: Stationens mand," *Jyllands-Posten*, March 4, 2001.

278 Police involvement with steroids was reported from Australia *Melbourne Age,* September 12, 1998; Mark Forbes, "Get-Tough on Steroid Sales," *Sydney Morning Herald,* July 10, 2000; Mark Dunn, "Police Probe Use of Steroids in Force," *Herald* (Australia), July 17, 2003.

278 "was not disciplined" Wangrin, "Steroid Use by Law Officers Raises Fears."

278 When Georg Andersen was banned See, for example, "Georg Andersen utestengt for livstid," *Nytt fra Norge* (Oslo), May 11, 1993. For the account of Andersen's evolution into a sympathetic underdog, I am indebted to Bjørn Barland and his personal communication (from Oslo) of December 22, 2003.

278 "We have no indication" Quoted in John C. Ensslin, "Officer Investigated for Allegedly Ordering Steroids," *Rocky Mountain News,* January 1, 2003.

279 In July 2003 a highly regarded police officer "Deputy Pleads Guilty to Having Steroids," *Cleveland Plain Dealer,* June 7, 2003.

279 The officer himself, a 1999 Stephen Hudak, "Steroids: A Threat to Police Officers," *Cleveland Plain Dealer,* July 27, 2003.

279 "The supplements I'm taking" Quoted in Renee Brown, "Roden Takes the Stand: Former Dover Officer Denies Using Steroids," *New Philadelphia Times Reporter,* January 16, 2003.

279 both the former Chicago police officer Wangrin, "Steroid Use by Law Officers Raises Fears." Ronny Coleman appeared on the cover of the January 2004 issue of *Flex* magazine.

279 "Bodybuilding," says one British expert Professor Russell Dobash of Manchester University, quoted in Ungoed-Thomas, "Police Taking Steroids to Counter Thugs."

280 "Steroids cross all barriers" Quoted in Gillon, "Questions for House—'Explosion' in Numbers Abusing Steroids."

280 An Australian expert confirmed Mark Dunn, "Three Groups Pinpointed as Steroid Users," *Herald Sun* (Australia), July 18, 2003.

280 "Don't you see" Quoted in Michelangelo Signorile, "The Incredible Bulk," *Out,* May 1997, 72.

280 "We were much more circumspect" Quoted in ibid.

281 "they're going to use them" Quoted in ibid.

281 "We struggle with [this issue]" Quoted in Gina Kolata, "With No Answers on Risks, Steroid Users Still Say 'Yes,' " *New York Times,* December 2, 2002.

281 "To rebuild muscle tissue" Signorile, "The Incredible Bulk," 72.

282 no "significant aphrodisical effect" "Ovaries, Estrogens and Libido," *JAMA* 113 (July 8, 1939): 168.

282 "normal men experience little" Carl G. Heller and Gordon B. Myers, "The Male Climacteric, Its Symptomatology, Diagnosis and Treatment," *JAMA* 126 (October 21, 1944): 475. In 1944 three other researchers referred to "[t]he failure of the androgen treatment to increase the performance of normal young men, in whom the sexual hormone production is at its maximum" (Ernst Simonsen, Walter M. Kearns, and Norbert Enzer, "Effect of Methyl Testosterone Treatment on Muscular Performance and the Central Nervous System of Older Men," *Journal of Clinical Endocrinology* 4 [1944]: 533).

282 Paul de Kruif reported Paul de Kruif, *The Male Hormone* (New York: Harcourt, Brace, 1945), 109.

282 "Testosterone supplementation produced" "Hormone Creams," *JAMA* 140 (May 21, 1949): 368.

282 "The prevailing experience," *JAMA* noted "Frigidity in Women," *JAMA* 117 (November 15, 1941): 1750–51.

282 Estrogen would reestablish "Cancer, Artificial Menopause and Libido," *JAMA* 129 (October 20, 1945): 584.

282 "congenital gonadal deficiency" "Use of Sex Hormones in Therapeutics," *British Medical Journal,* January 29, 1949, 168.

282 "In women who menstruate" "Hormone Creams," 368.

283 "the therapy of age changes" Alex Comfort, "On Research and Support in Geriatrics, Including Design for a Study of Muscular Strength in the Aged," *Journal of the American Geriatrics Society* 15 (1967): 428, 429, 430, 433.

283 "the largest and most depressing" Ibid., 430.

284 the publication in November 2003 of a report In a National Institutes of Health news release of November 12, 2003, the National Institute of Aging both commented on and endorsed the IOM report. The final paragraph of this commentary reads as follows:

> Finally, although some older men who have tried these treatments report feeling "more energetic" or "younger," testosterone therapy remains a scientifically unproven method for preventing or relieving any physical or psychological changes that men with testosterone levels may experience as they get older. Except for a relatively few younger and older men with extreme deficiencies, testosterone treatment is not deemed appropriate therapy for most men at this time. For now, the risks and benefits of testosterone therapy for most men who do not have extreme deficiencies of the hormone are unknown, and there is insufficient evidence for making well-informed decisions on whether this therapy is suitable in these individuals. The clinical trials and other studies recommended by the IOM could do much to clarify the future role of testosterone therapy in aging men. ("NIA Statement on IOM Testosterone Report" [November 12, 2003], www.eurekalert.org/pub _releases/2003-11/nioa-nso111203.php [accessed March 2004])

284 "People are really looking" Quoted in Alice Dembner, "Testosterone Use Grows Despite Possible Risks," *Boston Globe,* November 13, 2003.

284 Dr. John B. McKinlay Gina Kolata, "Panel Recommends Studies on Testosterone Therapy," *New York Times,* November 13, 2003. For McKinlay's work on the concept of male menopause, see John B. McKinlay, "Is There an Epidemiologic Basis for a Male Climacteric Syndrome? The Massachusetts Male Aging Study," in *Menopause: Evaluation, Treatment, and Health Concerns,* ed. Charles B. Hammond, Florence P. Haseltine, and Isaac Schiff (New York: Alan R. Liss, 1989), 163–92.

284 "What we are about to do" Quoted in Dembner, "Testosterone Use Grows Despite Possible Risks."

284 While most users of testosterone Ibid.

285 Prescription sales of testosterone drugs Ernani Luis Rhoden and Abraham Morgentaler, "Risks of Testosterone-Replacement Therapy and Recommendations for Monitoring," *New England Journal of Medicine* 350 (January 29, 2004): 482.

285 The IOM committee reported Marc Kaufman, "Testosterone Derided as a Health Supplement," *Washington Post,* November 13, 2003.

285   "There is a disconnect"   Morgentaler, quoted in ibid.

285   "Among those of us"   Morgentaler, quoted in Dembner, "Testosterone Use Grows Despite Possible Risks."

285   Morgentaler's debunking   Rhoden and Morgentaler, "Risks of Testosterone-Replacement Therapy and Recommendations for Monitoring," 482–92. It is worth noting that the commentary that accompanied this article reiterated the cautious approach that had been the norm in the medical literature. See Peter J. Snyder, "Hypogonadism in Elderly Men—What to Do Until the Evidence Comes," *New England Journal of Medicine* 350 (January 29, 2004): 440–42.

285   "Female hormone replacement therapy"   Carruthers, quoted in "Call for Men to Get HRT," *BBC News* (December 5, 2000), www.bbc.co.uk.

285   "prescribed testosterone implants"   Whitehead, quoted in Bernard Mallee, "Who's on the Testosterone? Women Trying to Survive in the Macho World of Politics Are Resorting to Hormonal Help," *New Statesman*, July 7, 2003.

286   "There is some degree of denial"   Bhasin, quoted in Kolata, "With No Answers on Risks, Steroid Users Still Say 'Yes.'"

286   Until 1984 the American Academy of Sports Medicine   See Jan Todd and Terry Todd, "Significant Events in the History of Drug Testing and the Olympic Movement: 1960–1999," in *Doping in Elite Sport: The Politics of Drugs in the Olympic Movement,* ed. Wayne Wilson and Edward Derse (Champaign, Ill.: Human Kinetics, 2000), 83.

286   A sports physician had already published   Daniel L. Cooper, "Drugs and the Athlete," *JAMA* 221 (August 28, 1972): 1007–11.

INDEX

AAAAM (American Academy of Anti-Aging Medicine), 14, 171, 291n
AARP (American Association of Retired People), 52–53
AAS. *See* anabolic-androgenic steroids
abortions, 153, 158
Abrahams, Adolphe, 184–85, 186
acne, 108
adolescents and preadolescents: androgens for (muscular dystrophy girl), 114; anxiety about drug use by, 263–64; new drug subculture of, 266, 351n; role models of, 181, 224, 226, 228–29; steroid use by, 27, 170, 171, 280; testosterone propionate to cure homosexual, 100–1. *See also* athletes, student; infants and children
adrenal extracts, effects of, 37. *See also* DHEA
adrenaline, as tonic vs. stimulant, 34
advertisements: athletes as role models in, 266; of caffeine as tonic vs. stimulant, 33; call for investigation of, 41; consumers as target of, 23, 125, 129, 168; of cosmetic treatments, 267, 292n, 329n; of female sex hormones, 50, 141; older people as target of, 124; physicians as target of, 41, 56–57, 126; sexual desire used in, 43; testosterone associated with

power in, 29; war on drugs subverted by, 228–29. *See also* commercialization; marketing
Afghanistan, friendly-fire incident and amphetamine use in, 5
aggression: steroids and amphetamines as producing, 26–27; testosterone associated with, 28–29, 278–79
aging: androgens to counter, 111; characteristics of, 43, 52; constructing narratives about, 124–25; as disease, 13–14, 17, 143, 171, 174; fatalism about, 108–9; gendered approach to, 139–40; hormone deficiency in, 9–10; sexuality ignored in, 9, 44, 73, 78, 81; "successful," 124–25, 146; as treatable, 44, 144–45. *See also* anti-aging therapies; older people
aging men: disorders of, 139; fatigue levels of, 51; idea of improving lives of, 105; as market for hormones, 49; methyl testosterone for, 50–51; rejuvenation of, 114–15, 317n; sexual demands of, 8, 54, 292n; vasectomies of senile, 42. *See also* hypogonadism; impotency; menopause, male
aging women: animal extracts for, 95; compulsory doping of, 7–8; interests of, 301n. *See also* menopause, female

Text:	10/13 Sabon
Display:	Sabon
Compositor:	Binghamton Valley Composition, LLC
Printer and Binder:	Maple-Vail Manufacturing Group